In the
School
of War

ROGER J. SPILLER

FOREWORD BY JOHN W. SHY

UNIVERSITY OF NEBRASKA PRESS • LINCOLN AND LONDON

Library of Congress Cataloging-in-Publication Data
Spiller, Roger J.
In the school of war / Roger J. Spiller ; foreword by
John W. Shy.
        p. cm. — (Studies in war, society, and the military)
Includes bibliographical references.
ISBN 978-0-8032-2816-0 (pbk. : alk. paper)
1. Military history. I. Title.
D25.5.S66 2010
355.0209—dc22
2009045142

Set in Sabon by Kim Essman.

This book is dedicated to James Pohl,
who really started all this.

CONTENTS

The field of military history has many worthy, assiduous, honest workers, historians who dig hard in the written record to re-create as accurately as possible the wars and military affairs that have inevitably been a central feature of the human experience. But imagination and originality are not qualities usually associated with military history and may appear to be subversive of the ideals of accuracy and objectivity, highly valued by all historians. Yet the history of war and military affairs is replete with great gaps and distortions in the evidential record, even for recent wars, when participants can be interviewed, and those gaps and distortions raise questions that can be answered only by informed speculation; in short, a few military historians with imaginative, skeptical minds are an invaluable asset if we seek to understand the aspects of war left murky or contested by the available evidence.

Roger Spiller has such a mind. I cannot now recall the time and circumstances of our first meeting, probably at the annual convention of the Society for Military History, but I do recall my early impression that he had a very sharp mind and was not afraid to use it and to say what he thought. Getting to know him and his work over the following decades, I saw that he was what might be called a "constructive contrarian," a historian who tends to look skeptically at the "official" version and at the generally accepted consensus on any aspect of military history that he considered important enough to question. And there was something more, something difficult to define, because it deals with stereotypes. Roger is a Texan, born and raised. He did his graduate study at Louisiana State University with a bold, stimulating teacher, T. Harry Williams. Fairly early in our acquaintance

I realized that Roger Spiller struck me as an impressive example of an American type: Wallace Stegner's "westerner."

Stegner was the late, great novelist of the American West. Like Spiller, he was clear-eyed and skeptical and did not always use "westerner" as a compliment. I use the term here cautiously in trying to get at an essential quality in Spiller and his work. His boldness can leave him open to counterattack, as he himself concedes in some of the essays in this book, for example, by those who think that "traitor" is not a term fairly applied to Robert E. Lee or who find value in the work of the military historian S. L. A. Marshall, whatever his faults as notetaker, statistician, or human being. I do not myself agree with every argument advanced in this book, but I am truly grateful that our beleaguered field contains a few bright members like Roger Spiller who provoke us to think again.

Roger Spiller spent a quarter century honing his skills teaching not twenty-year-old undergraduates but mature adults, military professionals in midcareer selected as the Army's best who knew more about the military than he did. Many of them had experienced war firsthand, and they formed a challenging audience who often seriously questioned the value of learning anything of professional value in a classroom from some civilian with a Ph.D. I suspect Roger Spiller arrived at Fort Leavenworth with many of the personal qualities I have sketched already in place, but meeting this teaching challenge day after day, week after week, year after year surely developed them to a high degree. Soldiers value appearance, and that aspect of Roger surely was an advantage. No paunchy professor he but as fit as his students, ready to rock climb or run a marathon. He must have been a perfect match for that remarkable institution.

Roger Spiller has not written many books, and I think I know why. Teaching for the U.S. government means being available to the people you are teaching; Major X with a chest full of Vietnam ribbons does not expect to come to your office and find a note telling him that you are, *on duty hours*, in the library doing research for your next book. Instead, with only brief intervals of available time one writes shorter pieces, lectures for delivery to students. His recent book, *An Instinct for War: Scenes from the Battlefields of History* (Harvard University Press, 2005), is also a collection of essays, only one of which ("Rain Stops Play") is reprinted here. I highly recommend *An Instinct for War* to all who find this volume valuable because it offers yet another side of Spiller's creative imagination. As the title of this volume announces, Leavenworth is a "school of war," but it is also a school with a smoldering internal conflict between teachers and taught. (Read the introduction on the near-mutinous class at the Command and General Staff College who invented the rubber-chicken treatment for instructors deemed unworthy.) In short, it was a tough but bracing environment, and Roger Spiller had the Right Stuff to survive and become the George C. Marshall Professor of Military History.

The essays in this book are essentially teaching documents, the kind of one-hour sound bites that reflect the best thought and self-education of the teacher himself. They reflect very well the wide range of interest and knowledge acquired by the author in his years teaching at Fort Leavenworth. They may also be read, including the introductory essays to each of the four parts, as an intellectual autobiography of Roger Spiller.

John W. Shy
Professor Emeritus of History
University of Michigan, Ann Arbor

Lunch had been over for hours, but the three of us were still at the table talking. Outside, the English countryside was the deep, picture-perfect green of spring. The house on the edge of Sandhurst's main parade ground hummed around us, full of a Sunday afternoon's happy business. From time to time children darted through the room. Elsewhere in the house, the chatter from other guests, coming and going, sounded like background music. Our conversation went on into the night, flowing from one subject to another. But the theme was constant: everything we talked about—history, literature, writing—touched in some way on war. Eventually, our host's wife stopped in to see how we were doing. Her polite reserve gave way to an outburst: how could three civilized human beings spend all that time talking about such a dreadful thing as war? Our reply was an embarrassed, puzzled silence. I wondered then, and later, if we had committed a crime against the day's beauty.

Our host that day was John Keegan, who was then still teaching military history at the Royal Military Academy, Britain's equivalent of West Point, and still some years away from receiving his knighthood. John and I had met earlier when he came to lecture at the U.S. Army Command and General Staff College, where I was the most junior professor. Having helped arrange his visit, I was detailed to act as his escort, which entailed little work but plenty of time to talk as I was getting him from place to place.

Three years later I was doing research in London and sent John a note when I arrived, asking him to dinner in town. "Why not come down here instead, this Sunday?" he answered. So down I went, where John collected me at the Camberley station. When we pulled up to his house, he told me to go directly in while he put away the car. I wandered in to find a kitchen full of people, just in from here and there, readying themselves for some sort of event on the Sandhurst grounds. As a drink was pressed into my hands, I introduced myself around.

"Oh," someone said, "you're the *other* American?"

Other American? You have more than one today?

Yes. The other's name is Fussell, due to arrive on the next train.

Paul Fussell?

Yes, that's it.

That was how I came to spend a day in conversation with the two living writers I most admired, whose books have had more influence over my way of thinking about war than any other. As this Sunday at Sandhurst unfolded, I felt that it was all very much in keeping with this accidental life of mine, and it's worth explaining here because most of the essays in this collection in one way or another really began that day.

When Keegan published his landmark book, *The Face of Battle*, in 1976, I was still in graduate school and wondering if I had made a mistake by choosing to concentrate my studies in military history. The standard fare of military history in those days—breezy narratives of campaigns and battles, biographies of commanders great and ordinary, deconstructions of this or that strategy, the technical arcana of warfare—seemed to leave out questions that most interested me. The human questions.

The military history I was reading had been taken prisoner by professional soldiers in the nineteenth century. That was when European professional officers began to think that what was known about war could be collected, organized, and analyzed scientifically. They built new organizations—general staffs—designed to translate their knowledge into victory. General staffs could, they hoped, reduce the uncertainty that bedeviled armies at war throughout history. Planned correctly, war could be won before the first shot was fired. The role of war itself, ideally, was merely to bring the plan to life.

The prospect of taking command of war, of exercising intellectual control over its fundamentally chaotic nature, corresponded nicely with the professional officer's faith in his own role. Elites in every field were seen in those days as the engines of historical progress, and their influence over events was thought to be exponential. They were not only important in their own right; they were more important than everyone else together. In the world of war commanders hoped they might take control of history as it happened. A perfect plan might determine the future. The commander could give orders, confident that they would be carried out without interference from surprise, bad luck—what Carl von Clausewitz would famously call "friction."

In the nineteenth century the recorded experience of past wars was the best ready source of knowledge for the general staffs, and battalions of staff officers were sent rummaging about military history for lessons that could be put to work in future wars. Military history could be useful. Used properly, military history might actually win wars. The only problem was it didn't work. After decades of laboring under these illusions, Europe's general staffs produced the Great War. The so-called lessons of history died in the trenches, the mud, the fire-swept expanses of no-man's-land.

The new social sciences gradually supplanted history as a source of soldiers' professional wisdom after World War II, but among scholars the old general staff approach to military history did not decline. If anything, military historians' tendency to organize their intellectual work in a way that would have been instantly recognizable to a member of the old Prussian General Staff became more pronounced. This kind of history was above all hierarchical: all action was conceived and directed by elites— the kings and statesmen and generals. Unimpeded from conception to action, military history majestically unfolded itself along its preordained narrative, assisted from time to time by the intervention of a major figure of heroic dimensions. This kind of military history is still deeply satisfying, its underlying conceptions and methods still very much on display in the megabookstores.

While I was in school, I was just on the edge of dissatisfaction with military history. I suspected that something important was missing in what I was reading, though I was unable to explain it, even to myself. But like all graduate students I did my apprenticeship, dutifully beavering along book after book. When I felt close to suffering an overdose on war books, I took refuge in other fields of history and in literature, where I saw bold, risky new work, real intellectual progress being made. In military history I saw stasis.

The appearance of Keegan's *The Face of Battle* in 1976 was a kind of deliverance for me. The book directly challenged the conventional approach to writing about the history of war. Rather than wishing away the fog and friction of war and instead of seeing war as a struggle between chains of command, Keegan took his mind directly into the source of war's confusions, battle itself—the threat of it, its conduct, and its aftermath.

Paradoxically, battle was the one subject that military history had done badly, and for good reason. The grand circumstances of war—their causes, their strategies and operations—had always been easier for historians to capture than what actually happened on the ground when the fighting began, when soldiers were fighting against the confusion, the exhaustion, the dangers of death or maiming or capture as much as their enemy. Their struggle to survive pushed all other instincts aside, not least the instinct to remember. When history tried to recount and explain battle, too often the result was clouded by sentimental imagining long after the event, wrapped in a cloak of romanticism.

What Keegan tried was risky. Keegan had never been in combat, had never been a soldier. Yet he took on a subject that has always ignited the most proprietary instinct among soldiers. Even if little was understood about battle, soldiers said, they at least had experienced it, and that counted for something. Those who had never been in a battle had no chance of understanding it. For Keegan to try his hand at it seemed presumptuous, even heretical.

If Keegan had written a medical book, catalogers would have

classed it as a kind of epidemiological study—the study of a disease from its point of origin and its transmission through its effect on its victims and their immediate circumstances. In three cases widely separated in time he created a picture of battle from the point of view—the "angle of vision," as he put it—of those who did the fighting. It was a picture in which the old general staff style of military history was *least* interested.

Since then Keegan's approach to military history has been both imitated and criticized. Keegan himself went on to write a great deal more and has become the world's best-known and most widely read military historian. Along the way I've come around to a more balanced appreciation for what he has done. Keegan reminded us that the face of battle is above all a human face, and if it is to be understood, we must not turn ours from its realities. The old style of military history reduced war to a play in which the actors were little more than stage props. Keegan returned the actors to center stage. *The Face of Battle*, for all its faults, showed me that war could be studied in ways that had been barely tried in three thousand years. Whatever else it accomplished, the book marked the beginning of a new school of military history and rejuvenated my interest in studies I was close to quitting.

Where would I have gone? I thought of leaving the academic life, even though at the time I had barely started. Unlike some of my classmates, I was never in love with the idea of life as an academic. I wouldn't have been missed. A great depression had settled over the academic world in the 1970s. Universities graduated far more historians than were needed. The few available appointments were fiercely contested. Untold numbers of bright and promising graduates would never get their chance at a life I held in such low esteem. And when I won my first appointment to teach history, I dismissed my success as nothing more than good luck. It confirmed my skepticism too. What kind of life was it that would reward my ingratitude?

So Keegan played an important part in rescuing me from my discontents. For several years I warded off those discontents by keeping two stacks of books beside the desk: the military history I had to read and the one I wanted to read—other kinds of history, and literature. I had long badgered classmates and friends about reading too narrowly, arguing that we were not in training to be technicians. The kind of military history then being written seemed to drive its students toward intellectual parochialism. The only antidote was to read as widely as possible, as far beyond our chosen field as we could. Our degrees said we were philosophers in history, didn't they? Why not take those diplomas seriously?

Paul Fussell's *The Great War and Modern Memory* landed in that second, more interesting stack of books because of Keegan. Fussell's book came out as Keegan's was in press, but Keegan added a footnote at the last minute, calling attention to Fussell's portrait of how the literature of World War I shaped Britain's sense of what happened on the western front. Keegan's verdict was quickly seconded: Fussell's book won the National Book Award for 1976, and if one searched for books written since that contained the words "and memory" in their titles, the list would go on seemingly forever. *The Great War and Modern Memory* gave rise to what seemed to be a new approach to history in which the literature of a period was taken as an expression of how a culture dealt with its collective memory. Edmund Wilson's *Patriotic Gore* had taken more or less the same approach to the Civil War in 1962, but Fussell's book had an edge to it that caught critics' eye. Fussell's own history was very much a presence in the book. A veteran of infantry fighting in Europe during World War II, he had graduated from that war with a decidedly skeptical, unromantic attitude that colored everything he wrote. As he said later toward the close of a long career as a professor and social critic, he still saw the world as "a pissed-off infantryman." Now in his eighties, Fussell is still pissed off.

At first, few military historians took notice of Fussell's book, and those who did criticized his use of history as tendentious, distorted, and incomplete. His refusal to make any concessions to sentimentality when thinking about war went too far for those who had been attracted to the study of war precisely because of its romantic, stylized history. Yet I thought then, and still do think, that *The Great War and Modern Memory* was one of the most important works about the history of war published during that decade.

Why? Despite the vast differences in their books, Keegan and Fussell were alike in challenging military history's deeply entrenched orthodoxy. Their knowledge, skill, and wit were not aimed at reducing the complexities of war for practical application. Their objective was understanding war, not improving its methods. They were, in fact, less interested in military history than in something quite different: the history of war itself. The distinction is not often made, but it constitutes a great divide in how military historians think about their work. More than a quarter century after these two books were published, arguments over them have barely faded. Keegan and Fussell convinced me that the study of war contained signs of life after all. Even now, when I write I imagine both of them looking over my shoulder, shaking their heads when I stray from what they taught me.

So that afternoon passed and so did our conversation, long into the night.

Fussell and I almost missed the last train back to London. Arriving at Waterloo Station, we said our good-byes and went our separate ways.

Walking back to my hotel that evening, I was glad that my discontents had not got the better of me.

In the School of War

One

On Combat

After artillery deploys for battle, arranges itself into batteries, a commander usually orders a ranging shot, a round or two meant to estimate how far his guns will reach. Or so it was before modern science intervened. Although we don't know for sure, someone among Henry V's archers at Agincourt—masters of the lethal, indirect firepower that would turn that day in his favor—must have fired such a shot, adding one more tactical detail to the King's picture of the field where he and his men were about to fight. Centuries later, Robert E. Lee reserved to himself the order for the first shot as he looked over the open fields at Fredericksburg and General Burnside's Grand Divisions forming for their attack. In those days, after throwing a few cannonballs in the enemy's direction, a commander could see for himself just when the enemy's advancing troops might fall under the shadow of his imaginary artillery fan. Then he could decide whether to open up his artillery to spoil the attack or, waiting longer, to kill it outright—the "it" being hundreds or even thousands of other human beings.

A ranging shot, which was as much an artistic as a technical feat, could tell the enemy commander something about you, too. If the shot sounded tentative or forlorn, if the crack of the gun and the snap of the explosion were somehow not so sharp, your enemy might think your defenses were too thin and then press his own attack that much more resolutely. Never mind that we've known for a long time that these sounds are influenced by atmospheric conditions, topography, and any number of other technical factors such as the quality of the gunpowder or the design of the barrel. So knowing, we might doubt cannon fire could be understood in psychological terms, but on the fields of classical battle impressions counted. Then the best commanders were said to have a knack for imagining the battle to come, sizing up the ground, their enemies, and the morale of both sides, and calculating all this in the blink of an eye—a *coup d'oeil*.

Whether any of this had any scientific credence, generals and soldiers readied themselves by the means—psychological as well as material—available to them. A few strands of a loved one's hair tucked away in a locket could be far more important to a soldier's performance than the most stirring oration by a well-fed bemedaled general or the elegant plans of a general staff. Before the battlefield exploded in spasms of violence, before the sweat-inducing stomach churning, tremors of fear coursed through the combatants' neural networks, rationality retreated to safer places, up the chain of command from one headquarters to the next, past the reports and letters and memoirs, finally coming to rest in the history books—a *coup d'oeil de dieu*, a god's-eye view.

Reaching back to where military history began, to its violent source, required some ranging shots.

My classrooms at the U.S. Army Command and General Staff College were full of professional officers, mostly majors with a dozen or more years of active service behind them, and at least a decade of service ahead. Almost all of them were veterans of the war in Vietnam.

Having seen war from the ground up as platoon leaders or company-grade officers, they reacted viscerally to even the slightest hint of sentimentality in their lectures. One important guest speaker was handled so roughly—catcalls and applause at all the wrong times—during an assembly that alarm bells sounded at Army headquarters back in Washington; an expedition of generals was hurriedly deployed from the Pentagon to "counsel" the class on its rebellious behavior. In the classrooms the sanitized general staff version of war was regarded indifferently, as irrelevant to what these officers already knew. Many officers caught up on their sleep. Elaborate maps at the front of the room overlaid with operational graphics—rectangles with a cross inside and two x's on top for an infantry division or maybe three x's for a corps, large blue arrows for friendly forces, always red for the enemy—were sometimes greeted with the question, "Are there any people in there?"

Legend has it that the inmates in one of the classrooms built a Rube Goldberg machine of pulleys and levers that dropped a rubber chicken from the rafters to the lectern so that the chicken came to a stop just in front of the instructor's face. When a lecture was going badly, someone would saunter to the back of the room, pull the lever, and drop the dreaded chicken, effectively terminating the class amid gales of laughter. Some of the poor instructors flatly refused to lecture to this notorious class. Even though many of them had seen as much of war as their students (and sometimes much more), their combat experience did not protect them if what they were teaching insulted the students' own knowledge of war.

I felt close to these students. We were about the same age then. I made no secret of having opposed the war, and they pretended not to mind. They were rough and likeable, and they often skated close to insubordination. They were not easily impressed, but they impressed me. During those years our roles were reversed: they didn't realize it, but they were my teachers.

You'd never think of them as vulnerable, but they were. Some of them did not understand what they'd been through in their war. Now they were in a school of war, where the war they knew firsthand <u>was hardly ever mentioned</u>. For years after the war in Vietnam the college offered no courses on it, as if the school's managers would do anything to avoid referring to the war. It might as well have been fought on Mars.

So they talked about their own real war in the spaces between their schooling—in the hallways, in the snack bars, between plays on the sports fields, and always during their parties in the student quarters, when two or three or four would drift away, holding an impromptu seminar at the edges of the light. By some unspoken agreement between them I was granted admission to these furtive meetings from time to time.

What they talked about was what Walt Whitman doubted would ever see light: a world so different from the high command's that it constituted an alternate universe. Their conversations slid away into subatomic reaches, their sentences trailing off as their listeners nodded knowingly. Speaking barely above a whisper, one of them told of killing an enemy soldier with his knife. He had gone too far ahead of his own men and found himself alone in a trench line facing several enemy soldiers. He fired until he ran out of ammunition, killing all but one. As the last enemy soldier ran toward him, he fumbled for his pistol. His hand found his knife instead. All the time he was speaking he was looking at the floor. No one else spoke. Then, as if returning from his memory, he looked up at the rest of us: "It was wet," he said quietly, "very wet."

How could military history encompass such knowledge as this? Some writers have tried, looking to soldiers' memoirs and letters, weaving them together to create a rational picture of battle. For the longest time even the best of these took their witnesses' memories for granted, as if these soldiers were in complete command of their faculties. But if you look carefully at how soldiers recorded their combat experiences, you'll see that they only go so far before, in the literary equivalent of throwing up their hands, they say, "Well, you just had to be there." And for the most part military history accepted this apology. We could figure out how Frederick the Great invaded Silesia or outwitted the prince de Soubise at Rossbach. We could follow the Marines into Belleau Wood during World War I or go ashore with the infantry at Normandy on D-Day. But did we really know what was happening to the human beings who were doing the fighting? Were there ways to penetrate war at its most elemental level?

"Fresh idioms" is what the poet and critic R. P. Blackmur called means of expression so radically new that they added to "the stock of reality." Military history seemed to have exhausted its idioms; fresh idioms, different ways of seeing the military past, were required. I was certainly not the only one who thought so. Already some scholars were breaking out of these confines in a movement that would come to be known as "the new military history," setting their work in much broader cultural and social context and ranging into other disciplines. The old general staff model that had guided how war was understood could not accommodate these new approaches. Some of these works drew on studies of human behavior that directly challenged orthodox military thought. They offered new ways of seeing into war's innermost workings and with a degree of precision that literature and even history could only approximate.

One of my best friends, Reggie Shrader, who was then a colleague at the staff college, had the idea of floating a seminar called "Men in Battle" in an effort to find new ways to understand the human experience of war. Keegan's *The Face of Battle* was our starting point, and Fussell's *The Great War and Modern Memory* convinced me that war literature—memoirs as well as fiction—could act as a powerful counterweight to military history's hierarchical, mechanistic depiction of war. So the seminar's readings in military history were leavened with classics of war literature such as Stephen Crane's *The Red Badge of Courage*, Robert Graves's *Good-Bye to All That*, and Erich Maria Remarque's *All Quiet on the Western Front* as well as memoirs such as Audie Murphy's *To Hell and Back*, John Muirhead's *Those Who Fall*, and Harold Leinbaugh and John Campbell's *The Men of Company K*.

Those officers who found their way into the seminar exuded more than a hint of rebellion. At the time the Army's version of their war was that it hadn't been lost in the field. Instead, a whole catalog of other causes was marshaled, the sum of which amounted to a modern American version of the old "stab in the back" excuse the Germans had constructed to explain their defeat in World War I. But a goodly number of these officers read their own war much more frankly and in a broader perspective than their discredited leaders. The younger generation had taken command of its own war history. By miscalculating the war so badly, their elders had forfeited any influence over their professional opinions.

Since leaving their battlefields behind these officers had constructed their personal histories by filing the rough edges from their memories, cobbling together their own experiences, trying to understand a war that had yet to be translated into knowledge. Their histories were therefore deeply personal, composed less of intellect than of emotion. Although they willingly discussed the old wars, their introspections seemed to paralyze them when we reached their war. That was when I assigned them to read Michael Herr's *Dispatches*. A piece of fiction that masqueraded as a memoir, Herr's book embodied virtually every discontent professional soldiers harbored in those days. Assigning *Dispatches* was like throwing raw meat to lions. Our meetings began to run long. Colleagues passing by the seminar room heard shouting and fists banging on desks. Other instructors complained that these students came late to their classes because they'd stayed behind to talk after our class was over.

The day after an especially intense discussion about Vietnam one of my students, an infantry officer, told me he and his wife had talked all night about his time in combat—something they'd never done in ten years of being together. To all appearances this officer was a steady, even-tempered professional in complete command of himself. But for nearly a decade, he confessed, he'd suffered nightmares, depression, and unaccountable outbursts of anger. Horrendous memories attacked him at odd moments. He had trouble fixing his mind on mundane tasks. Frequently, he felt on the verge of tears for no reason. He feared he was losing control of himself. He'd spared his wife no details while recounting what he'd gone through. Now somewhat relieved, he thought he might be able to talk his way through his problems. He had decided to seek professional counseling.

As he talked, I mostly listened, asking questions from time to time to keep him talking, keeping my opinions to myself. I feared I might do more harm than good if I presumed to do more than sympathize with his illness.

And it was an illness.

Our conversation took place at a time when any discussion of the war's psychological costs met with deep skepticism. Heated debates among psychiatrists and psychologists were entangled with public confusion over trends that purported to show high incidences of suicide, depression, and destructive behavior among Vietnam veterans. Inside the medical profession, a movement led by antiwar psychiatrists argued that this war was uniquely responsible for a constellation of psychological disorders—a "Post-Vietnam Syndrome." In an eerie replay of the debates after World War I over "shell shock," PVS was adopted as a public diagnosis, a shorthand that seemed to explain these veterans' dysfunctional behavior.

The medical profession finally compromised on how to define these disorders in 1980. The symptoms described to me by my student were not, the profession decided, the consequence of only this war. What came to be known as post-traumatic stress disorder, or PTSD, could appear after any war. Indeed, PTSD might be the result of *any* sort of mental trauma at all.

Regardless of scientific or public opinion, inside the Army a profound suspicion held sway. Men who stayed in the Army after the war feared that if they took their complaints to their own medical service their professional standing was at risk. Soldiers have a fondness for gossip that would make a bridge party gasp. Word was sure to get out. Like the officer who visited me that day, they believed that if they were going to find any help, it would have to be concealed from their fellow soldiers. I was sure that the only reason this officer had come to me was that I was an outsider. Talking to me was professionally safe.

Nothing in my formal education prepared me for this encounter—the first of several over the next few years. During my own time in uniform, however, I had served as a medic and later had worked my way through college as a medical attendant in an emergency room. Along the way I dealt with patients in various stages of mental distress, from mild discomfort all the way to complete psychotic collapse. For me, mental illness was no myth. Now, quite unexpectedly, my earlier experience was intersecting with my work as a military historian.

I had no ambition to become an amateur therapist, but these cases led me to an accident of understanding. They reflected combat experience largely ignored by military history, but scientists had taken notice. Ever since the advent of modern medicine in the nineteenth century, medical pioneers had slowly constructed a new body of scientific knowledge about human behavior, especially behavior under conditions of acute stress. A library full of this work waited for anyone who took the trouble to draw from it.

Armies were having none of this. Military conceptions of human behavior were—and are—little more than an assortment of hoary traditions, folk wisdom, myth, and prejudice. By the end of the nineteenth century, physicians across the landscape of Western science had taken notice of war's psychological costs, but as armies marched off to the First World War, their old beliefs marched with them. When the western front produced tens of thousands of psychological casualties that these old beliefs could not accommodate, the gulf between official and scientific explanations narrowed, but only temporarily. Hard-won lessons about the psychodynamics of combat from World War I were quickly set aside only to be relearned during World War II. Between World War II and Vietnam armies forgot these lessons again.

By then the contest between the military and scientific worlds over how to define soldierly conduct was nearly a century old. This contest turned on the question of whether a soldier's behavior was volitional, whether soldiers were in complete control of their own actions, even—especially—when their own survival and their comrades' were at stake. Scientists had long since decided that one's actions were not entirely governed by free will; just as one's breathing doesn't depend on thinking about it, some of the mind's operations do not depend on conscious decisions.

But armies live and die on their discipline. They train their soldiers to act collectively at the extremes of human performance; by surrendering their individuality, soldiers are taught that they can achieve results together they could never win singly. If some part of a soldier's behavior is beyond his army's reach, however, long-held assumptions about how to manipulate and manage him disintegrate. In professional military circles this was too far to go. Accepting scientific conceptions of human behavior was tantamount to overthrowing a body of military thought that had been centuries in the making. To many professional soldiers denial seemed the safest course of action.

This great divide between science and military tradition intensified my curiosity, pushing me in a direction I'd never expected to go. My experiment with the seminar convinced me that literature could be used to get at parts of war that military history had hardly touched. But the war one saw in those parts was war beyond the footnotes. However compelling Remarque's descriptions of life in the trenches of the western front, and however stimulating Crane's account of the soldier's inner torments, there always remained the question of how their insights could be translated into precise historical knowledge. At times our seminar discussions collapsed into generalities. Whitman's shadow seemed as impenetrable as ever. So the experiment went on.

My encounters with officers suffering from the traumas of their combat experiences drove me to different parts of the library. The spaces on my shelves next to the military history and literature began to fill up with histories of military medicine, psychiatry, and psychology, learned articles from medical journals, psychiatric case histories, accounts of treatments and therapies, and studies of social psychology during wartime. Their cumulative effect was a depressing awareness of my own ignorance and an equal determination to fuse this body of knowledge with my own.

A certain artifice attends any collection of essays. Lining them up suggests the thought behind them is driven by a constancy of mind that isn't clear when they're written. They fit, if at all, only in retrospect. The essays that follow are like ranging shots into the dark, feeling for the boundaries of my ignorance, hinting at how to arrange my formations, and deciding which direction to march. But the battle was just beginning, and even now it goes on.

ONE. Isen's Run

Human Dimensions of Warfare in the Twentieth Century

On the wall of my office at the U.S. Army Command and General Staff College there hangs an official U.S. Marine Corps photograph from the battle of Okinawa. Private Paul Isen of the Fifth Marines is crossing a blasted landscape known as "death valley" to those who fought there in May 1945. On the day the photograph was taken "death valley" was raked with Japanese machine gun fire. Isen is running through the fire at full tilt, his body in the attitude of a sprinter just off the blocks. His rifle is at port arms, held in the usual way across his chest, and his right hand grips the stock of his weapon at the balance point.

All the angles described by Isen's figure suggest the most intense concentration and speed. As if to confirm the danger of the scene, the photograph has been taken from the relative safety of a nearby hole. One can see the lip of the cameraman's haven in the foreground of the shot. When I look at this picture, I think of it as the essence of soldiering.

Isen is alone in the picture. Although combat soldiering is an affair of groups, the members of which sustain one another, often at the risk of their own lives, the final proposition of soldiering in modern times is that it is an intensely personal struggle against death and destruction. Isen is alone in another respect as well—that is how history has left him. Across the long march of military history the combat soldier has often been the last and least important consideration of those who make war and those who study it.

Some have gone so far as to argue that men who do Isen's kind of work are incidental to the conduct of war. During an army's campaign, so the argument goes, few days are spent in actual battle, and those who actually do the fighting are only a small part of the vast numbers required to sustain an army in the field. Mathematically correct, of course, this proves once again that the ability to count is not necessarily evidence of higher learning. The same writer who poses these equations goes on to assert that "battle is not the logical culmination of military operations." He does not inform us, however, what is.

Such terms of reference are useful only as long as they encourage, not inhibit, understanding. When we think about modern war in mechanistic terms, mathematical arguments about the logical culmination of military operations seem reasonable to us, and cold logic makes its usual promises. I think such an approach to understanding war is far off the mark, and in this I claim the support of Carl von Clausewitz, who wrote that in war one senses that "here ideas are governed by other factors, that the light of reason is refracted in a manner quite different from that which is normal in academic speculation." Anyone who thinks seriously about war is certainly obliged to master its mechanical aspects, but mechanics alone will never master the subject of war. That is why it is often called an art.

The modern evolution of war has conditioned us to think in terms of mechanics—technology, systems, organization—and we can see why. At the beginning of the nineteenth century a revolution in the technology of warfare, a feature of the industrial revolution itself, burst upon the military scene. Until then military technology had been a near constant factor in the conduct of war. The standard weapons used by soldiers at the battle of Waterloo in 1815 were based upon patterns essentially unchanged for 125 years. Only a few years after Waterloo new weapons appeared that altered the very character of combat. The new weapons could fire faster, more accurately, and at far greater ranges. In the wake of these the old forms of warfare were swept aside.

Associating the revolution in warfare with the industrial revolution is a common refrain among military historians. The interpretation seems to encompass what we know about the history of modern battle. Because of the new weapons—rifles and quick-firing artillery—the old, densely packed battle formations fell slowly out of fashion, and other tactics were conceived to correspond with the new combat power that technology had placed in the hands of the soldiers.

Even the power of command dispersed; under the old style, a commander could make his directions be heard and obeyed. As soldiers scattered over the battlefield, the commander's direct power was diminished, and battle leaders grappled with this new geography of combat for the better part of a century. The new style of war demanded more of the individual soldier. Decisions in combat that once were reserved for the aristocracy of battle—the commanders—were pushed down to the ranks of the ordinary fighter: Do I advance? Do I take cover? Do I fire now? Do I retreat? Do I surrender? Technological change seemed to be the proximate reason the responsibilities of the soldier had changed so vastly.

Yet another revolution was in the making—the democratic revolution. This was a cultural transformation of the first magnitude, one whose significance to our present lives dwarfs all others. One upshot of this revolution was the overturning of the notion that history was the exclusive property of those who supposedly controlled events. The ordinary, individual man began to matter. What he did, what he said, what he wrote, and how he behaved became important. If we insist that technology alone determined how the new soldier fought, then we discount the influence of the democratic revolution upon the battlefield. Perhaps this new revolution made certain technological alternatives possible. Inventions are merely the material reflections of a culture. Should we be so quick to believe that inventors and military theorists are immune from these influences?

I cite this problem because it emphasizes how a particular orientation shapes our understanding. If we believe that technology is at the root of all events, then we seek our understanding there. Because technology has played such a large and obvious role in modern military thought and practice, and because the connections between technology and war are so direct and simple, we are inclined to think that understanding war lies exclusively down that road. I think we have misled ourselves.

I believe that Isen might even agree with me, for if one listens carefully to how soldiers talk about war, it immediately becomes evident that the world they inhabit is entirely different from the one military experts write about. Let me demonstrate what I mean.

Sometime early in 1916 Capt. W. P. Neville, a company commander in the Eighth East Surrey Regiment of the British Army, made a curious purchase while on home leave from the western front. He bought four footballs (soccer balls), one for each of his platoons, and when he rejoined his unit he parceled them out. The footballs were for a special, one might even say unique, purpose: Neville was going to use them against his enemy. For several weeks the troops in the trenches on both sides had seen signs that a big attack was in the making along the Somme River in France. One week before the attack 1,537 artillery pieces began firing barrages without letup. Before the bombardment had ended 1.5 million shells had been fired. At 0730 on the morning of 1 July 1916, 110,000 Allied soldiers attacked along a front that was 13 miles wide.

Somewhere among the throngs of British soldiers Neville's footballs came into play. His idea was that each of his platoons would kick its football toward the enemy's trenches. Whoever kicked the ball deepest into the enemy positions won. As the attack began an observer down the line watched the Surreys jump off. "As the gun-fire died away, I saw an infantryman climb onto the parapet into no man's land, beckoning the others to follow. As he did so he kicked off a football. A good kick. The ball rose and traveled towards the German line. That seemed to be the signal to advance."

Neville was killed instantly, and within the next fifteen minutes so were 20,000 other soldiers. Before the day was out more than 60,000 men had been killed or wounded. Even so, one of Neville's footballs allegedly had made it a mile and a half into the enemy's defenses.

This remarkable incident, recounted in Paul Fussell's *The Great War and Modern Memory*, strikes us today as unusual, to say the least. Neville appears to have been out of touch with the very deadly reality that he and his company faced. However, the athletic feats of Neville's Surrey troops were not unprecedented. Footballs had led other attacks in this war. And if we know that for some time in England gamesmanship had been used as a way of talking and writing about war, we are a little closer to understanding what Neville was about.

Now it is highly unlikely that one would find Neville's stunt in a formal treatise on warfare. The military historian might call this story forth to show that Neville was a blockhead in the mold of those who ordered this disastrous attack, but to do so would miss the point. Neville and his troops were speaking to us in the soldier's voice, dealing with their war in terms that— although they corresponded in no way with those of the theoretician or the historian—nevertheless were as legitimate as any other point of view.

Neville had turned war into a game. He attempted to make his war understandable, an event so far outside his normal range of understanding that it was otherwise incomprehensible. He could contend with sport but perhaps not with the war that lay in undisguised ugliness beyond his own trench line. In the very same spirit airmen in World War II painted cartoons and happy designs on their aircraft. Later still, in Vietnam, soldiers used their helmets as billboards, advertising their own way of contending with war in signs and symbols that their generation had made available to them.

Who has the better claim on reality, the theoretician at the staff college or the combat soldier? We assume the theoretician's view of battle is legitimate: at least he makes the confusions of war orderly. At the staff college the progress of campaigns is mapped in big red and blue arrows. Fixed lines everywhere describe territory held and contested. Assembly positions, routes of march, and whole units are reduced to symbols.

A fighting division of 10,000 or 15,000 men becomes a square, easily moved here and there. Interestingly, no symbols show how effective a unit is after days of battle. If a unit can no longer fight, the staff officer simply moves the square to an inactive part of the map. Sometimes the staff officer's detachment from battle leads to a soul-shattering frisson. A story from World War I goes that when a certain staff officer was shown no-man's-land on a visit to the fighting line, he looked out over the wire at the shell holes, wrecked equipment, debris, and corpses and said, "My god. Did we actually send men into this?"

Imagine, then, how detached history and social memory can become from war. Soldiers have often been dismayed to see how history has treated battles in which they actually fought. The novelist James Jones, himself a veteran of the Twenty-fifth Infantry Division's Pacific campaigns in World War II, declared after reading accounts of his unit's operations, "History is always written from the viewpoint of the leaders." Jones had since conceived his own succinct history of war in the Pacific. He wrote: "I went where I was told to go, and did what I was told to do, but no more. I was scared shitless just about all of the time."

"But no more . . ." Jones wrote. The picture of a soldier's life in battle as one continuous round of dramatic heroics, fighting on bravely for a cause, is one for which Jones and perhaps most combat veterans still alive would only have contempt. Studs Terkel called World War II "The Good War," but that was a portrayal soldiers at the time would have thought was a silly contradiction in terms.

Societies invest sentiments in war that on the combat lines have little or no meaning. Ideology or patriotism or some other cause may well get the recruit to the enlistment station when the war breaks out, and these motives are not to be discounted. In the early days of World War I men threw themselves under trains at Waterloo Station in London after being refused for military service. Once in combat, however, the blush of patriotic fervor fades, overcome by the immediate stresses of battle. An Army psychiatrist who served in North Africa during World War II found that front-line lectures on the cause of freedom thoughtfully arranged by rear headquarters only succeeded in irritating combat infantrymen. Other motivations derived from combat itself had long since superseded any prewar enthusiasm that might have moved recruits to join the colors. And, after all, who could be so presumptuous as to lecture men on a cause for which, whether or not they acknowledged it, they daily risked their lives?

Of course, armies invest a great deal in their own myths and, what is more, have the power to impose them upon their soldiers. Armies have had a great and abiding faith in the idea that military training can prepare a soldier for combat, and many soldiers have testified that training can physically toughen the man destined for the fighting lines. Good training can show a soldier how to use the tools of combat, including his fellow soldiers. However, even the best training is never equal to combat. When training is deficient or indifferent or misguided, based upon an ill-founded idea of what combat may be like, it is as dangerous to the fighting soldier as an enemy bullet.

Before Neville and his men went over the top that day on the Somme, they no doubt had been drilled in the best parade ground fashion, and their manual of arms was no doubt of a high standard. However, they had also been instructed to climb calmly out of their trenches and walk forward, upright, with their bayonets fixed, since military doctrines held that such intense artillery bombardments would have utterly destroyed the enemy's defenses. The casualty lists that day told of the great distance between training and the realities of combat.

Our faith in training is part of a larger belief that experience counts. Even if training falls short, we believe that once a man goes into combat he constantly accumulates the special kind of experience that will defend him. Military historians are particularly fond of writing about units that are "battle hardened" or "battle tested" or "seasoned." Seldom do we admit that "seasoning" entails the suffering of casualties. How many casualties are necessary to "season" a unit? The more the better? How "seasoned" may a unit be before it literally falls apart? When I see such terms, I think of the characters in Stephen Crane's *The*

Red Badge of Courage who begin their war anxious to see battle and then in a blast furnace of a fight between two regiments only yards away from one another exclaim, "Oh, I say, this is too much of a good thing!"

Studies during World War II found that most casualties were suffered by men who were new to a fighting unit, leading some to conclude that experience was a vital factor in survival. Combat soldiers do indeed educate themselves to battle, learning to handle their weapons in ways their trainers never anticipated, learning how to use the slightest bit of ground for shelter, indeed, learning a whole catalog of practical skills that never find their way into training manuals. However, the sad fact is that even if one soldiers perfectly, one may not live out the day.

The soldier's life in combat is one in which his defenses, fragile to begin with, are slowly torn apart. If the cause for which he fights and the training he receives are insufficient to withstand the fortunes of battle, what is left to sustain him?

Only his comrades remain. In war after war soldiers have testified that the presence of their fellow soldiers enabled them to carry on when all other protections failed them. Yet comrades extend the soldier's vulnerability in an important way: comrades become casualties too. A soldier may invest all the faith he has left in his friends only to see them die one by one, as did Erich Maria Remarque's Paul Bäumer in *All Quiet on the Western Front*. They are friends whom, made early in his combat life, he does not replace. Histories make much of a combat unit's esprit de corps, but all too often we forget that a combat unit is an ever-changing human organism. One savage artillery barrage or one well-sited machine gun can wreck the most spirited unit.

When a military unit enters combat, all the forces of battle work toward its destruction, to break its cohesion and render it useless, and unless great care is taken by its leaders, that unit will not regenerate itself. Units long in combat are made up of small cliques of veterans who do not easily admit replacements into their ranks. World War II replacements were ordinarily put to work carrying rations, ammunition, and the wounded. This kind of work could easily be more dangerous than the veteran's: it was carried out in that zone just behind the active firing line, where enemy patrols operated and artillery shells routinely dropped, all at a time when the opportunity for protection was minimal. Many men died before anyone in the unit knew their names. They were not so fortunate as the new soldier taken under a veteran's wing and taught the ways of combat. But then he could become a casualty anyway.

Today, when veterans of World War II greet each other at reunions, they do so as fellow survivors of a disaster might, in a congratulatory fashion. Surely their common experience is their bond, but so too is the simple, profound fact of their survival. By contrast, Vietnam veterans seem to come together differently, if at all. During their war a soldier was largely trained as an individual, sent to war as an individual, and, as an individual, was required to serve in combat for one year. From the day of his arrival in Vietnam the soldier counted down his remaining days on his own personal calendar.

The camaraderie of World War II was based partly on a traditional soldier's contract: soldiers would fight until they were killed or wounded or until the war was over. The limited tour of duty in Vietnam virtually ensured that all a soldier's relationships, no matter how intense they seemed at the time, were conditional. When his tour was finished, he would have no compunction about abandoning these wartime relationships. He returned home alone. In a curious reversal of soldierly tradition, Vietnam veterans may have experienced more sustained fellow feeling with their comrades after leaving their war than they ever had while they fought it.

The soldier's relationship with his comrades is not the only association he establishes in combat, however. From the moment he steps inside the recruiting hall until the day he escapes from the world of combat, the soldier constructs the most elaborate relationship with his enemy. At first, of course, the enemy is ill defined, the product of wartime propaganda. In modern wars we have insisted particularly that the enemy be evil as well.

John Dower's brilliant study of attitudes toward the Japanese in World War II, *War without Mercy: Race and Power in the Pacific War*, makes plain how racism was put to use during the Pacific campaigns. There the stresses of intense jungle combat compounded the hatred U.S. soldiers felt for their enemies, whom they often regarded, in the words of another writer, as "a species of animal pest." However, in modern war, when so much of combat depends upon individual action, a wary mutual admiration develops even between the most dedicated enemies.

Remarque's *All Quiet on the Western Front* stated a proposition that doubtless startled many of his readers: soldiers in his war did not fight each other—they fought against the war itself. Half a century later in Vietnam soldiers would sometimes refer to their enemies in grudgingly respectful tones and talk about their skill, dedication, and courage, not so different from the young Union soldier in *The Red Badge of Courage* who thought of his Confederate opponents as "machines of steel."

Outsiders—those who have never been in combat—would think it strange to learn that on Christmas Day in 1914 French, German, and British soldiers on the western front climbed out of their trenches to meet in no-man's-land, where they exchanged cigarettes, food and drink, photos and addresses and sang songs. A company of the Second Battalion, Lancashire Fusiliers, and a Saxon company even played football. One wonders if Neville was available. On other, perhaps countless occasions soldiers have arranged delicate local truces. Very near where Neville attacked in 1916 the trench lines had been so quiet earlier that soldiers walked about freely during the day, well within range of enemy guns, without being molested. High commands naturally were alarmed by such practices and did their best to prevent them.

I do not agree with those who have suggested that this sort of behavior is the result of civilized upbringing or that society's normal injunction against killing somehow finds its way onto the battlefield and discourages wanton slaughter. That notion seems to have been disproved by the experience of our wars in the twentieth century.

I think the reasons for soldierly conduct lie elsewhere. Within the world of combat a peculiar and highly specialized society is created, one where rules, rituals, codes of conduct and behavior, standards of success and failure are in force that are confusing and strange to the casual observer. If this society of combat is volatile and transitory, and if its characteristics are uncharted by theorists and historians, that is not to say that it does not exist.

In the society of combat war itself assumes shapes altogether different from those concocted by society, government, or even one's own high command. A society might aim for the triumph of an ideology or revenge for a great wrong such as Pearl Harbor. Governments resort to war as the means of achieving those aims. Commanders look always to victory, which in the twentieth century was defined as the destruction of the enemy's will to resist. History commonly assumes that the aims of society, the means of government, and the ambitions of the commander are those of the soldier as well.

If we allow the soldier to speak for himself, however, we see a different set of standards altogether. The concept of victory is too abstract, too distant to be of much practical use to the soldier. For society, victory means the survival of the cause, and we have already seen that causes do little to help the soldier in combat. If the commander works mightily toward dominance on the battlefield, he assumes that he naturally serves the best interests of the soldiers under his control. However, the greatest commanders in history littered battlefields with their own dead as well as with the enemy. How then do the commander's objectives correspond with those of his soldiers?

The commander might argue that casualties have to be taken for the greater good, for a defeat would mean the death or capture of many more of his soldiers. The argument is a compelling one that conveys the hard task of battle commanders throughout history, but we should not expect soldiers, whose concerns are more immediate and whose standards of behavior are set by combat itself, to have much sympathy for their commander's problems. Especially in modern times soldiers have been a good deal more cynical about the men who enforce their participation in battle. Listen to these bitter lines from World War I by Siegfried Sassoon titled "The General":

"Good morning! Good morning!" the General said
when we met him last week on the way to the line.
Now the soldiers he smiled at are most of 'em dead,
and we're cursing his staff for incompetent swine.

What, then, constitutes victory for the soldier? In the first instance survival itself. If he can survive without debilitating wounds that torture him for the rest of his life, so much the better. Soldiers in both world wars developed an elegantly precise scale of which wounds were better than others and even the kinds of weapons they preferred to inflict them. In modern wars, when combat medical care has developed to a high pitch of life-saving efficiency, soldiers have come to regard wounds as not the worst thing that could happen to them. Modern soldiers have seen wounds as a legitimate way to escape combat, for a wound honorably received absolves the soldier from all responsibilities to his comrades. World War II medical officers were puzzled when they first saw stretcher cases coming in from the front lines; wounded men, even some wounded disastrously, were smiling. "Million-dollar wounds," the men called them, wounds that ensured they would not return to the world of combat. Then there were the poor soldiers who could not wait for chance or the enemy and simply shot themselves. SIWS (self-inflicted wounds), so recorded on the casualty reports, created anger, self-righteous indignation, and even courts-martial in the rear areas. At the front, however, SIWS were more pitied than hated by their fellow soldiers.

"Up there" or "up front" was what U.S. soldiers in World War II called the front lines, as if a higher form of existence awaited. Before going into combat soldiers worried whether they would be killed outright. After the initial shock subsided they wondered whether they would disgrace themselves or let their buddies down. During their initiation to combat they would often become paralyzed with fear, lose control of their bowels, become drenched with cold sweats, or experience tremors immediately after the crisis had passed. Sometimes a kind of trance took over, and time became distorted. Memory did not always function, and soldiers often could not recall what had happened or in what sequence events had occurred.

These were normal reactions to combat. A fatal sameness of events closed in on the soldier if he stayed in combat long enough. Combat consisted of taking each minute as it happened, each day, each mile. "To one who has been up there," one officer observed in World War II, "there is no such thing as getting used to it."

How do men stand it? Many do not. Modern armies have recognized that fighting men have their limits. The one-year tour in Vietnam perhaps was intended to see that men did not wear out under the strain of combat, but how the Army arrived at this figure and why are still open questions. In World War II the U.S. Army officially set 250 days of combat as a soldier's maximum; for the British Army the figure was fixed at 400 days. Long before these official limits were reached, however, the few soldiers who remained were no longer of much military use.

From the beginning of the twentieth century armies were forced to deal with soldiers who simply collapsed under the stresses of combat. The Russo-Japanese War of 1904–5, in many ways a precursor to World War I, first produced officially recognized combat stress casualties. Never known for its humane treatment of its soldiers, the Russian Army had no choice but to provide for men who, though outwardly unharmed, had been so mentally destroyed they could no longer function. The Russian Army's central psychiatric hospital in Harbin, China, reported more than 1,700 cases at the end of 1904; by early 1905 the cases were so numerous that they had to be distributed among regular field hospitals. Before that war was over nearly half a million Russian soldiers fought against a like number of Japanese. Whether officially recognized or not, the actual number of combat stress cases was very likely four or five times higher than those who were lucky enough to make it to the hospital.

When the Great War broke out, armies on the western front

had to contend with thousands of cases of what came to be called "shell shock." The discovery of soldierly limits clashed directly with old romantic views of how a soldier was supposed to conduct himself in battle, and some commanders flatly refused to admit these newer, scientifically defined standards of combat behavior. Even medical treatment for psychiatric casualties seemed at times to hold to the old standards, but the statistics were so overwhelming that they could hardly be ignored.

From 1916 to 1920 the British Army reported 41,746 psychiatric casualties, or 4 percent of all casualties taken. One of those cases was that of a twenty-four-year-old private who had been mute for nine months. He had fought in the retreat from Mons, the battles of the Marne and Aisne, and the first and second battles of Ypres. He had fought at Hill 60, Neuve-Chapelle, Loosen-Gohelle, and Armentières. Then he went to fight at Gallipoli, where he collapsed from heat exhaustion. When he awoke, he could not speak. His medical treatment, intended to return his psychological planets to their rightful orbits, was electric shock and the application of "hot plates" and lighted cigarettes to his mouth.

Well into World War II a soldier's breakdown in combat was regarded as evidence of a deficient character. The widespread view that men with good characters made the best soldiers is an innovation of modern war. Earlier, commanders believed just the reverse and so attempted to recruit men from the dregs of society whose hard upbringing supposedly shielded their less-sensitive natures from the trials of combat.

Whatever official and scientific explanation happened to be in vogue at the time, the U.S. Army seemed powerless to prevent soldiers from collapsing under the strains of battle. Furthermore, many soldiers showed no signs of psychiatric illness until well after their war was over. In 1942 American veterans' hospitals held more shell shock patients from World War I than any other category—68,000 men, or 58 percent of all patients.

The Army in World War II was no better at dealing with these casualties than its predecessor. In 1944 shell shock, or "combat fatigue," as it was called, was the leading cause of evacuation of soldiers from the overseas theaters of war to the United States. By then more than one million men had been relieved from service for psychiatric reasons.

The Vietnam War gave these illnesses a new name, one more in accord with our scientific presumptions: post-traumatic stress syndrome. At first officials were encouraged by the extremely low incidence of psychiatric casualties in Vietnam: compared to 23 percent in World War II, the casualty rate in Vietnam was only 1.5 percent. However, the brief tour of duty and the widespread availability of ways for a soldier to "medicate" himself seem to have simply postponed the eruption of personality disorders until the soldier was safely back home and out of service. About a million soldiers saw combat in Vietnam during our eight years there. Some investigators estimate that between 560,000 and 700,000 of these men will suffer some form of post-traumatic stress, and one claim pushes the figure to as many as 800,000 men, or eight of every ten men who actually saw combat in the war.

Yet old romantic notions about war and what it is like to have fought in one have remarkable staying power. The vast body of knowledge about how men behaved in combat during World War I was discarded promptly after the armistice, only to be relearned in World War II. I suspect that in Vietnam the problem was generally ignored, but to be fair I should point out that even the American Psychiatric Association did not finally agree on a definition of post-traumatic stress until 1980. However, not so very long ago I had conversations with professional military officers who preferred to believe that post-traumatic stress is a sign of weakness in one's character. Significantly, none of these officers has himself been in war. "Hell hath no fury," Charles E. Montague said, "like a noncombatant."

The competition between science and military tradition to explain the human dimensions of combat makes clear that our knowledge after 3,500 years of recorded military history is still very crude. Confronted by what they perceive as an ever more stressful combat environment, some writers are wondering now whether combat has lost its usefulness in warfare. However, speculations of this kind are possible only if one confuses the mechanics of war with its essential human character. "The tactical fact," S. L. A. Marshall once wrote, "which is at once the simplest and most complex topic in the military art—man himself as a figure on the field of combat."

What I have tried to do here is offer a glimpse inside the combat soldier's very special world, a world largely undiscovered by either military theory or history. To have any hope of understanding this world one must adopt a way of looking at war that is at variance with traditional views. Since much of this essay is about standards, I should say that the only standard that makes sense to me comes from that young Marine whose picture I mentioned earlier. For me, Isen's run represents the soldier's real world frozen in midstride. I have not had the courage to inquire whether Isen survived his war. If, however, when I am writing in my office I can imagine Isen nodding his head approvingly, my standards for remembering war will have been met.

TWO. **My Guns**

I was born in 1944, toward the middle of October, when a lot of people were getting killed for me, or blown up, or shot, or captured, or worse. Worse? "The shell hit him about here," said a veteran not long ago, remembering that time and place. "He disappeared."

The ones who survived their military service in those years eventually got their discharges, went home, went to work, raised families, and are now of an age to retire. Old age is beginning to do what the war could not, or would not. All these people, men and women, living or not, are part of what must be the most written-about generation in American history. As generations come and go this is a particularly distinguished one compared, say, with my own.

What, then, should one of my generation say in commemoration of those who fought in this war, most of the important things—presumably—already having been said? We know where all these people went and what they did. Any military atlas will show very large colored arrows, pointing this way and that. This is how the Australians and the Yanks traversed the Kokoda Trail to split New Guinea in half. On another page we can see Guadalcanal, an inconsiderable island, so far out of the way. Still farther on there is the campaign in North Africa and then inexorable progress across the Mediterranean to Italy, another jump into France (the "dash across France" is a perennially favorite phrase). Over in Poland, Byelorussia, and the Ukraine the situation becomes a test of the cartographer's art; everything seems a little messier. Back in the Pacific the friendly arrows multiply and advance toward the top of the page, "stepping-stones" to victory against Japan. Anyone can see how simple it is; anyone can criticize what was done, saying this was a better way. Why couldn't they see it then?

We have the numbers too. Nearly to a finality we can calculate the people involved, those killed and wounded ("disappeared" poses greater difficulties), where they were mostly killed or wounded, and what mostly killed or wounded them. For soldiers, artillery seemed to be the killer of killers. For civilians (let us not forget that more civilians were killed in this war than soldiers), gas or bombs, in that order. Indeed, all those matters that can be reduced to numbers have been, the tangibles as always being the most easily approached without understanding. Ships, planes, tanks, artillery pieces, "small" arms—"small" always referring to the size of the weapon and its projectile, not the damage it could do to a person—all these fill up the very large picture books found on the remainder shelves of local bookstores.

If all this leaves us less than satisfied, we can know so much about the statesmen and generals of World War II that they seem like members of our own families. Their lives are so well accounted for that in the unlikely event a gap appeared in their wartime chronologies, it would constitute a mystery sufficiently great to set battalions of historians into frenzied activity. The fraudulent "Hitler diaries" of a few years ago come to mind; we were nonplussed that something so potentially significant could have escaped notice, so accustomed were we to knowing everything about this war.

Even a certain dislike of reading should pose no impediment to knowing about the war. Virtually every night of the year television broadcasts some program on the war—the bigger, more visually dramatic pieces of the war, of course, but conveying a kind of recognition all the same. It is just possible that our present knowledge of the war comes mostly from this source, condensed, trivialized, and certainly very highly organized in digestible segments (one hour on "Barbarossa," the German invasion of Russia).

With all these rather insistent intrusions of war history upon our modern consciousness, it might seem strange to argue that we have lost sight of the real war altogether. That was precisely the thesis Studs Terkel meant to convey when he wrote *"The Good War": An Oral History of World War II*, bracketing his title in quotation marks that dripped with irony. But irony turned back on Terkel: it was a good war even to many who participated in it, and, furthermore, it got better all the time as the decisiveness of the Allied victory slowly revealed itself. Our very human impulse is to negotiate constantly with our memory, to domesticate it and manage it, remembering the good parts. With every passing year the old, real war loses another round in the negotiations.

The fiftieth anniversaries of the war are upon us. As in the real war, Americans are the latecomers. Europeans have been taking notice for a good two years, but the rush of events behind the old iron curtain has left precious few energies for commemorating the past. If our commemorations repeat the pattern of the war itself, our consciousness of the war will build to a kind of crescendo by about 1994. How, then, at a half-century's remove, can we make a new approach on that time and its people, especially when its evidence and effect are still so much a part of us and still so meaningful to the events we see unfold on the nightly news? How do we pay proper attention to the old war and what it means without further contributing to what Paul Fussell has called the "disneyfication" of the war?

The answer for me cannot be wholly historical; such an answer implies an emotional distance from the war that I do not enjoy. My connection to this war is one of long and personal standing, and my connection to its people is so close that I dread reading obituaries for fear that one of my old war people has died. Those who made history so fresh for me are disappearing one by one.

Exactly when I became sentient about war in general or particularly about this war I cannot say. It never seems to have been far away. I recall, imprecisely, photographs of relatives in uniform, well scrubbed, creased, and confident, very much younger than I thought they ever could have been. Growing up in the fifties, my friends and I always had at hand an old helmet, a shirt, or a bayonet to complement the imagination of the playground. Bloodstained items were a great premium to us. No one thought for a moment about the cost of these things. The father of one of my playmates was missing several fingers, lost in combat somewhere, torn away by a stream of machine-gun fire—or so it was rumored among us. He was otherwise a calm, respectable adult presence on the fringes of childhood life, but his debility added immeasurably to his mana, a piece of secret knowledge to be conveyed in whispers on the playground. Sometimes we played him in action, traumatic amputation and all.

Since then I have studied war more seriously, or so I think. I would like to think as well that I grew out of that childish infatuation with the play of war, but I often wonder if that is true. Once I began to study war in earnest I wondered whether I had made any intellectual progress at all. The questions that still interested me were a child's questions, really, chief among them, What is it really like? Not the war of the statesmen or the generals. Not the war of the scientists or the staff officers. Not even the war of the field commanders. To verge on being unkind as well as ungrateful, all these people were really office workers. I wanted to know about war at the darkest corner of its heart, that one quality that so differentiates war from all other human activity: combat itself.

For years now I have moved through the world of soldiers and soldiering as a privileged spectator, and it is from them that I have inherited a certain interest in the practicalities—what Fussell would call the actualities—of war, not to mention a certain impatience with the more domesticated versions of war that one finds so much in modern American life. Too, my privilege is complicated by a certain responsibility. I teach soldiers the history of war and so contribute to their vision of what war is. Soldiers, and especially professional soldiers, carry with them into their first combat an expectation of what their war will be like. My responsibility is to see that the distance between what they expect and what they get is as small as possible.

A decade and a half ago the British military historian John

Keegan wrote *The Face of Battle*, the kind of book for which historians reserve the word "seminal," really meaning that the author created a new way of thinking about an old problem. Keegan's view differed markedly from conventional military histories that interpreted wars from the top down. Regardless of the ways in which war had changed over the centuries, he wrote, what all wars have in common is that they are human enterprises, conducted, it is true, at extremes of human behavior and tolerance but human all the same. Even if understanding war does require some measure of technical knowledge, it is also true that any understanding of war that does not recognize its essential humanness is flawed. The "face of battle" has always been, finally, the human face itself.

When we reduce war to an affair of numbers or great men or grand strategies, when war's humanness finds it difficult to make its way past the trivializing negotiations of memory, we have lost sight of what war is and have begun to interest ourselves in what it is not. Paradoxically, war is most human and reveals its essential character at the very place where humanness is in the greatest danger of extinction: in the killing grounds, the zones of combat where men devote every impulse of their mental and physical energy to destroying one another. Making sense of this world is a singularly demanding undertaking. And for any exploration of this world, expert guides are essential.

Those guides are all around us in the form of books, certainly, but they are around us in person as well—perhaps our fathers and mothers, our relatives, our neighbors. Only a couple of years ago I discovered that a close relative, a sweet and decent man, had done the worst kind of fighting in the Pacific and had never uttered a word about it to me—until I asked. The soldiers of the old war, notoriously laconic as they are, have begun to speak more and more. They are even beginning to return to the deadly old places where they fought, visiting comrades they left behind in the ground or elsewhere. What they, in written and personal form, have taught me about this war is beyond calculation, perhaps even beyond my expression. I remember this war—its most important parts—through them. I think it must be, in the end, the best way of all to know a war. What have they taught me?

Twenty million Americans were examined for military service in World War II; fourteen million were accepted. Yet in World War II, as in all modern wars, the fighting part of this vast number was relatively small. Most Americans in uniform during this war knew less than nothing about combat and, what is more, were not particularly anxious to find out. The service one entered and when one entered had a great deal to do with whether one would actually fight. In the Navy the chances of engaging in seaborne combat were very high if one happened to be part of the fleets deployed to contested waters or on convoy duty in the Atlantic, and indeed the bulk of early American casualties came from just these sources. As the war wore on, the casualty rate slowed. Next came the air forces, whether Army or Navy. Like the convoy sailors, they saw combat relatively early; unlike the sailors, they did not see their casualties decline until nearly war's end. The story among the ground forces, the Marines and GIs, was precisely the reverse of the naval war: their early casualties were "light"—always in war the most relative of terms—and intensified throughout the war until, like those of the air forces, their casualties declined at the end of the war.

Regardless of the medium in which they fought, the American combatants of World War II were not relentlessly fighting. In the naval war combat was a series of episodes that interrupted days and sometimes months of steaming from one position to another. Surely the catastrophes of naval combat could kill or wound or drown several thousand sailors at one time, and the possibility just as surely preyed upon those who manned these ships, working its own special kind of stress on them. Aerial warfare had its own particular rhythms, and for the air crews there was at least a hint of war's end in certain commands that allowed for a maximum number of combat missions for each flier. Yet on any one of their missions war's end was never far away, and, what is more, the air crewmen were often unwilling witnesses to the end of someone else's war. If the "flyboys" seemed to have more opportunities to get away from their war than other combatants, as many foot soldiers grumbled, that only means we have misunderstood how their real war was composed. We do not hear the muffled sobs of fear in the squadron barracks on the night before a thousand-plane raid against Germany.

The war on the ground was predominantly the infantryman's war. Despite notable advancements in the equipment and techniques of armored warfare, this war belonged to the GI. If one is searching for a picture of those in something close to sustained combat for long periods of time, this is where one finds it. Here, too, the disparity between those who fought and those who did not seems the greatest. Of the millions of Americans sent overseas by the Army during World War II, only 14 percent were infantrymen. Those 14 percent took more than 70 percent of all the battle casualties among overseas troops.

Even among the fighting parts of an army, a relatively small proportion actually suffered combat. The most combative of all the combat units was the infantry division. Within these American formations combat troops of all categories counted for only 68 percent of the whole. One wartime study by a division commander, Lucian Truscott, estimated that 95 percent of his losses were sustained by his line troops. Harold Leinbaugh and John Campbell, officers of a rifle company in the fall of 1944 and into 1945 who later wrote *The Men of Company K*, put it less clinically: "We were the Willy Lomans of the war."

All this means that during World War II there existed on this planet men in all varieties of uniform who belonged to a vast military underclass and that still millions more of their fellow citizens were in the stands, so to speak, cheering them on. They fought in the service of causes that were radically, one might even say mortally, different, but the essence of the daily lives they led was not. It consisted, as Fussell reminds us, of "the experience of coming to grips, face to face, with an enemy who designs your death." Under these circumstances the popular wartime phrase "We're behind you all the way" takes on a rather different meaning.

Surely, then, it was the cause that made it all worthwhile. At first glance one might think that the nobility of one's cause had an important and easing effect upon those who fought in its service or even that a soldier who fights for a great and moral cause is a superior soldier, so protected by his nobility. It isn't true, and it was no closer to being true in the Second World War than in any other. Soldiering is a morally neutral act, so designed by centuries of tradition. Soldiers have fought bravely and well for the most despicable of causes, and the Second World War lasted for six years because millions of soldiers did exactly that. The great wartime cartoonist Bill Mauldin discerned among the GIS a grudging respect for the fighting qualities of enemy troops, even if they were "skunks." Some critics since the war have said that enemy troops, especially German troops, were far better soldiers than the GIS, but this is a contention far from being proved.

Assuming—only for the moment—that some enemy troops were better at their trade than American troops, should we not then view our relative lack of ability as a mark of honor, all the more indicative of sacrifice in the name of a great crusade? Then the GIS become noble amateurs or even martyrs to the cause of freedom. Surely no American armed force ever took the field for better reasons than the defeat of the Axis powers. Was this motivation not a powerful force in our favor? Evidently not.

Field research during the war showed that frontline troops were notoriously impatient with "morale lectures" laid on by well-meaning staff. Appeals to patriotism or cause met with little response from men who were constantly on the verge of physical or mental exhaustion because their lives were threatened every day. No doubt the same well-meaning commanders and staff officers who thought troop lectures were a good idea dismissed the lack of frontline enthusiasm as unwholesome cynicism, as evidence of suspiciously low morale. Still, the troops did fight on. Why?

For most of the world's noncombatant population the war may have been about one cause or another, but for the Willy Lomans the war was about staying alive. To ordinary men in such circumstances no amount of morale building could offset this fundamental fact, and to such men all those who were not with them were in no position to lecture. Combat consumed too much energy to allow any left over for higher considerations of national philosophy. All the defenses their society had given them in preparation for their war—the national and popular support they received, their training and their equipment, even the official sanction to kill—were found by the soldiers to be altogether too fragile to withstand the grind of combat. The sustenance of one's own comrades, today understood by professionals as the essential cement of any combat unit, proved to be unequal to the demands of combat. Leinbaugh and Campbell's rifle company began its war with two hundred men; by war's end combat had used up four hundred. Their casualties equaled twice their original strength. This rifle company, Leinbaugh and Campbell insist, was a wholly typical unit of its kind.

A kind of solidarity did exist on the front lines, one that commanders found threatening and attempted to suppress whenever possible; in the Great War and after this solidarity would have been called "the brotherhood of the trench." It was a feeling best expressed by Erich Maria Remarque in *All Quiet on the Western Front* when he has his character Paul Bäumer realize that all the soldiers on the front line, friendly and enemy alike, are not fighting each other so much as they are fighting against the war itself.

My impression, but only that, is that those who fought in World War II came to this realization much sooner than their predecessors in World War I because they expected much less from this war. When the war broke out, they knew it was going to be a bad one and suffered fewer illusions about what it could do for, or to, them. Harold Bond, a young infantry officer who fought with the Thirty-sixth Division in Italy, wrote years afterward: "My generation, brought up on *A Farewell to Arms, All Quiet on the Western Front*, and plays such as *Journey's End*, was not easily persuaded that modern war made any sense at all.

Most certainly none of us thought any longer of glory and military heroics." For all that, Bond needed no lectures on morale to tell him why he fought: "One has to fight against a clear and palpable evil; the Nazis were both vicious and degrading, appealing as they did to the worst side of human nature." What moved Bond in the end, however, was his simpler conviction, one that was closer to war's practicalities, that "young, unmarried men should be the first to go." The "go" in Bond's memory is ambiguous. Bond seems to have meant to go overseas, but going could also mean never coming back, given the possibilities inherent in his particular situation. Infantry officers, especially junior ones, were a highly expendable commodity along Italy's Gustav Line in those days. A division on the line could easily spend its complement of lieutenants (137 of them) in a month or two.

And in those days, late in 1944 and early in 1945, the Allied victory was by no means a sure thing. One reads in the histories of the war pronouncements that after a given battle—say, Stalingrad, or D-Day, or the Schweinfurt raid, or the battle of the Coral Sea—the Allied victory was "only a matter of time." For those who fought, the matter of time was more than incidental; it was everything. One of Harry Brown's characters in his novel *A Walk in the Sun* sees the war continuing forever, one day of combat after the other, until decades later he will fight in the "Battle of Tibet."

In late 1943 and early 1944 the war was very much in control, the human beings fighting against it not having arrested its murderous progress. So the war assumed a certain monotony for those who fought in it at sea, in the air, on the ground, and we should not be startled to discover a sense of futile wonderment and perhaps even fatalistic bitterness among them. Not surprisingly, after the war ended such feelings were suppressed. While the war was on they were very much alive. One infantry scout in Italy remembered that "we felt simply that we had been left to die. Men in our division gave up all hope of being relieved. They thought the Army intended to keep them in action until everybody was killed. . . . All the men have hope of getting back, but most of the hope is that you'll get hit someplace that won't kill you. That's all they talk about."

All wars contain their own particular human secrets. One such secret in this war was the hostility those in "the line" felt for those who were in "the rear." The rear was both a place and an identity, it was "any sonofabitch whose foxhole is behind mine," remembers J. A. Croft, who served as a rifleman in Leinbaugh and Campbell's Company K. The gulf of misunderstanding that existed between those who fought and the thousands of uniformed spectators who milled around any combat zone most often manifested itself in brutal insensitivity. Elliot Johnson was an artillery officer with the Fourth Infantry Division five days into the Normandy invasion when a close friend was accidentally killed by one of his own men. Overcome by grief, Johnson sought medical aid for his dead friend at battalion headquarters, where a drunken colonel ordered Johnson to "get that goddamn hunk of rotten meat out of here!" But there were other, less dramatic evidences of animosity between the line and the rear, and indeed no particular incident was required to keep the animosity alive. The distinguished classicist Bernard Knox, a combat veteran of both the Spanish Civil War and World War II, has written only lately but still with much feeling that "while it is true of every war that much as he may fear and perhaps even hate the enemy opposing him, the combat infantryman broods with deep and bitter resentment over the enormous number of people in his rear who sleep safely at night."

And so they soldiered on until they were killed or wounded or captured or disappeared, having little choice in the matter—or at least no choice most cared to make. The Army recorded only forty thousand deserters during the war, and of these about twenty-nine hundred were actually court-martialed. Forty-nine received the death penalty, but only one such sentence was actually carried out. The numbers of AWOLs—"absent without leave," a bureaucratic rendition of the "straggling" of older wars—was much higher, and when the American Army bypassed Paris, James Jones reports, the city acted as a giant magnet for ten thousand or so troops. How many of those were actually in contact with the enemy Jones did not know, but that kind of behavior was much less likely among the combat soldiers than among those in the rear echelons.

Sometimes when talking with my students, I ask them to calculate the number of a combat soldier's enemies, and at first they do not understand what I mean. But the sources of mayhem in any modern war reach dizzying numbers, and the enemy's work is only one. The anxious trigger finger that killed Elliot Johnson's friend in Normandy was all too common. When one arms thousands of men and confines them in a concentrated battle area, such incidents are inevitable. Our own artillery fire, mistakenly calculated, killed its share of friendly soldiers and probably was the source of the old artilleryman's fatalistic comment: "Looked good when it left here." Of course, the artillery could be dead on its designated target when, in a friendly version of mechanical ambush, a ground unit could walk right under it.

An additional danger threatened if one's fighting happened to involve a complicated machine. Military versions of industrial accidents were all the greater because these machines were operated in the excited atmosphere of real or potential danger. Sailors came to understand that a single enemy shell could set off a round of secondary explosions on their ships, killing and maiming far more of them than the original attack; but even when they were not under attack, the dangers of manning a modern warship were significant and ever present. In the same way aerial combat was only one of several ways to die. "There are a variety of possible deaths which face a member of a bomber crew and each man is free to choose his own pet fear," wrote John Bennett, a squadron commander in the Eighth Air Force. "A tire could blow out or an engine could fail on take-off. The oxygen system or electric heating system might fail at high altitude. There is the fear of explosion or midair collision while flying formation." Or, as sometimes happened, a gunner could accidentally hit another plane in formation while testing his guns before the run to target.

Back on the ground, the killing of friends could be far more intimate. Eugene B. Sledge's memoir of the Pacific war, *With the Old Breed on Peleliu and Okinawa*, one of the best of its kind, records how one night, when a soldier became hysterical and threatened to reveal their positions, his comrades killed him with an entrenching tool because they couldn't keep him quiet any other way. "Christ a'mighty. What a pity," said one of Sledge's comrades after hearing the shovel find its mark.

Looking at the war from the vantage point of the combatants, one can easily envision one's own commander and staff as enemies. They are the ones, after all, who assist the enemy in creating the deadly environment, and if they do not look after their men, much as a doctor his patients in intensive care, the natural alienation between line and rear can sour into sullen, refractory behavior. Harold Leinbaugh saw his regimental commander on the line only once in more than a hundred days of combat, and as Leinbaugh's own confidence as a company commander increased, he was less than reluctant to see to the welfare of his company according to his own lights rather than follow the dictates of a remote command. In *Wartime*, Paul Fussell's acerbic rendition of the war that has infuriated so many spectators and no doubt has pleased just as many combat veterans, a view of the staff as being completely ignorant of war's actualities can be found throughout. "There is a 'staff solution' to the fear problem," Fussell writes, "when under shelling and mortar fire and scared stiff, the infantry should alleviate the problem by moving—never back but forward. This will enable trained personnel to take care of the wounded and will bring you close enough to the enemy to make him stop the shelling." So far so good. Then Fussell adds: "That it will also bring you close enough to put you within rifle and machine-gun and hand-grenade range is what the theorists know but don't mention. The troops know it, which is why they like to move back."

All these testimonies and more leave little doubt that the real engines of combat are not mechanical but human. Fear and fatigue give combat its true character. Whether it is in the actual or the historical rear, neither is present, and so the distortions begin. Human beings are adaptable, we think, and can get used to anything; haven't they done so? Soldiers on the line did not think so. As the war went on combatants and almost no one else knew that everyone would break under the strain of combat at some time or another, provided always they are not otherwise harmed. Break they did. At one point in the war more "neuropsychiatric casualties" were shipped home from overseas than those who were physically injured. Significantly, these soldiers received more understanding care close to the fighting line than they did as they went to the rear, where facile moral judgments about courage were still unsullied by the realities of war.

Inevitably, some of these misunderstandings of what war is really like have infected the history of the war. Misunderstanding the humanness of war, historians and other commentators have superimposed upon it judgments whose weight is too great a burden for the war to bear. Sometimes in the soldiers' memoirs we hear the old war strain under its modern burdens when notes of embarrassment sound about actions that in combat no one would have blinked at. For most of the veterans, however, the domestication of the war seems not to matter so much; they are mostly indifferent to the meanings we impose upon it.

Having talked with so many of these men over the years, I still find it surprising that they will talk at all to one from "the rear." It is something like asking a person to discuss his medical record. What is even more interesting is that once they do begin to talk, it is clear they see their war as the single greatest event in their lives, no matter how distinguished their postwar careers. They would agree with Eugene Sledge, the youthful combatant turned college professor who long after his first amphibious assault against the beaches at Peleliu still regards that event in no uncertain terms: "Everything my life had been before and has been after pales in the light of that awesome moment." Sledge's view is remarkably similar to an old friend's, well respected in his postwar profession when I first met him. In moments of confidential conversation he always turned back to the days when he flew B-17s against the Germans, his memories vivid and detailed and not at all sentimental but more significant to him than anything he had done since.

The study of war in our colleges and universities has never been a popular subject with our professors, and the academy will disdainfully ignore the anniversaries of this war if at all possible. And because the most dramatic kind of history is being made daily before our eyes, the rest of our society may find it all too easy to turn its attention away from the old war. Yet from Xenophon and Thucydides onward war's interior landscape has posed a great mystery, and those men who made war were the most mysterious of all, their experiences perceived as impenetrable to those who were not there. The Second World War, so close at hand in time, is now only a bit more familiar to us than the wars fought by the ancient Greeks, and our limited familiarity is fading daily. Our commemorations over the next few years may postpone our forgetfulness, but eventually our most important war will take its final place in the histories, there to be investigated by the chance encounters of scholarship.

By then my old war friends will be gone as well, but their war will live with me as it always has. For one who plies a trade that makes so much of detachment, the impression of a sentiment is close to heresy, but these men of World War II will have been the closest of my friends. How close were we? Writing in *Dispatches* about a far different war in Vietnam, Michael Herr asked the same question of himself and the soldiers he encountered. How close? "But of course we were intimate," he wrote. "They were my guns. . . ."

I n the spring of 1947 a new book entitled *Men Against Fire: The Problem of Battle Command in Future War* began seri- alizing in the American military periodical *Infantry Journal.* For the next twelve issues of the journal the author, journalist, and sometime soldier S. L. A. Marshall quite deliberately turned away from the preoccupations of modern military thought. As postwar military commentators puzzled over the implications of Bernard Brodie's famous axiom on deterrence, published in *The Absolute Weapon* the year before, and contemplated a world in which the existence rather than the actual use of military force was the mainstay of national defense, Marshall took his readers back to the war just won.[1] To his mind, the new atomic age had changed little except to seize the official and public imagination. "The fatal idea continues to spread," he wrote, "that nothing counts except the future use, or non-use, of this one weapon." Marshall argued that "the tactical and human lessons of the past" still applied in modern warfare. As his theme in *Men Against Fire,* therefore, Marshall chose to address "the tactical fact which is at once the simplest and most complex topic in the military art— man himself as a figure on the field of combat."[2]

Little in *Men Against Fire* was original; it owed much to clas- sic works on the order of Maurice de Saxe's *Mes rêveries* and Charles Ardant du Picq's *Études sur le combat.* Upon these clas- sics Marshall superimposed his own observations from the war. Few of those observations would have seemed strange to a vet- eran of infantry combat: that he was often the last and least con- sidered element of modern warfare, though he bore the greatest burdens; that ignorance, alienation, and chance governed the fighting soldier's existence more than the elegant strategies of the high command; and that men under fire cleave to one another as to a mast in a stormy sea. The veteran knew all too well that his training was never equal to the demands of actual combat and knew that combat was a lethal race to understand how to survive and function in a world organized for his death. The veteran understood, too, that even if he soldiered perfectly, he might not live out the day. What the veteran soldiers of the Second World War knew had seldom been addressed in intellectual venues; it was the folk knowledge of warfare, learned anew with each war and handed down from soldier to soldier. Marshall attempted to codify and translate some of this special class of knowledge for those who were innocent of combat.[3]

The centerpiece of *Men Against Fire* had less to do with Marshall's sympathetic and humanistic interpretation of modern combat, however. Soldiers would have nodded approvingly, and did, at seeing in print lessons they had learned at such high cost, but Marshall had an allegation to make that startled even some veterans. Citing evidence he had gleaned from interviews with rifle companies fresh from combat, Marshall concluded that only one soldier in four fired his weapon while in contact with the enemy:

> In an average experienced infantry company [Marshall wrote] in an average stern day's action, the number engaging with any and all weapons was approximately 15 per cent of the total strength. In the most aggressive infantry companies, under the most intense local pressure, the figure rarely rose above 25 per cent of the total strength from the opening to the close of the action.[4]

The "ratio of fire" between those soldiers who used their weapons and those who did not consummated Marshall's argument in *Men Against Fire*. Marshall's concept of victory depended upon a series of simple calculations: victory in battle was merely the sum of successful combats, like a team playing toward a pennant. He reduced the whole art of tactics to a fundamental proposition— "how much fire can be brought to bear." For Marshall, fire represented "tactics in a nutshell." The guarantor of success in battle was an elementary truth. "I say that it is a simple thing," he wrote. "What we need in battle is more and better fire."[5]

Marshall had no use for the polite equivocations of scholarly discourse. His way of proving doubtful propositions was to state them more forcefully. Righteousness was always more important for Marshall than evidence. One wartime friend described Marshall as "an intuitive thinker" and remembered that he "was always absolutely sure he was right."[6]

The foundation of his conviction was not scholarship but his own military experience, experience that he inflated or revised as the occasion warranted. Marshall often hinted broadly that he had commanded infantry in combat, but his service dossier shows no such service. He frequently held that he had been the youngest officer in the American Expeditionary Forces during the Great War, but this plays with the truth as well. Marshall enlisted in 1917 and served with the 315th Engineer Regiment—then part of the Ninetieth Infantry Division—and won a commission after the armistice, when rapid demobilization required very junior officers to command "casual" and depot companies as the veteran officers went home. Marshall rarely drew such distinctions, however, leaving his audiences to infer that he had commanded in the trenches. Later in life he remarked that he had seen five wars as a soldier and eighteen as a correspondent, but his definitions of war and soldiering were rather elastic. That he had seen a great deal of soldiers going about their deadly work was no empty boast, however. This mantle of experience, acquired in several guises, protected him throughout his long and prolific career as a military writer, and his aggressive style intimidated those who would doubt his arguments. Perhaps inevitably, his readers would mistake his certitude for authority.[7]

46

Approving reviews of *Men Against Fire* soon appeared; more important for the book's success, it found a sympathetic audience in soldiers.[8] The *Infantry Journal*'s 1948 issues routinely carried testimonials to the book. Sgt. First Class Frederick Lurie called upon the Army to make the book required reading for "all recruits, noncoms, and officers." The editors replied, rather fulsomely, that "Lurie's opinion of the Importance of *Men Against Fire* is in large part shared by General Omar Bradley, Chief of Staff, and every other soldier of any rank who has read it."[9] Before the year was out, an *Infantry Journal* reader enlisted Marshall's "cold, hard facts" in a letter to the editor and quoted Marshall's statistical findings at length.[10]

By 1950 Marshall was satisfied that the book had been taken seriously in military circles. B. H. Liddell Hart heard from Marshall that the book "has been accepted by the Army as doctrine, more or less, and is being put to increasingly greater use."[11] Much later, in a new preface to *Men Against Fire*, Marshall recalled that "at centers like Forts Benning, Knox, and Riley, during the years 1948–49, to overcome weapons inertia, imaginative trainers instituted wholly new methods, some of which were suggested in the book." Marshall clearly understood that the reason for the book's popularity was his provocative and seemingly precise findings about combat performance. "Ratios of fire," he remembered, "drew main attention and stirred initial controversy."[12] The ratio of fire had already evolved from soldierly wisdom to military cliché. After a temporary tour of duty at the Korean front, Marshall reported with his usual confidence to the Secretary of the Army in April 1951 that the ratio "had risen beyond 55 per cent both in night defense and daytime attack—more than doubling the World War II output."[13]

No one seems to have disagreed with Marshall, at least in print. Precise evidence systematically collected by an experienced observer of men in combat forestalled any instinctive disagreements or personal observations that might have been offered. Beguiled by the potent combination of Marshall's style and experience, scholars have frequently and approvingly cited *Men Against Fire* as well as his other works. When Roger A. Beaumont and William P. Snyder wrote that "Marshall's great achievement rested on imaginative and careful research" and that "his influence . . . stemmed from his credibility as a soldier and avoidance of abstract sociological and psychological concepts," they were quite in accord with the judgments of their colleagues.[14] Russell F. Weigley had no compunction about accepting Marshall's findings without cavil. In *Eisenhower's Lieutenants* Weigley used Marshall's ratio to substantiate the American high command's impressions during the Second World War that "the infantry on which they would rely as their main combat resource was not particularly aggressive."[15] Comparing German and Allied infantry effectiveness in Western Europe in 1944, John English argued in *On Infantry* that the German emphasis upon combat as a group affair accounted for the critical difference in the tactical performance of the two armies. In this case Marshall was given as the authority on *Allied* performance.[16] And while the ratio of fire provided an apparently inviolable standard of measurement for the combat performance of American soldiers in the Second World War, on occasion the claim has been elevated to the status of a general principle of tactics. One perceptive student of the human dimensions of combat has proposed that "Marshall's insights into the motives and behavior of combatants in World War II are also valid for those who fought in the First World War."[17]

A more measured view of Marshall's work came, appropriately enough, from John Keegan, whose *Face of Battle* has done so much to rejuvenate an interest in understanding warfare from the combatant's "angle of vision." To Keegan, Marshall was "an American du Picq," and he felt when Marshall spoke at the British Staff College in Camberley that Marshall "was touched by genius."[18] Even so, Keegan refused to believe that Marshall's "revelations about the effective fighter and group loyalty are a sufficient explanation of how battle burdens are borne."[19]

After Korea Marshall was at the height of his powers. *Men Against Fire* was his fourth book; he eventually wrote thirty in all as well as countless articles and essays. His writings, his friendship with American officers of ever higher ranks, and his tireless advocacy of the soldierly view made him an important figure in the armed forces of the United States and several other countries. He was a fixture in the American Army, speaking regularly at the war and staff colleges and at officers' calls from post to post. He never needed an introduction to those audiences, and if anyone thought to question his observations, as Keegan remembers from Marshall's Camberley performance, the hapless interrogator was treated to a display of bad manners, "aggressive, hectoring, and rude . . . cheerfully insult[ing] those who asked him what he thought were stupid questions."[20]

By then Marshall's reputation was fortified by the scope and sheer quantity of his work, and few could compete with his passionate interpretations of the American fighting man in the crucible of combat. No one who encountered S. L. A. Marshall, in print or in person, would forget his authoritative manner, but if one were to fix upon the source of Marshall's acclaim, the "ratio of fire" and how he uncovered the truth of battle formed the pivot of his authority. Indeed, the ratio and the method by which he deduced it, more than any other facet of his work, set Marshall apart from his contemporaries.

Marshall had developed his ideas on infantry combat performance without resorting to a statistical pose well before he wrote *Men Against Fire*. In *Island Victory*, a book derived from his tour as a combat historian with the Twenty-seventh and Seventh Infantry Divisions during operations on Makin and Kwajalein islands in late 1943 and early 1944, Marshall explained a technique he had conceived that later was hailed as the basis for "an entirely new kind of military history"—the combat after-action interview.[21] Marshall went to the Pacific as part of the Army's attempt to capture the history of the war as it was being made. As one of a handful of writers and historians made officers for the duration, Marshall was a member of the Army's G-2 fledgling historical division. He and his colleagues insisted that they must get to the operational theaters of war if they were to make a start at this unprecedented official history enterprise. Marshall was one of the first to escape Washington.[22]

When Marshall went ashore with the fourth wave at Makin, the confusion of battle overwhelmed him. Struggling to make sense of the 165th Infantry Regiment's tactical operations, Marshall found that he could not reconcile even the most elementary situation. Then Marshall called all the survivors of the action together and began questioning them en masse.[23] Years later Marshall recalled, "Piece by piece we put it all together. The story of the night's experience came clear as crystal. It was like completing the picture of a jigsaw puzzle. At last I knew that, quite by accident, I had found what I had sailed west seeking."[24] The interview would begin with the initial contact with the enemy and move from soldier to soldier, tracing the action as it progressed. Anyone in the assembly was free to challenge a recollection in the interests of refining the picture of the action. Marshall always held that, in the company of his comrades, no soldier would enlarge or misrepresent his own role in the fight.[25] The first group interview took four days, but Marshall later recommended three days of interviewing for one day of combat.[26]

The concept of reconstructing a battle from participants' memories was not new. Well after Waterloo the British Army commissioned Capt. William Siborne to construct a terrain board of the battle. Although Siborne's objectives were antiquarian and celebratory, he took his work seriously, living in a farmhouse near La Haye Sainte on the battlefield for eight months and studying all the documents he could obtain. He then sent out a circular letter that solicited specific operational and tactical details from all the surviving officers. Fourteen years after Siborne began he published a two-volume history of the battle that drew upon the recollections his inquiries had gathered.[27] Although Siborne would have been reluctant to say so, his approach contradicted the conventional wisdom that the commander somehow contained within himself the power to control every event in battle. Siborne's project nonetheless anticipated the as yet poorly articulated need by professional soldiers in the nineteenth century for increasingly precise information about what really happens in combat. These same motivations inspired the work of Ardant du Picq nearly half a century later. Du Picq had employed the same technique as Siborne, canvassing his own officer corps by questionnaire for the facts of battle, but du Picq's experiment was an unhappy one. The very nature of du Picq's questions was considered impertinent by some of his colleagues, and they refused to cooperate. Turning to history instead, du Picq wrote what is still one of the most insightful works in this minor class of military literature.[28]

Marshall certainly knew of du Picq but never acknowledged his debt to the French officer. *Men Against Fire* refers in passing to du Picq, but the suggestion that Marshall's own work was somehow derivative rankled him.[29] In 1964 Stephen Ambrose wrote to Marshall, asking him to read a draft paper that drew comparisons between du Picq and Marshall; "What has amazed me is how similar your conclusions are," Ambrose wrote.[30] Sometime later Marshall penciled a screed on the flyleaf of his own copy of du Picq: "I think it a bad book and far from a 'classic.' . . . [Du] Picq is ignorant of his subject and simply guessing—tho[ugh] he travelled a distance on little gas." But du Picq was not alone in being rejected by Marshall as an intellectual forebear; Marshall recognized no one as his equal on the subject of men in battle.[31]

Marshall had in fact created a new method for military history. The difference between Siborne, du Picq, and Marshall lay in the promptness with which recollections of combat were gathered and from the orientation of Marshall's inquiries—the combat soldier himself. His approach insured that the combat narratives he eventually produced would "democratize" the interpretation of battle. Marshall's method was, as John Keegan points out, suitably American not only in voice but in object, for Marshall meant that his work should have an immediate tactical effect.[32] "*The fighting men do not know the nature of the mistakes which they make together,*" Marshall wrote in *Island Victory*, "and not knowing, they are deprived of the surest safeguard against making the same mistakes next time they are in battle."[33] What the soldiers and their commanders learned about their own combat performance during the course of the "interview after combat," as Marshall called the technique, was at least as beneficial for its tactical as for its historical findings.

Oral history, as scholars know it today, was not an accepted historical technique during the early days of the Second World War, and in any case Marshall never counted himself as a conventional scholar.[34] His conception of the new technique on Makin Island was inspired first by the confused face that battle inevitably shows to outsiders and participants alike. Yet the man who had come to Makin to record the history of combat was, above all, by professional upbringing and temperament a journalist. His career in a trade well suited to the recording of chaos, mayhem, and human tragedy was the vital additive required to accomplish what his more traditionally trained colleagues in the historical division had thus far failed to do.[35]

On Makin and Kwajalein and later in Europe Marshall drew upon the prewar trade he knew so well. The approach to knowledge was the same: get to the scene quickly, survey the location, and talk to the principal figures involved and as many survivors, singly or in groups, as can be found. Reconcile their accounts, withdraw, and compose their story at deadline speed. The simpler the picture, the better. Subtleties, nuances, wit, and a fancy prose style were best left to the editorial page.

Even so, Marshall was no city desk hack: he had a clipped, declarative, and aggressive style that was well suited to his subject and was very much the vogue prose of the 1940s. On the eve of the war he was a very successful journalist earning $10,000 a year.[36] He had learned his craft in the wild border town of El Paso, Texas, in the 1920s and covered revolutions and disasters in Latin America. In 1927 he had won a prized place on the *Detroit News*, a paper he was connected with for the rest of his life. His editors learned to indulge his wide taste in subjects: during his childhood in El Paso before the First World War Marshall was fascinated with sports and developed a liking for the polo games at Fort Bliss. By the Second World War he was an habitué of polo grounds around the country, and while analogies between sports and warfare are, though often used, both invidious and trivializing, sorting out the details of group action was a problem with which Marshall was certainly familiar.[37]

Marshall was commended for his work in the Pacific. Brig. Gen. A. V. Arnold, then commanding the Seventh Infantry Division, asked the War Department's permission to keep Marshall for the future training of the division. "It is difficult for me to express in words his value to the division," Arnold wrote. If the division could not keep Marshall, Arnold asked for "someone of Colonel Marshall's calibre."[38] The commander of the Twenty-seventh Infantry Division offered the opinion that Marshall had set the "pattern . . . for collecting historical data on the spot" and concluded that "if the Historical Section can send officers on such missions who are the equivalent of Colonel Marshall in judgement and tact, I think they will always be welcomed by commanders."[39] Although Marshall did not serve as an infantryman during the Pacific campaigns, the Seventh Infantry Division awarded him the coveted Combat Infantryman's Badge.[40]

Ever the dynamo, Marshall returned to Washington in April 1944 and immediately wrote *Island Victory*, which *Infantry Journal* first serialized and then published in cooperation with Penguin Books.[41] By then the Army's newly formed military history detachments had been sent to other operational theaters of war, and preparations were being made for extensive coverage of the impending cross-channel invasion. With his successful Pacific experience, Marshall regarded himself as the pioneer of field historical operations, and he did not hesitate to proselytize the technique he had conceived. In a postwar study of the Army's historical division, the Civil War historian Bell Wiley recalled:

> Enthusiastic reports that [Marshall] made to the Historical Branch concerning mass interviews in the Pacific may have had considerable influence in promoting interviews of individual and small groups by historical officers everywhere.[42]

Marshall's creation of the "interview after combat" convinced him that he could lift the veil of mystery that until then had concealed the most elementary truths of how men conducted themselves at the sharp end of warfare. The immediate, first-person voice of combat had never spoken in historical literature. Henceforth, the hidden knowledge of the hard trade of soldiering could be uncovered and analyzed and its precepts laid down for future application. Marshall's ratio of fire was the very incarnation of this new approach.

Marshall's "restless nature" and his "distaste for routine" virtually guaranteed that when D-Day finally arrived, Marshall would be close at hand.[43] He landed in Europe in late June 1944. Marshall expected and indeed insisted that his "interview after combat" method would work as well in Europe as it had in the Pacific. The historian for the European Theatre of Operations, Col. William A. Ganoe, asked Marshall shortly after his arrival in England to write a summary of his methods for use by Ganoe's historical officers in the field. Ganoe cautioned his historians "to adapt the methods herein disclosed to your personality. The principles certainly are inviolable."[44] Less than a month later Ganoe saw fit to retreat on the question of inviolability, instructing his historians that when Marshall's methods were "not applicable," they should be adopted as far as possible.[45]

Marshall had rank: he was a lieutenant colonel by then. More important, he had the cachet of being a veteran of the Pacific campaign, and, not least, he had a confidence in his mission bordering on evangelical zeal. Yet even Marshall could not always reckon on being well received by the line troops or their commanders. Although Marshall was an unabashed admirer of the elite American parachute divisions and made them his special province while in Europe, Gen. James Gavin and the men of his Eighty-second Airborne Division had a nearly visceral reaction to Marshall's probing. Gavin met Marshall shortly after D-Day and thought "he did not seem to know much about the infantry." Later, in Holland, Gavin was asked by one of his old sergeants in the 505th Parachute Infantry Regiment:

> General, who is the s. o. b. who comes around asking questions, wearing the insignia of another division, and who doesn't seem to know what he is talking about? Is he an IG? We are not telling him anything.

Evidently, the young historians who attempted to apply Marshall's techniques met with resistance from combat troops who doubtless were mystified and sometimes resentful of these "rear echelon" investigators.[46]

In addition to these substantial obstacles, the very nature of combat in Europe differed sharply from that which Marshall had seen on the Pacific Islands. On Makin and Kwajalein operations were physically contained, and combat was an affair of congested places and positions. The vegetation of the islands dictated extremely close combat, usually only a matter of yards. The enemy's culture and tactical habits often required suicidal battle discipline on all sides, and the islands provided little opportunity for American infantrymen even to pull back to the relative safety of reserve positions. European combat, on the other hand, allowed for a much greater dispersion of units, and in an Allied campaign whose chief objective was operational movement, the prospect of catching up with and then actually being allowed enough time to conduct a detailed interview with an infantry company was limited at best.[47]

Convinced that his technique would work, Marshall set off on a round of interviews. Capt. John Westover, a veteran of the North African, Sicilian, and Italian campaigns, was in tow as Marshall's military assistant. "I'm not sure just what my part will be," Westover wrote to his wife, "but it's going to be work. The Colonel is a slave driver—I'm probably going to be the slave." Without question, Marshall was peripatetic, spending time first with the units that had landed in Normandy, then returning to England to interview the companies of the 101st Airborne, then working with the Eighty-second in Holland and Belgium, and finally interviewing the units that had defended Bastogne in the Battle of the Bulge.[48]

In *Men Against Fire* Marshall claims to have interviewed "approximately" 400 infantry rifle companies in the Pacific and in Europe, but that number tended to change over the years. In 1952 the number had somehow grown to 603 companies; five years later his sample had declined to "something over 500" companies.[49] Those infantry companies—whatever their actual number—were his laboratories, the infantrymen his test subjects, and the focal point of his research was the ratio of fire. "Why the subject of fire ratios under combat conditions has not been long and searchingly explored, I don't know," Marshall wrote. "I suspect that it is because in earlier wars there had never existed the opportunity for *systematic collection of data*."[50]

Opportunity aplenty existed in Europe: more than twelve hundred rifle companies did their work between June 1944 and V-E Day ten months later. But Marshall required by his own standard two and sometimes three days with a company to examine one day's combat.[51] By the most generous calculation, Marshall would have finished "approximately" four hundred interviews sometime in October or November 1946, or at about the time he was writing *Men Against Fire*.

ON COMBAT

This calculation assumes, however, that of all the questions Marshall might ask the soldiers of a rifle company during his interviews, he would unfailingly want to know who had fired his weapon and who had not. Such a question, posed interview after interview, would have signaled that Marshall was on a particular line of inquiry and that, regardless of the other information Marshall might discover, he was devoted to investigating this facet of combat performance. John Westover, usually in attendance during Marshall's sessions with the troops, does not recall Marshall's *ever* asking this question. Nor does Westover recall Marshall ever talking about ratios of weapons usage in their many private conversations.[52] Marshall's own personal correspondence leaves no hint that he was ever collecting statistics. His surviving field notebooks show no signs of statistical compilations that would have been necessary to deduce a ratio as precise as Marshall reported later in *Men Against Fire*.[53] The "systematic collection of data" that made Marshall's ratio of fire so authoritative appears to have been an invention.

Historians and writers as a class are no better or worse at documenting their life and work than anyone else. The absence of evidence for Marshall's statistics is only negative proof, and that is why Marshall's observation on combat performance must be examined on its own ground—the character of infantry combat itself.

The battleground required to accommodate Marshall's ratio of fire was one in which, first of all, every soldier could use his weapon at some time during the action if he chose. Whether in a defensive action of the kind Marshall saw on Makin Island or in the advance against local resistance, the primary function of Marshall's soldier was to fire his weapon. The highest tactical ambition a commander could aspire to in Marshall's view was the employment of all weapons, presumably in concert, during any given action.

Any factor that would intrude upon an improved ratio of fire was discounted. Terrain, that most intimate and beloved companion of modern soldiers, played no role in Marshall's formulations. That the ground itself could govern and shape the tempo and rhythms of a combat action, preventing some men from firing and demanding performance from others, Marshall dismissed by examining actions that for the most part "had taken place under conditions of ground and manoeuvre where it would have been possible for at least 80 per cent of the men to fire, and where nearly all hands, at one time or another, were operating within satisfactory firing distance of enemy works."[54]

Marshall understood very well that modern infantry combat is asymmetrical. "It is never the case," he wrote in *Island Victory*, "that all parts of a company are actually fighting at one time though all may be there on the battlefield." Further, he wrote, "Battle is never a maelstrom into which all are drawn equally but is rather a continuing line of small eddies, small fights, which are sometimes tactically related and sometimes not."[55] The "line" of combat is merely a conceit; infantrymen are deployed in tactical arrangements that have more to do with enemy strength and ground than with staff college geometry. Thus, infantry combat is above all intensely relational but hardly uniform. The infinite varieties of encounter between infantry make it possible for one part of a unit to be heavily engaged while another is left completely alone.[56] And although small unit leaders are drilled to see that the whole power of their units is properly employed, the range of their control, not to mention that of the soldiers themselves, during combat is extremely constricted. Indeed, some of Marshall's most astute passages in *Men Against Fire* are devoted to overcoming limitations that the lack of immediate tactical information imposes on combat commanders and their men. But by claiming that most of his interviews were concerned with actions in which four-fifths of those engaged could fire, Marshall negated the problem of combat asymmetry. Indeed, Marshall insisted that there were no physical limitations on combat performance. "The results," he wrote in *Men Against Fire*, "appeared to indicate that the ceiling was fixed by some constant which was inherent in the nature of troops or perhaps in our failure to understand that nature sufficiently to apply the proper correctives."[57] The "constant," however, may not have been so certain after all. After Korea, musing before an audience in 1952, Marshall said, "I think perhaps I came out of the war [World War II] with too much of a conviction that our basic difficulty was in the development of fire." But he quickly added, "I would not retreat from any of the propositions that I made in the writing of *Men Against Fire*." Marshall had very nearly admitted in a moment of weakness that his interpretation, fixed in its scientific pose, was too frail a vessel to bear the weight of explaining a soldier's conduct in combat.[58]

Yet the rhythms and tempo of combat are governed not only by the soldiers but also by the *type* of weapons they employ. A given infantry company in the Second World War employed a whole suite of weapons with a descending succession of power designed for particular range, volume, and effect. Mortars, heavy and light machine guns, bazookas, automatic rifles, grenades, semiautomatic rifles, and submachine guns—all had a specific role in infantry combat, a role that ultimately was decided upon not by weapons designers or field manual writers but by the soldiers themselves in constant experimentation. American theory and training during the Second World War held, for instance, that automatic weapons established and protected a company's flanks on the defense and provided suppressive fire for infantry in the advance. Inexperienced companies in Europe quickly found, however, that automatic fire immediately brought down upon them a deadly counterfire and that in the defense one certain way of revealing one's flanks was to employ automatic weapons prematurely. Higher commanders would complain that doctrines were not being observed, but the men themselves preferred by far to let their supporting artillery break up enemy formations. Harold P. Leinbaugh, coauthor of *The Men of Company K*, is not in the least apologetic that he was uninterested in getting his company in the Second World War to lay down suppressive fire. Whenever he could he called for artillery, and he found that a good lie about approaching enemy tanks always brought the guns to bear.[59] Such practices, very likely prevalent in every war and most certainly in modern war, are "soldier's doctrines," consisting of the hard-won, practical folk knowledge of combat itself. As one who made his career on his intimate knowledge of soldiering, Marshall should have known that there are times in combat when one should *not* fire his weapons.

Marshall reported that once a soldier fired his weapon in combat, he tended to fire in all successive combats. The "active firers," he believed, "in the main were the same men who were carrying the fire fight for each company day after day." The successful combat soldier's performance in Marshall's mind was composed of only two stages: an apprenticeship, during which the soldier is "seasoned," after which he uses his weapon consistently. In this scenario, once the infantryman reaches the second stage, he attains something akin to a state of soldierly grace. Looking around at the men in the companies he interviewed, Marshall wrote, "You could pick out your man who would probably keep going until he was dead."[60] The soldiers of the Second World War knew better, knew that a graph of a man's time in combat would describe a ragged trajectory, knew that a hero one day could be a coward the next, and in their very special world knew that consistency was the last thing they could expect.[61]

S. L. A. Marshall's ratio of fire cannot be proved. The foundations of Marshall's claim lay not in statistical formulations or scholarly research but in his own experiences and observations of war. "Contemptuous of people only interested in methodology," Westover remembers, and "intensely practical," Marshall considered statistics "an adornment" of belief.[62] Ironically, Marshall chose to voice his belief in the idiom of science, as if to confer an absolute authority on his findings—the science that even then called into question the continuing utility of soldierly combat and moved him to write *Men Against Fire*.

History has a savage way about it. A reputation may be made or unmade when history seizes upon part of a life and reduces it to caricature. S. L. A. Marshall was one of the most important commentators on the soldier's world in this century. The axiom upon which so much of his reputation has been built overshadows his real contribution. Marshall's insistence that modern warfare is best understood through the medium of those who must actually do the fighting stands as a challenge to the disembodied, mechanistic approaches that all too often are the mainstay of military theorists and historians alike. "That lesson," Marshall wrote in *Men Against Fire*, we are "at the point of forgetting."[63] Forty years later, as the quest for universal laws of combat continues unabated, Marshall is still right.[64]

Notes

1. Brodie's elegant formulation of nuclear deterrence read: "Thus far the chief purpose of our military establishment has been to win wars. From now on its chief purpose must be to avert them. It can have almost no other purpose." Bernard Brodie, ed., *The Absolute Weapon: Atomic Power and World Order* (New York: Harcourt, Brace, 1946), 76. See also Lawrence Freedman, *The Evolution of Nuclear Strategy* (New York: St. Martin's Press, 1981), 3; Colin Gray, *Strategic Studies and Public Policy* (Lexington: University of Kentucky Press, 1982), 30–32; and Gregg Herken, "The Not-Quite-Absolute Weapon: Deterrence and the Legacy of Bernard Brodie," *Journal of Strategic Studies* 9, no. 6 (1986): 22.

2. S. L. A. Marshall, *Men Against Fire: The Problem of Battle Command in Future War* (Washington DC: Infantry Journal Press, 1947; repr., Gloucester MA: Peter Smith, 1978), 20, 26.

3. From the turn of the century onward and corresponding roughly to the rise of modern psychiatry and the behavioral sciences, a body of knowledge grew up that addressed the human dimensions of modern warfare. During the Second World War the American armed forces made a substantial investment in an attempt to understand how and why soldiers fought. Unfortunately, during that war and since, this body of knowledge has not been synthesized, nor has it been integrated with the broader military arts. Military historians, with few exceptions, are ignorant of the insights readily

available on the soldier in combat from the behavioral sciences. The best-known and most widely cited study, dating from the Second World War, is Samuel Stouffer et al., *The American Soldier*, vol. 2, *Combat and Its Aftermath* (Princeton NJ: Princeton University Press, 1949).

4. Marshall, *Men Against Fire*, 56.

5. Ibid., 51, 53. Marshall's association of fire with élan was hardly new. Ferdinand Foch in particular would have applauded Marshall's fixation upon fire. See Michael Howard, "Men Against Fire: Expectations of War in 1914," *International Security* 9, no. 1 (1984): 41–57; and Stephen Van Evera, "The Cult of the Offensive and the Origins of the First World War," *International Security* 9, no. 1 (1984): 58–61.

6. Interview with Professor John G. Westover, 15 June 1987. Westover was Marshall's assistant in Europe from July 1944 until the end of the war and was a lifelong friend. See also Westover's recollections of Marshall in "Describing the Colonel," *Newsletter of the S. L. A. Marshall Military History Collections*, no. 11 (Summer 1985): 1–4 (hereafter cited as *Marshall Newsletter*); "The Colonel Goes Interviewing," *Marshall Newsletter*, no. 12 (Winter 1985–86): 1–3; and "Marshall's Impact," *Marshall Newsletter*, no. 13 (Summer 1986): 1–3.

7. See Marshall, "Genesis to Revelation," *Military Review* 52, no. 2 (1972): 17; S. L. A. Marshall, "The Human Equation in Combat, 16 October 1952," in S. L. A. Marshall, *S. L. A. Marshall at Fort Leavenworth: Five Lectures at the U.S. Army Command and General Staff College*, ed. Roger J. Spiller (Fort Leavenworth KS: U.S. Army Command and General Staff College, 1980), 3; and Dale L. Walker, interview with S. L. A. Marshall, 18 May 1972, typed transcript, 11, S. L. A. Marshall Military History Collection, Library of the University of Texas at El Paso (hereafter cited as Marshall Collection). On the matter of Marshall's commission see Mrs. C. C. Marshall to the War Department Adjutant General's Office, 13 March 1933; and BG James F. McKinley to Mrs. C. C. Marshall, 24 March 1933, BG S. L. A. Marshall Military Personnel File, National Personnel Records Center, St. Louis MO (hereafter cited as Marshall 201 File).

8. P. J. Searles, review of *Men Against Fire* by S. L. A. Marshall, *New York Herald Tribune Weekly Book Review*, 19 October 1947, 23.

9. Sgt. First Class Frederick J. Lurie, "Everybody in the Army Should Read It: Men Against Fire," *Infantry Journal* 63, no. 6 (1948): 47; see also the "Editor's Note" in the same issue.

10. "A Lieutenant," in "Letters to the Editor," *Infantry Journal* 62, no. 3 (1948): 66–67.

11. S. L. A. Marshall to B. H. Liddell Hart, 8 February 1950, Papers of B. H. Liddell Hart, B. H. Liddell Hart Centre for Military Archives, King's

College, University of London. I am indebted to King's College for permission to quote from these papers.

12. Marshall, *Men Against Fire*, 9.

13. See also S. L. A. Marshall, *Commentary on Infantry Operations and Weapons Usage in Korea, Winter of 1950–51* (Chevy Chase MD: Johns Hopkins Operations Research Office, 1951), 4–5. In this restricted (now declassified) report Marshall was a good deal more equivocal about the ratio of fire in Korea than his preface in *Men Against Fire* would have had readers believe; even so, with qualifications Marshall reported that "when the ground and situation permit it, the measure of willing participation is more than double World War II averages. . . . The chronic non-firer is an exception under the conditions of Korean fighting."

14. Roger A. Beaumont and William P. Snyder, "Combat Effectiveness: Paradigms and Paradoxes," in *Combat Effectiveness*, ed. Sam Sarkesian (Beverly Hills CA: Sage Publications, 1980), 24.

15. Russell F. Weigley, *Eisenhower's Lieutenants: The Campaigns of France and Germany, 1944–1945* (Bloomington: Indiana University Press, 1981), 26.

16. John English, *On Infantry* (New York: Praeger Press, 1984), 145.

17. Ibid.; Eric Leed, *No Man's Land: Combat and Identity in World War I* (New York: Cambridge University Press, 1979), 10.

18. John Keegan, "The Historian and Battle," *International Security* 3, no. 3 (1978–79): 145.

19. Ibid., 147. British scholars are more reserved in their acceptance of Marshall's axiom. See, for example, Richard Holmes, *Acts of War: The Behaviour of Men in Battle* (New York: Free Press, 1985), 13. John Ellis, *The Sharp End: The Fighting Man in World War II* (New York: Charles Scribner's Sons, 1980) does not cite Marshall's ratio at all. See also David Rowland, "Assessments of Combat Degradation," *RUSI Journal* 131, no. 2 (1986): 33.

20. Keegan, "The Historian and Battle," 145.

21. S. L. A. Marshall, *Island Victory* (Washington DC: Infantry Journal Press; Penguin Books, 1944), 14–26, 201–13. Martin Blumenson, one of Marshall's combat historians in the European theater, believes Marshall "invented a literary form, the reconstruction of battle on the personal terms of the participants," and "thereby dissipated the traditional fog of war." See Martin Blumenson, "My Recollections of S. L. A. Marshall," *Marshall Newsletter*, no. 11 (Winter 1986–87): 2.

22. S. L. A. Marshall, *Bringing up the Rear*, ed. Cate Marshall (San Rafael CA: Presidio Press, 1979), 57–59, is Marshall's posthumous autobiography and describes his part in the Army's nascent official history program. For a rather more balanced view of events see Stetson Conn, *Historical Work*

in the United States Army, 1862–1954 (Washington DC: U.S. Army Center of Military History, 1980), 76–93; Kent Roberts Greenfield, *The Historian and the Army* (New Brunswick NJ: Rutgers University Press, 1954; repr., Kennekat Press, 1970), 11–13; and Bell I. Wiley, "Historical Program of the Army from 1939 to Present," unpublished typescript, part 3, undated (ca. 1953), 2–3, Historical Records Collection, U.S. Army Center of Military History, Washington DC.

23. Marshall, *Island Victory*, 15–26.

24. Marshall, *Bringing up the Rear*, 72.

25. Marshall, *Island Victory*, 18, 22; and Marshall, *Men Against Fire*, 55.

26. Marshall, *Island Victory*, 25.

27. Keegan discusses Siborne in *The Face of Battle*, 118, 120. In 1881 Siborne's son, Maj. Gen. H. T. Siborne, edited his father's collection of letters. His preface describes his father's work on Waterloo and reproduces the circular letter Siborne the elder sent to his fellow officers. See H. T. Siborne, ed., *Waterloo Letters*, 2 vols. (London: Cassell and Company, 1891), i–xi. See also "W. T. Siborne," in *Dictionary of National Biography*, ed. Sir Leslie Stephen (London: Oxford University Press, 1897), 18:185–86.

28. Charles Ardant du Picq, *Battle Studies: Ancient and Modern Battle*, trans. John N. Greely and Robert C. Cotton (Harrisburg PA: Military Service Company, 1946). For appraisals of du Picq's place in modern military thought see Michael Howard, "Men Against Fire," 41–57, esp. 40–50; L. Nachin, "Ardant du Picq," *Revue militaire française* 16 (July–September 1925, October–December 1925): 358–71, 54–67; and Stefan T. Possony and Étienne Mantoux, "Du Picq and Foch: The French School," in *The Makers of Modern Strategy*, ed. Edward M. Earle (Princeton NJ: Princeton University Press, 1943), 206–18.

29. Marshall, *Men Against Fire*, 154.

30. Stephen E. Ambrose to S. L. A. Marshall, 12 August 1964 and 21 August 1964, Correspondence Files, Marshall Collection.

31. Note in S. L. A. Marshall's hand, flyleaf of Ardant du Picq's *Battle Studies*, in Library of Marshall Collection. See also Walker, Marshall interview, 18 May 1972, Marshall Collection.

32. Keegan, *The Face of Battle*, 72.

33. Marshall, *Island Victory*, 21, italics in original.

34. Marshall had a checkered educational record. By his own account he was an indifferent student and did not finish high school before enlisting in the Army in 1917. After the war he put in a semester or two at the Texas School of Mines. Later he was happy to tell his military audiences that he had no professional military schooling. See Marshall, *Bringing up the Rear*, xii, 2–3, 9, 12–13.

35. As the Second World War began, the Historical Section of the Army War College, under the direction of Gen. Oliver L. Spaulding, was still working on the Army's official history of the First World War. Doubtful that Spaulding's longer view of doing official military history promised any hope of success in the current conflict, several officers held a rump session in early 1943 and began a campaign of their own to capture the operational history of the war. Lt. Col. John Mason Kemper became the chief of the new "Historical Section" of the Army's G-2 (Intelligence) in July of the same year. Kemper was the first historical officer to attempt combat reporting. Unfortunately, Kemper chose the Kiska operation in the Aleutian Islands, an operation notable for the unobliging departure of the enemy before the arrival of American troops. Marshall, *Bringing up the Rear*, 58. See also Conn, *Historical Work*, 76–93.

36. S. L. A. Marshall, "Personnel Placement Questionnaire," 24 August 1942, 3, Marshall 201 File.

37. See Marshall, *Bringing up the Rear*, 18–45, for an account of his interwar career in journalism.

38. BG A. V. Arnold to MG Clayton Bissell, 9 April 2944, Marshall 201 File.

39. MG Ralph C. Smith to MG George V. Strong, 12 December 1943, Marshall 201 File.

40. HQS, Seventh Infantry Division, Special Orders number 30, paragraph 2, 1 March 1944, Marshall 201 File.

41. Conn, *Historical Work*, 95.

42. Wiley, "Historical Program," 3.

43. The characterizations are Wiley's (ibid., 2–3).

44. William A. Ganoe, "Methods of Interviews based on success of Lt. Colonel S. L. A. Marshall in the Pacific," Memorandum to the Members of the Historical Teams, HQS ETO, 26 June 1944, Marshall Collection.

45. William A. Ganoe, Memorandum to Historical Teams in the Field, HQS ETOUSA, 15 July 1944, box 33, ETO Historical Division Administrative Files, RG 332, National Archives.

46. Lt. Gen. James Gavin (U.S. Army, ret.) to author, 24 June 1987.

47. In each of the theaters of war combat had its own peculiar characteristics, making special demands upon those who did the fighting. Samuel Stouffer and his colleagues attempted a comparison of combat in the Pacific and the ETO, but the results, inevitably, were equivocal; the study found that while in terms of the duration of intense combat and the casualties the Pacific battle was less severe than those in Europe, "in nearly every other respect . . . the men in the Pacific faced conditions which severely tested morale and combat efficiency." All of which is to say that, to the combatants, such distinctions are meaningless. See Stouffer, *The American Soldier*, 2:69–70.

48. Westover, "Describing the Colonel," 1–4. See also n. 8.

49. Marshall, *Men Against Fire*, 53. See Marshall, "The Human Equation," 5; and Marshall, "Salesmanship for the Army, 20 May 1957," in Marshall, *S. L. A. Marshall at Fort Leavenworth*, 5, 39.

50. Marshall, *Men Against Fire*, 53, italics added.

51. "To reconstruct one day of vigorous battle will usually take about two days of briefing (five to six hours each day), provided the men are given the opportunity to do most of the talking. They will always be keener and will participate more freely on the second day, and if a third day is needed, the response will again rise" (Marshall, *Island Victory*, 22, see also 211). Interestingly, Marshall's summary of his interviewing techniques when written for Ganoe did not include the time required to accomplish a company interview.

52. Interview with Professor John Westover, 15 June 1987. Westover is sure Marshall "never ran any statistical survey." Another Marshall intimate, Dr. Hugh Cole, who was deputy theater historian, first under Ganoe and then under Marshall himself, wrote in his obituary for Marshall that the statistic "was open to grave question." See Hugh M. Cole, "S. L. A. Marshall (1900–1977): In Memoriam," *Parameters* 8 (March 1978): 4.

53. The S. L. A. Marshall Military History Collection at the University of Texas at El Paso is the main repository for Marshall's official and personal correspondence, draft manuscripts, and ephemera. A considerable body of correspondence between Marshall and B. H. Liddell Hart is collected at the B. H. Liddell Hart Centre for Military Archives, King's College, University of London. The U.S. Army History Institute, U.S. Army War College, Carlisle Barracks PA, holds several of Marshall's field notebooks. Some administrative records from the G-2 Historical Division bearing upon Marshall's wartime career are held at the National Archives and in the Historical Record Collection of the U.S. Army Center of Military History, Washington DC. The U.S. Army's Personnel Records Center, St. Louis MO, holds Marshall's personal service, or "201," file. None of these documentary sources indicates Marshall collected statistics that could be used in establishing a ratio of fire.

54. Marshall, *Men Against Fire*, 54.

55. Marshall, *Island Victory*, 205.

56. Marshall, *Men Against Fire*, 64–65, 89–90.

57. Ibid., 57.

58. See Marshall, "The Human Equation," 8–9; and Marshall, "Problems in Combat Leadership, 3 December 1962," in Marshall, *S. L. A. Marshall at Fort Leavenworth*, 35.

59. I am indebted to Harold P. Leinbaugh and, indeed, to all those combat veterans from the Second World War, Korea, and Vietnam who accepted

the heavy burden in many discussions over the years of educating me to the mysteries of modern infantry combat *in practice*.

60. Marshall, *Men Against Fire*, 59.

61. During the Second World War two researchers attempted a scientific description of the soldier's life in combat. See Roy Swank and Walter E. Marchand, "Combat Neuroses: Development of Combat Exhaustion," *Archives of Neurology and Psychology* 55 (1946): 238–41. Various Allied armies during the war at least acknowledged and attempted to operate on standards that implicitly recognized that soldiers in combat, however adept, had their limits. See Edward J. Drea, "Unit Reconstitution," CSI *Reports No. 3*, December 1983, 16–19.

62. Interview with Professor John Westover, 15 June 1987.

63. Marshall, *Men Against Fire*, 63.

64. See John W. R. Lepinwell, "The Laws of Combat? Lanchester Reexamined," *International Security* 12, no. 1 (1987): 89–134; and Thomas F. Homer-Dixon, "A Common Mis-application of the Lanchester Square Law," *International Security* 12, no. 1 (1987): 135–39.

The woods were infested with German soldiers, and the men knew it. On the day before their sister unit, the Thirtieth Infantry Regiment, Third Infantry Division, had entered the Alsatian forest known as the Bois de Riedwihr and—having gone too far too fast, outrunning their artillery supports—been blown to pieces. The remnants of the Thirtieth took refuge beyond the Ill River, in the direction of Holtzwihr, and awaited reinforcements. That was why, on January 24, 1945, the men of Company B, 115th Infantry Regiment, took up the approach march.

As Company B entered the woods, they encountered extremely heavy resistance in the form of sniper nests, artillery bursts fused for treetop detonation, mines, booby traps, mortars, and machine guns sited for cross fire. The company had to fight their way tree to tree, and by the end of the day they had little ammunition left. When the company commander was seriously wounded by a mortar round, a fresh-faced second lieutenant who looked more like one of Norman Rockwell's newspaper boys than someone you'd trust your life to was ordered to take command and resume the advance at first light.

The life of a second lieutenant in command of an infantry company during World War II was usually very short. The chances of surviving to become a first lieutenant were slim; of surviving the war, slimmer still; and of emerging physically unhurt, almost nil. In one fifty-day period as this particular division fought its way through the hills of Italy, line units reported a 152 percent loss in second lieutenants. The greatest likelihood of casualty occurred during a combat infantryman's first ten days in battle, but that of course did not mean that if he kept whole bones for ten days he would not be killed or wounded on the eleventh or even that his experience would somehow shield him from what lay ahead in the days afterward.

The new commander of Company B was, as Bill Mauldin's Willie and Joe—and even he—would later say, "a fugitive from the law of averages." The lieutenant had joined the Third Infantry Division as a private in North Africa. After serving for a time as a battalion runner because he was considered too frail for line duty (his friends called him "Baby"), he was eventually permitted to join the line as a combat rifleman with Company B in July 1943, during the Sicilian campaign. For nineteen months he had been pushing his luck, a quality that he appeared to possess in abundance. Only the day before he assumed command his right leg had been sprayed with fragments from a mortar burst. But compared to the mayhem he had already witnessed, his wound seemed so slight to him that he simply pulled out what fragments he could, applied his own field dressing, and continued his duties. Two officers who had been commissioned with him were killed in the same barrage.

Now, on January 26, the lieutenant moved his company through the Bois de Riedwihr. By early afternoon they had made their way to the edge of an open field, and as they walked into the clearing, the Germans opened fire with their usual murderous precision. In the barrage an American tank destroyer operating in support of the company was set afire and abandoned by its crew. Company B had gone to ground with the opening shot, and the lieutenant called for artillery counterfire. In the meantime, large numbers of German infantrymen and six tanks advanced across the open ground, making for the American position. The lieutenant ordered his men to withdraw to the relative safety of the woods while he remained to direct the artillery fire. The Germans were not to be dissuaded, however, and they pressed their advantage. Despairing of any more help from artillery, the lieutenant crossed ground swept by enemy fire, leaped aboard the burning tank destroyer, and turned its .50-caliber machine gun against the advancing Germans. As he worked the fearsome weapon, those of his comrades who could see him from the woods were sure that the lieutenant would soon be killed by ammunition exploding in the tank destroyer. By this time enemy tanks were actually abreast of his position, and he was under attack from three sides.

For the better part of an hour an estimated 250 German infantrymen—two reinforced rifle companies—devoted themselves to killing the lieutenant, the only American then in their sights. As many as fifty of them paid for their devotions with their lives. Finally, the Germans broke off the attack, and the lieutenant, unscathed, left the still-burning tank destroyer to rejoin his men.

Four months later, in Salzburg, Austria, 1st Lt. Audie Leon Murphy of Hunt County, Texas, stood nervously as Lt. Gen. Alexander Patch draped the Congressional Medal of Honor around his neck. On that day Murphy became the most highly decorated American fighting man not just in World War II but in all of U.S. military history. The Medal of Honor was Murphy's twenty-eighth decoration. He had been awarded every other medal for valor in battle that the Army had to offer and several twice. He was alive, more or less in one piece, and he was not yet old enough to vote.

Extraordinary valor in mortal combat has been celebrated in verse and rhetoric since Troy. The hero's deeds are commemorated and held up as examples of manly behavior worthy of imitation. A man who models his life on the hero, so the reasoning goes, prepares himself for the moment when his own finely schooled qualities will be called on. At the moment of decision the hero-aspirant must risk the possibility of annihilation, and in that moment his self-knowledge is pitted against forces beyond his control. No wonder men who have performed in these uncertain regions of behavior have long had an air of mystery, as if their valorous acts were beyond reason or understanding.

The institutionalization of valor—the elevation of the soldierly hero as a publicly honored figure—originated about two hundred years ago, when, in an age of enlightened reason, there evolved an attitude in the military that a soldier deserves something more than minimal pay, death, or crippling wounds in return for the honor of serving his country. Napoleon, for example, although he thought little about marching his soldiers into the ground or wantonly spending their lives if doing so fit his plans, nonetheless was aware of the practical need to reward his men for heroic service. But in this, as in so many other matters, Napoleon was precocious.

The British occasionally struck a medal to commemorate this great battle or that. The Waterloo Medal allowed its bearer two years' credit toward his pension. No doubt the ranks applauded even the smallest emolument for especially hard service. When, during the Indian Mutiny, Sir Colin Campbell—a very conservative commander when it came to handing out awards—implored his old regiment to make a special effort to break through enemy lines to rescue the British Residency at Lucknow, one soldier cried out, "Will we get a medal for this, Sir Colin?" But it was not until the Crimean War that Britain established the fabled Victoria Cross. The Americans adopted a similar practice later still, creating the Medal of Honor in 1862. In the early days the medal was relatively easy to win: one Federal regiment was given the award en masse simply for extending its Civil War enlistment, although the award was later revoked.

The institutionalization of valor also served ulterior purposes. Medals were given to foster morale among the troops and support for the war back home. Partly for this reason, with the proliferation of medals, their credibility became suspect among combat veterans. When pressed, modern soldiers will admit that it is better to have a medal for valor than not, but the medal mongering of the Vietnam War, for example, has created a cynical attitude toward battle decorations. Most soldiers today do not feel that, with the exception of the Medal of Honor itself, awards mean very much. One highly decorated officer said recently that during his own experience in Vietnam "the Silver Star was essentially a company commander's good-conduct medal."

What can heroes tell us about themselves other than that they are brave? By revealing the details of their own behavior, they can tell us something about all soldiers in battle and about the phenomenon of battle itself. Since their lives are documented more than others', they offer us a window not only on themselves but on the hidden lives of ordinary soldiers as well. The difference between the two is not as great as we used to think.

Throughout history the most notable feature of the heroic act is that it transcends its military objective. Commanders experienced in leading men into battle, for instance, are not at all certain that heroes are militarily useful. Most, given a choice between leading a battalion full of heroes and one of ordinary soldiers, would prefer the latter. Successful military action depends on the commander's ability to impose order on the chaos of battle, to turn his tactical ambitions into reality. This requires discipline and regularity of behavior, and neither quality seems to be common among heroes.

Clearly, it is not the lure of a medal that drives a man headlong into combat, risking death or dismemberment. Profounder motivations are required. The great puzzle is that most soldiers already possess these motivations and have acted on them through centuries of hard campaigning.

"The men know who deserve the medals and who don't," wrote S. L. A. Marshall in *Collier's* during the Korean War. Marshall remembered one commander from the North African campaign of World War II who stopped recommending his men for decorations because invariably those least deserving awards received them while true heroes did not. Marshall claimed that during World War II an unwritten rule prevented a combat medic—the one class of soldier whose life expectancy was actually shorter than the combat rifleman—from receiving any award higher than the Silver Star. Thus, the awarding of medals was too erratic to be just. There could be little assurance among the men that the ribbons over a man's pocket told the real tale, and most men were a little bashful about wearing them at all.

A hero's immediate comrades tend to know the truth about him, but among other soldiers he is naturally somewhat distrusted. An officer who served in the Third Infantry Division admitted that

Murphy "was not the most admired guy in the world." There are good and practical reasons for the ordinary soldier—whose first ambition is to survive the day, the next day, and perhaps even the war—to cock an eye at the consistent hero. Even though his actions are public, the hero is often a solitary soul who depends chiefly on his own passions, skills, and luck. It is his aloneness that singles him out. He tends to get killed, and his comrades with him. Worse, he sometimes survives while his comrades do not. Of course, this may be only luck—the bullet or shell just did not have his name on it that day—but you can easily sympathize with the suspicions of the ordinary soldier.

The bonds among the men in the smallest fighting units of World War II were extremely strong. The great wartime cartoonist Bill Mauldin, a perceptive observer of men in combat, believed that "you will seldom find a misfit who has been in an outfit more than a few months." (Those who could not fit in usually ended up dead or invalided to the rear.) And as for those occasions when someone in a unit is a candidate for an award, Mauldin added that "his friends are so willing to be witnesses that sometimes they have to be cross-examined to make sure they are not crediting him with three knocked-out machine guns instead of one."

After Murphy's action in the Bois de Riedwihr, he was pulled out of the line. Witnesses provided affidavits, and, within the month, the division had begun processing his award. By taking Murphy away from his unit (infantrymen were in very short supply in those days), the division signaled its view that the award would probably be the Medal of Honor. None other was sufficient to warrant relief from combat. Murphy was, after all, a rare commodity—a living and relatively undamaged candidate—and the authorities very likely did not want to risk losing him. (Capt. Maurice Britt, also of the Third Division, had been recommended for the Medal of Honor during the Italian campaign, but he had stayed on the line, only to lose an arm in a subsequent action.) Murphy was promoted to first lieutenant, given a leave to Paris, and, upon his return, reassigned as a liaison officer to his regiment. This change of duty improved by a large margin his chances of surviving the war. There is no evidence that he complained.

In his letters home about this time Murphy frequently mentioned his medals, especially the Purple Hearts. But he seems to have regarded them more as war souvenirs, booty to be sent home, than as badges of soldierly courage. He understood that a Medal of Honor would get him out of the line, and that was the main reason for his enthusiasm when he learned he might get one. On April 1, 1945, he wrote to friends that he had been given the Distinguished Service Cross, a Silver Star, and a Bronze Star and then was waiting at regimental headquarters for the Medal of Honor to be awarded "so I can come home." That, along with the Legion of Merit he was about to receive, meant that "since that is all the Medals they have to offer i'll [sic] have to take it easy for a while."

Eleven days after receiving the medal Murphy stepped off a plane at San Antonio and, in company with other military notables from Texas, began a round of parades, toasts, speeches, and interviews, slowly working his way north to his home in Hunt County. To the crowds that gathered around him that summer Murphy was no doubt befuddling and endearing. He was not the iron-eyed, athletic, self-contained warrior Americans seem to expect their military heroes to be. He was not tall and muscular, and he did not swagger. He was very slight, soft-spoken, and wearily uncomfortable with all the attention. But for the tan officer's uniform, bristling with ribbons, he could have been the kid next door. The actor James Cagney, soon to be instrumental in helping Murphy get his start in motion pictures, said that what was appealing about Murphy was his "assurance and poise without aggressiveness."

Murphy certainly did not look like the kind of man who might have spent nearly two years fighting his way from the hills of Sicily to the German frontier in the worst kind of infantry combat. In the story that accompanied his cover photo in *Life* magazine in July there is a picture of the lieutenant getting a haircut at Mrs. Greer's barbershop in Farmersville, Texas, near his home. Outside the big plate-glass window there stands a crowd of more than a dozen men, simply staring at him. There is an expectant air about the crowd, as if Murphy might suddenly bolt from the chair and do something herolike. His head is bowed, and the barber's bib drapes across his knees. He looks very young and mortally tired.

What Murphy was about to discover is that the hero's deed is only the down payment on the price he must pay for acclaim. Frequently, the medal becomes a curse for the man who wears it. Some 111 men won the Victoria Cross during Britain's nineteenth-century campaigns. Seven of these subsequently took their own lives, a horrendous rate for a time when in the general population there were only 8 suicides per 100,000. Still more had utterly disastrous postwar lives, finding that they were unequal to the more pacific rhythms of life beyond the battlefield. We know of the sad fate of the popular Marine hero Ira Hayes, who assisted in the raising of the flag on Iwo Jima's Mount Suribachi, but no complete study of the postwar fates of medal winners has ever been done. Of course, you need not be a certified war hero to suffer problems after a war, but the hero may carry a heavier burden than the ordinary soldier. As it was put by Capt. Ian Fraser of the Royal Navy, a Victoria Cross winner in World War II, "a man is trained for the task that might win him a vc. He is not trained to cope with what follows."

It is when you consider Murphy's record in context that his valor becomes truly impressive. During World War II 433 Medals of Honor were awarded, 293 of them to soldiers. Thirty-four, or 11.6 percent, went to men in Murphy's own Third Infantry Division during campaigns from North Africa to Germany. Fourteen were awarded to Murphy's 115th Infantry Regiment alone.

The division's record naturally poses questions. Compared to others, was the Third somehow a better fighting organization? Did it have a more difficult, longer war? Were its leaders especially sensitive to the benefits of soldierly morale, and therefore did they apply more often for awards? And did Murphy's membership in the Third somehow encourage him to perform valorous deeds repeatedly?

Unquestionably, the Third Infantry Division was a fine fighting organization. It was a "heavy" infantry division as it entered the war during the North African campaign, carrying more than fifteen thousand troops on its rolls. During the war it participated in four amphibious landings, fought in ten separate campaigns, and was in contact with the enemy on more than five hundred days, with few opportunities to rest and refit. According to the testimony of one of its wartime commanders, Lucian K. Truscott Jr., "few divisions have ever entered action in a higher state of combat efficiency." Truscott was a very plainspoken cavalryman, not given to hyperbole, and he was one of the very best division commanders of the war. But the appraisal of one's enemies always carries more weight. After Field Marshal Albert Kesselring, the German theater commander in Italy, was captured, he was asked to rate the quality of the units his armies had fought. He replied that the Third "was the best division we faced and never gave us a rest."

And then there are the numbers. Recently, when an officer who served with the division early in the war was asked about the official view of the awards, he agreed that the Third had more than its share; then he added, "Have you looked at the casualty figures?" Essentially, the division's membership turned over five times during the course of its campaigns. Battle and nonbattle casualties amounted to a staggering 74,044 soldiers by the division's own count. Of these losses, Truscott reported during the fighting in Italy, 86 percent were in the infantry battalions. After the first thirty days of fighting the infantry companies were at half strength, "although," recalled Truscott, "it had not seemed from day to day that losses were excessive."

Unfortunately, divisional battle streamers and casualty figures tell us very little about what the soldiering—the ordinary soldiering—was like. Well after the war one Army psychiatrist attempted to profile "normal" combat reactions; the result was a picture of a bedraggled and haggard near neurotic suffering from vague physical complaints, an inability to concentrate on the task at hand, constant irritability, and, in general, uselessness for any sort of strenuous activity—certainly not combat. During the war both Bill Mauldin and Ernie Pyle tried to describe for the public back home what the front was really like. In the end both would have agreed with the British Army's Capt. Athol Stewart: "Do *you* know what it's like? Of course you don't."

In their reminiscences veterans often despair of recalling the details of actual combat. Threading throughout their attempts at memory are references to "dreamlike states" and "floating" and in the more modern language of Vietnam "out-of-body experiences." The novelist John Steinbeck, working as a war correspondent in Italy during some of the campaigns Murphy fought in, believed that combat is beyond the powers of memory to reproduce. "You try to remember what it was like, and you can't quite manage it," he wrote. "The outlines in your memory are vague. The next day the memory slips farther, until very little is left at all. . . . Men in prolonged battle are not normal men."

So combat riflemen like Murphy stood at the farthest and most dangerous end of grand military enterprises, where elegant strategies and refined tactics count for little. Those matters belong to a world bounded by traditional military science. When a soldier moves forward against fire, he steps beyond the boundaries of anything we understand. Then, centuries of military science are at the mercy of one bullet, and if reason is at play, it must expend its power in forms so different that they have eluded us thus far.

For Murphy and his comrades in Company B the authors of all their miseries were, of course, the Germans. From the time Murphy entered the line until his last day in combat his enemies were on the strategic defensive and largely on the tactical defensive as well. In the terrain he had to cross the advantage naturally rested with the defense, and at this the Germans were very, very good. After the fighting around Mount Fratello Murphy wrote, "I acquired a healthy respect for the Germans as fighters" and "an insight into the furies of mass combat." That action, he recorded, had "taken the vinegar out of my spirit."

The Italian campaign was the worst yet for the Third Division. Casualties between the Allied landings at Salerno and Anzio amounted to more than the authorized strength of the division; as usual, the line units suffered the most. Because of the atrocious weather and the limitations it imposed on motorized tactical movement in monotonously hilly terrain, troops were often stranded in the lines for several days without food or water. Mules were pressed into service to carry needed supplies when enemy fire subsided. The enemy gave ground grudgingly. Murphy participated in several attacks during this time, attacks that succeeded less because of the power of assault than because of shrewd maneuvering. Often the enemy seemed impervious to anything the Americans tried. "If the suffering of men could do the job, the German lines would be split wide open. But not one real dent do we make," Murphy wrote later of the fighting around Monte Lungo. When the enemy did give ground and the Americans occupied it, the Germans routinely shelled their old positions.

Murphy survived the Italian campaign as a staff sergeant, with two Bronze Stars for valor, in command of a platoon—a position normally held by a second lieutenant. He had not been wounded, although he had been one of his division's twelve thousand "nonbattle casualties." Meanwhile, he had come to the attention of his commanders as a canny soldier who possessed extraordinary combat sense. Insofar as a soldier could be battle wise, Murphy was.

The wisdom of battle exacts its price, however. During the war researchers found that after the initial fear of combat passed the ordinary soldier was likely to relax somewhat, take more chances, and in some cases harbor a feeling of indestructibility. That feeling would be challenged eventually by the grind of daily action or, more promptly, by two dramatic events: a wound or a near miss, or the death of a close friend. Both were about to happen to Murphy.

On the morning of August 15, 1944, Allied troops invaded southern France, coming ashore south of Saint-Tropez. Military historians would later debate how relatively light the German defenses were compared to those at Normandy and how easily the Sixth Army Group moved northward along the Rhone against a rapidly retreating German Army. But invasion day was a very bad one for Murphy. Near the town of Ramatuelle his best friend was killed when enemy troops played a false surrender. After his friend died in his arms Murphy embarked upon a frenzied and single-handed assault, eventually killing or wounding thirteen German soldiers. "I remember the experience as I do a nightmare," he wrote. "The men . . . tell me that I shout pleas and curses at them, because they do not come up and join me." Murphy won the Distinguished Service Cross for his mad spree at Ramatuelle; no doubt he would have preferred the survival of his friend.

After a quick and cheering advance along the Rhone, the Sixth Army Group entered the Vosges Mountains, and all of a sudden the fighting seemed reminiscent of Italy. By this time nearly all of the original members of Company B were gone—killed or wounded. Murphy began to withdraw into a fatalistic alienation from his fellow soldiers. The comradeship that had originally sustained him had been gradually shot away and could not, would not, be regenerated. Although still in the midst of his fighting company, Audie Murphy was essentially alone.

Remembering this bleak time, in his autobiography, *To Hell and Back*, Murphy wrote:

> So many men have come and gone that I can no longer keep track of them. Since Kerrigan got his, I have isolated myself as much as possible, desiring only to do my work and be left alone. I feel burnt out, emotionally and physically exhausted. Let the hill be strewn with corpses as long as I do not have to turn over

the bodies and find the familiar face of a friend. It is with the living that I must concern myself, juggling them as numbers to fit the mathematics of battle.

As remarkable as his survival was the fact that Murphy had not by then succumbed to combat fatigue. Among the frontline troops the conventional wisdom was that everyone had his "breaking point" if he stayed in the line too long. Nor did respite from battle, such as Murphy had had while training for the landing in southern France, particularly help in warding off that breaking point. Paul Fussell recalls his experience after he returned from the hospital to the combat lines. His convalescence "helped me survive for four weeks more but it broke the rhythm and, never badly scared before, . . . I found for the first time that I was terrified, unwilling to take the chances that before had seemed rather sporting."

By October 1944 both of the opposing armies were wearing down. Maj. Gen. Wolf Ewart, the commander of the German 338th Infantry Division then opposing the Sixth Army's advance, reported losses as high as 60 percent in the battles for Alsace. The casualties among the officers and noncommissioned officers were especially high. On the American side of the lines infantrymen were at a premium, and as the winter approached manpower shortages became severe. Having earlier refused a battlefield commission because it would separate him from his men (newly commissioned officers were routinely transferred to another unit), Murphy accepted his commission on October 15 with the understanding that he could stay with Company B. His regimental commander, Col. Hallett D. Edson, pinned the gold bars on Murphy's shirt and told him to get a shave, take a bath, "and get the hell back to the front lines."

Twelve days later Murphy was seriously wounded by a sniper. Getting to the field hospital took too long; Murphy's infected wound became gangrenous. He remained hospitalized for the rest of the year. When he finally returned to Company B, the unit was getting ready to penetrate the Colmar Pocket in the direction of Holtzwihr. However, the Bois de Riedwihr lay across their line of march, and it was within these woods that Murphy's fame awaited.

During World War II battles often took place inside what the Germans knew as *der Kessel*, "the cauldron." The phrase evokes the stuff of close combat in confined spaces, the abiding and numbing fear of the next step that grinds down the swift movement of armies. To a degree perhaps not appreciated by modern military historians, World War II was one of places and lines. The rapier's thrust, typified by the dash across France, was an exception in this war. Eventually, the men who did Murphy's kind of work had to take the ground away from their counterparts on the other side of the main line of resistance. For the better part of two years Murphy lived inside *der Kessel*. As we shall see, he went to some lengths to get there, believing, as many do, that within war were mysteries of self to be discovered and of worlds beyond the life of a Texas sharecropper.

In Stephen Crane's classic story of the soldier's rite of passage, *The Red Badge of Courage*, the young hero, Henry Fleming, is overtaken by a desire to see war. He frets that war might be too modern to permit the attainment of real glory. He wonders if "he might be a man heretofore doomed to peace and obscurity, but, in reality, made to shine in war." Remarkably—all the more so since Murphy later played Henry Fleming in the movie version of Crane's book—Murphy seems to have been "made to shine in war."

No one tried harder than Murphy to see, as Henry Fleming did, "the great Red God of War." Whether Murphy had a predisposition for war is a problematic question, but there is little doubt that he saw the war, as innocents often do, as a way of escaping the grinding poverty that had so far dominated his young life. He was drawn to the elite units: The Marines were first on his list. Rejected twice, he tried to enlist for duty with the new airborne units, but he stood 5 feet 6 inches tall and weighed only 112 pounds—less than the battle gear the troops were often obliged to carry. Finally, he was made to settle for the infantry—unhappily, as "the infantry was too commonplace for my ambitions," he wrote later. Caught up in the great mobilization, Murphy was shifted from one post to another; at each place well-meaning superiors attempted to protect him from a combat assignment. "Fuming," he recalled, "I stuck to my guns." He was still just a child, really, when "finally the great news came. We were going into action."

Audie Murphy was so adept at infantry combat that we are compelled to look for reasons. He was certainly willing, even earnest, to join the rush to the colors, but most recruits are willing in the first flush of war. Reality quickly cools the new soldier's ardor. Murphy did not cool quite so quickly. Despite his small size he had the stamina that comes from years of farm work, but it cannot be said that he was any better prepared for the physical rigors of combat than anyone else. After a few weeks on the battle lines infantrymen are usually in terrible physical shape. Long before he was wounded Murphy spent several days in hospitals suffering from respiratory ailments acquired in Sicily and Italy. He had plenty of company.

Murphy appears to have believed, and his home state was quick to claim, that having been born and reared in Texas had something to do with his military success. But pride in origins should not be confused with some sort of predestination. He was a rural boy, of course, accustomed to hunting in the hills and valleys of North Texas. The countryside and its forms held no mysteries for him. But these advantages, if advantages they were, can be noted only as indecipherable factors. Most Americans who fought well in the war were not from Texas and had been no closer to the country than the city park before they enlisted. How they performed in combat had more to do with what the great German military historian Hans Delbrück would have called "the material possibilities of the moment." And despite a great deal of official interest by the U.S. Army since World War II, a psychophysical profile of "the natural fighter" has never been done.

Whether Murphy's behavior predisposed others to think of him as valorous is another question. It is true that even the most ordinary rifleman took terrifying risks day after day, but Murphy's practices were not typical. During his war Murphy developed certain habits that automatically brought him to the approving notice of his superiors. Before the war he had been pugnacious, and this temperament served him well during his campaigns. And although he was as comfortable with his comrades as any combat soldier might be, he was given to independent action. He often volunteered for patrols to gather information or to take prisoners. Frequently, he would "go hunting," and, when he did, enemy snipers were in danger. As he gradually acquired command responsibilities he usually would see his men safely placed, then go forward alone or with a couple of others to reconnoiter the ground ahead. For Murphy, then, the sequence of events during his action at the Bois de Riedwihr was not so unusual.

Nor was his endurance of notorious stresses unusual. One officer of the First Scots Guards who fought in Tunisia recalled seeing "strong, courageous men reduced to whimpering wrecks, crying like children." Murphy never seems to have had such a breakdown, although he had more than his share of reasons to do so. He seems, on the contrary, to have been able to redirect his reaction to stress against the military objective at hand. Obviously, stress was at play during the incident at Ramatuelle. Since the last century military theorists have recognized that one of the many ways to escape immediate danger in combat is to move forward; Murphy did that more than once.

All of which is not to say that Murphy escaped suffering, either in the war or after it. After the sniper's bullet in Alsace proved he was not, after all, invulnerable, he adopted the fatalistic attitude common to soldiers long at war. From his hospital bed he wrote home that "these Krauts are getting to be better shots than they used to be or else my lucks [sic] playing out on me. I guess some day they will tag me for keeps."

After he was recommended for the Medal of Honor and reassigned to his regimental headquarters, Murphy's luck was tested less often; but there was plenty of war left, and on several occasions he was drawn into combat, despite the Army's desire to preserve the life of a Medal of Honor winner. And then, finally, the war ended. But Murphy's private war did not.

In ages past, once the colors were furled, soldiers gratefully went home. The signing of the peace was a signal for nation and individual alike that normal life could be resumed. But during the twentieth century there were disturbing signs that the psychological effects of war are rather more persistent than anyone wants to think. The medical world has devised increasingly sophisticated interpretations of the spiritual lassitude, and worse, that seems to affect so many veterans. What was "shell shock" in World War I was gradually redescribed as "combat fatigue" or "neuropsychiatric casualty" in World War II and finally as "post-traumatic stress" in the Vietnam War. So, too, did the supposed causes of the malaise change. Whereas shell shock was thought to be the result of concussions and gas from high explosives, combat fatigue was believed to be a pernicious mixture of the soldier's personality and the immediate stresses of combat. In the years since Vietnam interpretations have tended to emphasize the stresses of combat alone as the cause of postwar emotional suffering.

Of course, there were vast differences among all these wars—the circumstances under which men fought as well as the conditions they found at home upon their return. Students of the Vietnam era have noted that Vietnam veterans did not have the advantage of returning World War II soldiers, who came home in troopships, where they could "decompress" for at least several days. The flight from Saigon to San Francisco took only about eighteen hours; afterward, soldiers were discharged and left to their own readjustment—or lack thereof. Murphy's experience more nearly matched that of the Vietnam vet. Even with his own generation's opportunity to relax before discharge, Murphy thought, returning vets were poorly handled. He told an interviewer in 1960 that "they took army dogs and rehabilitated them for civilian life. But they turned soldiers into civilians immediately and let 'em sink or swim."

To be sure, Murphy's own postwar experience was unusual.

Few other vets became national institutions. As his fame spread, one Dallas newspaper sought to tell the public "what Murphy is like—a swell kid, absolutely modest, sincere and genuine and unaltered by terrible experiences." Well, not quite, because while other veterans were allowed to contend with their personal demons in private, every event in Murphy's life after the war was played out in public. His skills did not easily translate into civilian life, and he clearly was unsure what to do when the cheering stopped.

Fortunately, before too long he was recruited by Hollywood, much as sports heroes are today. His photograph on the cover of *Life* had inspired James Cagney to invite him west. Originally intending to register Murphy at a hotel, Cagney was so startled by Murphy's fatigued appearance that he offered the young man the use of his pool house instead. Murphy was Cagney's guest briefly, went home for a visit, and then returned to spend nearly a year at the actor's home. Within five years Murphy had parlayed his wartime fame into a peacetime career.

His movie career has been depicted as modest. Film histories do not mention his work—perhaps wrongly, for he was cast perfectly in John Huston's *The Red Badge of Courage* and Joseph L. Mankiewicz's *The Quiet American*. Murphy himself took a dim view of his acting ability and did not seem to think of his career as more than a way to make a decent living. "I didn't want to be an actor. It was simply the best offer that came along," he recalled long after the war. But he certainly did well enough: by the early 1950s Audie Murphy had enough box-office power to demand script and director approval (as well as the lead role) for any movie he was in.

Yet the two years he spent in the cauldron of war dominated his life and, to an extent that could be known only by himself, determined its course. His wartime heroism overshadowed everything he did, although by most standards he made a greater postwar success of himself than his early history would have suggested. Without that vital identity as a military hero, Murphy might well have returned to a quiet life in rural Texas, never to be touched by fame. Ironically, perhaps, it was that fame that kept the war too much alive for him. Decades after the war he still could not relax. He had chronic stomach complaints, sensitivity to loud noises, and frequent nightmares. He always kept the bedroom lights on at night and a loaded pistol by his bed. Sometimes he carried the pistol.

Murphy's fortune declined in the 1960s. He had always gambled, but the habit began to get the best of him then. As bankruptcy threatened he grasped at dubious business schemes and acquaintances. His political outlook, always on the conservative side, verged on the extreme. But none of these difficulties strike us today as particularly the effect of trauma. Indeed, we are so accustomed to heroic figures who fall from public grace that the concept of heroism itself has devolved. When Murphy was killed in a plane crash near Roanoke, Virginia, in 1971, he still seemed incomplete, searching for something elusive. Once asked whether men get over a war, he had replied reflectively, "I don't think they ever do."

FIVE. Cherry Blossoms Falling

Japanese Combat Behavior at War's End

In October 1944 the United States Army published the *Handbook on Japanese Military Forces*. Its appearance, organization, and language suggested a field manual, authoritative, unambiguous, a text to be relied upon. The manual was a feat of intellectual "reverse engineering," drawing upon intelligence gathered from two years of fighting in the Pacific. It was also a text meant to demystify the mysterious, to make intelligible the inscrutable. So the handbook is not the place one expects to find a note of surprise. "Despite the opportunities presented during 6 years of active combat," the text reads, "the Japanese have continued to violate certain fundamental principles of accepted tactics and technique. Their tendency to persist in such violations is based primarily upon their failure to credit the enemy with good judgment and equal military efficiency. Whether or not they have profited by recent experiences remains to be seen."[1] Farther on under the heading "Forms of Attack" one reads: "The Japanese will attack in many cases where the orthodox decision would call for less positive action. The attack may be rash and costly but will never lack vigor and determination." For the Japanese Army, the "meeting engagement" is said to be the preferred form of attack, which the handbook defines as "the collision of two hostile forces in motion." This form of attack was believed to be "the optimum development of the alleged Japanese aptitude for swift and decisive offensive action."[2]

If we look behind the clinical language of the handbook and into the history of the Pacific War, at the history of combat itself, then the idea of a meeting engagement takes on a terrifying reality. Such an engagement occurred at the Ilu River on Guadalcanal. Capt. Nicolai Stevenson was moving his company of

Marines through kunai grass along the river when intense small arms fire erupted to his front. Seventy yards from the Japanese lines he called for a bayonet assault. When his enemies realized what Stevenson was doing, they too fixed bayonets and charged. The two forces crashed into one another and intermingled in a horrifying frenzy of hand-to-hand combat. Not a single soldier of the Ichiki Detachment, veterans of Singapore and Malaya, picked troops all, survived the collision.[3]

Is this what the authors of the Army's handbook meant by the tendency of Imperial Japan's forces "to violate certain fundamental principles of accepted tactics"? What happened at the Ilu was a singular event for Stevenson's Marines and for the men of the Ichiki Detachment, but approximations of it would be repeated throughout the Pacific War. One is therefore constrained to ask, Whose fundamental principles? Whose accepted tactics? Perhaps not those of the soldiers and sailors of Japan, perhaps not even those of the leaders of Japan.

One cannot inquire very deeply into the history of the Pacific War without experiencing a different sort of meeting engagement in which two histories collide on a battlefield of cultures where so little of each seems understandable in terms of the other. To Captain Stevenson that day the behavior of his enemy seemed suicidal, not sensible. Had the situation been reversed, Stevenson would have seen first to the protection of his men and his position by preparing his defenses to receive the charge. He would have tried to employ every weapon at his disposal and artillery too, if it was available. He would have abandoned this stance only if in his judgment a profitable counterattack could be mounted against the enemy. Even under the circumstances as he found them, Stevenson's training had come into play. That training would have taught him that one acceptable response was to advance toward the source of the enemy's fire and silence it, not shrink from it. That, at least, was an "accepted principle" to Stevenson but not, evidently, to the men of the Ichiki Detachment. Their comrades in the Sendai Division had been told by their commander that in the coming attack they and all the

ON COMBAT

other members of the command now rushing to defend the island would be "undaunted by the mass of the enemy," that they would not "bow to material substance." By displaying "a combination of fortitude, perseverance, and steadfastness," he assured them, they would "inflict a terrible blow upon the heads of the enemy." The concept of victory does not seem to have appeared in the commander's address.[4]

Even so, this commander faithfully reflected the sense of discussions between the empire's strategic leaders in the months before the Pearl Harbor attack. At liaison meetings among representatives of the various ministries and at conferences in the presence of the emperor himself, Japanese strategists concluded that they had little choice but to embark upon a new phase of the war, expanding toward the "southern resources area" and against the United States. Years afterward the phrase "window of opportunity" would become a cliché in American strategic circles, but in the councils of 1941 Japan the compulsion to act against all odds that this cliché implies was very much present. In July the Navy's chief of staff, Admiral Osami Nagano, contemplated the prospects of war with the United States. "Although there is now a chance of achieving victory," he argued, "the chances will diminish as time goes on. . . . [I]f we conclude that conflict cannot ultimately be avoided then I would like you to know that as time goes by we will be in a disadvantageous position." Later, at a seventeen-hour liaison meeting on 1 November, Nagano was less circumspect. "The time for war will not come later," he said.[5]

The same deficiencies in national resources that induced this sense of strategic vulnerability and crisis in late 1941 foredoomed Japan's capacity to conduct a war of sufficient scope and duration to achieve its ambitions. Even in the beginning of the Pacific War, the best that Japanese leaders expected was to fight their way toward a negotiated peace that would leave Japan in a favorable position as a world power, but these ambitions were the very definition of what Paul Kennedy would later call "strategic overstretch." After the war the Army's last chief of staff, Lieutenant General Kawabe, said bluntly: "This war was the kind of war which should have been avoided at all costs according to the theory."[6] The theory was simply that, in war, there should be some correlation between ends and means, and this the forces of Imperial Japan did not enjoy. Prime Minister Hideki Tojo himself thought that Japan might steal a momentary success, but, like Nagano, he believed that if the war went on for much longer, "there would be no end of difficulties."[7]

Yet the theory of which Kawabe had spoken was a Westerner's theory, and, anyway, difficulties were made to be overcome. Other sources of behavior in war were available to Japan's strategic leaders and to its soldiers in the field. Japanese culture and tradition possessed a rich storehouse of idioms that could be, and were, mobilized in the service of this new war.[8] The materialistic Western military style that Japan had adopted only seventy-five years earlier was nowhere near as serviceable. In extremis, Western modalities of warfare could not withstand the stresses of Japan's Pacific War, whether at the strategic, operational, or tactical level. Deeper reserves of belief and behavior were drawn upon from the very first days of the war, and they would predominate at war's end.

Westerners who relied upon their own cultural terms of reference to understand Japanese behavior sooner or later disposed of their puzzlement by dismissing it as irrational or otherwise unique, a characterization that one frequently encounters in the literature of the time.[9] As Ian Buruma has observed, "Japan provokes a sudden urge in many foreigners to express their culture shock in writing."[10] Back on Guadalcanal, Captain Stevenson fretted about the holes in his defensive perimeter along the beach and rejoiced, half a century later, in "the incredible luck that inspired the Japanese always to attack at those points where we were dug in instead of the vast empty spaces where we were not."[11] Perhaps Stevenson has forgotten that the American combat infantryman's cardinal tactical principle in the Second World War was that he should "close with and destroy the enemy," which was what he had done and would do for the rest of his war and which was not, in effect, different from his enemy's actions. If this catchy phrase did not carry with it the force of an absolute imperial injunction, if it was often not followed for good and sufficient reasons, that was only the manifestation of the individualism that influenced all the Western armies, combining their efforts when they must, reverting to type when they could.[12]

In the armed forces of Imperial Japan traditional sources of behavior had long since been appropriated. The "Imperial Rescript to Soldiers and Sailors" of 1882 explicitly bound the armed forces to the emperor himself. Perhaps the fullest expression of the ideology of the communal nation as a great uniracial family thoroughly identified with the imperial deity appeared in 1937, with the publication of a pamphlet entitled "Fundamentals of Our National Polity." Imperial subjects were enjoined to subordinate the self to the greater whole (*kokutai*), embodied in the divine imperial presence. "Our relationship between sovereign and subject is by no means a shallow, horizontal relationship such as implies a correlation between ruler and citizen," the pamphlet read. Rather, the self is transcended "and is that of 'dying to self and returning to [the] One.'" So the reader would not miss the point, the authors of the pamphlet added, "This is a thing that can never be understood from an individualistic way of thinking."[13]

Only a short leap was required from conceptions of racial uniqueness, harmony, and purity to one of racial superiority. As many scholars have observed, the culture of Showa had postured itself to denigrate the strength of other cultures. And in the highest councils of war planning, confidence in one's own superiority contributed importantly to strategic miscalculations. Japan's most powerful enemies, not being Japanese, were thus not so powerful after all. Strategic planners sought, and naturally found, reason to believe that the power of the United States, beset by domestic disagreements over its own involvement in foreign affairs as well as economic and racial strife at home, was fragile after all. Those who listened to Prime Minister Tojo at an imperial conference in November 1941 heard him attempt to allay anxieties in precisely such terms.[14]

In order to avoid succumbing completely to Japanese perceptions of themselves, it is necessary to recall that strategic miscalculations were just as effectively rationalized elsewhere in the world at the time. Hitler's conception of Germans as the master race required, as any such conception does, that one designate specifically whom one is to be master over. Of course, he had enlisted the Jews for his conception, but he also capitalized upon the readily available "Slavs," the Russians, who unlike the Jews had a nation and an army to contend with and, he expected, to conquer. That was ideology, but in practice there were important differences in the way Germany and Japan applied it. No matter how skillful and ruthless his drive to mobilize the ideology of the master race, the most that Hitler was ever able to do was to create specialized supramilitary organizations such as the ss, which served as an ideologically pure army within an army. As for the rest of the Germans, old-fashioned nationalism would have to serve. The armed forces of Japan managed a much more thorough ideological mobilization. Every part of the military establishment was enlisted in the cause.[15]

The mechanism by which this transformation was accomplished was of course the ancient way of the warrior, or *bushidō* which had been codified by Yamamoto Tsunetomo in the early eighteenth century in a kind of vade mecum, the *Hagakure*. However, regarding the *Hagakure* as the purest expression of *bushid- bushidō*, as it was practiced in the Pacific War is misleading, for this concept was itself significantly modernized after the restoration. In its original form *bushidō* was feudal and local and, by comparison to its newer variations, rather individualistic. Adherents of the old way of the warrior were adjured to conduct themselves righteously even at the cost of life and cause. So important was this principle that reason, or "calculation" in the words of the *Hagakure*, was regarded as an impediment, a corruption of the true and righteous way.[16] Yamamoto recounts a soliloquy by one Lord Aki: "On the battlefield, once discretion starts it cannot be stopped. One will not break through to the enemy with discretion. . . . [I]f one were informed on military tactics, he would have many doubts, and there will be no end to the matter. My descendants will not practice military tactics."[17] Other philosophers of *bushidō* were not so resolutely anti-intellectual as Yamamoto, however.[18] Yet *Hagakure* was the most widely read of all tracts on the *samurai* ethos, wherein the warrior consummated honor through his death. It was in the act of dying that he would reveal his true spirit. All other goals, calculation, reasons, were subordinated to the act of righteous self-sacrifice.

Of all the characteristics of the Japanese way of war, this one has been the most resistant to Western understanding. One need only compare the outlook of the French military writer Charles Ardant du Picq, whose *Études sur le combat* was the most widely read book in the trenches of the Great War in France. "Man does not enter battle to fight, but for victory," he wrote. "He does everything he can to avoid the first and obtain the second."[19] One could hardly imagine a passage more opposed in spirit and philosophy to the code of *bushidō*, and it was a philosophy that Western soldiers in battle had long since embraced.

Like the code of chivalry in the West, *bushidō* was a military aristocrat's creed. After the Meiji Restoration the task for Japan's modernizers, as for their Western counterparts a century earlier, was to suffuse the new national army with the precepts of this code. In this way classes that before had little association with these sacrificial codes could now be mobilized to serve the interests of the new order. In Japan this was accomplished quite handily, so that in the "Fundamentals of Our National Policy" one sees *bushidō* in new dress, designed for the masses. It was said to have "developed into a spirit of self-effacement and of meeting death with a perfect calmness. . . . In effect, man tried to fulfill true life by way of death."

The most distinguished of the old *samurai* are honored as "bringing *bushido* to perfection," but, significantly, the text reads further: "It is this same *bushido* that shed itself of an outdated feudalism at the time of the Meiji Restoration, increased in splendor, became the Way of loyalty and patriotism, and has evolved before us as the spirit of the imperial forces."[20]

All this was very well and good, but Japan was certainly not the only nation that militarized deeply rooted cultural principles in order to fight this war. Like Germany, the Soviet Union quickly discovered that appeals to the new principles of Marxism possessed nothing like the motivation power of nationalism. This, along with the help of the police state, which soon regained its equilibrium, seemed quite sufficient to move more than twenty million Soviet citizens to give their lives to the war.[21] In the United States the invocation of "the Four Freedoms" seemed a sufficient organizing cry, but, as national slogans went, it rather lacked intensity. Paul Fussell has written: "For most of the troops, the war might just as well have been about good looks, so evanescent at times did its meaning and purpose seem."[22] For all intents and purposes, Fussell and his comrades entered the war as individuals, and as individuals they trained and fought and often died, and if they came home with whole bones they thought it was only because of the sheerest luck. The armies in which they fought not only tolerated but shaped their fighting styles around this sensibility, which was that if machines could do the job, then men would not have to. The approach did not produce the most stylish armies, but then, as du Picq had observed, fighting was not the point. Victory was the point.

It has long been a cliché among military historians that armies are a reflection of the societies that give them birth. But if it is so, the reflection is more what one sees in a funhouse mirror at a carnival, refracted and distorted and partial. Armies make up their own kind of society, aimed at a single purpose, which is often quite distant from the culture that breeds them.

The Imperial Japanese Army (IJA) took great care to see that its soldiers were thoroughly indoctrinated with the values symbolized by *kokutai*. Over the years the Army's masters had come to believe that young rural lads, strong of body and uncorrupted by much formal education or association with the debilitating cosmopolitanism of urban life, made the best raw material for soldiers. The physically hard life and the hierarchical family structure of the villages fitted into a uniform quite literally. The Army's regiments recruited upon specific districts and localities, much as other armies have, and in the course of a brutal training regimen supplanted the social and psychological requirements of village life with their own. No recruit ever had cause to doubt his place in the world of the regiment or to doubt the reason for his presence. The imperial chrysanthemum was forged on the bolt action of his Type-38 (Sanpachi) rifle, and each morning he greeted his emperor by bowing in the direction of the imperial palace. Every day he was made to read the "Imperial Rescript to Soldiers and Sailors" and at mess to recite the "five principles" derived therefrom: loyalty, propriety, valor, righteousness, and simplicity.[23] For causes great and small and sometimes for no reason at all, he was beaten by his superiors, who believed that one's will was strengthened by physical trial. In addition to the trials of the formal training schedule, the demands of hierarchy were felt in the barracks as well, for after the NCOs departed, senior privates assumed the role of superior and exacted their own demands upon the junior recruit, a practice that was countenanced by the chain of command as an additive to the rigors of the day.[24] Once possessed of willpower and discipline, the soldier was considered equal to any task, no matter the physical or material obstructions he might encounter. Foreign military observers with imperial units during the decade before the war routinely professed their astonishment over the physical and psychological demands made of these soldiers—demands that were met. An American officer recorded in 1938 a regiment's forced march in cold and rain and mud with rifle, pack, and 150 rounds of ammunition that covered 122 miles in 72 hours.[25]

The officers who marched at the head of the column, who with swords drawn charged rifle lines, machine guns, and artillery firing over blank sights, had taken on a different character during the early years of Showa, when the old aristocratic clans were gradually replaced by young men drawn from the lower middle classes, made up of shopkeepers and small landholders. Upward of 30 percent had been educated in military prep schools, which they had entered at age twelve or thirteen.[26] Their higher military education was relentlessly focused on tactics taught by rote. One American officer who attended the Imperial General Staff College before the war recalled: "The pronouncements of the Staff and Faculty were accepted with awe and even reverence. During the entire year of my attendance I never heard an instructor's decision or solution criticized, or even discussed or questioned." He added, rather needlessly, that his own army's staff college was not like this.[27] When the officers did debate among themselves, rhetorical assertiveness was more valuable than knowledge.[28] Thus, an officer corps was created that lacked imagination and little experience at improvisation but that possessed a tendency to adhere to a course of action to the bitter end.[29] In the French Army before the First World War officers extolled similar virtues that were nicely captured in the notorious phrase *offensive à outrance.*

Both at home and abroad this officer corps behaved in ways that revealed its uneasy accommodation to modern military practices. The psychological structure of command relationships was profoundly influenced by the very different role of the leader in Japanese culture. When a Westerner reads the IJA's depiction of the infantry company as "one household in the one village that is the regiment" and that "the heads of household are the father and the mother," with the officer as the equivalent of "a strict father, and the NCO a loving mother," the reaction is likely to be incredulousness.[30] Few Westerners with experience as a subordinate to a noncommissioned officer are likely to have confused him with a "loving mother." To a Japanese recruit, however, such phrases carried a comforting subtext, one that assured him of a secure place—in a severe hierarchy, to be sure, but a secure place nonetheless. Such a subtext was not comforting only to Army recruits, for its writ ran well beyond, throughout Japanese society to its very center. Long before the term *network* was used as a descriptive term in Western society, the Japanese had constructed for themselves the most elaborate of networks, one that fixed every individual in relation to another. The terms of reference for this relationship are *oyabun* and *kobun*, the former meant to signify one with the status of a father, the other that of a child, and nearly every Japanese played at least one role and sometimes both. The terms *sempai* and *kohai* are much more familiar to Westerners, but only the *sempai* who enjoys a very special relationship with a *kohai* possesses the status of *oyabun*. This familial network did not disappear when it was clothed in the uniform of the imperial forces. But it competed directly with and sometimes overruled the mechanistic command relationships required of a modern army.[31]

Japanese linguists tell us the language has no word for "leader," that one must employ terms referring to the *oyabun-kobun* relationship. And indeed the functions of the one a Westerner would call a leader are of a very different order, for the leader is expected to subsume himself in the activities of his group "to the point that he has almost no personal identity." One attains a leadership position by virtue of status, not merit. Unlike Western leaders, Japanese leaders make no pretence of superior merit, knowledge, or ability. Indeed, to Western sensibilities, Japanese leaders are defined by those who follow them. These subordinates are also bound by rules of comportment that do not resonate in Western behavior. An aggressive favored subordinate may assume de facto leadership in a group, but he must do so in the name of the leader, never his own. Direct public challenges to leaders by their subordinates were impermissible. No matter how grave the situation, the subordinate must never offend his superior's status.[32]

One might think, therefore, that here was a corps of officers whose upbringing suppressed any hint of indiscipline. But the prewar officer corps was riotous, faction ridden, notorious for taking foreign as well as domestic matters into its own hands, not merely reactionary but downright atavistic. How, then, is one to understand the downright mutinous behavior of subordinate officers that punctuated prewar Japanese politics and continued through the war to the very end? If one's motives were sincere and honorable, directed toward what one conceived to be the best interests of the emperor (or any superior), the concept of *gekokujo*—"the overpowering of seniors by juniors"—was readily at hand.[33] So expansible was this concept, for instance, that it accommodated the Kwantung Army's attack on Manchuria in 1931 over the objections of the civil government in Tokyo and a year later the assassination of the premier, Inukai Tsuyoshi, who opposed it.[34] It accommodated, too, a spectacular stunt by an aide to the military attaché at Shanghai the following year. By staging an assault on Japanese priests, he hoped to create an incident that would divert world attention from Japanese operations in Manchuria. The aide's incident got out of hand and required the deployment of a naval brigade and three divisions to quell the fighting that broke out in the city.[35] It was possible, of course, to go too far. In 1936, when the Young Officers' Revolt erupted in Tokyo with the killing of several senior government officials, the leaders of the conspiracy defended themselves with claims to righteous motives (*makoto*), but they were quietly executed and their followers purged.[36]

The Japanese place a great value upon nonverbal behavior and pride themselves on being able to "read" the true intentions of their conversant.[37] A Japanese may say one thing to preserve harmony (or *ninjo*, usually rendered as "human feelings") by avoiding personal confrontation while privately believing something else. The difference between what is said and what is felt is encompassed by the concepts of *tatemae* and *honne*. Ian Buruma has written: "When the Japanese talk about being able to communicate without using words, they really mean that they can read each other's *honne*, while keeping to the *tatemae*."[38] It is because of the potential conflict inherent in the overt expression of *honne* that the Japanese value silent communication.

The armies of the Second World War—including those of the Japanese—were in one sense huge industrial organizations whose Western aesthetics demanded that they be handled in certain mechanistic ways if they were to function properly. Professional soldiers like to speak of "operational necessity," a phrase

98

in which are subsumed sets of sequenced "if-then" propositions. "If I wish to start a machine, then I first must turn it on," to use a mundane example; or, more pertinently, "If I wish to fight a war, then I must acquire the means to do so." But as we have seen already this most vital of propositions was violated almost from the outset of the Pacific War, and the clash between cultural and operational necessity continued to plague the Japanese throughout the conflict.

One of the more remarkable instances of competition between cultural and operational necessity occurred during the Imphal-Kohima campaign of 1944, when Lieutenant General Mutaguchi, commander of the Fifteenth Army, had privately decided that his army's situation was hopeless. Losing ground to General Slim, his men starving, his casualties disastrous, holding out no hope for reinforcements or resupply, and facing the onset of the rainy season, he nevertheless did not tell his superior, Lieutenant General Kawabe, that the campaign should go over to the defensive. Kawabe understood the situation as well as Mutaguchi did, but neither would admit it. Instead, Kawabe "read" his field commander's thoughts and submitted a frank report to General Headquarters, although he did not recommend calling off the offensive. In late June Slim's forces broke through to the Imphal Plain, and this gave Mutaguchi's chief of staff the opportunity to prepare a telegram for Kawabe that acknowledged the true state of affairs in Burma. Mutaguchi approved the telegram without further comment. Staff officers in both headquarters understood their commanders were attempting to preserve the fiction of success while attending to the realities of Allied successes. Nearly three months were consumed by delicate psychological negotiations between the high commanders and their staffs in the interests of preserving their "human feelings" before they could respond. Their subordinates, understanding the necessity to avoid any circumstance in which their superiors might be required to confront unpleasant or discordant facts, delicately arranged for the Fifteenth Army, now virtually a wreck, to assume a defensive posture. Of course, by then it was too late, but "human feelings"—at least those of Mutaguchi and Kawabe—had been preserved.[39] In the meantime, the Fifteenth Army was dying: by the time it retreated across the Chindwin River, it had lost 53,000 of its original 85,000 soldiers. By the end of the war 150,000 Japanese had died in Burma. Seventeen hundred had been captured, but only 400 had been fit when they were made prisoner. No regular officer was ever taken prisoner and no officers of any sort below the rank of major.[40]

Historians customarily regard the summer of 1944 as the beginning of the end of the Pacific War. One day after Mutaguchi's troops began withdrawing across the Chindwin River the island of Saipan fell, and on 18 July Tojo resigned as premier. In the central Pacific the Bonin Islands were already under intense bombardment. The battles for Guam, Tinian, and Peleliu were on the horizon. Hopes of holding the strategic "outer perimeter" were replaced by fears that not even Japan's "inner perimeter," protecting the home islands, could be held. Seen from the strategic perspective of high policy, the Pacific War is rich with candidates for the dramatic "turning points" historians are so fond of.

Time works differently for the soldier in combat, whatever his culture. His career is measured by a much more compact cycle, from his initiation in combat to whatever end the war has in store for him. During the Normandy campaign psychologists with American troops described the structure of a soldier's life in combat as an arc of effectiveness that reached its apogee after about fifteen days in contact with the enemy. At that point the soldier operated on a plateau where his behavior and skill were optimized. Ten days or so later, however, both skills and behavior began to erode as combat exhaustion set in. After about a month in combat the soldier had become more of a burden than a benefit to his unit. Assuming that he survived all the while, the soldier would eventually descend to a completely dysfunctional state.[41] By then the U.S. Army had decided that no soldier should be kept in combat longer than 240 days. The British Army had decided that 400 days were about right for a combat tour. Both figures blithely assume a near-miraculous survival, of course.

But, as usual, the soldiers themselves were considerably ahead of the psychologists, not to mention their own commanders. As early as the campaigns in North Africa, soldiers on the line had come to understand that if one stayed on the line long enough, one would succumb to combat stress.[42]

Studies such as the one at Normandy were concerned specifically with the behavior of American troops, of course, but most assume without going further that their findings apply to all American troops, regardless of where they fought—a very dubious proposition, indeed. As for the behavior of their enemies, American military psychologists seem not to have targeted any studies against them. Social and behavioral scientists in the United States did undertake strategic-level analysis against the Germans and the Japanese, but in the Pacific operational areas tactical-level studies of enemy combat psychology, based on captured enemy documents and prisoner of war interrogations, were left to the operational types, mostly language and intelligence officers serving with combat formations.[43]

How, then, might one describe the structure of the Japanese soldier's life in combat? Historical studies tend to assume that the Japanese soldier's psychological career in action corresponded with Japan's strategic fortunes, and the increasing desperation of the battles in the last year of the Pacific War does correlate with ever more dramatically sacrificial behavior by the imperial forces. But this does not also mean that this behavior was unique to strategic misfortune, for it certainly was not.

At this remove it is easy to forget how quickly certain parts of the Pacific War went so badly for the soldiers of Imperial Japan. Not only on Guadalcanal but in New Guinea Japanese soldiers were soon outmaneuvered, outmanned, outgunned, and certainly outsupplied. The strategic perimeters were very early on proven to be little more than an ambition, dissolving into points of defense that the Allies attacked or ignored as they thought best. It was at these points of defense that the nature of the Japanese soldier's combat experience is best revealed.

By comparison with combat experiences elsewhere, marked

as they were by physical as well as psychological movement, the impression one has of the structure of the Japanese soldier's experience is one of inevitability. It was as if the script had already been written, and all that was wanted was a proper stage upon which it could be enacted.

And, indeed, an element of theatricality pervaded the structure of the Japanese soldier's combat experience. The entire family was watching how one comported oneself. In the unlikely event that a recruit infected with a Western-style iconoclasm survived training, the regulations of his army would have reminded him that surrender under any circumstances was punishable by death.[44] The Army's Field Service Code of 1941 did its part to emphasize these values, reading: "Meet the expectations of your family and home community by making effort upon effort, always mindful of the honor of your name. If alive, do not suffer the disgrace of becoming a prisoner; in death, do not leave behind a name soiled by misdeeds."[45] Certainly toward the beginning of the war, send-off gatherings for soldiers leaving for the front were punctuated by such exhortations. And in the field, if a soldier was lucky enough to receive a letter from home, it might well read like this one, intercepted by the Allies: "You are my son—and yet you are not my son. You are the son of the Emperor. Your body is not yours—it belongs to the Emperor." Yet this mother was not quite ready to give him up completely. She added: "Therefore you must take good care of yourself. Day and night I am praying for your safety. God and I, your mother, will always be with you."[46]

Whether in the Solomons, New Guinea, or the Philippines or on the numberless islands of the Pacific, the attrition of disease, malnutrition, exhaustion, or the actions of the enemy brought the Japanese soldier face-to-face with the prospect of the death that had been so glorified that it could hardly be denied. The cohesive familial structure that had been so painstakingly and brutally recreated in the units began to disintegrate. The course of the war drove the individual soldier toward the threat of abandonment, first by his nation and his strategic commanders and then by his comrades as they died one by one. The diaries and letters of soldiers who faced this abandonment commonly express their admiration for their emperor, their gratitude to their family, and the hope that ultimately their spirit would return to the Yasukuni shrine, there to rest with all of Japan's fallen sons. From an all too typical diary entry dated 3 December 1942 we read:

> I have fought with all my strength. I believe by all means that the violent efforts of Basa Garrison will be handed down to posterity. . . . But now my fighting strength is weakened and I am about to expose my dead body on the seashore of Basa. My comrades have already died, though my heart is filled with joy because I can become the guardian spirit of my country. I will fight and crush the enemy. I will protect the seashore of Basa for ever.[47]

This diary entry brings to mind another soldier's farewell written under similar circumstances: "The [enemy] have broken through everywhere. Our troops, weakened by long periods of hunger without possibility of [illegible; relief?], engaged in the heaviest fighting since the beginning of this battle, without a day's relief, and in a state of complete physical exhaustion, have performed heroically. None of them surrenders." It was written by a German soldier during the battle of Stalingrad.[48]

The Japanese understood very well the consequences that would follow from the destruction of a fighting unit's cohesion. Formations so dependent upon leadership and cohesion would inevitably suffer if their leaders were killed and the cohesion disrupted by the costs of battle. An army whose very being revolved around a romantic concept of war as a set of discrete events whose purpose was the acting out of selfless sacrifice rather than winning was fragile, liable to break into fragments of stylishly heroic but militarily purposeless actions. At least since their disastrous encounter with the Soviets at Nomonhan in 1939, select officers in General Headquarters had understood the deficiencies in their national style of war. Still, the Army's high command persisted in believing that the Yamato spirit would triumph over all material adversity.[49]

On the Pacific battlegrounds as well as in the highest strategic councils this conception of war seemed more appropriate as the war went on. It was a conception that could be defined as a collection of spiritual confrontations, not as the processional unfolding of engagements, one linked to another, which was how the Allied command elites saw the matter. To the Japanese the Allied style of war was little more than a giant machine going about its merciless work, and indeed theirs was a blue-collar approach to war. All over the Pacific War the Japanese conducted what came to be called *banzai* charges of the kind Stevenson met at Guadalcanal. When students of war ask whether any of these did any good, meaning, did the Japanese advance their cause in any material way, the answer is almost uniformly no. Although many Allied lives were lost defending against these charges, much the great part of the cost was always borne by the Japanese.[50]

Thus, this spiritualistic conception of war quickly revealed its military shortcomings. Before Imphal, the men of the Thirty-third Division were ordered to attack; they were also told by their commanders that they would certainly be annihilated but that they would gain a victory too.[51] The subtext of these instructions was a belief in the "spiritual charge," the effect supposed when the spirits of all the dead reunited themselves to fight on against the enemy. This, it was said, was what happened at Attu in 1943. Although the war had already furnished numerous examples of forlorn attacks on the ground, at sea, and in the air, Attu seems to have resonated with imperial military leaders. On Attu, with no hope of relief or evacuation, 2,500 Japanese soldiers fought to the last man, outnumbered five to one. Back in Tokyo, Attu inspired a new concept denoted by a word that had not been familiar in Japanese, lifted from an aphorism in a sixth-century Chinese classic, where it was held that "a man of moral superiority would break his precious jade rather than compromise to save the roof tiles of his home." The concept was expressed by the word *gyokusai*, or "jewel smashed."[52] It was venerable, and it was far more dignified than the rough-and-ready phrases that had been employed to describe sacrificial attacks—"body smashing," "flesh bullets," "self-blasting."[53] And it was official. Following *gyokusai*, the spiritual charge was expected to overpower the enemy by virtue of its righteous energy and force the enemy to retreat. The spiritual charge was no invention of the moment, a lapse into the hysteria of mortal futility. After a unit was obliterated by the Russians at the battle of Nomonhan, one officer observed: "The enemy must have felt uneasy, for they gave up the position and retreated." For that reason, the officer thought, "the departed souls were still making a charge. Is it not a fact that the enemy retreated?"[54]

Faced with the choice of a solitary, unobserved death or one in the company of one's comrades, Japanese soldiers by the thousands chose the latter if they could. This preference, available from the beginning of the Pacific War and indeed long before, was co-opted by officialdom and institutionalized as an essential element of national strategy. The disaster at Attu in 1943 occasioned this change, although in truth many other examples of individual and mass sacrifice were available by then. Very early on in the war, from Burma to New Guinea and the Solomons, Allied troops routinely encountered enemy behavior that eluded all their cultural points of reference. Everywhere the Japanese were usually unable to treat or evacuate their wounded. In Burma and on the larger islands they were harried from place to place by enemy artillery and air attacks. One medic who fought on New Britain remembered his year on the island as "our wild flight for five hundred kilometers," which his army called "changing directions." Virtually without medicine, this soldier's aid station became instead a facility for mercy killing, where a fatal injection or a grenade, pressed hurriedly into his patients' hands as they broke camp, became the only relief he could offer.[55]

One hundred and forty-eight thousand Japanese soldiers died on New Guinea. One soldier of the Seventy-ninth Infantry Regiment of the Twentieth Division who miraculously survived his unit's retreat following the Australian attack at Finschhafen in

1943 described an experience that was all too typical. Habitually short of every kind of supply and equipment, he came to wonder what the Japanese infantryman was actually for. "It often seemed to me," he recalled, "to increase the number of victims. . . . [W]e didn't know what was killing us. Who killed that one? Was it death from insanity? A suicide? A mercy killing? Maybe he just couldn't endure the pain of living."[56]

By the end of 1943 soldiers and civilians all over the world could be found who had been driven to the extremities of their existence. Allied troops on New Guinea found firsthand as well as documentary evidence of cannibalism among the Japanese troops. This evidence suggests that such incidents were more than the isolated act of soldiers driven mad by fear, disease, or hunger. Australian soldiers testified that they had found the remains of comrades who had been cannibalized, and enemy orders were captured in which one Japanese general officer reminded his troops that "eating anyone except an enemy soldier" was an act punishable by death.[57] What seems to have occasioned this remarkable order was the general's concern that his soldiers were preying upon their own kind. The soldier of the Seventy-ninth Regiment came to learn that, of the many sources of danger he had to contend with, one was his own comrades. "Near the end we were told not to go out alone to get water, even in daytime. We could trust the men we knew, but there were rumors that you could never be sure what would happen if another of our own soldiers came upon you. . . . [T]he stories I heard made me shiver and left me chilled to the bone," he remembered.[58]

Of course, Japanese soldiers went mad, but in this war the concept of madness was highly elastic and depended mostly upon whether one was able to carry on with some semblance of effectiveness. The character of Japan's Pacific War permitted very little attention to what other armies were calling "neuropsychiatric casualties." On the more static fronts, such as the North China area of operations, IJA medical statistics showed soldiers suffering from "mental diseases" at a rate of more than 20,000 a year. Under the more general category of "other nervous diseases" the number rose above 30,000 a year between 1942 and 1945. Gross statistics from the "South Areas" of operation reached 100,000 in 1943 and 1944. Little else is known of these cases, how these data were collected, or their disposition. In any event, medical considerations were never allowed to interfere with field operations.[59]

In these transactions the enemy seemed somewhat beside the point, so remote from Japanese frames of reference that they seemed to exist only to contribute to the hellishness of the war. One soldier remarked, rather typically: "The 'enemy'? I often wondered what that meant. We didn't hate the enemy. We seemed to fight them only because they showed up."[60] John Dower has observed that while Western racism focused upon the denigration of others, "the Japanese were preoccupied far more exclusively with elevating themselves."[61] Considered deficient in spirit from the beginning, enemy identities eventually merged into a great machine that produced dizzying magnitudes of violence. And when such people committed the sin of being taken prisoner, they were far from being human at all.

Allied prisoners of the Japanese fortunate to survive their first meeting with their captors often doubted how fortunate they had been. They were beyond consideration as humans. To the Japanese, any meager spirit these foreigners may have possessed had been extinguished by the fact of their captivity. They were then vulnerable to any outrage their captors could devise. As scholars have learned, guarding prisoners was "almost as dishonourable as being one," and for such disreputable duty "misfits, troublemakers, alcoholics, and even the insane" were more than sufficient.[62] General Slim believed atrocities occurred most often when Japanese officers failed to exercise military discipline, but one would have to go far to find any Japanese soldier who was punished for what he did to a prisoner or for that matter to a civilian who fell under his power.[63] Remarkably, one former POW found it possible to be philosophical: "Sure the Japs beat you with baseball bats," he said, "but they beat each other with baseball bats too."[64] It is also true that atrocities and outrages against humanity were being committed by combatants all over the world between 1941 and 1945. The Japanese betrayed an aptitude for particular kinds of behavior, but other nationalities accomplished much the same end by the different means their cultures had given them. The worst atrocity the Japanese may have perpetrated was on themselves.

If by some chance Japan's strategic leaders had been accused of overdignifying the needless battle at Attu to the level of state policy, in July 1944 they were to witness on Saipan an event whose magnitude of sacrifice was adequate to strategic considerations. Five years after Nomonhan one can see the sense of the "spiritual charge" on display in the Imperial General Headquarters (IGHQ) Army Section's Confidential War Diary entry for 24 June 1944: "The Saipan defense force should carry out *gyokusai*. It is not possible to conduct the hoped-for direction of the battle. The only thing left is to wait for the enemy to abandon their will to fight because of the '*Gyokusai* of the One Hundred Million.'"[65] Two weeks after this entry was written the island was the site of an orgy of self-induced slaughter, where 3,000 Japanese soldiers joined in a *banzai* charge against prepared defenses. Some of these came from their aid stations on makeshift crutches or leaning on their comrades for support, trailing bandages. Inspired by this example, whole units later submitted to mass beheading by their officers, who then committed *seppuku*. Still others attended to the matter individually, with pistols, knives, or grenades. Still worse yet, hundreds of Japanese civilians trapped on the island hurled themselves off cliffs and dashed themselves to death on the rocks or drowned in the waves below.[66] While newspapers back home extolled the virtues of those who had given their lives in this apocalypse, none mentioned that more Japanese soldiers had been captured in this battle than ever before, some 1,780 taken after more than 23,000 had been killed. More than 14,000 civilians had survived and had been interned by the Americans. Japanese newspapers reported that virtually all had died in glorious defense of the island.[67]

Mitsuharu Noda, a sailor who was trapped on the island

by the invasion, participated in the mass attack and survived. After consuming all the whisky and cigarettes they could find, he and about twenty others from his unit joined the assault at four o'clock on the morning of 7 July. "We are not going to attack enemies," he recalled. "We were ordered to go there to be killed. . . . [I]t was a kind of suicide." He was hit in the stomach by two machine gun bullets. As he was lying on the ground, he watched as several others crawled toward one another until their heads were touching. Then one of them detonated a grenade as he cried, "Long live the emperor." "I held my breath at this appalling sight," Noda writes.[68]

Saipan was sufficiently apocalyptic to bring down the Tojo ministry, and Saipan certainly astonished the enemy. But Saipan opened the way for a campaign whose extravagance has ever since blinded us to the patterns of culture and combat behavior that served as its essential foundation. That campaign entailed the creation in the fall of 1944 of the first "Special Attack" units (Tokkotai), best known to Westerners as the *kamikaze*.[69] Originally the invention of Vice Admiral Onishi, commander of the First Naval Air Fleet based in Manila, the first such units were formed from the 201st Air Group and used against the American fleet. On their first outing the men of the 201st sank one carrier and damaged six more. Their actions not only galvanized the public back home but attracted the attention of the emperor himself, whose reaction was communicated to the 201st: "Was it necessary to go to this extreme? But they have certainly done a good job."[70]

What followed could only be described as a kind of fad. Although officers in Imperial Headquarters were skeptical at first, not six months had passed before substantial amounts of war production in the home islands were diverted to the construction of various sorts of "Special Attack" weapons for sea, land, and, most dramatically, air.[71] Even Onishi himself was said to regard the whole enterprise as a "tragic necessity." Soon after the first units were formed, Onishi told a comrade: "The fact that we now have to resort to [such a method] shows how poor our strategy has been since the beginning. . . . You know, this really is a violation of [proper] command."[72]

Set alongside the psychodynamics of ground combat, those of the *kamikaze* seem altogether different, rather more like a Shinto purification rite than an act of combat. Indeed, on the eve of the first attacks Admiral Onishi told his pilots: "You are already gods, without earthly desires."[73] Young, romantic, unmarried men were preferred for this honor. Initiates contemplated the meaning of their fate cloistered in austere barracks, composing meditations and *haiku*. It was to these doomed young men that the cherry blossom conceit best applied. What one scholar has called "that quintessential Japanese image" celebrated "the special beauty inherent in evanescence, worldly misfortune, and the 'pathos of things' [*mon no aware*]."[74] How very unlike this refined, choreographed image from the hell-bent-for-leather visions conjured up during the "Firecracker attack" of 1941. The Divine Wind made "belly slitting" seem vulgar, too chaotic to contain the purity of the cherry blossoms.

Armies that are losing often betray certain characteristics. Impending disaster may give birth to a dissonance between strategic intent and tactical events. One need only recall the maniacal orders that issued from Hitler's bunker during the battle of Berlin. Even in the best of seasons, however, armies can be quite fragile. On the verge of defeat they may simply shatter into so many individuals. A certain reluctance to fight on can be punctuated by episodes of raw bloody-mindedness. Of course, armies like these suffer higher casualties if they do not quit soon enough. Under these circumstances unit cohesion can only suffer. Officers gradually lose any moral authority they might have possessed and come to be regarded with even more hostility than usual by the other ranks. One also sees in such armies an appetite for depredation if the opportunity allows.

Modern nations have taken pains to send their soldiers to war armed with the right tools, but that is not all a soldier carries into combat. His culture has supplied him with a kit of psychological defenses, beliefs, and values. But it is a rare memoir, at least among Westerners, that does not depict the soldier's acculturation to war as a degenerative process in which these prewar defenses are literally stripped away, one by one, until he is left with little of his old identity and now has one better fitted to the imperatives of the world of combat.[75]

So it is all the more interesting that the Japanese soldier's behavior in the Pacific War did not conform to these patterns of behavior so well understood in the West. The strategic disasters of 1945 seem not to have excited substantive changes either, as one would expect in a Western-style army.[76] The defenses with which the Japanese soldier's culture had armed him remained intact, persisted, and ran their course with no evident systemic degradation of individual fighting effectiveness. Thus, as late as the battle for Okinawa, what Westerners saw on the killing grounds was different only in degree, not kind, from what had been seen in 1942.

The island-bound character of the Pacific War seemed fitting for the Japanese way of war, which was less a process than a collection of tactical events. The islands served as stages upon which Japanese strategy could devolve, much more so than the vast landscapes of Manchuria or China. Far from a dissonance between Japanese strategy and tactics, there appeared a kind of harmony. The personal apocalypse that individual Japanese soldiers had suffered all along during the war was, toward the end, a version in miniature that scholars tell us some of Japan's strategic leaders had planned for the defense of the home islands.[77] These plans, while appearing to violate common sense, were regarded by those who made them as wholly acceptable responses to the strategic situation as they knew it to be. Westerners were quick to say then, and have been saying so ever since, that a national *gyokusai* would have been unprecedented in military history, unique to the Japanese. When thinking about a war that consumed fifty million lives, I am inclined to believe that no act was beyond any part of humankind in 1945, no act at all.

Notes

1. *Handbook on Japanese Military Forces*, United States War Department Technical Manual TME 30-480 (Washington DC: GPO, 15 September 1944), 85.

2. Ibid., 86.

3. Nicolai Stevenson, "Four Months on the Front Line," *American Heritage* 36, no. 6 (1985): 49–52. Stevenson commanded Company C, First Battalion, First Marine Regiment, First Marine Division. This engagement was part of a larger operation known generally as the battle of the Tenaru River, because the Marines' original maps transposed the rivers' names. Stevenson refers throughout his memoir to the Japanese unit as the "Ischiki Battalion," but it was part of a regimental-size formation. The battle occurred on 21 August 1942. The commander of the formation, Col. Ichiki Kiyono himself, was killed in this action. See "Reports of General MacArthur," in *Japanese Operations in the Southwest Pacific Area*, vol. 2, pt. 1 (Washington DC: GPO, 1966; facsimile reprint, Washington DC: U.S. Army Center of Military History, 1994), 148 and nn. 92, 93.

4. Lt. Gen. Maruyama Masao, "Address of Instruction, 1 October 1942," quoted in *American Samurai: Myth, Imagination, and the Conduct of Battle in the First Marine Division, 1941–1951* by Craig M. Cameron (Cambridge: Cambridge University Press, 1994), 103.

5. Nagano is quoted in Alvin D. Coox, "The Effectiveness of the Japanese Military Establishment in the Second World War," in *Military Effectiveness*, vol. 3, *The Second World War*, ed. Allan R. Millett and Williamson Murray (Boston: Unwin Hyman, 1988), 13, 14.

6. Ibid., 28.

7. Ibid., 14.

8. For a discussion of how tradition resisted modernism in the prewar period see Kato Suichi, "Taisho Democracy as the Pre-stage for Japanese Militarism," in *Japan in Crisis: Essays on Taisho Democracy*, ed. Bernard S. Silberman and H. D. Harootunian (Princeton NJ: Princeton University Press, 1974), 227.

9. Scholars are by no means immune from this tendency. Alvin Coox writes of the irrationality of Japanese strategic estimates on the eve of the war ("Effectiveness," 19). Even the Japanese historian Ienaga Saburo, in his *The Pacific War* (New York: Random House, Pantheon Asia Library, 1978), 33, employs this term.

10. Ian Buruma, *Behind the Mask: On Sexual Demons, Sacred Mothers, Transvestites, Gangsters, and Other Japanese Cultural Heroes* (New York: Meridian Books, 1984), ix. For a sampling of contemporaneous views see John Dower, *War without Mercy: Race and Power in the Pacific War* (New York: Random House, Pantheon Books, 1988), 94–97.

11. Stevenson, "Four Months," 51.

12. See Paul Fussell's discussion of this tactical principle in his "Thank God for the Atom Bomb," in *Thank God for the Atom Bomb and Other Essays* (New York: Simon & Schuster Summit Books, 1988), 14.

13. Japanese Ministry of Education, "Fundamentals of Our National Polity," in *Sources of Japanese Tradition*, comp. Ryusaku Tsunoda, William T. de Bary, and Donald Keene (New York: Columbia University Press, 1958), 785–95. For a discussion of the concept of the Yamato Race (*Yamato minzoku*) during the Second World War see Dower, *War without Mercy*, 204–6.

14. Tojo is quoted in Coox, "Effectiveness," 23–24. See also Tadashi Fukutake, *The Japanese Social Structure: Its Evolution in the Modern Century*, trans. Ronald Dore (Tokyo: University of Tokyo Press, 1982), 32, 42, 52–53, 55–56, and 64–68, which discusses the social dynamics of "familistic" groupings in Japan and the process by which a "group egoism" is created.

15. See an elaboration of this point in Richard J. Smethurst, *A Social Basis for Prewar Japanese Militarism: The Army and the Rural Community* (Berkeley: University of California Press, 1974), 180–81.

16. Law and higher authority were corrupted by reason and thus in the most famous stories were often defied in the interests of righteousness. To the authorities, however, the offenders were outlaws, as were the "Forty-seven Ronin." For the story of another legendary *samurai* see that of Shoin (Yoshida Toajiro) in Tsunoda, de Bary, and Keene, *Sources of Japanese Tradition*, 616–18.

17. Yamamoto Tsunetomo, *Hagakure: The Book of the Samurai*, trans. William Scott Wilson (Tokyo: Kodansha International Ltd., 1979), 155.

18. Tsunoda, de Bary, and Keene, *Sources of Japanese Tradition*, 606–18.

19. "L'homme ne va pas au combat pour la lutte, mais pour la victoire. Il fait tout ce qui depend de lui pour supprimer la première et assurer la seconde." Charles Ardant du Picq, *Études sur le combat: Combat antique et combat moderne* (Paris: Éditions Berger-Levrault, 1942), 7.

20. Tsunoda, de Bary, and Keene, *Sources of Japanese Tradition*, 791–92. How the values of the *samurai* were inculcated in the Imperial Army recruit is detailed by Edward J. Drea, "In the Army Barracks of Imperial Japan," *Armed Forces and Society* 15, no. 3 (1989): 329–48.

21. See Adam Ulam's rendition of Stalin's famous 3 July 1941 speech to the nation in *Stalin: The Man and His Era* (New York: Viking Press, 1973), 539–40. See also Isaac Deutscher, *Stalin: A Political Biography*, 2nd ed. (New York: Oxford University Press, 1972), 485.

22. Paul Fussell, *Wartime: Understanding and Behavior in the Second World War* (New York: Oxford University Press, 1989), 129.

23. Ruth Benedict remarks that "men appointed to read [the imperial rescripts] have killed themselves because they misread a sentence" in *The Chrysanthemum and the Sword: Patterns of Japanese Culture* (1946; New York: New American Library, 1974), 209.

24. Drea, "In the Army Barracks," 332–36; Coox, "Effectiveness," 34–36.

25. Lt. Col. Warren J. Clear, "Close-Up of the Jap Fighting Man," printed lecture delivered at the Command and General Staff School, Fort Leavenworth, Kansas, October 1942, 23. Clear had served as a military observer with the Second Division at Aizu-Wakamatsu in north-central Honshu. See also Capt. Harold Doud, "Six Months with the Japanese Infantry," *Infantry Journal* 64, no. 1 (1937): 18–21; and M. D. Kennedy, *The Military Side of Japanese Life* (Boston: Houghton Mifflin, 1924).

26. Suichi, "Taisho Democracy," 227–28.

27. Substantial portions of Col. E. S. Bratton's official report are quoted in Clear, "Close-Up of the Jap Fighting Man," 37–43. Bratton was the only Westerner ever to graduate from the Riku-gun Dai Gakko.

28. Edward J. Drea, "U.S. Army and Japanese Imperial Army Doctrine during World War II," typescript provided by the author, 17.

29. One Marine officer who fought from Guadalcanal onward thought the Japanese commanders deficient in "headwork." Quoted in Cameron, *American Samurai*, 121. See also Ronald Spector, *Eagle against the Sun: The American War with Japan* (New York: Random House, Vintage Books, 1985), 35–36; and Coox, "Effectiveness," 34–36, for a succinct evaluation of the IJA's operational and tactical effectiveness.

30. This passage is from the IJA's 1908 edition of its squad administration handbook, quoted by Drea, "In the Army Barracks," 335.

31. The anthropologist Chie Nakane discusses *oyabun-kobun* relationships at length in *Japanese Society* (Berkeley: University of California Press, 1972), 42–43, 63–69, but within the context of civil, not military, society.

32. I have observed the same characteristics in my own army and suspect they must exist in every army to one degree or another. In the U.S. Army these extrahierarchical and lateral relationships are a good deal less compulsory and more consensual than those that existed in prewar Japan. Even so, one can discern their influence if one looks with sufficient care.

33. This is how Richard Storry renders the concept in his *A History of Modern Japan* (London: Penguin Reprints, 1990), 185.

34. Ibid., 187–92.

35. This first Shanghai incident is recounted in Saburo, *The Pacific War*, 65–66.

36. Storry, *History of Modern Japan*, 196–200.

37. Yasuko Tohyama, "Aspects of Japanese Nonverbal Behavior in Relation to Traditional Culture," in *The Empire of Signs: Semiotic Essays on Japanese Culture*, ed. Yoshihiko Ikegami (Amsterdam: John Benjamins Publishing Company, 1991), 181–218.

38. Buruma, *Behind the Mask*, 221–22. See also Doi Takeo, *The Anatomy of Self: The Individual versus Society*, trans. Mark A. Harbison (Tokyo: Kodansha International, 1985), 35–47, and also *The Anatomy of Dependence*, trans. John Bester (Tokyo: Kodansha International, 1971).

39. This account is drawn from a contemporary study of the Japanese high command in the Burma campaign by a serving officer in the Japanese Ground Self-Defense Forces, Lt. Col. Urai Hideo, "Characteristics of Japanese Imperial Army's Leadership and Its Background in the Imphal Operation," conference paper presented at the JGSDFUS Army Military History Exchange, 8–12 February 1993, Tokyo, 31–37. Copy in possession of the author.

40. Louis Allen, *Burma: The Longest War, 1941–1945* (New York: St. Martin's Press, 1984), 611.

41. Roy L. Swank and Walter E. Marchand, "Combat Neuroses: Development of Combat Exhaustion," *Archives of Neurology and Psychology* 55 (1946): 236–47.

42. Capt. J. W. Apple, "Prevention of Manpower Loss from Psychiatric Disorder: Report of a Trip to North Africa Theater of Operations, 12 May–29 July 1944," typescript, n.d. [22 May 1945], 2, copy in U.S. Army Center of Military History, Historical Records Collection. See also William S. Mullins and Albert J. Glass, eds., *Neuropsychiatry in World War II*, vol. 2, *The Overseas Theaters* (Washington DC: Department of the Army, Office of the Surgeon General, 1973).

43. The best examples of these reports are to be found in the collected reports of the Allied Translator and Interpreter Section for MacArthur's South-West Pacific Area. See, for instance, Col. Sidney F. Mashbir, coordinator, "Self-Immolation as a Factor in Japanese Military Psychology," ATIS Information Bulletin no. 14, typescript, originally classified as confidential, General Headquarters, Southwest Pacific Area, 4 April 1944.

44. Coox, "Effectiveness," 37.

45. Quoted in Haruko Taya Cook and Theodore F. Cook, *Japan at War: An Oral History* (New York: New Press, 1992), 264.

46. Extract quoted in Mashbir, "Self-Immolation," 6.

47. Extract quoted in ibid.

48. Franz Schneider and Charles Gullans, trans., *Last Letters from Stalingrad* (1962; Westport CT: Greenwood Press, 1974), 54.

49. The foregoing is based upon Alvin Coox, *Nomonhan: Japan against Russia, 1939* (Stanford CA: Stanford University Press, 1985), 2:991–1092.

50. Spector, *Eagle against the Sun*, 265, 267, 283–84, 316–17, 319.

51. Allen, *Burma*, 610.

52. Dower, *War without Mercy*, 230–32.

53. For a discussion of the changing metaphysics of death see Ivan Morris, *The Nobility of Failure: Tragic Heroes in the History of Japan* (New York: Farrar Straus Giroux, 1975), 288.

54. Hirose Minami, *Psychology of the Japanese People*, trans. Albert R. Ikoma (Toronto: University of Toronto Press, 1971), 138–39.

55. Ogawa Tamotsu, "Soldiers' Deaths," in Cook and Cook, *Japan at War*, 277–79.

56. Ogawa Masatsugu, "The 'Green Desert' of New Guinea," in ibid., 271.

57. "Japanese Soldiers Practiced [Cannibalism] during World War II," United Press International press release, 11 August 1992. This press release is based upon the research of Toshiyuki Tanaka, Associate Professor, Melbourne University, as reported by Kyodo News Service, Tokyo.

58. Masatsugu, "The 'Green Desert' of New Guinea," 273–74. See also Saburo, *The Pacific War*, 192.

59. United States Navy, *United States Naval Technical Mission to Japan*, 1946, pt. 10, "Studies in the Field of Psychiatry," Report #M-D: "Neuro-Psychiatry in the Japanese Imperial Forces," Enclosure C, 164.

60. Masatsugu, "The 'Green Desert' of New Guinea," 271.

61. Dower, *War without Mercy*, 204–5. See also Allen, *Burma*, 268.

62. Spector, *Eagle against the Sun*, 398.

63. Allen, *Burma*, 610.

64. Quoted in Spector, *Eagle against the Sun*, 399.

65. Quoted in Haruko Taya Cook, "The Myth of the Saipan Suicides," MHQ: *The Quarterly Journal of Military History* 7, no. 3 (1995): 18; see also Morris, *The Nobility of Failure*, 284–85.

66. See Morris's rendition of Saipan in *The Nobility of Failure*, 299.

67. Cook, "The Myth," 15–16.

68. Noda's account is reprinted in ibid.

69. The term normally employed was *shimpu*, or "divine wind."

70. Morris, *The Nobility of Failure*, 183.

71. Saburo, *The Pacific War*, 183.

72. Quoted in Morris, *The Nobility of Failure*, 284.

73. Ibid., 287.

74. Ibid., 40.

75. The divestiture of prewar identity is a leitmotif in modern war literature as well, beginning with Stephen Crane's *The Red Badge of Courage* and Siegfried Sassoon's *Memoirs of an Infantry Officer* and running well

past the Second World War's *The Naked and the Dead* by Norman Mailer into the Vietnam War.

76. Dramatic though it is, I do not regard the appearance of the *kamikaze* as a substantive change on either the strategic or the tactical level.

77. Edward J. Drea, "Previews of Hell," MHQ: *The Quarterly Journal of Military History* 7, no. 3 (1995): 74–81.

George C. Scott was furious. Tim Considine, the young soldier at the end of the ward in the casualty clearing station, had just told the general that his nerves couldn't take the shelling anymore. Calling Considine a goddamned coward, Scott knocked the soldier's helmet off and stepped back, about to draw his revolver. By this time the attending physicians and Scott's aides had pulled him away from the young man, who was still seated, sobbing. Scott screamed at the soldier, "You're a disgrace to the Army and you're going back to the front to fight, although that's too good for you. You ought to be lined up against a wall and shot. In fact, I ought to shoot you myself, God damn you."[1]

Of course, this is a scene from the motion picture *Patton*. Scott and Considine had just played a critical moment in the movie and, indeed, in Gen. George S. Patton Jr.'s World War II career. The scene was more or less accurately done, although there was more to the story.

This was actually the second of two incidents, happening a week apart in early August 1943 at the height of the Sicilian campaign. The first was played out in the Fifteenth Evacuation Hospital, then near Nicosia, among newly arrived wounded from the First Armored Division. Patton set upon Private Charles H. Kuhl of Company L, Twenty-sixth Infantry Regiment. Kuhl, who was later diagnosed as "high-strung," was also suffering from malaria and diarrhea. Patton had cursed Kuhl, slapped him, picked him up by his collar, and kicked him out of the tent. Later that night Patton wrote in his diary that he had met "the only arrant coward I have ever seen in this Army" and that such men "should be tried for cowardice and shot."

The second soldier, twenty-year-old Private Paul Bennett of the Thirteenth Field Artillery Brigade, had by then been on the front lines for nearly six months. Bennett had exhibited symptoms of "extreme nervousness" after seeing a fellow soldier wounded, but he had begged to remain with his unit and was ordered back to the Ninety-third Evacuation Hospital by his battery surgeon.[2]

And there the matter would have remained if it had been left to the chain of command. The day after the first incident the hospital commander reported it to the II Corps chief of staff, who gave it to the corps commander, Omar Bradley. Bradley locked the report in his safe because, as he said later, "Patton was my Army commander—I couldn't go over Patton's head."[3]

But news of the incidents would not be so easily contained. At every point the chain of command tried to excuse Patton's behavior, but the story made its way through medical channels to Eisenhower, who himself at first thought a private reprimand might be sufficient chastisement for an Army commander. He was wrong. By then three American war correspondents attached to the Seventh Army had the story. They flew to Seventh Army headquarters in Algiers and gave Walter Bedell Smith, Eisenhower's chief of staff, a summary of the story. At that point Eisenhower had no choice but to treat the incidents seriously. He appealed to the correspondents to keep the story out of their papers, and they agreed. Nearly four months later a radio correspondent back in the States, Drew Pearson, broke the story, and Patton was relieved of command. Well into the next year Eisenhower was still dealing with the aftermath of the two slapping incidents.[4]

The Second World War was composed of many battlefields, not all of them recorded in the morning reports or tactical summaries or message traffic. Some of the battles began before the war itself, traversed the war, and were fought on well beyond the war. The scientific war, which has attracted relatively little scholarly attention, could be seen in this way, and so too the intelligence war. The medical war has remained hidden away in the official histories, histories, it must be said, that are among the best of their kind. And deep inside the medical history of the war we can see glimpses of the psychological battlefield.

Of course, soldiers have always been affected by their wars in one way or another. Before the twentieth century traditions everywhere held that visible wounds were the only wounds. A soldier might not be in control of his fate on the battlefield, tradition said, but surely the soldier must control himself. The soldier may shrink from the terrors of battle, so tradition said, but in the end he must go forward and face down those terrors even at the cost of his life. For if he did not, if he surrendered to those terrors, if he lost control of himself, he rendered himself beyond the pale of manhood. He was a coward, a thing to be despised by all those who did not surrender and by all those who would die rather than give into their instincts to survive. By these traditional standards the most important weapon a man carried into battle was his own upbringing, because battle's genius was to discover a man's weakness and to work at that weakness until the man failed. Only a man's inner strength could save him from this fate.[5] This complex of ideas, prejudices, and self-congratulatory fantasies persisted well into the twentieth century and very likely into the twenty-first. Lord Moran, who learned his prejudices in the Great War and became Churchill's personal physician in the Second World War, reduced this complex to an aphorism: "A man of character in peace is a man of courage in war."[6]

And it appeared that most men did not lose their self-control in battle. History does, of course, record many instances in which groups of soldiers failed, instances in which whole formations were seized by panic and fled their enemies or surrendered en masse. But wars run their course because most soldiers face death and dismemberment against all rational impulse to save themselves. For the greater part of military history, disease, death, or wounding intervened long before most soldiers failed themselves or their comrades. So the question is whether those who did fail are worth much attention at all. If soldierly failure is a problem, has it been an important problem? Could not this problem, such as it was, be dealt with in the traditional way, as Patton threatened his soldiers he would deal with them, up against a wall, before a firing squad?

Until the Great War tradition held sway, but that war famously challenged conventional wisdom, and nowhere more than in the British Army. That army recorded 100,000 cases of what was popularly called "shell shock" in that war, and by the end of the war 38 percent of all hospitalized soldiers suffered from neuropsychiatric disorders.[7] Two years after the war the British had 65,000 veterans on pension for shell shock, 9,000 of whom were still being treated.[8] "The World," Lloyd George said, "is suffering from shell-shock."[9]

Even among the Americans, whose experience in the Great War was considerably less costly, shell shock became a household term. As the British and German experience revealed, this problem simply would not disappear with the war's end. Only 2 percent of those Americans on active service in the Great War were neuropsychiatric casualties. But the cases tended to increase with the passage of time. Between 1923, when the Veterans Administration was established, and 1941, the United States spent $282,000,000 for treatment and another $61,850,000 for compensation for shell-shocked veterans. Just after Pearl Harbor 58 percent of all the patients in America's VA hospitals were shell shock victims from World War I—68,000 patients in all. One psychiatrist reported seeing new cases of World War I veterans who had been excited by the current struggle. "The neuropsychiatric casualties are overlapping," he wrote. The problem "reaches from war to war."[10]

During the Great War the Allied armies had attempted to screen recruits in the hope of eliminating men whose physical and mental attributes made them unfit for military service. The American Army rejected 12.9 recruits per 1,000 examined for mental and intellectual debility, close to 600,000 men in all.[11] On the eve of America's new war Dr. Harry Stack Sullivan, one of the most influential psychiatrists in the country, enlisted as an advisor to the Selective Service. Sullivan used his considerable influence to convince the Selective Service that the psychiatric costs of the Great

War could be avoided by means of a rigorous induction examination that would eliminate persons of "substandard mentality and physique." Once these inductees were rejected, the Army could get on with its work without further concern.[12]

The examiners at the induction stations enthusiastically went about their work, purifying the future American Army. Sullivan had detailed the kind of men not wanted: low-grade morons, psychopaths, the eccentric, subversives, the emotionally unstable, sexual deviants, and others with "inadequate personalities." Physicians at the induction stations had three minutes at most. They were untrained in any form of psychiatry, and their questions usually came down to "Do you like girls?" A group of Harvard physicians, who were better trained, concocted their own formula for the properly inducted soldier: "Normal, masculine men had flat, angular bodies, narrow hips and pubic hair running towards the navel, whereas cowards had soft bodies, wider hips, and pubic hair that spread laterally."[13]

Armed with such knowledge, examiners saw 15,000,000 men at the induction stations during the war, 4,650,000 of whom were rejected. Of these, 1,825,000 men—39 percent—were rejected for some form of personality disorder.

Screening did not work. Leaving aside for the moment the premise of screening, that psychiatric problems could be predicted, there was the question of the medical examiners themselves, most of whom were general practitioners, not psychiatrists. In 1940 the American Psychiatric Association counted only 3,000 members, most of whom worked in state hospitals for the insane, where psychotic patients dominated caseloads.[14]

The prospect of fighting a war freed of psychiatric burdens certainly appealed to the army. Early in 1941 Col. Patrick Madigan, a neuropsychiatrist who was an assistant to the Army's Surgeon General, wrote:

> There is no place in the Army for the physical and mental weakling. The Army should not be regarded as a gymnasium for the training and developing of the undernourished and un-

derdeveloped, nor a psychiatric clinic for the proper adjustment of adolescents who need emotional support.[15]

The Army Medical Corps counted thirty-five psychiatrists at the beginning of the war.[16] Psychiatrists once had been assigned to each of the Army's divisions, but just before Pearl Harbor these positions had been eliminated, perhaps in a rush of confidence about screening. The Army's Surgeon General had no psychiatric consultant until February 1942, and when the chief surgeon assigned to Operation Torch, the force that was to invade North Africa, was asked whether a psychiatrist should go along, he replied he hoped one could be found if needed.[17]

One was needed. Despite what psychiatrist William Menninger recalled was "a complete blackout on all information with regard to psychiatry and its role in the Army," reports of very high psychiatric casualties on all the early battlefronts of the war were impossible for authorities to ignore.[18] Early cases from the Guadalcanal campaign were so severe that specialists at first thought they were a "new and unique psychiatric malady," which they designated "Guadalcanal Neurosis." One psychiatrist described

> soldiers reduced to a pitiable state of military ineffectiveness after prolonged exposure under severest tropical conditions to exhaustion, fear, malaria, and sudden violent death at the hands of an insidious and ruthless enemy.[19]

And such debilitating cases were numerous: 40 percent of all those medically evacuated from the Guadalcanal campaign to the United States were neuropsychiatric casualties.[20] More than 6,000 neuropsychiatric casualties were evacuated to the States from the South Pacific theater during the war. Elsewhere in the Pacific the story was much the same. During the last two months of the Buna-Gona campaign in New Guinea neuropsychiatric admissions in the Thirty-second and Forty-first Infantry Divisions ranged from 60 to 70 per 1,000 strength per year, four times as high as the average admission rate for the AEF in World War I.

For reasons much the same as those cited for Guadalcanal, the Southwest Pacific theater of operations began losing as many men through medical evacuation as it gained new troops coming in from the States. Then, one physician recalled, "persons other than psychiatrists took an interest."[21]

In one particular case an entire division was wrecked by neuropsychiatric casualties. Fighting its first action on New Georgia island in mid-1943, the Forty-third Infantry Division's neuropsychiatric casualties consumed 15 percent of its strength, coming apart at the seams under conditions no more severe than those met elsewhere in the Pacific. The entire division was pulled from the line and sent all the way back to New Zealand to be reconstituted.[22]

For the rest of the war operations in the Pacific turned in the highest neuropsychiatric rate of all: 43.94 cases per 1,000 average strength per annum.[23] The unforgiving tropical environment, the constrictions of island fighting, tropical diseases, and an opponent who excited the deepest racial enmity and horror all contributed to this high rate. All the more remarkably, however, the Mediterranean theater of operations had a case rate not that far below the Pacific's.[24]

American forces invaded North Africa several months after ground operations began in the Pacific, but news of what happened there seems not to have made any impression on either the American chain of command or the Army's medical service. American forces were as woefully unprepared for psychiatric casualties as they were for the enemy, and combat operations produced rates that took everyone, doctors included, by surprise. The psychiatric casualties rose steadily as the Tunisian campaign went on, from 20 percent to 34 percent of all nonbattle casualties suffered.[25] At one point in the campaign medical evacuations for psychiatric reasons exceeded the number of replacements, just as they did in parts of the Pacific.[26]

Not only had the Americans ignored their own experience in the Pacific, they managed not to learn from the experience of their British allies, who, of course, had been fighting in North Africa since 1940. What would the Americans have learned from the British? Not so much, as it happens. Winston Churchill was not at all reluctant to voice his skepticism about the practice of psychiatry in general and in the military services in particular. He thought psychiatrists should not be allowed too much access to the services, "fearing that their work often degenerated into 'charlatanry.'"[27]

The British medical services needed no urging from their prime minister. What British authorities did perhaps remember was the crushing financial burden imposed on Britain's postwar budgets by pension claims arising from shell shock. Furthermore, even elite specialists in psychiatry could not agree on the nature of these casualties. The prevailing view of these cases was that their real point of origin lay in the patient's own prewar psychology, which governed how he would react to the extraordinary stresses of combat. In this construction combat merely excited the patient's real disorder. This view, which fit very nicely with the widespread suspicions among line commanders that these men were weaklings to begin with, persisted throughout the war. By 1945 the senior psychiatric consultant to the Royal Army Medical Corps, Brig. J. R. Rees, could still speak without blushing about men "keep[ing] control of their anxieties" in combat.[28]

The few American psychiatrists who actually made their way to the Pacific and North Africa brought with them all the theoretical and methodological preconceptions of their civilian practices. Roy Grinker, who with John Spiegel was to produce a classic study of neuropsychiatric casualties during the war, arrived in North Africa and immediately began practicing as he would have back home: long sessions of abreactive psychoanalysis, reaching over several months. Several hundred miles behind the lines in Algiers, Grinker saw only the most intractable psychiatric cases and experimented with hypnosis and new drugs such as sodium amatol and sodium pentothal as well as insulin in his treatments. For Grinker, the prospect of a soldier's returning to the front lines was beside the point.[29] As a group, such patients as Grinker and others far to the rear did see were held under medical treatment for an average of forty-six days.[30]

But for the armies, returning soldiers to the line was exactly the point. As these casualties mounted, reality began to intrude on the medical services. Classical approaches to psychoanalysis were of little practical use on the battlefield. A long-forgotten lesson of the First World War was that the greater distance a psychiatric casualty was removed from the front line, the greater the chance his condition would worsen. In the great majority of such cases it was far better to keep the soldier as close to his unit as possible, allow him to rest for twenty-four hours, and return him to duty.[31] Now the American Army was learning this lesson all over again.

And in the process of learning, the Army's medical service seemed to be of no help whatsoever. Historical, theoretical, or methodological guidance was confined to medical bulletins that were often irrelevant or simply too late to be of use.[32] Physicians in the field with the line units, rarely trained in psychiatry, gained practical experience working with their soldiers. Any advances in the field of psychiatry emitting from the American experience in the Second World War came from them, not from their professional seniors, certainly not from the Army's medical infrastructure.[33]

From the first time neuropsychiatric casualties in war were noted by medical researchers, an abiding question had been how they should be classified as a disorder. From the late nineteenth century on psychiatry had retreated very gradually from the idea that all mental disorders had a physical basis. The conception of a person's mental life had changed too, from the belief that one could always control oneself, or should, to the view that certain parts of a human being's mental life lay beyond control and that processes were at work that could only be approached professionally by a psychiatrist, if at all, in a long treatment protocol based on psychoanalytical principles. Allied armies had carried this conception into the Second World War, but it wasn't working on the battlefield. Normal soldiers were suffering from symptoms common to acute forms of hysteria and neurosis. Were these cases simply civilian breakdowns in which the patients happened to be wearing a uniform, or was the phenomenon unique to the world of combat, as some physicians on the line began to suspect?

No one had a definitive answer, but opinions were everywhere, and the nosology reflected the confusion. A dictionary's worth of diagnoses evolved as the war went on. "War neurosis" was an early favorite, and so was "shell shock," despite having been discredited. Case notes sometimes used the diagnosis "NYD (N)," or "Not Yet Diagnosed (Nervous)," also a leftover from the Great War. After two years of war "psychoneurosis" had come to be regarded by line officers and practitioners alike as a "waste basket diagnosis," something a harried battalion surgeon might scribble on a patient's identification tag. One doctor counted no less than sixty different terms for neuropsychiatric casualties in his command alone.[34] In a professional and intellectual sense commanders and doctors on the line had to fend for themselves.[35]

The single most practical innovation in the diagnosis and treatment of neuropsychiatric casualties occurred in North Africa in the spring of 1943, just when the fighting was most intense. Capt. Frederick Hanson had been a neurologist practicing in Montreal when the war began in Europe. In 1940 he joined the Canadian Army and soon found himself on the Dieppe raid. By now in the American Army, he shipped out to North Africa in early 1943 and began working at the II Corps' casualty clearing station. His own combat experience along with his observations at II Corps convinced him that physical exhaustion was the primary cause of psychiatric casualties and, further, that the predisposing causes that were so important to theoreticians had little to do with most of the cases he saw on the line. He rejected the prevailing view that these cases required the elaborate treatments common to prewar theories and instead promoted rest for the patient as close to the front line as possible. He thought forty-eight hours at most was enough for these soldiers to regain their energy and return to duty. Using this approach, Hanson managed to return 70 percent of these cases back to the fighting line.

Armed with these results, Hanson and his II Corps surgeon, Perrin Long, managed to convince Omar Bradley that the term *exhaustion* be used as the initial diagnosis for all such cases. Only the most intractable cases would be sent farther down the medical evacuation chain. In effect, Hanson had removed both the mystery and the stigma from the mental effects of combat.[36]

Unfortunately, the II Corps policy seems not to have traveled to other commands or up the chain of command. Diagnoses continued to vary from command to command, even formation to formation. As the scope and intensity of fighting increased everywhere in the summer of 1943, psychiatric casualties rose as well. By September 1943 the medical discharge rate from the Army reached 70,000 per month—roughly the same as the rate of induction into the Army—and 40 percent of all these discharges were for psychiatric causes.[37] In November 1943 the Army finally authorized the assignment of a psychiatrist to each division.[38]

As the dimensions of the psychological battlefield revealed themselves, commanders and physicians tried to understand why, after rejecting so many unsuitable draftees, the armed forces were suffering so many more of these casualties now than in the First World War. Despite a rejection rate 7.6 times higher in World War II than in World War I, the discharge rate was still 2.4 times higher.[39] The answer, some thought, lay in the basic human material available to the armies. The British general Sir Alan Brooke was heard to say: "We are not like anything as tough as we were in the last war. . . . There has been too much luxury."[40] In North Africa it was said that "not a few psychiatrists . . . were dismayed by the high prevalence of severe passivity in young American manhood."[41] No less a figure than George C. Marshall, the Chief of Staff of the Army, ventured his own opinion:

> Perhaps the most important factor contributing to the spread
> of psychoneurotics in our Army has been the nation's educa-
> tional program and environmental background since 1920.

While our enemies were teaching their youths to endure hardships, contribute to the national welfare, and to prepare for war, our young people were led to expect luxuries, to depend upon a paternal government for assistance in making a livelihood and to look upon soldiers and war as unnecessary and hateful.[42]

Rather than indulging in blimpish remarks about modern American manhood, high-ranking officials might have been better served by attending to some elementary questions about the making of modern war. Despite several years of preparing for the coming war, not until after Pearl Harbor did anyone at Army headquarters consider at what rate soldiers would be killed or incapacitated and might need to be replaced. The official assumption seemed to be that if one were not killed, wounded, captured, or sick, one might fight on forever.[43] But the key to understanding most of these casualties lay not so much in the psychology of the soldier as in the environment of combat itself. The problem was most acutely felt in the world of the infantry soldier.

The experience of the infantryman was most decidedly not that of the majority who wore the Army's uniform between 1942 and 1945, for of the huge military machine America assembled, a surprisingly small percentage of men actually had to fight. That the physical and mental costs of battle fell disproportionately on the infantry seemed obvious enough, but just how disproportionately did not become evident until deep into the war. The infantry made up only 14 percent of all its troops overseas, yet they suffered 70 percent of all battle casualties. Even in those formations supposedly designed for infantry combat, the infantry divisions themselves, infantrymen made up only 68 percent of the formation's total strength. But infantrymen took 95 percent of all casualties, and the disparity was all the greater because rifle companies within those divisions routinely fought at two-thirds or less of their official strength.[44]

Toward the end of 1943 Maj. Gen. Lucian Truscott, perhaps the best American division commander of the war, commissioned a study of casualties in his Third Infantry Division, which had just been relieved from action after fifty-nine days of combat in Italy. During that period the division had suffered 3,144 battle casualties and 5,446 nonbattle casualties. Within Truscott's division the infantry suffered battle casualties at a rate seven times that of his field artillery and six times that of all other division elements. Of all the casualties in this division, 93 percent were infantry, while 35 percent of all battle casualties were riflemen. Under Truscott's command the division was handled better than most, but his casualty rates were not appreciably different. About 75,000 men fought with this division during the war; in effect, the division consumed its own weight five times.[45]

At the time Truscott's report was being prepared, American ground forces had been in action for about two years, and the effects of prolonged exposure to combat were everywhere evident. While it may have been possible to dismiss psychiatric casualties early in these campaigns as poor human material, men who had been on the front lines for months began to break down as well. In contrast to the anxiety reactions seen in North Africa, the symptoms of these men were subdued and not at all dramatic. After months of combat these men all of a sudden began freezing under fire and were suddenly unable to think quickly in situations that before would have moved them to prompt action. One regimental commander in Italy sent a soldier to the rear with this note: "This man passes out when he hears shells, he can't march, he can't hike, he can't dig foxholes, he has varicose veins and exhaustion. Get him the hell out of here." The men themselves usually just said they were "all burned out" or "no good to the boys anymore."

Capt. Raymond Sobel, a psychiatrist with the Thirty-fourth Infantry Division at Anzio, proposed a wholly new diagnosis— "The Old Sergeant's Syndrome."[46] Sobel's division had been in combat 136 days by the time it reached Anzio in early 1944. His old sergeants had broken down because they had seen too much, but there remained the question of how much combat a soldier could, or should, take.[47]

At the same time Sobel was formulating his new diagnosis, Capt. John Appel, a psychiatrist with the Office of the Surgeon General in Washington, was on a six-week tour of the Italian battlefield. His report was valuable not because its findings were new but because of its codification of practical knowledge already understood by experienced line officers and doctors and its redefinition of the soldier's life in combat. Tradition held that a soldier who managed to survive his first contact with the enemy had experienced a "baptism of fire." After this critical initiation the soldier was supposed to attain a state of military grace in which he functioned as a fully adept member of his unit. In this conception the soldier's physical and psychological life played itself out on a plateau of highly adaptive behavior until his war was over. Appel saw quite a different picture: "To one who has been 'up there,' it is obvious that there is no such thing as 'getting used to it,'" he wrote. "The simple fact [is] that [the] danger of being killed imposes a strain so great that it causes men to break down." Against the static picture of the soldier's world Appel posed a highly dynamic life in combat. A soldier attained his peak of effectiveness at ninety days, after which he experienced a physical and psychological erosion that continued until he lost his capacity to function. The only answer to this problem, Appel thought, was to limit the soldier's exposure to combat. The combat tour for an infantryman ought to be no more than 240 days.[48] This was not asking too much. Only 7 percent of infantrymen on the line lasted that long without being killed or wounded.[49]

The Army never really decided on the optimum combat tour before the war ended. After V-E Day, Army planners preparing for the invasion of Japan advocated a 120-day combat tour for infantrymen. From first to last, GI's on the line were truly "fugitives from the law of averages."

Neuropsychiatric casualty rates had always correlated closely with battle casualty rates. During the campaigns in Northwest Europe rates ran an average of 10 percent of all casualties suffered by U.S. and British troops, but by then 80 percent of combat fatigue cases were being returned to duty.[50] In the Pacific the same case patterns persisted. Among Army forces on Okinawa neuropsychiatric cases ran to 13.3 percent of all hospital admissions. Col. Ralph Kaufman, a psychiatrist who was then XXIV Corps surgeon, thought the correlation of such cases with artillery fire "was so close, that one could tell from the admissions as to which unit was under fire."[51] During the ten days before the capture of Sugar Loaf Mountain, the Sixth Marine Division alone lost 2,662 battle casualties and 1,289 cases of battle fatigue.[52]

Ten million men served in the Army in World War II, 213,000 men were killed, and 723,560 men were wounded. For every five men wounded, one was killed and one was "psychologically disturbed."[53] Almost a million men were admitted to Army hospitals for neuropsychiatric reasons during the war; 400,000 of these were in the overseas theaters of operation.[54] In the Army's ground forces 504,000 men were permanently lost for psychiatric reasons—about seven and a half lost divisions. From January 1942 to the end of 1945, 380,000 men were discharged from the Army for neuropsychiatric reasons, or 39 percent of all medical discharges. By V-E Day Army hospitals counted 50,000 neuropsychiatric patients.[55] By the end of 1945, 240,000 men were already receiving pensions for neuropsychiatric disabilities. William Menninger predicted that in the future 42 percent of all veterans' disabilities would be for psychiatric causes.[56]

The psychological battlefield in World War II, like the greater war, was littered with casualties. Nearly a million Americans were killed or wounded in this war, but the mental battlefields of the war produced at least as many of its own casualties. The soldier's battle with his enemies followed the traces that modern industrial warfare had long since laid down. The soldier's battle with himself, however, was only dimly understood at the outset of the war. Traditional military knowledge and ancient custom made no allowances for this newly discovered dimension of war. Gradually and uncertainly, a new and more scientifically grounded understanding of the soldier's war intruded on military tradition, and the battle for the soul of the soldier would be fought in the company kitchens and battalion aid stations, all the way back to the hospitals in America itself.

But this particular battle ended with no clear winner because the psychiatrists themselves had finished the war not quite sure of where it had taken them. Their experiences in the war had steadily turned them away from the classical psychoanalytic approaches toward far less doctrinaire models of practice that emphasized environmental and social influences on a soldier's performance in combat.[57] Elite psychiatric theorists and practitioners found it difficult to acknowledge that the war had added anything to their own professional knowledge, and one will search in vain for any genuine advances in either psychiatric theory or practice during these years.[58]

Our historical picture of the Second World War has been governed by grand histories, campaign histories, studies in generalship, and memoirs. This is the war that literary critic and onetime lieutenant of infantry Paul Fussell was referring to when he wrote, "For the past fifty years the Allied war has been sanitized and romanticized almost beyond recognition by the sentimental, the loony patriotic, the ignorant, and the bloodthirsty."[59] Little of what Fussell saw on the library shelves betrayed any understanding of what he called the "actualities" of war—the combat soldier's daily struggle against those who design his death.

The psychological battlefield is important for our understanding of World War II not only because of its influence on the war's conduct or because it challenged fundamental psychological theories and practices but because it produced an unprecedented body of knowledge bearing on the actualities of the war—the inner life of the soldier in combat.[60] Walt Whitman famously said once that the soldier's war, what he called the "real war," will never get in the books, but history can never surrender to the idea that any part of the human experience is beyond its reach. It is still possible to get the real war in the books.

Notes

1. The real Patton is quoted here from Carlo D'Este's *Bitter Victory: The Battle for Sicily, 1943* (New York: Dutton, 1988), 484. D'Este's account is by far the most complete rendering of the slapping incidents.

2. Ibid., 483–84, 484 n. 1.

3. Bradley is quoted in ibid., 486.

4. Ibid., 484–86. Drew Pearson broadcast the Patton story on November 22, 1943. See Eisenhower to George C. Marshall, November 23, 1943, in *The Papers of Dwight David Eisenhower: The War Years*, ed. Alfred D. Chandler Jr. (Baltimore MD: Johns Hopkins University Press, 1970), 3:1571–72. See also Eisenhower's report of January 29, 1944, to the Chief of Staff of the Army, George C. Marshall, on his policy for evacuating "psychoneurotics" from his theater back to the United States, in ibid., 1697–98.

5. Psychiatrists and psychologists would refer to a patient's "predisposition."

6. Lord Moran, *The Anatomy of Courage* (London: Constable & Company, 1945; New York: Avery Publishing, 1987), xviii.

7. Capt. H. J. C. J. L'Etang, "A Criticism of Military Psychiatry in the Second World War," *Journal of the Royal Army Medical Corps* 96, no. 1 (1951): 317. See also Ben Shephard, *A War of Nerves: Soldiers and Psychiatrists in the Twentieth Century* (Cambridge MA: Harvard University Press, 2001), 152.

8. Ted Bogacz, "War Neurosis and Cultural Change in England, 1914–1922: The Work of the War Office Committee of Enquiry into 'Shell-Shock,'" *Journal of Contemporary History* 24, no. 2 (1989): 227–55.

9. George is quoted in Shephard, *A War of Nerves*, 142. The German Army had treated 313,000 cases of neurological disorder during the Great War, a number that should be regarded as highly conservative, given the prejudice most physicians held against such cases. As a matter of course, German doctors would not approve psychological casualties for disability pensions after the war. In 1932, with the economy failing and National Socialist ideology rapidly gaining popularity, German pension laws were revised, and 16,000 German veterans suffering psychiatric disorders were summarily dropped from the rolls. From this point on the Germans would take their own unique road in dealing with such cases. Robert W. Whalen, *Bitter Wounds: German Victims of the Great War, 1914–1919* (Ithaca NY: Cornell University Press, 1984), 53, 59; James M. Diehl, "Victors or Victims: Disabled Veterans in the Third Reich," *Journal of Modern History* 59 (December 1987): 723 and n. 53. See Lothar Kalinowski, "Problems of War Neuroses in the Light of Experiences in Other Countries," *American Journal of Psychiatry* 107 (November 1950): 340–46, which takes a rather benign view of German psychiatric practices during the war. See also Robert

Jay Lifton, *The Nazi Doctors: Medical Killing and the Psychology of Genocide* (1986; New York: Basic Books, 2000); and Geoffrey Cocks, *Psychotherapy in the Third Reich: The Göring Institute*, 2nd rev. ed. (New Brunswick: Transaction Books, 1997), esp. 306–27.

10. Douglas Thom, "War Neurosis: Experiences of 1914–1918; Lessons for the Current Emergency," *Journal of Laboratory and Clinical Medicine* 28 (1943): 499–502.

11. Eli Ginzberg, *The Lost Divisions* (New York: Columbia University Press, 1959), 61.

12. In August 1940 the War Department issued Mobilization Regulation 1-9, prescribing physical and mental standards for all recruits. Albert Glass, "Psychosomatic Medicine," in *Internal Medicine in World War II*, vol. 3, *Infectious Diseases and General Medicine*, ed. W. Paul Havens Jr. (Washington DC: Department of the Army, Office of the Surgeon General, 1968), 677–78. See also Shephard, *A War of Nerves*, 197–200.

13. Quoted in Shephard, *A War of Nerves*, 200.

14. William Menninger, "Psychiatry and the War," *Atlantic Monthly* 176 (November 1945): 107–14, reprinted in Bernard M. Hall, ed., *A Psychiatrist for a Troubled World: Selected Papers of William C. Menninger, M.D.* (New York: Viking Press, 1954), 518.

15. Madigan is quoted in Glass, "Psychosomatic Medicine," 689.

16. Menninger, "Psychiatry and the War," 504–5.

17. Albert Glass, "Military Psychiatry in Korea," [1982?], Historical Records Collection, U.S. Army Center of Military History, 67–72. See also Lt. Col. Calvin S. Drayer and Col. Albert J. Glass, introduction to *Neuropsychiatry in World War II*, vol. 2, *The Overseas Theaters*, ed. Col. Albert J. Glass (Washington DC: Department of the Army, Office of the Surgeon General, 1973), 5.

18. William Menninger, "The Future Role of Psychiatry in the Army," *Military Surgeon* 100 (February 1947): 108–13, reprinted in Hall, *Psychiatrist for a Troubled World*, 526–27. The "publicity blackout" on all matters involving neuropsychiatric casualties as well as malaria cases was imposed by the War Department toward the end of 1943, but pressure from the American Psychiatric Association forced a reversal of this policy in late 1944. See Larry Bland, ed., *The Papers of George Catlett Marshall* (Baltimore MD: Johns Hopkins University Press, 1996), 4:225 nn. 1–5. Great Britain and Germany similarly embargoed all information relating to neuropsychiatric casualties, and after the war Allied Occupation authorities in Germany "discouraged publications on military psychiatry." See Kalinowski, "Problems of War Neuroses," 340.

19. Maj. Albert A. Rosner, "Neuropsychiatric Casualties from Guadalcanal," *American Journal of Medical Science*, no. 207 (June 1944): 770.

These cases were severe indeed. Rosner saw his patients ten months after they left Guadalcanal.

20. Ibid. See also Theodore Lidz, "Psychiatric Casualties from Guadalcanal: A Study of Reactions to Extreme Stress," *Psychiatry* 9 (August 1946): 193.

21. S. Alan Challman and Henry A. Davidson, "Southwest Pacific Area," in Glass, *The Overseas Theaters*, 525–27.

22. Maj. K. G. Fuschak, "The 43rd Infantry Division: Unit Cohesion and Neuropsychiatric Casualties" (Master of Military Arts and Sciences thesis, U.S. Army Command and General Staff College, Fort Leavenworth KS, 1999). The New Guinea Occupation Force, of which the Forty-third was a part, counted 2,500 neuropsychiatric casualties for the whole force while on the island. John Miller Jr., *Cartwheel: The Reduction of Rabaul* (Washington DC: Department of the Army, Office of the Chief of Military History, 1959), 121.

23. Frank A. Reister, *Medical Statistics in World War II* (Washington DC: Department of the Army, Office of the Surgeon General, 1975), 44.

24. For the entire Mediterranean theater of operations, the rate stood at 40.84 per 1,000 average strength per annum. See ibid.

25. Drayer and Glass, introduction, 9.

26. W. Hausman and D. Rioch, "Military Psychiatry: A Prototype of Social and Preventive Psychiatry in the United States," *Archives of General Psychiatry*, June 1967, 727–39, cited in Larry Ingraham and Frederick J. Manning, "Psychiatric Battle Casualties: The Missing Column in a War without Replacements," *Military Review* 60, no. 8 (1980): 19.

27. R. H. Ahrenfeldt, *Psychiatry in the British Army in World War II* (New York: Columbia University Press, 1958), 26 and 27 n.

28. Maj. Gen. Sir Henry Letheby Tidy, *Inter-Allied Conferences on War Medicine: 1942–1945* (London: Staples Press Ltd., 1945), 224. The British armed forces counted 118,000 psychiatric cases for all three services during World War II. This number constituted one-third to one-half of all medical invalids. But by one account only three of every twenty neuropsychiatric patients had frontline duty before they were diagnosed. L'Etang, "A Criticism of Military Psychiatry," 237–38.

29. See Shephard's discussion of Grinker in *A War of Nerves*, 212–13.

30. Reister, *Medical Statistics*, 43.

31. Shephard, *A War of Nerves*, 123–32, contains a brief account of the American psychiatrist Thomas Salmon's 1918 report on shell shock.

32. Roy Grinker and John Spiegel's *War Neurosis in North Africa* began its life as a U.S. Army medical bulletin. While useful for treating the most acute and chronic cases of neuropsychiatric debility, its value for frontline practice was limited.

33. William Menninger, who spent the war as the chief neuropsychiatric consultant to the Surgeon General, admitted as much. See his "Psychiatry and the War," *Atlantic Monthly* 176 (November 1945): 107–14, in Hall, *Psychiatrist for a Troubled World*, 513.

34. Douglas Bond, "General Neuropsychiatric History," and Donald B. Peterson, "China Burma India," both in Glass, *The Overseas Theaters*, 873, 848; see also Challman and Davidson, "Southwest Pacific Area," 523. This nosological confusion was by no means confined to the Allies. By 1944 the head of the German Wehrmacht Health Services prohibited the use of the term *neurosis*, proposing *abnormal mental reaction* instead. See Cocks, *Psychotherapy in the Third Reich*, 319–20.

35. After the war two leading psychiatrists complained that "the literature on war neurosis shows that very few investigators felt much need for a psychodynamic frame of reference. Hence, in its absence they can rely only on presenting symptoms and on fitting the syndromes into preexisting categories. This amounts to classification by descriptive resemblance. . . . Furthermore, systems of therapy have been devised that have no relation to any system of psychopathology. The situation is without equal in any other branch of medicine today." Abram Kardiner and Herbert Spiegel, *War Stress and Neurotic Illness* (New York: Paul B. Hoeber, Inc., 1947), 27.

36. See Shephard, *A War of Nerves*, 216; and Drayer and Glass, introduction, 3–11. In July 1940 the First Australian Corps, then in Palestine, established the same policy, using "exhaustion" "for acute neurotic casualties arising in action." It recommended that "all other terms suggesting bodily or mental damage should be avoided." Whether Hanson or the other policy makers in II Corps knew of the Australian practice is an unanswered question. See Allan S. Walker, *Clinical Problems of War* (Canberra, Australia: Australian War Memorial, 1952), 677.

37. *Bulletin of the U.S. Army Medical Department* 2 (December 1944): 52–55.

38. *War Department Circular*, no. 290, November 9, 1943. See Jules Coleman, "Division Psychiatry in the Southwest Pacific Area," in Glass, *The Overseas Theaters*, 623.

39. Glass, "Military Psychiatry in Korea," 71.

40. Quoted in Shephard, *A War of Nerves*, 172.

41. Drayer and Glass, introduction, 8–9; see also Maj. William H. Kelley, "War Neuroses," *Infantry Journal* 59, no. 2 (1946): 20.

42. George C. Marshall, memorandum for General [Alexander] Surles, December 30, 1943, in Bland, *The Papers of George Catlett Marshall*, 4:222. Marshall very wisely classified this draft memorandum as secret, and it seems never to have been published.

43. Edward Drea, "Unit Reconstitution: A Historical Perspective" (U.S.

Army Command and General Staff College, Combat Studies Institute, Fort Leavenworth KS, 1983), 16.

44. "Battle Casualties," *Infantry Journal* 65, no. 3 (1949): 19. This article abstracts a report on World War II battle and nonbattle casualties by the Planning Section, Headquarters, Army Ground Forces, in 1946.

45. "Headquarters, Third Infantry Division, to Commanding General, NATOUSA, U.S. Army; Subject: Casualties and Replacements, 17 December 1943, orig. Secret." Typed manuscript in the author's possession.

46. Albert J. Glass and Calvin S. Drayer, "Italian Campaign (1 March 1944–2 May 1945), Psychiatry Established at Division Level," in Glass, *The Overseas Theaters*, 49–52. These patients were normally noncommissioned officers who had been on the line for four or five months and who presented "preexisting social and emotional adjustment of a high degree; marked sense of responsibility; long combat in a responsible position such as noncom or officer; excellent group consciousness and motivation . . . with resultant contraction of the personality and marked guilt feelings over having left the group."

47. Lloyd J. Thompson, Perry C. Talkington, and Alfred O. Ludwig, "Neuropsychiatry at Army and Division Levels," in ibid., 332.

48. Capt. John W. Appel, "Prevention of Manpower Loss from Psychiatric Disorders: Report of a Trip to North African Theater of Operations, 17 May–29 July 1944, orig. confidential." Typed manuscript in the author's possession. See also Drea, "Unit Reconstitution," 17–18; and Shephard, *A War of Nerves*, 245. Appel's prescription of a 240-day combat tour for infantry was clearly too much, but even that constituted a measure of progress; previously, the Army had no policy at all. Roy Swank and Walter E. Marchand conducted a much more rigorous examination of combat fatigue during the Normandy campaign and described a bell curve of effectiveness of much shorter duration. See their "Combat Neurosis: Development of Combat Exhaustion," *Archives of Neurology and Psychology* 55 (1946): 236–47.

49. Shephard, *A War of Nerves*, 245.

50. William Menninger, "Psychiatric Experience in the War, 1941–1946," in Hall, *Psychiatrist for a Troubled World*, 534. See also Leo Bartemeir, Lawrence Kubie, Karl A. Menninger, John Romano, and John C. Whitehorn, "Combat Exhaustion," *Journal of Mental and Nervous Diseases* 104 (July–December 1946): 361–62.

51. Oscar B. Markey, "Tenth U.S. Army," in Glass, *The Overseas Theaters*, 643.

52. Ibid., 663.

53. Bartemeir et al., "Combat Exhaustion," 372.

54. Reister, *Medical Statistics*, 4, 43.

55. Menninger, "Psychiatric Experience," 530.

56. William Menninger, "Readjustment of the Handicapped Veteran," in Hall, *Psychiatrist for a Troubled World*, 547.

57. The Freudians were the most doctrinaire of the classical psychoanalytic school of thought, but in Great Britain they were not invited to contribute to wartime psychiatry at all. Ernest Jones, who was Britain's leading Freudian, later wrote that "advertising men had more influence on the running of the war." Roy Grinker, despite his own experiences in North Africa and later in the United States Army Air Corps, very much disapproved of Frederick Hanson's rough-and-ready approach to combat exhaustion. Grinker had been one of Freud's analysands, and his extensive treatments of neuropsychiatric cases virtually presupposed that his patients would never return to combat duty. Shephard, *A War of Nerves*, 168, 212, 216.

58. Toward the end of the war William Menninger led a five-member commission on a tour of the European theater of operations to examine and report on psychiatric casualties and their treatment. The commission's report equivocated on the question of whether a soldier's predisposing temperament or the environment of combat was more influential in a soldier's breakdown. While they acknowledged that the diagnosis of "combat exhaustion" was practical for frontline psychiatry, they did not consider the diagnosis useful for treating more acute cases in the rear. Yet a year later Menninger would write that "far more impressive in the adjustment process than the history or the personality make-up or the internal psychodynamic stress was the force of factors in the environment that supported or disrupted the individual." See Bartemeir et al., "Combat Exhaustion," 380; and Menninger, "Psychiatric Experience," 532.

59. Paul Fussell, *Wartime: Understanding and Behavior in the Second World War* (Oxford: Oxford University Press, 1989), ix.

60. See, for instance, Samuel Stouffer et al., *The American Soldier: Combat and Its Aftermath* (Princeton NJ: Princeton University Press, 1949); Ginzberg, *The Lost Divisions*; as well as Stephen Ranson, "The Normal Battle Reaction: Its Relation to Pathologic Battle Reaction," in *Combat Psychiatry: Experiences of the North African and Mediterranean Theaters of Operation, American Ground Forces, World War II*, ed. and comp. Frederick R. Hanson, Bulletin of the U.S. Army Medical Department, vol. 9, supplemental number (November 1949).

Two

In the School of War

My colleague, a very senior professor, was curious. He had just heard I would be leaving the history department before long for a new teaching position at the U.S. Army's Command and General Staff College at Fort Leavenworth, Kansas. I could stay where I was for another year or two before moving on, but I'd decided to move now.

Those were bleak years in the academic professions. Appointments in any field were rare; in the humanities, especially history, they were almost nonexistent. If by some miracle you had a teaching position, even one as temporary as mine, you held onto it as long as you could.

Why would I take such a chance? he asked. Was there a prospect of tenure?

No, no chance at all. One year and out.

Then why?

Imagine a place, I said, that seemed to be built around your own interests, with a library full of works on your specialty, a large faculty whose work was related to your own, and students who practiced what you studied. What would you give up to spend a year in such a place? If one were a religious historian, it would be a little like teaching at the Vatican.

So I went, expecting to stay the year but no more. Twenty-seven years later I left.

When I joined the faculty at the staff college, most of the civilians worked as administrative staff. The exceptions were a distinguished visiting professor of military history—the Civil War scholar Dudley Cornish that year—and two visiting associate professors with one-year terms. I was one of the associate profs.

The rest of the faculty was made up of active duty military

officers, senior majors or lieutenant colonels serving three-year teaching tours. Once these were highly prized assignments, and the roll call of former staff college instructors read like a who's who of the old Army's most distinguished leaders. But after World War II the prestige of teaching at the staff college had dimmed. Before the war faculty had been handpicked, recruited for their experience, professional knowledge, and promise of future service. Now assignments were made by a bureaucracy in Washington that simply requisitioned bodies to fill whatever position came open, frequently without regard to whether the candidate had any educational background or intellectual proclivity. The common perception in the Army was that this was a place to send its less competitive officers. Faculty morale was what you'd expect.

The staff college had no history department, although several history courses were in the curriculum. My new home was the Department of Joint and Combined Operations, whose faculty of about thirty military officers taught strategy, planning, and the conduct of operations in company with the other armed services as well as with other nations. Within the department the three visiting civilian academics and five officers, mostly majors, made up a subcommittee for military history. We filled up two offices. I shared my part of one room with the coffeepot. I could not think of any other place I would rather have been.

In their never-ending struggle for a larger part in the curriculum, the military historians were in retreat. The year before, history electives had been reduced to make room for more "relevant" courses. A survey course in American military history was all that was left, plus a few elective courses.

Everyone had to take the survey course, which really only amounted to the Army's organizational history with a few battles thrown in to relieve the boredom, and the class was neither interesting nor especially demanding. A strict college policy limited how much reading and written work we could require.

Our students were mostly majors, although captains and lieutenant colonels occasionally showed up on class rosters. Most of them were in their twelfth or thirteenth year of service, they were in their early thirties, and the greater part of them came from the combat arms—infantry, artillery, and armor officers. In contrast to their faculty, these officers competed to attend the school; roughly 40 percent of eligible officers in a given year were chosen. Selection marked an officer as having potential for high rank and wider responsibilities. Those who did not survive the competition understood that the institution had sent them a signal: dreary assignments from then on, late promotions if any, early retirement. Foreign officers—sometimes as many as a hundred from fifty nations or more, some of whom had never traveled beyond their own countries—attended the school too. Female and minority officers were a rarity.

Most of the classes were taught in sixteen large "section" rooms that accommodated sixty students. In the front of the room a large projection screen and a lectern flanked a raised stage. From this perch lecturers held forth to a room full of students who took refuge behind long tables. Smoking in class was allowed, and the students' weapon of choice was a cigar going at full blast. On warm days in late summer a Beijing-like pall hung over the class. Sometimes from the higher altitude of the stage you could hardly see the students' faces. After one or two tries I decided never to use the stage again and descended into the haze to lecture, feeling vaguely like a policeman walking his beat, disturbing the sleeping homeless. More than a few of the instructors used the lecterns as if they were sandbags and talked toward the slides they projected onto the giant screen or simply read their lecture notes. Only the electives, kept at about sixteen students, allowed for discussion.

The academic year ran for ten months. Every summer officers from around the world descended on Fort Leavenworth, moving vans and trailers packed to the limit. Many of them came from tours of duty that allowed them little free time. Even in less demanding staff positions, officers put in preposterous hours. In the combat units officers' days were longer. At the beginning of the academic year all the students gathered for a grand assembly to hear the commandants—lieutenant generals who were assigned for two years at a time—depict their coming year as "time off from the *real* Army" and "a good time to reconnect with your family." Any hint that their time at the staff college might be put to use advancing their professional knowledge was rarely mentioned, and then only apologetically. "I'm afraid you'll be doing a lot of reading, but it's only a lot of reading if you do it," was the common refrain from the succession of commandants.

A good many students were happy to take the commandants at their word. Well over half of them in any given year had advanced degrees and were no strangers to demanding intellectual work. Occasionally, students showed up who held doctorates in one field or another. They were all certainly smart enough to do anything we asked of them, so they were not long in learning how little would be asked of them. Happy exceptions kept us from tearing our hair out.

The Army that gave us these officers was in the professional doldrums, only a few years past its defeat in Vietnam. The officers commiserated with one another and dealt with their own demons in private, rarely talking about the war. Soon enough I learned how to read their uniforms, résumés in the form of multicolored ribbons and metal badges. Purple hearts with clusters told of multiple wounds. Distinguished Service Crosses and Silver and Bronze Stars abstracted acts of heroism spelled out in an officer's service file. And always the patch sewed on at the right shoulder, designating the unit that took them into battle. If you knew those unit histories, an educated guess would tell you when the officer's career had intersected with the war: Ia Drang, Pleiku, the A Shau Valley, Khe Sanh, Tet, and hundreds of other fights. Later, when the number of Vietnam veterans in the class declined, I thought I could tell which of my students had been in combat simply by looking at their eyes. At the moment, however, the Army's experience in Vietnam would play no part in the high command's plans for the next conflict except as an example of how not to fight a war.

Not even the most bellicose policy maker in those days would have sent this army off to war. In the late seventies the Army was not prepared to do much of anything, and there was a brooding anxiety that it might be called on to fight sooner than it was ready—if it was ever ready again.

But an army must have an enemy to measure itself against, however remote the chance of actually going to war against it. The Soviets had served this purpose for years, but while we were preoccupied with Vietnam the threat they posed seemed less compelling. Once the war was over the Army rediscovered the Cold War, and the Soviet Union took center stage again; it was the only threat that might summon the Army from its garrisons too soon. Consigning Vietnam to history best forgotten, the Army's leaders reimagined a Russian juggernaut, superbly armed and trained, lurking just beyond the iron curtain, waiting for the right time to sweep across Western Europe. For an army at low ebb, the Soviet threat was enlisted once again as its raison d'être.

At first these issues barely interested me. My professional upbringing conditioned me to strictly separate the past from the present. Unencumbered by the distortions of the present—so the thinking went—you could set your mind against interesting historical puzzles at your own pace. In return the world outside made no demands on what you were doing; no one waited impatiently for you to finish your work. Nor had I found the routines of my earlier life as a beginning academic particularly stimulating. I happily dozed through faculty meetings about textbooks or parking spaces or who got how much time with the department's copy machine. Now, however, I was becoming entangled in a world I'd never imagined for myself.

A movement to reform the Army was in motion by the time I got to the staff college. The Army was lobbying for a new suite of modern weapons, but Congress was less than enthusiastic. So soon after Vietnam, the Army's professional credibility in the halls of government was far from convincing. A small circle of general officers began looking for ways to make their case for the Army's reconstruction.

A new military doctrine proved to be the answer. Military doctrines were hardly unknown in the U.S. Army, existing in one form or another for more than a century. But official doctrine had rarely if ever influenced the Army's policies. Doctrine was a derivative minor class of professional military literature that responded to change; it merely ratified practices decided by a much less formal process. Although published as official Army regulations, doctrines were routinely ignored by commanders who called on their own experience as a guide to actions or simply responded to the exigencies of the moment.

The reformers had the idea that doctrine could be used for other larger purposes. It could set—and enforce—standards of organization, training, and even a style of operation, matters that doctrine had always addressed. But it also offered a new language with which the Army could be promoted to a wider but skeptical official audience. For the first time in American military history the doctrine business was about to become public business.

Inside the Army doctrine became a growth industry. Formerly, officers detailed to tend doctrine regarded such an assignment as the kiss of death for their careers. Now field-grade officers across the Army were recruited for small ad hoc think tanks to analyze recent military operations around the world. All across the military landscape, and particularly at Fort Leavenworth, conferences debated arcane questions of military practice. Sometimes you couldn't get to class without tripping over a general and his entourage, hurrying through the halls in a trance of self-importance.

A bantamlike four-star general named William DePuy was the engine of the reform movement. As a three-star general he had been the architect of a wide-ranging reorganization of the Army after Vietnam, and now he commanded one of his creations, the Training and Doctrine Command. The staff college and most of the Army's other schools fell under his authority.

DePuy was an accomplished if controversial soldier, an intense, self-absorbed autocrat who in the course of his long career had learned to navigate—and manipulate—the Byzantine defense establishment. Even though he was a kingpin in the Army's bureaucracy, he did not hesitate to subvert it when it got in his way. Having designed the huge bureaucracy he now ran, he lost no time in creating a shadow network of trusted acolytes whose talents he could use.

DePuy's leading protégé, a young major general who had himself enjoyed an accomplished career, was Donn Starry. A tanker who as a young officer had learned his trade under Gen. Creighton Abrams and later led the offensive against North Vietnamese sanctuaries along the Cambodian border, Starry had as quick a mind as anyone in uniform. A voracious reader, an unapologetic intellectual, and a close student of history, Starry's impatience with bureaucracy was exceeded only by DePuy's. And, like DePuy, he was something of an insurgent. When DePuy retired in 1978, Starry pinned on his fourth star and took DePuy's place. For the next four years he drove the Army's reforms as relentlessly as his predecessor.

But Starry was not DePuy's clone. He was more tolerant of ambiguity and nuance than DePuy had ever been. DePuy's mind was closed to any ideas but his own. He was more interested in convincing than understanding, ruthlessly sweeping aside any suggestion that he might be wrong. Although Starry was just as strong-minded and quick-tempered as DePuy and was just as quick to decide a question when the time came, he was never threatened by different ideas. For all his success, DePuy seemed deeply insecure, always searching for validation and approval. Starry never was.

For the greater part of the seventies the discipline of history played no part in the Army's reinvention of itself. The historical community inside the Army was made up mainly of the military faculty at West Point and civilians at the Army's Center of Military History in Washington. Scattered here and there in commands around the Army, a few other historians, mostly civilians, tended to official history. My military colleagues at the staff college had been sent off to graduate school by the Army and served their apprenticeships at West Point.

Like their colleagues all across the Army, these young officers were restive. Themselves veterans of the war, they believed the

Army had suffered above all an intellectual defeat. If they could not agree on whether their army had been outfought, some of them concluded it had been outthought. For them, the first step toward reform was understanding what had happened not only in the immediate past but in the broadest possible context, across the sweep of modern military history. Historical knowledge could then open the door to what should happen next not by reproducing the past but by stimulating the professional imagination. Driven as much by their passions as by their intellect, they meant to return military history to what they regarded as its rightful place at the forefront of the Army's professional thought.

The recent reductions in history's share of the curriculum marked a low point in its status at the school. Its fortunes were about to improve noticeably. Efforts to create a new department of military history were already under way, the result of a coalition formed in the early seventies between several leading civilian military historians, the history faculty at West Point, and official historians from around the Army. One of those was Brooks Kleber, the command historian at the Training and Doctrine Command who served as the leading advocate for history within the command. A veteran and former POW of World War II who held a reserve commission until his retirement as a colonel, Kleber was already a fixture at the command's headquarters in Fort Monroe, Virginia. His World War II service in the same infantry division as General DePuy guaranteed Kleber a degree of access to the general that few civilians enjoyed. When Starry replaced DePuy, Kleber's influence in the command only increased. The two men liked each other, shared an intense interest in history, and understood how it could be used as a force for institutional progress. They were now in a position to translate their understanding into action.

Fort Leavenworth was the ideal place to begin. The Army's future leaders studied there, year after year. If they could be shown that an understanding of military history had professional utility, the next generation of generals might not be so intellectually defenseless as the last. History could again serve as one of the intellectual tools in an Army officer's kit.

The burden of enacting this reform at the school fell on the shoulders of one major, Charles Shrader, a logistician, a Vietnam veteran, and a former faculty member of West Point's history department. He was also a graduate of Vanderbilt and held a doctorate in medieval history from Columbia. His intellectual gifts were formidable. He was about to prove that his bureaucratic skills were equally impressive.

Shrader and I met at a professional conference in 1977. An old friend from graduate school, T. R. Young, who then held one of the visiting professorships at the staff college, invited me to breakfast to meet Shrader. I arrived on time but in some disrepair, having spent most of the previous night at a raucous dinner party. But Shrader and I soon discovered a common interest in medieval history, and the breakfast lasted for quite a while.

Breakfast had been a pleasant cure for my hangover, but afterward we went our separate ways. A month later, much to my surprise, I was invited to audition for the position Young was about to vacate at the staff college. Surely this was a mistake. The position called for an associate professor. I was barely an assistant professor. Then the professor who'd directed my graduate work, T. Harry Williams, called; he'd been asked to recommend someone to replace Young and had put in my name. Go, Williams said. Have a good time and see what happens.

I already knew of Fort Leavenworth's history and the school's role in the Army. I was certain the school would want a more seasoned scholar, but neither did I want to disappoint my old prof. I accepted the invitation. Whatever happened, I thought, a visit would be interesting.

The audition entailed giving a lecture. Young asked what I would like to talk about. "The changing nature of the nineteenth-century battlefield," I suggested, might be worth the audience's time, although I really had no idea what kind of audience I would face.

On the day of the lecture a newly promoted lieutenant colonel, Hal Nelson, took charge of me, showing me around the college and introducing me to the heads of the school's other departments. As we were walking to another meeting Hal said he imagined I was nervous about the lecture. I shouldn't be, he said. "You've already got the job." Later on I wondered what would have happened if the lecture had fallen flat.

In the event I survived the lecture. Looking over the room full of soldiers before starting, I wondered how much credibility a young civilian could possibly have, talking about war in this place. But as the lecture went on I grew more comfortable and completely forgot my hesitation. Here was an informed, experienced audience whose interest was not only academic but practical. I had landed in the world my studies represented.

Much later, still puzzled by my appointment, I asked Shrader why I'd been taken on. He said he'd made up his mind at our first meeting. "Anyone who could discuss medieval history with your kind of hangover had to be hired," he replied. Never underestimate the power of drink.

One of the essays in this part, "War History and the History Wars," describes our campaign to rejuvenate history in the officer corps during the seventies and eighties. My temporary position having been made permanent a year after I arrived, I began studying the Army's folkways and tribal customs and worked at learning its peculiar language and its peculiar dialects. Other civilian scholars began joining the faculty. Two of them, Edward Drea and Robert Berlin, were to become lifelong friends. The sight of a civilian rushing down the hall to make class on time no longer drew startled looks. I settled in, more or less, but no matter how acculturated I was, I would always be an outsider, caught between the Army and the world beyond.

The truth was that this ambiguous role appealed to me, but it confused—and aggravated—my military and academic friends. As the bureaucratic battles raged over the new department's creation, I came to know and admire Brooks Kleber. At several critical times he deployed his bureaucratic skill with an artfulness C. P. Snow would've recognized: Kleber was a master of what

Snow called "closed politics," the politics of the boardroom, the kind in which there is no appeal to a higher representative assembly. I was no good at it.

My skills were of a decidedly lower order. I lived on my convictions—"gusts of emotion," Snow would've said—not my reason. Argumentative, impatient, abrupt, and intolerant of opinions other than my own, I was naive enough to think that given half a chance, right ideas would always win. I saw the new department as the only medium by which our ideas about history could be advanced. All other solutions were misguided, wrongheaded, or ignorant. Those who opposed us were simply reactionaries. Kleber understood—as I did not—that in an institution bound above all by rules of deference my convictions might alienate those who could be won over to our side.

To friends scattered about academia I was dangerously close to being a kept man. Claiming military history as a field of study was bad enough. Some thought it gave off a whiff of militarism. The easy prejudices of the day held that military historians were simply closet fascists who simply hadn't come out yet. If against all odds you found a place in the academic world, you stood a chance of respectability, assuming good and correct behavior. But those who worked with the armed forces were beyond the pale. We were hazarding our professional souls. You could not survive such an environment, they believed, without compromising your principles, violating the sacred canons of historical practice, or perhaps even surrendering your morality. More than once I was earnestly advised to make good my escape before it was too late. The irony of my position was not lost on me. I was living between two worlds, not quite tenable in either.

But I liked what I was doing. I was engaged with problems that I had once understood only on a theoretical, intellectual level, problems that I now saw in their practical shape. The stakes of my knowledge, such as it was, were going up; something I said or wrote might influence action, might have mortal consequences. The distance between thought and action was reduced to a very narrow margin, and that margin posed a responsibility that rarely if ever troubled the sleep of my fellow historians.

Historians of all stripes are very reserved when asked to apply what they know to contemporary problems. From our professional infancy we are taught the dangers of using historical knowledge as a guide to present action. The historian's mind is created by the past, and that is where it should remain, quarantined—as far as possible—from the present. Or so the argument runs.

These principles work well enough where most historians live. In lecture halls and seminar rooms injunctions against using historical knowledge for any purpose other than understanding the past are rarely challenged. Historians happily argue about methods, means of discourse, and interpretation but not about utility; on this, at least, historians seem to have agreed long ago. I was taught—"indoctrinated" might be the better word—that history, of all the disciplines, must stand majestically alone, unencumbered by the heresy of "presentism." But this principle has led historians to husband their knowledge and to stand by smugly as history's intellectual stature declined and other disciplines laid claim to how we understand the world we live in.

By the end of the seventies the campaign to return history to the curriculum in the Army's professional schools was making headway but against heavy weather. As much as we wanted to dismiss our detractors as philistines or bureaucratic reactionaries, we had trouble making our case. Our high-minded justifications too often struck critics as little more than academic clichés.

Even Kleber, then at the forefront of the campaign, kept his rationale well within the limits of the profession's dictates. In a *Military Review* essay at the time he wrote, "One must not expect too much from history. Its study does not provide blueprints or precise formulas for future action. Rather, its understanding brings about a state of historical mindedness, a part of the overall professionalism desired in the officer corps. This is reason enough for the study of military history."

You have to wonder why we were as successful as we were. We

were demanding that the Army accept our faith in the value of history and refusing to make any concession to practicality. We might just as well have defended our case by citing pronouncements of the Delphic oracle. At the time we were satisfied by these arguments. In this way we were not different from those young—and mistaken—reformers in the French Army before the Great War, "convinced of the justice of our ideas, of the superiority of our theories and our methods, and resolved to make them prevail despite all opposition."

All the while I was gradually being drawn into work more and more removed from the orthodox practice of history. Two years into my tenure I was assigned the extra duty of serving as the command historian for the lieutenant general, William Richardson, who was then overseeing the school and the fort. Part of this work entailed writing studies or background analyses on issues in which the command had an official interest. Soon after I took on this role the general asked me for a historical perspective on several plans then in play for the Army's reorganization. The paper I wrote kept strictly to recounting how similar reforms had fared. It didn't touch on the contemporary problem at all. In due course the paper came back. Across the bottom the general had written, "Yes, but what do *you* think?"

What indeed? History offered no sure answer, no guideline or blueprint, as Kleber insisted. It wasn't supposed to, was it? Nevertheless, the general wanted an answer—my answer—all the same.

I did finally manage, not very confidently, to answer the general. But, I thought, it was a staff officer's answer, not history's. I couldn't see that it had much to do with history. I was completely wrong. The general knew very well that history did not shed enough light on the question to act as some sort of tiebreaker. He would consider my views alongside all the others he'd collected and then reach his own conclusions. He knew that history and the historian were not the same things. He did not mean to apply history so much as to apply the historian.

The distinction is important, and it holds the key to unlocking the trap many historians have made for themselves. In the long struggle to master the discipline, unique habits of thought and worldview are created in the historian's mind. Other scholarly disciplines work the same effect on their practitioners. We have no trouble believing in a "scientific mind" or a "legal mind." We ascribe certain qualities to those kinds of minds derived from the knowledge they acquire, how they customarily deal with questions or problems, the standards by which they function, and what they expect to accomplish. We can find scholars of science and law in occupations far removed from their fields because society values the habits of mind their disciplines have instilled in them. Historians rarely see themselves in this way, but it is as suitable to conceive of a "historical mind" as any other.

What does this historical mind look like? What are the qualities of "historical mindedness" Brooks Kleber wrote about? Its leading quality may be an innate suspicion of reductionism, of treating the complex nature of reality as an obstacle to understanding. Other disciplines use a variety of tools—models, rules, formulas—to disassemble reality, to make it manageable. The historical mind, by contrast, tolerates a degree of complexity that drives others mad. To this sort of mind complexity and understanding are not mutually exclusive but interactive.

When the historian studies a question, the first step entails mastering its larger context, the unique circumstances that brought it to life. At first these circumstances may appear as little more than a bewildering array of isolated incidents, with no evident relation among them. The pieces don't seem to fit together at all. At this point the historian's skill and training come into play, showing how those pieces interact to create results that no model or formula could predict or explain.

Historians are usually happy with this outcome, but they do not see that the intellectual skills with which it was achieved can be just as valuable when applied to contemporary problems. Their ability to reconstruct and understand a past reality can be used to assemble a picture of the present free of the encumbering preconceptions other disciplines impose on it. And their suspicion of simplistic explanations can act as a check on equally simplistic projections of the future. History does not repeat itself, but the fundamental, dynamic properties of history in the past and history in the future remain the same. That is why historians may be just as well equipped to deal with the future as any other discipline, perhaps even more so.

Talk like this makes historians nervous. They object that applying the historical mind to present-day problems sacrifices what may be the historian's most important tool of all—perspective, the chronological distance between the historian and what he or she studies. Knowing how the story ends, so the argument goes, is critical to how it is understood—the weight of the present always shapes our weighing of the past. We seldom acknowledge, however, that if our historical judgments are to be of much value, we ought to have an equally acute understanding of the present. We seem to invest a good deal less intellectual energy in that side of the transaction. If we were to acknowledge our responsibility to understand the present as well as we do the past, what we know and how we know it would assume an altogether different and more useful character.

Such questions are not only theoretical; for me, they were very practical indeed. I was spending as much time dealing with history in the making as with the making of history. Many of the issues I dealt with were history-less: precedents, analogies, and metaphors—the idioms historians commonly use when forced to think about the present—carried no weight at all in the Army's boardrooms. Even when history did inform a problem, a question remained: So what next?

Sir Michael Howard, himself well schooled in the ways of modern armies, wrote once that although armies are always thinking about the future, what they expected almost always fell short. The real trick, he thought, was to not get the future "too far wrong."

How far wrong was I about the future after all? My reasons for leaving the comforts of civilian academic life seemed right at the time, but I was far from seeing what came next. The distance between what I expected and what I got—Paul Fussell's definition of true irony—defied measurement. What I got found its way into what I wrote. My school of war grew well beyond its original boundaries to encompass a broader world than the life I'd expected. Some of what I learned in this unconventional school can be found in these essays.

Establishing the Combat Studies Institute

At an annual meeting of Army historians in the spring of 1978 at the U.S. Army War College, Maj. Charles R. Shrader, a member of the history faculty at the Command and General Staff College (CGSC), delivered a paper on military history instruction at his college. Military history at the staff college had suffered a reverse during the past year, Shrader reported. Earlier, upward of a dozen officers had taught military history, including twenty electives. In 1978, however, the history faculty at the staff college had been reduced to officers and two civilians and was known as the Applied Military History Team within a much larger academic department whose chief interest was military strategy. The historians had called upon the services of a distinguished visiting professor of military history, the late K. Jack Bauer of Rensselaer Polytechnic; together, they taught a small required course to the one thousand officers who made up the student body at the staff college. In addition, the faculty offered seven military history electives, electives so well subscribed that students often had to be turned away. Shrader forecast further reductions during the coming year. The chief of the team, Lt. Col. Harold Nelson, was transferring and would not be replaced by an officer of like rank. Shrader was to assume leadership of the team.

Despite his gloomy report, Shrader believed that military history had made important inroads at the staff college. He thought there was a measure of institutional acceptance for military history because of the high standards of instruction in the discipline and its popularity with students. Moreover, the officer in charge of the day-to-day affairs of the staff college, Brig. Gen. Robert Arter, had taken an interest in the small band of military historians and protected their program from even more extreme reductions. "Last year at this time," Shrader said, "there was some trepidation as to our survival in any form at CGSC."[1] As Shrader made clear, the threat of extinction had been turned aside this time by a combination of faculty performance and high-ranking patronage, but the state of military history at the staff college was fragile indeed. Should the military history team lose another skirmish, the history wars would come to an unhappy end.

More skirmishes lay ahead for Major Shrader and his team, yet within a year a new military history department called the Combat Studies Institute (CSI) had been established at the staff college. The Combat Studies Institute is now nearly nine years old. Both within and beyond the American armed forces, CSI is a unique organization. The institute is chartered to act as the military history department for the staff college, to conduct official historical research on issues that bear upon the present concerns of the Army, to oversee military history instruction in the other schools that make up the Army's professional officer education system, and to act as a professional resource for those who teach military history in the more than four hundred ROTC detachments in the United States.

The institute has thirty-three military and civilian historians; all of the civilians hold doctorates, and nearly everyone has some training beyond the master's degree. These historians have expertise in Russian, German, Japanese, Chinese, Latin American, Eastern European, Middle Eastern, and African history as well as most of the periods of U.S. history. The members of the institute are qualified to do original research in all the languages required by their fields, and everyone is skilled in that dialect of English peculiar to the Army. One interest binds all these talents together, an interest in military affairs, past and present.

Since its establishment in the summer of 1979, the institute has published fourteen monographs in the Leavenworth Papers series, five CSI Research Surveys, and a large number of lesser special studies, reports, and staff appreciations. All of this work was official, that is, supported by the Army, and the Army apparently uses it. The institute has printed more than 210,000 copies of its Leavenworth Papers and research surveys alone. At the same time, the members of the institute have independently published about a dozen works for academic and commercial presses, very likely a hundred scholarly articles, and a host of reviews, essays, and other ephemera.[2] Few major historical meetings occur without a presentation by a member of CSI. Considering the brief life of the organization, the official and personal accomplishments of its members have been noteworthy.

The story of how this unique historical organization came to be established is worth telling on three counts. First, history wins. To a fair degree, the Combat Studies Institute of today corresponds to the ambitions of its founders. The institute also represents an important step in the evolution of historical study in the U.S. Army at large and at the staff college in particular. Finally, the establishment of CSI serves as an interesting case study in what C. P. Snow calls "closed politics," or "any kind of politics in which there is no appeal to a larger assembly."[3]

The real war over war history began long ago, as the British military writer B. H. Liddell Hart noted when he wrote in *Military Affairs* that "official history" was a contradiction in terms. "The worst examples of suppression and distortion," he wrote, "have been in the field of military history—since this has usually been entrusted to, or undertaken by, men who were brought up in a profession where obedience and loyalty to authority are inculcated as the prime virtues."[4] Liddell Hart was taking aim at James E. Edmonds's official history of the British Army in the Great War and Edmonds's confessed inability to criticize old comrades in public as he did in private. Liddell Hart would not have admitted that Edmonds's shortcomings had less to do with official history than with Edmonds himself.[5] Even so, when Liddell Hart wrote this essay in 1959, there was evidence aplenty in the other direction. Britain and the Commonwealth Countries and the United States, among others, had their official histories of the Second World War well under way. None ever merited the kind of criticism Liddell Hart leveled at Edmonds's work.[6]

No official history enterprise was more ambitious than that of the American Army. Yet even as the Army's official histories of World War II were being written, within the Army itself there was a gradual alienation from the notion that a knowledge of history, military history in particular, was an essential element in the making of a professional officer corps. Even at this remove the reasons for the Army's alienation from history are not entirely clear. The advent of nuclear weapons had definitively challenged the traditional foundations of military knowledge, but disciplines other than history had arisen to compete with history's preeminence as the soldier's laboratory of war. The sense that history had somehow come to an end encouraged a presentist orientation that history could not, or would not, adopt. By the 1970s the study of military history, once considered de rigueur for any serving officer, had virtually disappeared from the Army's professional life. With the exception of West Point's history department, military history appeared in Army schools only when there was an interested and energetic individual to take up the cause, and then only at the sufferance of local officials.[7]

By the mid-1970s a group of historically trained, like-minded young field-grade officers had collected at the staff college. Nearly all of them had taught European history in West Point's newly created department, and all of them were veterans of the war in Vietnam. To say merely that they were interested in history is perhaps not enough. The faith of this generation of Army officers had been severely tested by Vietnam. They seemed to believe that their Army's defeat in Southeast Asia was as much intellectual as military and that an alienation from historical knowledge lay at the root of that failure. The restoration of history in the Army was to them tantamount to restoring the Army itself. A certain reformist, insurgent, impatient attitude united these young officers. One who had come to the staff college in 1972 as a student and stayed to teach wrote after a year on the faculty: "This year I have witnessed a paucity of creative thought, initiative and imagination from the faculty as we continuously react to useless bureaucratic trivia." Admitting that some progress had been made toward offering more military history, he wrote: "It is not my intent to spend any time in this document justifying the need for the study of military history by our students, or army officers in general. I am assured that such study for an army officer is necessary and I have yet to encounter anyone who felt we were doing it well today."[8] Below the surface of this criticism lay the assumption that the Army's fixation upon "useless bureaucratic trivia" had doomed its performance in war. As they looked about their Army, these officers saw little prospect for change; the more they looked, the more their frustrations rose. "Goddamn this Army, anyway," one said. "We ought to abolish it and start one of our own."[9]

Yet these officers were true believers, and they believed above all that good historical deeds would convert the unfaithful. That military history survived at all during the early 1970s at the staff college indicates that their beliefs had some basis. Even so, the record of military history studies at Fort Leavenworth during the 1970s, depending as it did upon individual officers, would not have been enough to inspire the creation of an independent academic department. What was wanted was a deus ex machina, one that would alter the uneasy relationship between the military history reformers and institutional power.[10]

As Major Shrader delivered his paper at the Army War College, the Army was in the throes of a great doctrinal reform, reshaping itself to fight on battlefields far removed from Southeast Asia. The high command was driving the Army with a relentlessness born of both a lost war and a fear that the Army had fallen behind its premier adversary, the Soviet Army. To matters of strategy, tactics, the integration of new equipment, and peacetime organization these leaders were bringing a certain impatience of their own with the old ways of the Army. One of those leaders was the newly promoted commander of the staff college's parent organization, the Training and Doctrine Command (TRADOC), Gen. Donn A. Starry.[11]

Unlike many of his contemporaries in the corps of general officers, General Starry was well and widely read, and not only in military history. Once asked for the title of his favorite book, Starry named *The Diary of Samuel Pepys*. His papers and speeches routinely employed historical and literary allusions, and his instructions often sent staff officers scurrying to their dictionaries. He was also extremely impatient with fools and, as he sometimes called them, "poltroons." At this moment Starry was guiding, with a firm and proprietary hand, the writing of field manuals designed to modernize the doctrines of a dangerously outmoded army. A good deal of this work was being done at Fort Leavenworth. Although the men were separated by many ranks, Starry's attitudes and those of the military historians at the staff college were similar. The presentist, mechanistic approach to military problems that so disturbed them apparently disturbed the general as well.[12] Thus, the general asked a question early in the summer of 1978: To what degree did historical knowledge inform the Army's current doctrines?[13]

Those who are not familiar with the military trades should understand that questions from four-star generals are never taken casually. A simple interrogatory from one of these men is sufficient to turn whole organizational routines on their heads. Often, generals ask questions when they very well know the answers merely in order to illuminate an unsatisfactory state of affairs for their subordinates.

In this case the general did still more. In July he dispatched two of his closest staff officers, lieutenant colonels James Braden and George Dramis, to Fort Leavenworth and charged them with discovering the answer to his pointed question. After a cursory inspection at the staff college, the two officers reported that any work being done in military history was wholly incidental to doctrinal affairs. They added that military history as it was being practiced was without much merit or relevance to the college's aims.

Dr. Brooks Kleber had been appointed the command historian of TRADOC in 1973. As such, Kleber was General Starry's special staff officer for all matters pertaining to official history within the entire command. Kleber had a paternalistic affection for the military historians at the staff college, many of whom he had met while they were on West Point's history faculty. Having heard of the unflattering report on military history at Fort Leavenworth, Kleber made his own inquiries of college officials. Their answers revealed quite a different state of affairs: although small, the Applied Military History Team performed to a high standard and was winning friends among both the students and the college's administration. Kleber soon informed Starry that the earlier report had been distorted.[14]

Of these disputes in the rarefied atmosphere of the high command the members of the Applied Military History Team were blissfully unaware. Neither of Starry's staff officers had seen fit to talk with the team; after all, the team was so small as to be nearly invisible. In addition to Shrader himself there were three other officers: Maj. Robert Doughty, Maj. Robert Frank, and 1st Lt. John C. Binkley (one of two lieutenants on the faculty). Two visiting associate professors who had just arrived for the year, Dr. P. D. Jones of Bradley University and this writer, completed the team. Although not officially part of the team, the Morrison Professor of Military History, Professor Dudley T. Cornish of Pittsburgh State University, naturally gravitated toward the younger historians and occasionally protected them from their enthusiasm. I think of them all now as a happy but impoverished lot with a simple, busy life.[15]

The dispute between Kleber and the staff officers was further complicated by the delivery in June of a study on the state of military history instruction throughout the officer education system. Written by Reserve Col. Jerry Haggerty, the study had argued for a progressive system of courses in all officers' schools, from ROTC through the staff college, which would oversee the system. Kleber had been discussing Haggerty's recommendations with the TRADOC chief of staff, Maj. Gen. Robert Hixon, but Hixon was far from being convinced that the idea was viable. A conference of general officers from the command was scheduled for the end of August at Fort Leavenworth. General Hixon and Dr.

Kleber asked the staff college for a meeting at that time to discuss Haggerty's study.[16]

However, General Starry was not content to leave the matter in the hands of his staff. He meant to discuss the whole issue of military history and its uses with his subordinate at Fort Leavenworth, Lt. Gen. J. R. Thurman, during the August conference. Whether Starry's instincts sounded a warning is not known; if so, however, his instincts were quite correct. Within the staff college, perhaps within the Applied Military History Team itself, there was resistance to the recommendations of the Haggerty study. Staff college memorandums, exchanged in preparation for Hixon and Kleber's briefing, indicate that the local staff was prepared to discuss Haggerty's recommendations but that the resources of the college would not be committed.[17]

In the meantime, the military historians' parent Department of Unified and Combined Operations (DUCO) was directed to prepare a background paper for General Thurman's conversation with Starry. Clearly, General Starry's interest in the affairs of the department was cause for some trepidation. The department director, Col. Richard Manion, was as aware as anyone that the spirit of retrenchment was still in the air. The direct interest of the commanding general of TRADOC in the department's affairs could easily spell trouble. Thus, the paper Manion prepared for General Thurman emphasized the "practical" nature of military history instruction at the staff college, not just, as he wrote, "history for history's sake."[18]

Three days later departmental officers briefed General Hixon and Dr. Kleber, but the pointed question raised by General Starry was not addressed. Still concentrating on the Haggerty study's recommendations, the panel "expressed general satisfaction with the CGSC military history program as it is presently being conducted" and solicited (but did not *order*) the college's assistance in setting up similar programs in the Army's officer education system.[19]

Starry's concerns were not so easily turned away, however. In the wake of Starry's visit General Thurman summoned the deputy commandant of the staff college, Brigadier General Arter, Colonel Manion and his deputy, and Major Shrader to discuss how Starry's concerns could be answered. The officers were required to present themselves at General Thurman's office on September 5.[20]

Naturally enough, these events excited much discussion within the military history team. The Haggerty study recommendations, while acceptable in theory, could not possibly have been implemented by a team made up of only four officers and two civilians. The sheer scope of such a task would have doomed historical instruction at the staff college and turned the historians into administrators. Starry's ideas, so far as they were known then, also seemed to pose a threat. The suggestion that military history could be directly employed as a source of wisdom for current military doctrines seemed to be a violation of the most fundamental canons of historical practice. And yet the members of the team were bureaucratically vulnerable. If the historians lost professional control of their discipline, if reasonable counterproposals could not be formulated, the high command, knowing or caring little for the nuances of historical practice, could eliminate the last vestige of military history at the staff college.[21]

The greater part of this burden fell to Shrader, who, as the team chief, had the task of educating Colonel Manion to these issues. And though the members of the team had many long and inconclusive discussions, Shrader was the one who had to articulate a policy recommendation. Perhaps an officer who had his eye on the main chance would have been more accommodating, would have fashioned the team's position along lines best calculated to please his superiors' vaguely articulated notions about history and doctrine. From the beginning Shrader suspected there was a very real chance that historical work at the college would be corrupted in this affair and that history would become a rummage bin for those who merely wished to prove or disprove a point of military doctrine. He chose not to compromise at all, reckoning that if his position failed to satisfy, it would fail on the grounds of professional honesty. He set about to devise an organization that would cleave to orthodoxy.

Shrader's scheme looked very much like the institute as it stands now. The plan called for a new academic department at the staff college devoted entirely to military history. The new department's research committee would address topics that had a bearing upon issues then confronting the Army. Which topics, exactly, the researchers undertook would be determined within the new department itself. Each year research plans would be approved by the commanding general of TRADOC, General Starry himself.[22] A teaching committee would continue with staff college classes much as before.

In all likelihood Shrader had his plan ready well before he and the other officers had to meet with Thurman. That Shrader was invited to participate in the meeting at all was a minor victory; majors don't often have serious discussions with lieutenant generals. Of all those present at the meeting with Thurman that September morning, Shrader had the most highly developed sense of what had to be accomplished. The memorandum recording the meeting suggests that Shrader was "masking his batteries," to use an artillerist's phrase, for Shrader had to convince not only General Thurman but also his immediate superiors of the plan's utility. Yet all the questions addressed in the manuscript version of Shrader's plan were discussed during the meeting. One entry, subsumed within the memorandum, indicated that Shrader's thinking about the new department was considerably ahead of those present. The name he had fixed upon for the organization was suggested as one of several candidates: the Combat Studies Institute.[23]

Still, the fictions and niceties of military punctilios had to be observed. Thurman had opened the meeting with a discourse on "his and General Starry's concerns in the area of historical investigations of army doctrinal matters." Shrader and probably the others present as well knew that General Thurman had little interest in history. But they knew, too, that General Starry was speaking through General Thurman and that if Thurman was not particularly interested in history, he was interested in satisfying General Starry. By the end of the meeting General Thurman had directed the staff college officers to devise a concept for the establishment of a "capability to conduct historical research and analysis at Fort Leavenworth."[24] On the same day General Thurman notified General Starry that several military historians at Fort Leavenworth were going to be set aside for research projects.[25]

In the meantime the memorandum of the meeting with Thurman was circulated throughout the staff college for comment, more perhaps for political reasons than any prospect of useful suggestions. None of the respondents objected to the notion that something had to be done, a testament either to the soundness of the idea or to the knowledge that General Thurman appeared to be in support of it. Ironically, the staff college's German liaison officer, Oberst Helmut Zedlick, took a line of argument that corresponded most closely to that of the historians themselves. "This institution deserves the best military historians the country can offer. There is no need to form a large group, but some outstanding personalities with passion and character will do the job. It needs character to do this as the killing of 'holy cows' is not so easy, and this seems to be one of the major tasks for the activity."[26] Other respondents expressed uneasiness that this organization would be too "academic." The colonel directing the logistics department at the college wrote, for instance: "If the army can accept an historical evaluation that cannot be precise; one that has uncertainty about how things will be; and, if the army will not insist that the historian become clairvoyant, then and only then will historical investigation be worthwhile." He added pointedly that the number of civilians involved should be strictly limited: "*History* may indicate that benefits usually thought to accrue from permanent civilian[s] . . . are illusory."[27]

On September 14 General Thurman heard of the college's plan for CSI and approved it without amendment. The general's approval launched a feverish search for resources, a matter that had hardly been touched upon during the last few weeks' deliberations. Shrader's plan called for eighteen new positions.[28] Since the college had only recently suffered faculty reductions, departments were hardly willing to donate officer "spaces" to the new enterprise. Four days after the meeting with General Thurman, Colonel Manion and Major Shrader flew east to gather information from official historical agencies and to make arrangements with personnel officials in Washington to recruit qualified historians in uniform.[29] General Thurman, meanwhile, sent a message to General Starry notifying him of recent developments and asking for authorization to add eighteen military and civilian personnel to his local roster. If General Starry wanted a new organization, General Thurman meant at least to try to convince his superior to pay for it.[30]

Starry's reply to Thurman no longer exists, but the substance of it was a four-star "no!" Evidently, Starry approved the concept for CSI but admonished Thurman to look to local organizations to provide the necessary personnel, including the drafting of staff college students if necessary. On the day that Thurman received Starry's reply, Thurman wrote a note to General Arter at the college: "We have *got* to get started in a modest way w/o [without] additional resources—Gen[eral] Starry is *not* going to give me any more spaces, so [we] will have to make do for now."[31] The generals had finished their work. The establishment of CSI now became an affair of bureaucracies.

Up and down the chain of command at the fort the commitment to the idea of CSI was rather more casual than that of the members of the military history team, who, it had been decided, would form the core of the new organization. Thurman himself was only as interested in the business as General Starry; the concept having been approved, he was no doubt only too happy to pass on to other matters.[32] Within the military history team's department officers not directly interested in the action except as an action looked for its advantages to their own interests.

While Shrader and Colonel Manion were on their eastern tour, Manion's deputy, Lt. Col. James Johnson, devised a scheme that would soften the blow to his department when the military history team achieved its independence. When Manion and Shrader returned, Johnson was waiting for Manion with a proposal to ask Thurman for two or three officers for a "planning and implementing group" to oversee the establishment of the new department. Once the group's work was done, Johnson expected to be able to keep these officers in his department.[33]

Quite naturally, Shrader had taken a proprietary interest in the creation of CSI. Upon hearing of Johnson's subterfuge, Shrader wrote a peremptory and vaguely insubordinate memorandum to his colonel. Shrader blasted "Johnson's scheme to obtain a 'hired gun'" as a "thinly disguised ploy" and an insult to the members of the military history team. In a veiled reference to Starry and Thurman, Shrader went further: "The necessity for satisfying the desires for immediate gratification of those providing the resources is recognized, but those desires *must* be subordinated to the need for considerable care in forming a lasting, vigorous organization." If current plans were allowed to play out, Shrader wrote, they could "only lead to the creation of an agency which will be crippled from the start." He could not be a part of an organization, he concluded, that was "certain to be the object of derision and ridicule by those whose judgment I value."[34]

Today Shrader does not recall sending this memorandum to his director. Perhaps the flat refusal of any office to give up officers for the project obviated the need for him to send it. In his memorandum Shrader had argued that he was the officer best qualified to oversee the creation of the institute. In any event, Colonel Manion had little recourse but to hand the action over to Shrader.[35]

As plans then stood, the new organization was scheduled to become "provisional" on January 1, 1979, and achieve full independence by July 1. In addition to fighting for the necessary staff, funds, and working space, the members of the history team had to find a director for CSI. The team members elected not to leave this matter to chance or the high command. Even before Starry and Thurman had approved the concept for CSI, the history team compiled a list of candidates. A lieutenant colonel, then a student at the Army War College, headed their list.[36] William A. Stofft was well known to the officers on the team. He had first come to the staff college as a student. During his student year Stofft had persuaded college officials to let him and other interested officers teach several military history courses. After graduation Stofft had joined the faculty and continued to teach within the strategy department of the college.[37] Although the list of candidate directors the team had compiled included an officer who is today a three-star general, the team had chosen Stofft from the first. During his consultative trip east Shrader had made a stop at the War College and, quite without authorization, recruited Stofft for the new position.[38]

The first term was the busiest time of the academic year for the historians. All save Professor Cornish were relatively new to the profession. The administrative work entailed in establishing a wholly new department of the staff college was considerable. Perhaps in other circumstances the team would have been happy to leave the bureaucratic details to someone else, but they had come to believe that officials outside the team were prone to treat the project as entirely routine. If no one else quite understood the implications of the project, the historians at least believed they did. As a consequence, the members of the team tended to adopt a beleaguered mentality, leavened with a certain cynical disdain for all who did not embrace the project with the same enthusiasm.

Outside the team Colonel Manion and no doubt others worried about the team's noticeably low rank. Lieutenant Colonel Johnson's earlier plan to create a "planning group" for CSI, which Shrader had regarded as a dark subterfuge, may have been only an expression of his concern about the bureaucratic inexperience of the team. And although the decision to make CSI "semiautonomous" at the beginning of the new year had been made, college officials could not bring themselves to deliver the new department wholly into the hands of three junior majors, a lieutenant, and two civilians; until CSI achieved complete independence the following June, Colonel Manion (and after his retirement in March his successor, another colonel) would, at least in theory, oversee the institute's activities.[39]

In keeping with these concerns, a proposal had been made quite early in the planning to form a consultative group of prominent military historians from outside the staff college. The group, including professors John Shy of Michigan, Jay Luvaas of Allegheny College, I. B. Holley of Duke, Robin Higham of Kansas State, Col. Roy Flint of West Point, Col. Don Shaw of the Military History Institute, and Dr. Kleber, convened with the members of the team at the staff college in early January. Stofft was on hand as well, having taken a break from his War College studies. Several days earlier the old Applied Military History Team had been transmogrified into the Combat Studies Institute (Provisional).[40]

Since the previous August Shrader and his colleagues had been living in an agitated state, spending hours in excited discussion as they attempted to anticipate every problem that might stand in the way of the project. If they believed they had accounted for every contingency, perhaps they should be forgiven for thinking that there was little chance the consultants could do more in two days of meetings. If they were a bit prideful and a bit protective in this attitude, it is also worth saying that they were right.

One issue seemed to dominate the proceedings of the conference: how and to what degree could military history play a role in the formulation of military doctrines? One conferee came close to suggesting that the military historians be made to write doctrine themselves. Another wondered whether CSI should be part of the staff college or be amalgamated with one of the other organizations at Fort Leavenworth, there to provide salient examples from history to the doctrine writers. These questions were bound up with how much freedom CSI would have to pursue research and exactly what sorts of subjects CSI would address. Dark forecasts were made about the deficiencies of "scholarship on demand," and doubts were expressed about the ability of relatively junior historians to withstand bureaucratic and administrative demands for quick answers.[41]

Not until the summary session was much said about teaching military history. Several conferees held that teaching should be incidental to doctrinal research. I. B. Holley thought that as much as three-fourths of the new institute's time should be devoted to doctrinal research. John Shy thought that if the new organization did not provide for at least half of its time in research at the very beginning, the chances of doing so later were small.[42]

Into these theoretical considerations Dr. Kleber injected a note of realism. When he first heard of the plan for CSI several months earlier, he considered it grandiose and impractical, an overreaction to General Starry's concerns. Since then he had kept a watchful eye upon events at Fort Leavenworth and from his position close to General Starry had interceded on behalf of the project despite his reservations. Kleber had not forgotten that Starry's original complaint focused upon the deficiencies of doctrine. Thus, he told the meeting: "This is a vehicle of General Starry's. He is a hard taskmaster. I am afraid that if you do not get involved in responding to the reason that you are existing fairly quickly, there will be trouble on high." Speaking more directly to the members of CSI who were present, Kleber added that when the enterprise was under way "you will understand that the real world exists and we must make ourselves known and useful. This is the main task."[43]

Throughout the meeting there was a barely subdued sense of urgency, as if an opportunity had appeared but only for a brief time. This sense had animated the members of the history team for several months as well. They knew well enough what the Army at large thought about their work; they were poor relations at the staff college, without protection from past and future retrenchments. That they had advanced the project this far they knew well too was due to the approval of one man who had no idea that his concerns would be translated into what the team had proposed. One of the conferees made this point very early in the meeting: "CSI can be destroyed by the next general." No one could reckon just how much time the new organization had to prove itself or, indeed, to evolve beyond dependence upon General Starry's patronage. All present felt there was little time to waste if CSI was to survive "the next general." If CSI was to succeed, that success had to be founded upon published research. Having sounded these warnings, the conferees left the members of CSI to get on with their problems.[44]

Even before the turn of the year, one member of the history team had stopped teaching and made for the library. Maj. Robert Doughty's doctoral dissertation was in its final throes. Although working against a deadline to finish his dissertation for the University of Kansas, Doughty embarked upon the survey of the Army's tactical doctrines from the close of the Second World War to the mid-1970s. Moreover, Doughty was slated to be transferred to Europe in the spring. Although he remembers this spring of 1979 as one of the worst in his life, it passed in a blur. At the end of it Doughty had finished his dissertation, and he had also completed what was to become in the summer of 1979 the first number of the Leavenworth Papers.[45] Doughty's monograph, *The Evolution of U.S. Army Tactical Doctrine, 1945–1975*, served both as a demonstration piece for those who were concerned about what CSI might produce and as a model for subsequent Leavenworth Papers—a study, founded upon primary sources, that shed light upon matters of present concern to the Army at large, longer than an article, shorter than most books, published locally, and widely distributed.

As Doughty's paper was being readied for publication, Lieutenant Colonel Stofft graduated from the War College and transferred to Fort Leavenworth in June 1979. Two days after he arrived CSI shed its provisional status and achieved formal independence as an academic department of the staff college. Of the original officers on the old Applied Military History Team, only Shrader remained. The others, their tours of duty completed, scattered around the Army, and new faculty arrived to take their places. For ten crucial months Shrader had guided the concept of CSI through a bureaucratic maze, acting as director of CSI in all but name. If he was reluctant to relinquish the organization he had created, good soldier that he was, he betrayed no signs of it.

The transfer of power from Shrader to Stofft was not dramatic, but Stofft's assumption of the directorship signaled a new stage in the evolution of the institute. Even before his arrival at Fort Leavenworth Stofft had been summoned from the War College to an audience with General Starry at his headquarters, where the general made clear that he expected the new organization to deliver on its promises, and quickly.[46]

Stofft faced three overriding, interrelated tasks in the summer of 1979: the establishment of an active research and publishing program, the expansion of CSI's constituency, and the requisition of the people and the money necessary to carry the program to fruition. Contrary to the expectations of the January consultants, research seemed to be the least of CSI's problems. CSI was left to plan its own research program; by the late summer of 1979 several more Leavenworth Papers were in progress and would be published promptly. The natural interests of CSI's researchers and their knowledge of current Army affairs were sufficient to insure that CSI studies would illuminate modern military problems. No one was dragooned into doing a study, and no historian was required to shape his study according to preconceived notions of what would please the Army.

Merely doing studies was not enough, however. If Shrader's genius had been to conceive and launch an idea, Stofft's talent was to institutionalize it. Stofft understood that CSI's work was the vital medium by which CSI's constituency could be broadened. Momentarily in the favor of the high command, CSI had to direct its campaign toward the middle and lower echelons of the officer corps—there, after all, was where "the next general" would originate. From the start, therefore, each of CSI's major studies required a first printing of ten thousand copies. Issues were mailed to all the Army's troop and organization commanders, to other research and doctrinal organizations, and throughout the Army's professional education system, reaching from the greenest lieutenant to the most senior colonel. The rapid promotion of CSI's program was only one effect of this campaign, however. Rather than submitting CSI's research program to the direct oversight of the high command, Stofft in effect offered CSI's work for the approval of the entire officer corps of the Army, a huge, critical audience that was not at all reluctant to state its view of the quality of CSI's work. In the meantime the corps of general officers, sensitive to the broad acceptance of CSI's work, had taken an active and positive interest in CSI's welfare. General Starry's confidence in the new organization, at first based on sheer faith, then upon what it was actually producing, supported the institute throughout his tenure. He relinquished his command in 1982. Since then "the next general" has come and gone many times, and each has followed General Starry's precedent without complaint.

Shrader, Stofft, and their colleagues in CSI encountered and contended with problems common to the practice of public history at large. The first and most important advantage they possessed and capitalized upon was an intimate working knowledge of their organization and its affairs. Moreover, they were committed to the proposition that history illuminated and informed those affairs in a way that no other analytical approach could hope to match. Finally, they never surrendered to the idea that utilizing history in this fashion required its subordination to preconceived organizational expectations.

Ultimately, the organizational indifference to history that Shrader and his colleagues worked against was not as intractable as they originally believed. In the past decade the Army has embraced the study of history as never before, and CSI has played an important part in this trend. Like Shrader himself, some of the junior officers who contributed significantly to this process did so at certain cost to their careers. Their sacrifice kept the art of history alive until the Army was ready to adopt it anew. Although they may not see these events so philosophically today, their reward may be greater than the high rank that every professional officer hopes for. They will have had a hand in changing the way their Army thinks.

Notes

1. Charles R. Schrader, "Presentation at Military History Conference, April 7, 1978, Carlisle Barracks PA," typescript in possession of the author.

2. Memorandum, Dr. Robert Berlin to author, "Leavenworth Papers and Research Survey Production," September 1986, Combat Studies Institute Historical Files, U.S. Army Command and General Staff College Archives, Fort Leavenworth KS (hereafter cited as CSI Files). Only an informal accounting of the private academic activities of the members of the institute is kept.

3. C. P. Snow, *Science and Government: The Godkin Lectures at Harvard University, 1960* (New York: New American Library, 1962), 53.

4. B. H. Liddell Hart, "Responsibility and Judgment in Historical Writing," *Military Affairs* 23 (Spring 1959): 35–36.

5. See also David French, "'Official but Not History?': Sir James Edmonds and the Official History of the Great War," *Journal of the Royal United Services Institution* 131 (March 1986): 58–63.

6. See, for instance, an appraisal of official history in John Keegan, *The Face of Battle* (New York: Viking Press, 1976), 22.

7. At the direction of Gen. William Westmoreland, then chief of staff of the Army, the head of the history department at West Point, Col. Thomas Griess, convened an investigation of the status of historical education in the Army. In the spring of 1971 the group of military educators produced a report that contained a survey of historical programs throughout the Army and of attitudes at various echelons toward historical studies, and it concluded with a volume's worth of recommendations. Throughout the decade this report served as an important reference for military historians in uniform, but it cannot be said to have instituted reforms. See Department of the Army, "Ad Hoc Committee Report on the Army Need to Study Military History," bound typescript, 4 vols., West Point NY, May 1971. Dr. Brooks Kleber, the only civilian on the committee, was to have an important role in the formation of CSI. See also Kleber's own accounting of the committee's activities in Brooks Kleber, "The Army Looks at Its Need for Military History," *Military Affairs* 37 (April 1973): 47–48.

8. Memorandum, Lt. Col. William A. Stofft to Deputy Commandant, CGSC, October 31, 1976, 6, CSI Files.

9. Remark to the author by a colleague (who will not be named) in the summer of 1978.

10. Although the "Ad Hoc Committee Report" has sometimes been cited as the catalyst for what happened at Fort Leavenworth in 1978, neither I nor my colleagues recall the report's being brought into play against the bureaucracy at the staff college. In May 1976 interested civilian and uniformed historians met at Fort Leavenworth to assess "what had gone wrong with

the Ad Hoc Committee recommendations." The meeting led to the establishment of what was essentially a lobby, devoted to exercising "unrelenting pressure on the army's education system to increase and improve the teaching of history." This meeting also was the genesis of the TRADOC Military History Conference, an annual meeting of representatives of historical agencies from across the entire Army. See Col. L. D. F. Frasche, "Educational Reform in the U.S. Army: The Integration of History, Training, and Doctrine since the Vietnam War," paper presented at the Annual Meeting of the American Historical Association, December 29, 1984, 4–5. Copy in the author's possession.

11. The history of the U.S. Army after the Vietnam War has yet to be written. The story of the Army's doctrinal reforms in the 1970s is the subject of a Leavenworth Paper, Maj. Paul Herbert's *Deciding What Has to Be Done: William E. Depuy and the Making of FM 100-5*, published in 1988. Ironically, these very doctrinal reforms were the proximate cause of much controversy among the young officers. The new doctrine seemed to them unnecessarily mechanistic and "system-oriented."

12. This characterization of General Starry is based upon several years' personal association. In 1983 I was required to retire the general's personal and official papers for deposit at the Military History Institute, Carlisle Barracks PA; as part of this process I read the entire collection, which includes an oral history conducted by Dr. Brooks Kleber upon Starry's departure from TRADOC in 1981. Another oral history project with General Starry is presently under way at the Military History Institute.

13. Author's notes, telephone interview with Dr. Brooks Kleber on events surrounding the establishment of CSI, August 20, 1980.

14. Ibid. I have since confirmed Kleber's account of events with one of these staff officers, George Dramis, now a colonel.

15. I joined the department in June 1978.

16. Memorandum, Col. Richard Manion to Brig. Gen. Robert Arter, Subject: Military History, August 10, 1978; and Memorandum, Brig. Gen. Robert Arter to Lt. Gen. J. R. Thurman, Subject: Military History, August 25, 1978, CSI Files.

17. Ibid.

18. Col. Richard Manion, "Background Paper for Lieutenant General Thurman for Discussions with General Starry," August 29, 1978, CSI Files.

19. Memorandum, Col. Richard Manion to Lt. Gen. Thurman, Subject: Military History Briefing for M. G. Hixon, September 5, 1978, CSI Files.

20. Memorandum for Committee and Team Chiefs from Director, DUCO, Subject: Rationale for Existence of DUCO for General Starry, August 29, 1978, CSI Files.

21. Ibid. Judging from General Starry's questions as they were represented in this memorandum, the threat was to the entire Department of Unified and Combined Operations. The department taught strategy, joint and coalition operations, as well as history; all were subjects taught at the War College, and appropriately so. This would not be the last time high-ranking officers would ask why the staff college was teaching strategy to mere majors.

22. Manuscript (in hand of Maj. C. R. Shrader), "Memorandum for Director, DUCO, Subject: Proposed Historical Studies Activity," undated, CSI Files.

23. Col. Richard A. Manion, Memorandum for Record, Subject: "Discussions with LTG Thurman, 1030 hours, 5 September 1978; Re: Establishment of a Combat Studies Research and Analysis Activity at Fort Leavenworth," September 5, 1978, CSI Files.

24. Ibid.

25. Memorandum of Record, Subject: Doctrinal Institutionalization, n.d. [September 22, 1978?], CSI Files, records a message sent by Lieutenant General Thurman to General Starry on September 5, 1978, signaling his intention to "fence some people in DUCO as a nucleus of historians whose job would be to study in a scholarly way the lessons of history and how these could affect our doctrine."

26. Disposition Form, German Liaison Officer to Director, DUCO, Subject: Establishment of a Combat Study Research and Analysis Activity, September 7, 1978, CSI Files.

27. Memorandum, Col. John E. Sutton to Col. Richard Manion, Subject: Comments on the Historical Research Group, September 8, 1978, CSI Files.

28. Memorandum for Record, Subject: Briefing for Lieutenant General Thurman on Military History Institute, September 14, 1978. A copy of the Briefing Slides is at Inclosure 1, detailing the request for eighteen additional positions.

29. Ibid. See also Disposition Form, Col. Richard Manion to Commandant [Lieutenant General Thurman], Subject: Combat Studies Institute, September 26, 1978, CSI Files, which details Manion and Shrader's trip to Washington, the War College, and West Point.

30. Message, Lieutenant General Thurman to General Starry, Subject: Military History Research, September 22, 1978; and Message, Lieutenant General Thurman to General Starry, Subject: Military History Research, September 29, 1978, CSI Files.

31. Handwritten memo, Lieutenant General Thurman to Brigadier General Arter, September 29, 1978, CSI Files.

32. To be fair to General Thurman, he made no pretense of a fondness for history. A few hours after he approved the concept for CSI on Septem-

ber 14, Thurman met with the staff college's faculty council. Apparently in a reflective mood, Thurman told the assembled officers that "he and his brother [Maj. Gen. Maxwell Thurman], while successful in the army, may represent the wrong kind of officer for the army today, in terms of specific professional expertise and educational background. They both are basically technicians with a strong background in technical or 'hard science' subjects. On top of this technical background a smattering of liberal arts education has been sprinkled. The reverse appears to be the ideal, i.e., a strong liberal arts foundation, providing an inquisitive, philosophical, and broad approach to the world, on top of which are built the technical skills required to meet specific needs." See Memorandum for Deputy Commandant, USACGSC, Subject: Minutes of the Faculty Council Meeting, September 14, 1978, CSI Files.

33. Memorandum for the Deputy Commandant from the Director, DUCO, Subject: History Project Status Report, September 22, 1978. Shrader composed his protest on the same day. See Memorandum for Director, DUCO, Subject: Formation of CSI, September 22, 1978, handwritten manuscript, CSI Files (hereafter cited as Shrader Memorandum).

34. Shrader Memorandum, 2.

35. Ibid., 3.

36. Decision Paper, Director, DUCO to Commandant, Subject: Combat Studies Institute, September 26, 1978, Inclosure 3 (Candidates for Position of Director, CSI), CSI Files. Three days earlier Shrader had included his appraisal of Stofft in his protest to Colonel Manion. "I believe LTC Bill Stofft is the best available candidate for the position of Director, CSI. He possesses the requisite academic skills and military background and enjoys the respect of both the military historians in the army and a significant portion of the civilian academic community. He also possesses the bureaucratic skills and contacts to make CSI work. The same cannot be said of other potential candidates" (Shrader Memorandum, 5).

37. Author's notes, Memorandum of a telephone interview with Brig. Gen. William A. Stofft, January 6, 1987.

38. Author's notes, Memorandum of a telephone interview with Lt. Col. C. R. Shrader, February 2, 1987.

39. [Maj. C. R. Shrader], "Combat Studies Institute Semi-Annual Historical Summary (January 3, 1979 through August 31, 1979)," September 12, 1979, typewritten manuscript, 1, CSI Files.

40. Ibid. CSI Conference Notes, "Working Session Organization," January 11–12, 1979, CSI Files.

41. CSI Conference Notes, "Minutes of Working Sessions," January 11–12, 1979, 4, CSI Files.

42. CSI Conference Notes, "Summary of Final Session," January 12, 1979, 10, CSI Files.

43. Ibid.

44. CSI Conference Notes, "Summary of Session III: CSI Organizations and Functions," January 12, 1979, 3, CSI Files.

45. Maj. Robert A. Doughty, *The Evolution of U.S. Army Tactical Doctrine, 1945–1975*, Leavenworth Paper, no. 1 (Fort Leavenworth KS: U.S. Army Command and General Staff College, 1979).

46. Author's notes, Memorandum of a telephone interview with Brig. Gen. William A. Stofft, January 4, 1987. Stofft and Starry met again before Stofft assumed the directorship. On May 24, 1979, Stofft, Starry, and Thurman convened at Fort Leavenworth to discuss the new organization in detail. Memorandum, Lt. Col. William A. Stofft to Brig. Gen. Robert Arter, Subject: Visit of General Starry (Combat Studies Institute), May 24, 1979, CSI Files.

EIGHT. **Armies in History, History in Armies**

Official military history can be defined as that form of historical work done within and for a military institution. Naturally, such a general definition obscures any number of reservations, conditions, and contingencies, but it is a good starting point for how one might see this subvariant of historical practice today. As a concept, official military history seems new; it seems to belong to the age of institutions, of organizations, of bureaucracies—in other words, to the modern age. Yet if one remembers the purposes of official military history—casting experience into useful form—the practice must be very old indeed. From the very beginning of historical practice in the West, history at large and military history in particular have been aimed at learning from one's mistakes or, better yet, the mistakes of others. Armies must always have wanted more information, more knowledge than they had. Armies that found themselves deficient in information could fight their way through ignorance, if they were lucky, but knowledge was a way of hedging one's bets. In the eighteenth century and gradually thereafter armies increasingly decided that knowledge was preferable to luck and that they should begin to invest some of their time and treasure in the disciplined, systematic collection and analysis of information. Other varieties of history might yet be dismissed as a luxury or, worse, as merely a hobby for the antiquarian, but military history was believed to possess certain operationally useful properties. By the nineteenth century, military officers were being chosen to serve as historians as an integral part of the new, evolving general staff culture in the West.

So we can date the appearance of modern official military history with some precision. Professor Jay Luvaas considers Baron

Henri Jomini the first official historian, working under Napoleon's patronage. We may suspect, however, that what Napoleon had in mind was his own good standing in the historical afterlife rather than good history per se.[1] Capt. William Siborne's Waterloo researches during the 1830s, supported by the British Army, falls close to official history, or at least official commemoration. Siborne's mission was to reconstruct in miniature the battle at the height of crisis, not to write a book, although he could not be prevented from doing that as well. He based his reconstruction on the straightforwardly tendentious notion that the winners of a battle knew more about the event than the losers, and in keeping with this notion he wrote letters chiefly to British survivors of the battle—survivors who had outlived the battle itself by an extra fifteen years or so. Later in the century Siborne's son, who had himself risen to the rank of major general, collected all his father's Waterloo letters and published what is still today one of the most compact, useful sources on the battle.[2]

Britain's official military histories date from just after the Crimean War. The first project was not very successful and was quite publicly condemned in—of all places—the pages of the *Journal of the Royal United Service Institution*. The two authors, both army officers who could not disentangle their regimental prejudices from their authorial responsibilities, disliked each other and would not agree about what were the "major lessons" of the siege of Sebastopol. Alas, now we shall never know.

Official history, as it evolved within the general staff culture, seemed to suit the Prussians and then later the Germans very well indeed. Almost at the outset, their official histories were regarded as having set the gold standard for such enterprises. Other European armies imitated their highly detailed approach and comprehensive scope. Given a choice between comprehensiveness or profundity, the Germans always chose the former and so did their imitators, so that a proper staff history, "crammed full of facts *and dull*," might depict "a picture of war on a gigantic scale, slowly unrolled before the reader, with all its complex purpose and involved action calmly traced by a master hand."[3]

The United States' first entry into official military history was inspired by a suggestion during the Civil War from Gen. Henry Halleck, President Lincoln's military advisor, a suggestion that led to the eventual publication of the 128 volumes of *The Official Records of the War of the Rebellion.* The whole *Official Records* project spanned nearly forty years, and some sort of official military history work has been under way in the United States ever since.[4]

By the time of the Russo-Japanese War, leading armies had recognized the need for obtaining and analyzing operational and tactical data that might be of practical use in future, and military history offered the best means by which these analyses could be conducted. Just at the turn of the century, however, we are seeing other fields beginning to make their first contributions toward the understanding of modern war. Ivan Bloch's six-volume magnum opus, arguing the futility of future war by means of innovative, if crude, econometric analyses, posed one of the first direct challenges to history as the best way of viewing war present or war past.[5] History would persist as the intellectual mode for some time still, however. Great multivolume official histories of this war were completed by both the Russians and the Japanese as well as by officers from several of the observing armies—the Germans, the French, and the British. The Americans reported their observations to headquarters, but one could not call these reports histories as such.[6] All these works possessed a kind of Victorian stateliness, proceeding along similar lines from strategic appreciation to operational analysis to tactical exposition, written in the bloodless style common to the professional's pose at the time.

These histories stand now as the very embodiment of that day's professional military knowledge. Legend around my own staff college has it that Gen. William T. Sherman contributed a number of military works from his own library in order to give our library a good start. But when I arrived, the foundation stones of what is now a magnificent library were these very official histories—the German, French, British, and Russian versions of the

Russo-Japanese and other recent wars. Given the state of military history in general and official military history in particular, one could not have done better at the time than acquire these works. Strange to say, at the beginning of the twentieth century, military history of the academic sort in the United States had some growing to do. Not until after World War II could it be said that civilian academicians were gaining any ground on either the volume or the quality of military history produced under official auspices.

Official history projects represented a considerable investment in a nation's treasure, but they carried a certain emotional investment too, as when an Austrian officer was removed from the active list because he dared criticize his country's official history of the Austrian campaign of 1849. There was the celebrated case of the German general who challenged a crippled veteran to a duel because the veteran had taken issue in print with the general's official historical work. By the turn of the century, however, official military historical work had transcended these eccentricities by producing books of real and lasting intellectual and professional military value.[7]

The impulse to commemorate the nation's sacrifice was perhaps the most elementary motive behind all these projects. The record of that sacrifice had to be collected and set down in some useful form. Perhaps behind these tasks lay the understanding that a kind of accounting had to be rendered not only for posterity but for the society that gave life and sustenance to the army itself. Modern official historians may be forgiven if they lay claim to the ancient fathers of history itself as their intellectual forebears. Motives such as these would not have seemed strange to Thucydides.

So, even though military history, officially committed, has been in operation for rather a long time, in my country one would search university curricula in vain for any mention of it. As far as I know, apart from programs in what is called "public history"—by which is usually meant foundation, park, museum, or memorial work—there are no courses in how the historian might ac-

IN THE SCHOOL OF WAR

tually practice in an environment that is not strictly academic. The conceit is that if one is up to doing the academic work necessary to stack up letters behind one's name, one is naturally qualified to practice in all possible environments—academic, institutional, commercial, or official. This is demonstrably not true. Perhaps, then, the academic might deign to pay attention to this matter, because while the craft of official history offers professional challenges unlikely to be encountered elsewhere, it is very poorly understood within the profession itself. I think the following case is very much to this point.

In the spring of 1959 the British military writer B. H. Liddell Hart published an essay in the journal *Military Affairs* entitled "Responsibility and Judgment in Historical Writing." He began by describing the several ways a historian might find himself subordinated to a raison d'être other than the pursuit of historical truth—the "scientific" pursuit of historical truth, as he put it. Standing in the way of truth, he wrote, were "so many people [who] are compelled to cover up truth, often against their inclination, by the requirements of their jobs." These were historians who had submitted to what Liddell Hart saw as "an inevitable condition of service for anyone who is a servant of Government or any other institution: a political party, a religious body, or a commercial firm." In all such cases the outcome was predictable: something less than truth, official truth masquerading as truth— or, the reader was left to infer, official lying.

While Liddell Hart was suspicious of historians with associations of any kind, he reserved his most trenchant remarks for those who worked as official military historians.[8] He thought it was time to say that "official history" is a contradiction in terms—the word "official" tends to qualify and often cancels out the word "history." Furthermore, "the worst examples of suppression and distortion," he wrote, "have been in the field of military history—since this has usually been entrusted to, or undertaken by, men who were brought up in a profession where obedience and loyalty to authority are inculcated as the prime virtues"—that is to say, military officers themselves. He did not consider the possibility that an officer's loyalties might actually assist in the discovery of scientific truth.[9]

As it happened, Liddell Hart had one particular officer in mind as an example. This was Brig. James E. Edmonds, who had been placed in charge of producing the British Army's official military histories of the Great War and in whom, Liddell Hart wrote, "the effect is all too strikingly illustrated." Liddell Hart did not tell his readers, however, that he and Brigadier Edmonds had a long and complex association that dated well back into the 1920s. In those days, before achieving public notice as a military critic with the *Daily Telegraph* and as a military historian in his own right, Liddell Hart saw Edmonds quite often. The relationship was important to Liddell Hart, who, having been medically decommissioned, was then making his start in journalism. It was also important because Edmonds was evidently something of a gossip. Today journalists might characterize him as "a source who wishes to remain anonymous."

And, indeed, Edmonds did have a curious working philosophy. When he met with Liddell Hart, he would reveal information—information of the sort that today would be regarded as "privileged," much as that shared by lawyer and client or doctor and patient—gleaned from his own official work on the history of the Great War. Edmonds clearly delighted in contributing to Liddell Hart's growing disillusionment with the war's generals, and in the 25,000 boxes of documents there was more than enough available to scandalize every meeting with Liddell Hart or anyone else for quite a long time. By the mid-1920s more and more knowledgeable criticism of the conduct of the war was reaching the general public, very little of it redounding to the credit of generals. But while Edmonds would tattle about his fellow officers to Liddell Hart and who knew how many others, he would not himself make the juicy bits public. Those who were really in the know, he said, would be able to "read between the lines" of his official history when it finally did come out.[10]

No doubt Liddell Hart was flattered to be included among the cognoscenti. Fed horror stories by Edmonds, thoroughly attuned to the critical histories and memoirs that seemed to appear daily, Liddell Hart grew less forgiving of Allied war leaders. In the earlier days of his relationship with Edmonds, Liddell Hart had been rather more forgiving of the generals. That, most assuredly, would change.

By the mid-1920s Liddell Hart had also formed an intellectual and personal alliance with the formidable J. F. C. Fuller, then a colonel in the British Army and very possibly the only human being Liddell Hart would ever regard as possessing an intellect and military knowledge superior to his own. Liddell Hart was very much the junior partner at the beginning of this relationship, just after the war. Reading through their earliest correspondence, while Liddell Hart was still on active service as a captain, detailed to write infantry tactical doctrine, one is impressed by his skillful dealings with the prickly Fuller. Liddell Hart's own intellect obviously impressed Fuller, and before long the two were corresponding as near equals. I believe it does Liddell Hart no disservice to observe that this was as much because of Fuller's own personality as because of Liddell Hart's brilliance. Fuller was incessantly critical, but for him only ideas seemed to be worth arguing over. He certainly refused to stand on the dignity of his rank alone. When he took up an appointment in 1923 as an instructor at the Staff College at Camberley, he amazed his students (and no doubt scandalized the rest of the faculty) by announcing, "Nothing clarifies true knowledge like a free exchange of ideas; consequently, because I happen to be a colonel and you a captain or major, do not imagine for a moment that rank is a bar to free speech."[11]

Toward the end of his tenure at Camberley, Fuller published *The Foundations of the Science of War*, an eccentric and not particularly successful book that aimed to reduce modern war to a universal principle that might guide the soldier's actions, regardless of where or when those actions might occur. As Fuller would admit later, the book was gratuitously complex, and the reviewers reacted accordingly. An anonymous review in the *Army*

Quarterly offered the hope that the young "might not take it too seriously."

Characteristically, Fuller would not contribute to his own defense. "I am trying to work out a science of war and not a *vade mecum* for fools," he said. No doubt this mulish behavior only encouraged the critics, one of whom was none other than Brigadier Edmonds himself. In a crushing, ridiculing review for the *Army Quarterly*, Edmonds belittled Fuller's so-called universal principle—a crackbrained, pseudomystical fantasy cribbed from his studies of the occult during his younger days in India. What is more amazing is that any part of Fuller's *Foundations* was regarded as worthy of any attention after such a public drubbing. But it was. Even with its defects, *Foundations* is worth anyone's time.[12]

By the late 1920s Liddell Hart was outgrowing his tutorials with both Fuller and Edmonds. His correspondence, always assertively confident, grew increasingly contentious, as did his journalism and his writing in general. Tolerated by an amazingly forgiving military establishment, Fuller could afford to play the intellectual buccaneer, but Liddell Hart, living by his wits, had no safety net to catch him if he imitated Fuller too closely. If Liddell Hart was coming to see Edmonds as the "kept man," that put Liddell Hart somewhere between the two men. No doubt Liddell Hart fancied himself as having created an environment of his own particular design, free from unwonted influences, one of near clinical purity. In reality, Liddell Hart alternated between these two models, Fuller the eccentric, Edmonds the insider, like a shuttlecock.

By the 1930s Liddell Hart's relations with both men had cooled. His correspondence with Edmonds grew quite adversarial. His judgment of British generalship had grown progressively more critical, so much so that he had alienated any number of his official contacts in the Army. At one point Liddell Hart wrote bluntly to Edmonds: "No one has given me clearer evidence of the deficiencies of our higher leaders as individuals than you have, yet you are inclined to pretend that, collectively, they were up to the problem they had to face." In effect, the two men had switched opinions with one another, with Edmonds then defending, Liddell Hart attacking, Britain's wartime leadership. Of course, Liddell Hart would have said he was right on either side and Edmonds was wrong. Edmonds was beyond the pale now. Everything he touched was corrupted or corrupting and in the process had become for Liddell Hart the very embodiment of the official military historian. Here is Liddell Hart, writing in 1933:

> Not a few military historians have admitted that they feel compelled by position, interest or friendship, to put down less than they know to be true. Once a man surrenders to this tendency the truth begins to slip away like water down a wastepipe— until those who want to learn how to conduct war in the future are unknowingly bathing their minds in a shallow bath.[13]

Here, as in his *Military Affairs* essay so many years later, Liddell Hart is begging several questions. Being part of an official establishment is not a precondition for self-censorship. Independent or academic historians have shown themselves to be quite capable of withholding all manner of information, even distorting it at times. So can those who work within large institutions. For the better part of fifty years official military historians produced huge multivolume studies of the Second World War. Information that has come to light since these were published quite often revises or even overturns the official story. To what degree should these histories be relied upon now? The answer, I think, is quite straightforward: official history is just as vulnerable to corruption or manipulation as any other sort of history.

The historian's environment is no guarantee one way or another of what Liddell Hart would see as "scientific truth." Those of us who use history, whether scholar or general reader, should not at any time surrender our own critical faculties. We are the ones Liddell Hart left out of his equation. In the end it is we who will decide whether the work in our hands has been corrupted. Liddell Hart seems to have imagined that we would give up the privilege of that decision to the historian. Why would he think so?

Liddell Hart insisted on being thought right at all times. A brief examination of his papers, dating from later in his life, reveals a near-obsessive compulsion to argue and reargue points he had made in books years before. I think this is because Liddell Hart, like Fuller, was essentially an autodidact, unschooled in the exchange of ideas and therefore much less interested in *explaining* than in *convincing*. There is a very strong polemical element in the work of both men. They consider themselves most successful when there are no more arguments for them to meet, and for Liddell Hart in particular success had very practical, personal consequences.

Ironically, Liddell Hart's own relationship to "scientific truth" has come under close examination in recent years. *Liddell Hart and the Weight of History* by John Mearsheimer appeared in 1988 to no small amount of controversy in the United Kingdom. Mearsheimer's thesis was that Liddell Hart conducted a very deliberate campaign to rehabilitate his reputation after the Second World War and that he did this in no small part by distorting and manipulating the record of his prewar activities.

It is no secret at all that Liddell Hart's dalliance in defense politics before the war led to his being banished from official circles during the war. Very much in keeping with the public opinion in Great Britain at the time, Liddell Hart championed very conservative defense policies while serving as a shadow advisor to Chamberlain's secretary of state for war, Leslie Hore-Belisha. Liddell Hart's so-called limited liability approach called for reducing Britain's commitment to Continental defense to an absolute minimum in order to avoid being dragged into another disastrous war. He was certainly not alone at the time, but after Chamberlain, after Munich, and after May 1940 he must have felt so.

At some point Liddell Hart had begun to consider himself a man of affairs as much as a man of ideas. His ideas and his writing had brought him greater and greater public attention. Those who were impressed by the workings of his mind and his pen solicited his views on subjects beyond the range of this historical research. Such was Liddell Hart's view of the functions of history that he would have seen these developments as merely the natural outgrowth of his historical work. Both Liddell Hart and Fuller were not unlike other historians of the day who believed that cautionary lessons could be deduced from any historical subject and that these lessons could be directly and rather literally applied to the present. Both men measured their success at least in part by the degree to which the lessons they promoted were adopted by modern military institutions. This is a self-deception perhaps as old as history itself and one that makes modern historians shift in their seats. In Liddell Hart's case the illusion led to his nearly complete eclipse as an influence on British military policy during the war.

For all his confidence and self-assured worldliness, I suspect Liddell Hart had a very incomplete view of what he was getting into when he began to involve himself in contemporary defense policy. He thought he had a storehouse full of lessons; if only blockheaded officialdom would take heed, the mistakes and miscalculations of the past could be avoided. This was his message to his readers almost from the beginning: the assumption of superior knowledge and the wisdom that was created by its acquisition. I do not think he understood that a subtle change in his relationship to officialdom had occurred. He believed he was applying history. In fact, he was applying himself—two very different things. If I seem altogether too completely convinced of this difference, I might add, by way of extenuation, that I have been convinced in quite a direct way.

In the late 1970s I joined a group inside the U.S. Army's staff college that in many ways would test Liddell Hart's dim view of official history. This group, which came to be called the Combat Studies Institute, had the idea that military historians might be used to investigate the historical and common sense of military doctrines as they were being written or, perhaps, even before. Our task required us to make ourselves into close students of contemporary foreign and defense issues, including innovations in military technology, in the military thought of other nations, and in any other matter of significance to the Army of the present. None of these ambitions could be said to have been very new. As I noted earlier, military history was until the twentieth century the dominating mode by which warfare was analyzed, if indeed any analysis was performed at all. Against our background of contemporary knowledge, we argued, our historical knowledge might once more prove itself as a useful means of analysis. I recall there was a great deal of enthusiastic talk at the time about what was called "historical mindedness" and references to the "historical mind," just as one might refer to the "legal mind" or the "scientific mind." The thought was that a certain frame of mind was imparted while preparing for a professional life in these other fields, so why not history? Indeed, the employment of military history in this way was very close to what Fuller and Liddell Hart thought they were doing in the interwar period. But there was no doubt, either, that several of us thought our historical souls were in danger. I was fairly certain I would never be admitted to the company of historians ever again.

But between this small group as I found it in the late 1970s and Fuller and Liddell Hart's circle between the wars were several important differences. Fuller and Liddell Hart had an agenda. We had none. For Liddell Hart perhaps even more than Fuller, being able to draw a straight line between what he has argued and what has been officially adopted was a matter of paramount importance. By contrast, when we received a problem, we studied it as comprehensively and objectively as possible and forwarded our findings without regard to any official positions then held. To my knowledge we never asked, nor were we ever told, whether "the Army" had a position on the question under review. Our attitude was that if our elders and betters did not want to know what we thought, they had better not ask us. Nor did we keep score on ourselves. We understood very well that we were not the only people being asked about these matters. We believed that the worth of what was being done would be evident over the long term.[14]

IN THE SCHOOL OF WAR

The formation of this group worked a subtle change on official military history as it was practiced then. I do not think we quite realized it at the time, but official military history was being "operationalized," for lack of a better word. We were conducting analyses of contemporary developments with the techniques and standards we had been taught as historians. We were not really in the business of applying history. We were really applying the historians themselves. I think that, in fact, was what Liddell Hart was actually attempting to do when he became entangled in military policy.

I did not really understand this distinction, oddly, until I left the staff college for an operational job at the headquarters of one of our joint commands. No one wanted to be lectured on history there. Things were moving too fast to retire to a classroom. Everyone's judgment was tested daily. In the case of some of my colleagues, the basis of their judgment was long field experience; in others, long experience at the national staff level. The basis of my judgment was a very long memory that was not entirely my own. When the in-box filled up, only good solutions counted. No one seemed to bother much with how one arrived at them. I discovered that staff work was interdisciplinary. No one mentality would ever be allowed to dominate it, nor, indeed, should it. But any staff work that occurs without a keen understanding of the historical foundation of the question under the glass is doomed to be stunted and less useful than it would be otherwise.

When I think of Liddell Hart in such a light, I believe he was asking too much of the history he wrote. When he expected his views to be adopted without cavil, he betrayed a fundamental misunderstanding not only of how modern historical knowledge worked but also of how modern bureaucratic government worked. He expected too direct a correlation between cause and effect, and he expected that the agency of change would always come in the dramatic form of a human being. But all too often routines and processes determined courses of official action. If the modern official historian means to traffic in this environment, he should not assume that this sort of work in these sorts of places will come to him naturally or automatically by virtue of his training. It does not.

I had occasion once to talk with an army officer who had served in Whitehall when Liddell Hart was at the zenith of his pseudo-official power. Every few days, he said, Basil would call up on the telephone, full of enthusiasm for this or that scheme, and go on at length. It was only necessary for the officer to reply occasionally "yes" or "hmm," "I see" or "most impressive." Then, having extinguished his enthusiasm, Liddell Hart would ring off. He always had something interesting to say, recalled this officer, but it was always rather remote from what he saw on his desk. When I asked him if he could remember just one thing from those conversations, he said no, he couldn't.

Years ago, C. P. Snow, later Lord Snow, wrote what I think must be the best description, drawn from his own long experience, of how policy is advanced in modern government. "One saw policy," Snow wrote, "shaped under one's eyes by a series of small decisions. (In fact, it was rare for policy to be clearly thought out, though some romantics or worshippers of 'great men' like to think so. Usually it built itself from a thousand small arrangements, ideas, compromises, bits of give-and-take. There was not much which was decisively changed by a human will.)"[15]

In his *Military Affairs* article Liddell Hart writes of the historian's responsibility toward his craft, and no historian would disagree. But I believe the military historian has an additional responsibility, one that does not much trouble the social historian or the medieval historian or the ancient historian. Military history distinguishes itself by the very intimate connection between thought and action. There is always the very real possibility that someone will actually be influenced by what one has written, and indeed that was what both Liddell Hart and Fuller wanted when both were at the height of their powers. But the exercise of influence is no proof of having achieved historical truth. Liddell Hart says nothing about his responsibility to those who listened to him or read his work and accepted its findings. A keen appreciation of that responsibility might well have encouraged a good deal more moderation on his part, just when he needed it the most.

Perhaps if Liddell Hart were with us today he would reconsider his position. He would see, I hope, that the practice of military history, whether in official or academic venues, has changed considerably in the last quarter-century and that we have learned (or remembered) a great deal about how to win for history the esteem it deserves and we need. Those of us who have been involved in these changes hope they are for the better, but we do not know for sure. Perhaps after a thousand small arrangements, ideas, compromises, bits of give-and-take, we will know how wrong we are.

Notes

1. Jay Luvaas, "The First British Official Historians," *Military Affairs* 26 (Summer 1962): 49–58.

2. William Siborne, *History of the Waterloo Campaign* (T. & W. Boone, 1848; London: Green, 1990), and Herbert T. Siborne, ed., *Waterloo Letters* (London: Cassell, 1891). See also John Keegan on Siborne and his contribution in *The Face of Battle* (New York: Viking Press, 1976), 120.

3. Luvaas, "The First British Official Historians," 51. The characterization is Luvaas's, and no one could disagree.

4. No history or official historical work in the United States has ever been published, but a widely available bound typescript, written by Stetson Conn, is a very good general view. Stetson Conn, "Historical Work in the United States Army, 1862–1954," U.S. Army Center of Military History, Washington DC, 1980.

5. Only a summary volume has been translated into English from the original Russian: Ivan de Bloch, *The Future of War in Its Technical, Economic and Political Relations*, trans. R. C. Long and with a conversation with the author by W. T. Stead and an introduction by Edwin D. Mead (Boston: World Peace Foundation, 1914). See also Michael Howard, "Men against Fire: The Doctrine of the Offensive in 1914," in *Makers of Modern Strategy from Machiavelli to the Nuclear Age*, ed. Peter Paret with the collaboration of Gordon A. Craig and Felix Gilbert (Princeton NJ: Princeton University Press, 1986), 51–526, for a view of Bloch in context.

6. U.S. War Department, Military Intelligence Division, *Reports of Military Observers Attached to the Armies in Manchuria during the Russo-Japanese War*, 4 vols. (Washington DC: Government Printing Office, 1906). See also John T. Greenwood, "The U.S. Army Military Observers with the

Japanese during the Russo-Japanese War, 1904–1905," *Army History*, Winter 1996.

7. Luvaas, "The First British Official Historians," 58.

8. As we shall see, Liddell Hart had been making this complaint for some time.

9. B. H. Liddell Hart, "Responsibility and Judgment in Historical Writing," *Military Affairs* 23 (Spring 1959): 35–36.

10. See David French, "'Official but Not History?': Sir James Edmonds and the Official History of the Great War," *Journal of the Royal United Services Institution for Defence Studies* 131 (March 1986): 58–63. See also John Mearsheimer, *Liddell Hart and the Weight of History* (Ithaca NY: Cornell University Press, 1988), 56–74, which contains a very valuable discussion on the evolution of Liddell Hart's judgments.

11. These remarks are based on my own reading of the Fuller–Liddell Hart correspondence at the Liddell Hart Centre for Military Archives, King's College, London. Fuller's remarks before his staff college students are recorded in Brian Holden Reid, *J. F. C. Fuller: Military Thinker* (New York: St. Martin's Press, 1987), 83.

12. Holden Reid, *J. F. C. Fuller*, 81–87.

13. Mearsheimer, *Liddell Hart*, 1 (facing).

14. I have written about this period elsewhere. See "War History and the History Wars: Establishing the Combat Studies Institute," *Public Historian* 10, no. 4 (1988): 65–81. However, Dr. Brooks Kleber, at the time the U.S. Army Training and Doctrine Command's command historian, was the author of the phrase "historical mindedness."

15. C. P. Snow, "The Light and the Dark," in *Strangers and Brothers* (New York: Charles Scribner's Sons, 1972), 244.

NINE. The Vietnam Syndrome

A Brief History

This essay addresses the origins, evolution, and consequences of the so-called Vietnam Syndrome, especially as it has influenced American military operations since the end of the war. The attacks on New York and Washington slightly more than a year ago and, indeed, events since then have made this subject rather less abstract than it might have been otherwise.

The United States was in shock for some time after the attacks of September 11, and what would be known as "the war on terror" was still in its first light. Our enemies had not yet shown themselves. No war had been declared in the constitutional way. No strategies had been revealed. But the scent of vengefulness hung in the air. The public seemed to assume that the United States would reply to these attacks, but no one was inclined to look very much beyond the immediate moment. When, later on, the war was announced—not declared—and given a name, it became clear that Washington planned more than a limited retaliation. Without specifying the strategic aims of the war—no Fourteen Points or Four Freedoms this time—leading American officials were quick to warn their fellow citizens that the war would last a good long time. That seemed to be a pretty good guess when we were taking so long to find an enemy. Clearly, a cruise missile strike would not assuage public anger.

As the initial shock dissipated and as the mass media broadcast guesses about the next military step, a certain question was never very far from the surface. Are the American people up to it? Can the Americans meet the demands of a new, protracted, and very unconventional struggle? Later on, will the Americans support the war as enthusiastically as they seem to support it now, or will that support slowly lose its edge?

The common point of reference for all these questions was the war in Vietnam, a war fought so long ago that it seems almost ancient now. But the influence of that war on the present opinion is assumed to be such that one might be forgiven for thinking the United States had hidden behind its oceanic walls ever since. Grenada, Panama, Beirut, Central America, the Balkans, Somalia, and even the Gulf War—none of these campaigns seem to have achieved the significance of the war in Vietnam. Only the memory of Vietnam is assumed to have had this kind of staying power, this capacity to influence our contemporary national policies. Are the American people up to it? This is a question that would not have been asked—indeed, was not asked—before the war in Vietnam.[1] This question, the body of assumptions upon which it is founded, and the effect the answer is supposed to exercise over American statecraft and American public sentiment are often referred to simply as the Vietnam Syndrome. I want to suggest that the Vietnam Syndrome has long outlived any real influence or usefulness it might have once had.

As with other such phrases, the Vietnam Syndrome has persisted because it has a certain elasticity. In its broadest sense the Vietnam Syndrome signifies the supposed reluctance of the people of the United States to support the employment of their armed forces in the service of their nation's foreign policy. An important, more recently fixed codicil of this loose collection of attitudes has to do with the time and cost of a given military action if it cannot be avoided: military action must be prompt, decisive, and as nearly cost-free as possible. The syndrome requires that few or preferably no casualties be taken. If those conditions are not met, the American public will insist on a prompt cessation of operations and an immediate withdrawal, without reference to its effect on American foreign policy. These notions constitute what might be regarded as the irreducible minimum of the Vietnam Syndrome. Of course, the phrase can be injected with a very wide range of additional meanings, depending on the argument it is meant to serve at the moment. Any attempt at a precise def-

IN THE SCHOOL OF WAR

inition rather defeats the purpose; the Vietnam Syndrome is not meant to serve as a thought but as a substitute for thought.

Among the claims to memory the twentieth century might make on the future, one seems to me to have been an extraordinary facility for cant, for the cheap, essentially meaningless political slogan. And it is their emptiness, their lack of meaning, that paradoxically make them especially pernicious. Almost half a century ago George Orwell warned that modern prose "consists less and less of *words* chosen for the sake of their meaning, and more of *phrases* tacked together like the sections of a prefabricated hen-house."[2]

The United States got a jump on the new century with "Remember the *Maine*," an exhortation to war against Spain inspired by what seems to have been a battleship's defective boiler rather than the act of sabotage it was believed to be at the time. No matter. In the Great War we heard the French call out at Verdun "Ils ne passeront pas!" (They shall not pass!). Both of these entries fall under the general category of war cries. They call frankly for retribution and little else. Once the urge is satisfied, they imply, everyone ought to go home. They make no contribution to political science.

The first great and particularly awful slogan of the century was *der Dolchstoss*, or "the stab in the back," often cast as an explanation of how Germany would have won the Great War if spineless politicians and weak-kneed civilians had only stuck it out, as German armies were supposedly doing in the trenches. *Der Dolchstoss* was infinitely expansible. The phrase was suffused with just the right mixture of failure, regret, guilt, betrayal, vengefulness, spite, envy, self-righteousness, and, yes, even hatred—all these emotions and more. Furthermore, the phrase "had legs"; it persisted in the political and public language. Hitler and his fellow criminals found the stab in the back myth very useful indeed when their turn to make their own contribution to national mythology came around during the 1930s.

Taking the prize for concision, deployment of meaning, and a very long public life, "Munich" will always come to mind, recalling Neville Chamberlain's "appeasement" of Hitler over Czechoslovakia in 1938. History has flogged Chamberlain ever since, and never again will Munich be known only as the principal city of Bavaria. Like the stab in the back slogan, "Munich" has staying power, and indeed the so-called lessons of Munich have been brandished several times lately—most recently over the direction U.S. policy should take toward Iraq.

Comparing the Munich Syndrome with the Vietnam Syndrome is instructive. Munich is used against those who do not act. The Vietnam Syndrome describes those who act too much, are disappointed by what their action produces, and then refuse to act more.[3] Munich is a metaphor for an event with known and largely agreed upon consequences. The Vietnam Syndrome has greater scope; it spans an entire decade. Munich works as a cautionary lesson—don't be intimidated or fooled by bullies—but the Vietnam Syndrome offers a kind of sad description for which few solutions seem to be available. Indeed, the use of the word "syndrome" imparts a medical tone, as if to suggest a disease. And that is not quite an accident.

The Vietnam Syndrome began its life in the 1960s as a diagnosis. In medical terminology a syndrome is a collection of symptoms whose patterns suggest a particular illness. These symptoms may be transient or temporary, and they respond to proper medical treatment. A syndrome that persists or takes on a chronic state is defined as a disorder and as such might be managed over the long term rather than cured.

The exact origins of the diagnosis are not entirely clear. One guess has the term originating as a kind of medical shorthand during the late 1960s among psychiatrists and psychologists of the Veterans Administration hospitals.[4] The public debut of the Vietnam Syndrome was in the *New York Times* for May 6, 1972, in an op-ed piece by one Dr. Chaim Shatan. Shatan was a director of psychoanalytic training at New York University. As a practicing psychoanalyst, Shatan had become interested in the nature, causes, and treatment of severe psychological shock, especially as these cases presented themselves among victims of Nazi atrocities during the Holocaust.

By the late 1960s Shatan was also an opponent of the war in Vietnam. At a university antiwar rally several Vietnam veterans approached Shatan, asking for his help. They complained of difficulty readjusting to civilian life after their combat tours. They did not expect a sympathetic hearing at the VA hospitals. They did not ask for therapy; they said they were "hurting" and just wanted to talk. So was born what came to be known as the "rap group," really only a collective therapy session by a new name.[5]

Before long Dr. Shatan was joined by another psychiatrist who was also interested in the nature and long-term effects of psychic trauma. Robert Jay Lifton taught at Yale and had served as a psychiatrist with the U.S. Air Force during the Korean War. Like Shatan, he also had come to oppose the Vietnam War. His research interests at the time focused on the psychological trauma experienced by the survivors of the atomic attack on Hiroshima. To Shatan and Lifton the victims of the Holocaust and of Hiroshima were special. The psychic traumas these patients had suffered so transcended the "normal range of human experiences" that their shock was capable of producing profound reactions. To Lifton such patients made up a "special contemporary group" whose experiences had created "special regenerative insight." Before long, Shatan and Lifton were beginning to think of the veterans in their rap groups in the same light as victims of Hiroshima and the Holocaust.[6]

To these analysts it seemed possible to think of the veterans as new and different sorts of patients, those whose psychological illness was the result of the stresses they experienced in war. Furthermore, these analysts found it possible to argue that a war whose origins, conduct, and expected outcome were so controversial would engender more psychological casualties than wars of a more straightforward kind.[7] None of this was correct, but during the 1970s some facts appear to have been inconvenient in American public discourse.[8]

One symptom of the Post-Vietnam Syndrome was advertised as

new and dangerous: these traumatic reactions were delayed, not showing themselves for months or even years after the traumatic event. Further, these reactions could supposedly occur without warning at any time. The *New York Times* published a story in 1975 of a case in which a Vietnam veteran was convicted of murdering his wife. The veteran's defense was that he had been startled awake by a combat flashback and had instinctively pulled the gun from under his pillow and defended himself. An unsympathetic jury gave him life in prison. Citing statistics gathered during what he called a "comprehensive series of stories" in *Penthouse* magazine, the journalist Tom Wicker informed the readers of his column in the *New York Times* that as many as 500,000 of the 2.5 million Vietnam veterans had attempted suicide, conveying the impression that every vet was deranged.[9] News like this routinely appeared during the 1970s, and Hollywood discovered Rambo as well.

Throughout the decade the American public was engaged in highly complex negotiations with the memory of the war in Vietnam. The process by which the Vietnam veteran became a metaphor for the nation as a whole began very soon after President Nixon ordered the withdrawal of American forces. In January 1970 Lifton and several other prominent psychiatrists were called to testify before the Senate on the care and treatment of wounded Vietnam veterans. Lifton devoted his testimony to the "psychological predicament of the Vietnam Veteran." Although Lifton did not employ the term "Post-Vietnam Syndrome," his testimony leaves little doubt that he considered his patients' complaints quite real, uniquely created by combat experiences.[10]

The finer technical points of Lifton's testimony are of less significance here than his broader argument; it was, simply put, that the United States itself was suffering from a collective kind of Post-Vietnam Syndrome, composed of symptoms that mimicked those of his individual patients—guilt, resentment, and alienation. "The Vietnam Veteran serves as a psychological crucible of the entire country's doubts and misgivings about the war," Lifton told the senators.[11]

This was not the first occasion a medical diagnosis had slipped past the boundaries of its scientific origins to enter common language. In Great Britain after the First World War "shell shock," although repudiated by the physician who coined the term, became a very public diagnosis, freighted with any number of extrascientific connotations. After that war leading British psychologists observed, just as did Robert Lifton, that although the term with which each became associated was medically useless, the terms had nevertheless captured the public's imagination.[12] However, not even shell shock rose quite to the level of national cliché, as the Post-Vietnam Syndrome would.

To finish this skein of the story, debates were to continue in medical circles for the rest of the decade over the legitimacy of the Post-Vietnam Syndrome. The debates were more or less resolved in 1980 with a new third edition of the psychiatric profession's diagnostic guide, the *Diagnostic and Statistical Manual of Mental Disorders*, or DSM-III. After an intense public lobbying campaign by Shatan, Lifton, and others DSM-III included a category of illness now designated "post-traumatic stress disorder," or PTSD.[13] A new chapter in the history of modern psychiatric disease classifications had been written. Well before then, however, the Vietnam Syndrome had made good its escape from the medical world and had been enlisted for nonscientific duty.

By 1970 public opinion polls showed a majority of Americans favoring withdrawal from Vietnam. Indeed, popular support for Richard Nixon's presidential administration was partly contingent upon U.S. withdrawal from Vietnam. Richard J. Barnet found it possible to write in 1970, without reservation: "It is safe to say that there is no one in the United States who is *for* the Vietnam war. . . . Although the war is far from over, the 'lessons' of Vietnam are filling volumes. The whole direction of American foreign policy for the next generation will depend upon which lessons are accepted as the new orthodoxy."[14]

When this was written, the United States had already started its slow retreat. President Nixon would not be able to make good on his campaign promise to abolish conscription for another year.

The war was still running, and it would continue to run, past the last American troops who left in April 1973 and on to that day in late April 1975, when NVA tanks crashed through the gates at the Presidential Palace in Saigon. On that day the last Americans were killed in Vietnam: two Marine corporals, Charles McMahon, 22, and Darwin Judge, 19. The war had sunk from view in America. Contrary to Professor Barnet's view, not many people seemed very interested in the lessons of the war.

"To the surprise of many observers," historian George Herring wrote several years later, "the traumatic climax of the Vietnam War in 1975 did not provoke a great national debate on what had gone wrong. Quite the contrary, the first postwar years were marked by a conspicuous silence on the subject, as though the war had not happened."[15] Indeed, the American people had already delivered their verdict on this war. In 1971 public opinion polls showed slightly more than 60 percent of Americans favoring the withdrawal of all U.S. troops from Vietnam. Four years later, during the week Saigon fell to the North Vietnamese, 53 percent of those polled still thought the United States should "help governments that might be overthrown by communist-backed forces."[16] Opinion had settled into what seemed to be a permanent divide: slightly more than half of all Americans supported their government's foreign policies, even if those policies meant using military force.[17] So it was not the use of military force in general that had fallen from favor; it was the *unsuccessful* use of military force.

That was public opinion. Elite political opinion was a good deal more wary of military commitments abroad. Congressional opposition to the war manifested itself most forcefully through votes on defense budgets. In 1970 defense expenditures consumed about 40 percent of all government expenditures. By 1976 (the vote was for FY 1977) that outlay had dropped to about 24 percent, a smaller proportion than any budget since before the Second World War.[18] Rather than fighting a futile delaying action against public and congressional sentiment, Secretary of Defense Melvin Laird tried to manage the inevitable reductions. His ambition was to posture the defense establishment for a rebuilding program several years hence, when the disappointments of the war might be muted.[19]

What public commentators were fond of calling the "process of national healing" had to compete with the Watergate scandals at home and a world that continued to make demands on official American attention. The Nixon administration had already promulgated what was called the "Nixon Doctrine," calling for a retreat from foreign obligations. This was just as well, for Congress passed the Church Amendment in 1973, forbidding any more Americans in combat in Southeast Asia. That was followed a year later by the War Powers Act, in which Congress asserted its constitutional powers by severely limiting presidential authority to employ military force abroad. The United States drew back from the global activism that President Kennedy had proclaimed so famously in his inaugural address.[20] Historians since have argued that, by contrast, the five years after the fall of Saigon constituted "the greatest deviation of U.S. policy from the basic . . . containment strategy of the past 35 years."[21]

Any war that takes as long to end as this one did defies those who like their history neat. How public figures interpreted the lessons of this war depended importantly on preconceptions. What we would recognize today as an objective view of the war—its origins, its conduct, and its outcome—was nowhere to be seen. This view would necessarily have included not only an appreciation for events as they transpired but also a clear-eyed reading of American public sentiment. Neither of those seemed to be in good supply.

Richard Nixon did more than any other single public figure to redefine the Vietnam Syndrome from diagnosis to political slogan. Five years after resigning from office during the Watergate scandals, Nixon published *The Real War*, in which he used "The Vietnam Syndrome" as a title for one of his chapters. Here he wrote:

> Unless the United States shakes the false lessons of Vietnam and puts "the Vietnam Syndrome" behind it, we will forfeit

the security of our allies and eventually our own. This is the real lesson of Vietnam—not that we should abandon power, but that unless we learn to use it effectively to defend our interests, the tables of history will be turned against us and all we believe in.[22]

By one count the United States employed its armed forces abroad in support of its foreign policy objectives more than 215 times between 1945 and 1976. This accounting does not include the Korean or Vietnam wars.[23] By this standard American military operations declined between the end of Vietnam and the beginning of the 1980s, when Nixon wrote this. The Soviets did indeed intervene in Angola's civil war during this period, but so did the United States—until Congress learned of the covert operations we were conducting. It is also true that President Carter and his administration were hesitant to react to the seizure of hostages at the embassy in Tehran and that the United States' covert attempt to rescue them misfired badly. Nor, at virtually the same time, was the United States capable of preventing the Soviet Union's invasion of Afghanistan. Even at this remove one wonders how the United States could have found a way to keep the Soviets at home. How, in this light, might one see the United States' reaction—or, more exactly, lack of reaction—to the Soviet Union's invasion of Czechoslovakia? These foreign policy reverses said more about official hesitancy and poor planning than a strategic retreat induced by a national malaise.[24] The Carter administration may have conceived its policies, thinking that it was reflecting the wishes of the American people; if so, it was going to pay for such miscalculation after the fact by losing the next election.

This was by no means the first time policy makers had projected their illusions onto American public opinion as rationale for policy, nor would it be the last. The new presidential administration of Ronald Reagan came to office in 1980 on a promise, among others, to "restore the military strength of the United States as quickly as possible." For this task the new president selected Caspar W. Weinberger to serve as secretary of defense and George W. Shultz to serve as the new secretary of state.

These two worldly, experienced, and strong-willed men had very different views of American military power. Shultz was very much the activist. To Shultz every international problem was in some respect an American problem, and calculated international engagement was Shultz's answer to the Carter administration's timidity. Not that Weinberger was a pacifist, far from it, but he disliked using military power as an adjunct to diplomacy. The differences between the two cabinet officers turned not on whether military power should be employed but on how, when, and to what purpose.

In retrospect, Shultz's and Weinberger's views were not so far apart in practice. Shultz was increasingly frustrated by a resurgence of terrorism in the Middle East, terrorism that seemed to benefit by the acquiescence or fearful tolerance of leading powers. He favored American participation in a multinational peacekeeping force that was deployed into Lebanon in 1982. Weinberger was most interested in rebuilding the armed forces. Contingency operations, peacekeeping or "nation-building" operations, and expeditionary operations could only dissipate American military power as far as he was concerned. Weinberger thought the Beirut expedition was poorly framed, its objectives too vague for practical use. For Weinberger, the attack on the Marine barracks the following year was the inevitable result of sending American troops on "show-the-flag" missions.

Furthermore, in the Reagan White House a third party often worked at cross-purposes to both the secretary of defense and the secretary of state—the national security advisor, Robert McFarlane. Weinberger was especially critical of McFarlane and his staff, all of whom he thought were "even more militant" than the staff at the State Department. To Weinberger, the NSC staff spent "most of their time thinking up ever more wild adventures for our troops."[25] All of them seemed to regard their fellow citizens as unreliable or at least as holding opinions so variable as to make any foreign policy initiative a risky proposition. To McFarlane and one of his most energetic staffers, Lt. Col. Oliver North, that meant covert operations. Their own covert operations.

Both Shultz and Weinberger would eventually take their arguments to the public. In October 1984 Shultz delivered an address in Manhattan in which he argued that the United States must "prevent and deter future terrorist acts. . . . The public must understand before the fact that occasions will come when their government must act before each and every fact is known—and the decisions cannot be tied to the opinion polls."[26] The cycle between national decision and national action was too fast to accommodate democratic participation, Shultz seemed to be arguing; you have to leave it up to me.

Weinberger answered Shultz the following month in a speech before the National Press Club that he called "The Uses of National Power."[27] He proposed six "tests" for the United States to pass before committing American troops to combat. The speech quickly and famously became known as the "Weinberger Doctrine," and because it has been variously interpreted and somewhat distorted over the past decade and a half, Weinberger's "tests" are worth repeating:

1. Our vital interests must be at stake.
2. The issues involved are so important for the future of the United States and our allies that we are prepared to commit enough forces to win.
3. We have clearly defined political and military objectives, which we must secure.
4. We have sized our forces to achieve our objectives.
5. We have some reasonable assurance of the support of the American people.
6. U.S. forces are committed to combat only as a last resort.[28]

To George Shultz, the Weinberger Doctrine was anathema. "This was the Vietnam syndrome in spades, and a complete abdication of the duties of leadership," he wrote in his memoirs. Ignoring the salient fact that in the American system of government, cabinet officers do not unilaterally promulgate fighting doctrines or indeed doctrines of any sort, Shultz speculated that Weinberger had been co-opted by the Joint Chiefs of Staff. The JCS, Shultz thought, held a "deep philosophical opposition to using our military for counterterrorist operations."[29]

However, if one were to inventory American expeditionary operations in the last two decades of the twentieth century, one might conclude that the United States was recovering handily from any syndrome it might have suffered. In addition to the Carter administration's attempt to rescue hostages in Iran in 1980, the Marines had been sent into Lebanon in 1983. Two days after a truck bomb destroyed the Marine barracks in Beirut, killing more than 240 people, the United States invaded the Caribbean island of Grenada, a dagger pointed at the heart of Trinidad and Tobago. In 1986 the United States launched strikes against Libya in reprisal for terrorist actions in Europe. In the following year the United States agreed to flag all tankers in the Persian Gulf during the "tanker war" between Iran and Iraq. And, as the decade drew to a close, the United States invaded Panama, overthrew the government, and installed another. All the while, the United States was covertly supporting the Afghan revolt against Soviet occupation. Not one of these operations adhered strictly to the Weinberger Doctrine's six tests; indeed, several of them directly violated Weinberger's principle requiring an unambiguous objective. Such accountings are always somewhat subjective, of course, but it seems to me the United States was not exactly quiescent during this period.[30]

The next, perhaps the last, variant of the Vietnam Syndrome appeared in the form of what has been called the Powell Doctrine. Colin Powell had served as one of Secretary Weinberger's military assistants before rising, eventually, to official fame as chairman of the Joint Chiefs of Staff during the Gulf War. Indeed, Powell was with Weinberger when the secretary delivered his speech at the press club. Although Powell's doctrine and Weinberger's are often spoken of as though they are the same, Powell's views as chairman evolved away from Weinberger's dogma and toward

Shultz's flexibility.[31] Powell's first major operation as chairman of the JCS was the invasion of Panama. How he depicts that operation in his memoirs is telling: "The lessons I absorbed from Panama confirmed all my convictions over the preceding twenty years, since the days of doubt over Vietnam. Have a clear political objective and stick to it. Use all the force necessary, and do not apologize for going in big if that is what it takes." All these lessons have to do with how to employ military force, not whether to use military force. This variant, like the original, also assumes that the object in war does not change while the war is being fought. So to Powell the objective did not much matter so long as it was clear and attainable. The Powell Doctrine did not seem to leave much room for Shultz-style operations, but that did not prove to be the case. Powell was not averse to using the armed forces; he simply wanted the forces to be so powerful, regardless of the mission, that there was no danger of failure.[32]

Just before retiring from military service, Powell approved a new joint doctrine that had a great deal more in common with Shultz's views.[33] After the Gulf War the orthodox American-style operation was in danger of being subsumed under the weight of emphasis on what were being called "operations other than war." Indeed, the Gulf War was beginning to look a bit old-fashioned in the middle 1990s. By then Powell was given to saying that decisive military victories were rare in the modern world and that the most an armed force could do was to ensure a conflict ended on terms that diplomacy could make favorable. Although he claimed to be guided by the "lessons" of Vietnam, he had no real reply when he and Madeleine Albright, then U.S. ambassador to the UN, were arguing over the intervention in Bosnia. "What's the point of having this superb military that you are always talking about if we can't use it?" she asked. Powell answered by citing the "more than two dozen times" American armed forces had been used in the past three years—"for war, peacekeeping, disaster relief, and humanitarian assistance." After his retirement from military life Powell would write, "There are times when American lives must be risked and lost. Foreign policy cannot be paralyzed by the prospect of casualties. . . . To provide a 'symbol' or a 'presence' is not good enough." The only American strategic doctrine in effect might just as well have been phrased this way: circumstances define action.[34]

One former policy maker who has been keeping watch calculates that "the pace of interventions has, if anything, picked up" in the 1990s.[35] After the Gulf War the United States intervened in Bosnia, Somalia, Haiti, Rwanda, and Kosovo, not to mention actions associated with the aftermath of the Gulf War itself— enforcing "no-fly" zones over Iraq for almost a decade as well as relief operations in northern Iraq. President Bush might have been too late with his cheer after the Gulf War that the Vietnam Syndrome had been "licked, once and for all." As a doctrinal basis for international action, the Vietnam Syndrome had been shredded already by the history of the 1980s.

The most persistent symptom of the Vietnam Syndrome has turned on the question of American casualties. This question alone has been made to serve on occasion as a crude measurement of success—sometimes employed as an argument against action, sometimes invoked after the fact in recrimination. As an instrument of statecraft, however, the casualty list is less than effective and sometimes self-defeating. The United States' withdrawal from Somalia after the killing of eighteen soldiers during the Mogadishu debacle of 1993 is often cited as an example of the fecklessness of American policy makers and public alike—the "cut and run" mentality that supposedly had its origins in 1973. In point of fact, we have seen accusations like this since the very beginning of the twentieth century. After the Boer War a French general observed that the British Army was suffering what he called "Acute Transvaalitis," which he defined as an abnormal dread of losses on the battlefield.[36] He thought of this dread as a "ravaging microbe" that fed upon the "floods of sniveling sentimentalism then in vogue."[37]

At the other extreme, however, one can find a case that seems to offer proof of a rather stolid acceptance of the butcher's bill. That was in the summer of 1990, when classified estimates of casualties in an anticipated war with Iraq were leaked to the press. These numbers were revealed well before the United States had committed itself to nothing more than defending Saudi Arabia against further Iraqi aggression. Simulations of an American offensive against prepared Iraqi positions had run out estimates of thirty thousand American casualties.

What happened when these estimates were leaked is telling. Nothing happened. The American public reacted not at all. Strategic planning proceeded at the normal pace, scheduled deployments were executed without pause, and lodgments in the operational areas were established at the necessary times and places. No one raised the casualty flag. Operations Desert Shield and Desert Storm were conducted more or less as planned. The Vietnam Syndrome was nowhere to be seen, except in the White House, where President Bush was promising the American public, "This will not be another Vietnam. This will not be a protracted, drawn-out war."[38]

If the Vietnam Syndrome has any life left at all, it is only in public discourse. Even then it is a defective medium for the expression of what are very complex public views. American policy makers no doubt had a catalog of reasons for withdrawing our troops after the fight in Mogadishu, but if they believed they were accurately reflecting the opinions of most Americans, they were wrong. Opinion polls showed at the time and later a decided public tendency to escalate, not withdraw, when Americans suffered casualties. No "Acute Transvaalitis" here.

This lack of correspondence between the views of the policy maker and the citizen extends to other, broader questions of American foreign policy. Recent studies have shown an American public that is a good deal more amenable to foreign aid than policy makers had long supposed. Most Americans also seem to support international engagement as much as ever. Contrary to official wisdom in the United States and indeed elsewhere around the world, most Americans are not interested in assuming the role of global hegemony. As for the "humanitarian operations" that were supposed to have fallen into disrepute since Mogadishu, the contrary is true. Americans do support such missions, especially if they are under United Nations authority.[39] All of this suggests that if we are to understand why some operations work and others do not, why some win support and others do not, we shall have to go well beyond casual guesses about domestic support and the influence of an old war. And yet even today one would have no trouble at all finding responsible officials and public intellectuals using the Vietnam Syndrome as a tool of argument.[40]

We may now ask ourselves, at a generation's remove, Did the Vietnam Syndrome make any real difference in the conduct of American statecraft? If we could somehow factor out the Vietnam Syndrome for a moment, would the American domestic temper, which is the real engine of our foreign policies, have pointed us in the same directions at about the same time? I think a case might be made that there would have been differences in degree, minor variations, but not in kind. No cliché should ever exercise much influence over a nation's affairs.

Such questions are, of course, no longer of theoretical interest only. So it is just as well that the power of the Vietnam Syndrome has faded to that of a rhetorical artifact.

As the metaphor is no longer capable of bearing too much intellectual or emotional weight, history has moved along in its unsentimental way. Perhaps this new century has a full supply of its own grand clichés, waiting to be requisitioned—but I hope not.

Notes

1. The United States' earlier wars had certainly provoked controversy and resistance, but on those occasions public resistance had a different shape. Only during our Civil War and during our brief involvement in the Great War were there any significant resistance movements, and none of these was strong enough to affect American national strategy or military policy in any substantive way. Put another way, until the war in Vietnam, American antiwar movements were fringe movements.

2. George Orwell, "Politics and the English Language," in *The Collected Essays, Journalism and Letters of George Orwell*, vol. 4, *In Front of Your*

Nose, 1945–1950, ed. Sonia Orwell and Ian Angus (New York: Harcourt Brace Jovanovich, Inc., 1968), 129. George Ball, undersecretary of state in the Kennedy and Johnson presidencies and an important figure in early planning for the war, found it necessary to write an opinion piece in the *New York Times* deploring the development of a new stab in the back thesis for the defeat in Vietnam. See George Ball, "Block that Vietnam Myth," *New York Times*, September 30, 1990, 4. The date is significant: debates on the American intervention in the Gulf were then under way.

3. Arnold R. Isaacs is among the many others who have made this comparison. Isaacs points out that North Vietnam's prime minister, Pham Van Dong, was "haunted by a Munich analogy" as well, vowing never again to allow himself to be misled because of unwise diplomatic concessions. Arnold R. Isaacs, *Vietnam Shadows: The War, Its Ghosts, and Its Legacy* (Baltimore MD: Johns Hopkins University Press, 1997), 67. See also Jeffrey Record, *Perils of Reasoning by Historical Analogy: Munich, Vietnam and American Use of Force*, Air War College Occasional Paper, no. 4 (Maxwell AFB, Alabama Air University Press, March 1998).

4. Ben Shepard, *A War of Nerves: Soldiers and Psychiatrists in the Twentieth Century* (Cambridge MA: Harvard University Press, 2001), 357, offers this impressive list of symptoms: apathy, cynicism, alienation, depression, mistrust and expectation of betrayal, inability to concentrate, insomnia, nightmares, restlessness, uprootedness, and impatience.

5. Chaim Shatan, "Post-Vietnam Syndrome," *New York Times*, May 6, 1972, 35.

6. See Shephard's excellent discussion on the ideas of Shatan and Lifton in *A War of Nerves*, 356–67. Lifton's earlier work, *Death in Life: Survivors of Hiroshima* (Chapel Hill: University of North Carolina Press, 1991) is quoted here. A much less generous interpretation of Lifton's work appears in D. G. Burkett and Glenna Whitley's *Stolen Valor: How the Vietnam Generation Was Robbed of Its Heroes and Its History* (Dallas TX: Verity Press, 1998), 141–61.

7. U.S. Congress, Senate, Committee on Labor and Human Resources, *Oversight of Medical Care of Veterans Wounded in Vietnam*, Hearings before the Subcommittee on Veterans Affairs, 91st Cong., 2nd sess., January 27, 1970, 498–99 (hereafter cited as Lifton Testimony). Lifton drew precisely this corollary in testimony before the Senate.

8. Several contemporary studies are summarized in Burkett and Whitley, *Stolen Valor*, 141–51. Wars have long known psychological casualties. Modern military medicine had itself hardly come of age before taking notice of such casualties. From the Russo-Japanese War onward, the medical services of most advanced armies struggled to understand psychological distress due to combat. The psychological casualties produced by the Vietnam War were

not inordinately high; by one count, they amounted to roughly half of those produced by World War II American troops—a fact reported once more in 1975 by David Lamb, "Vietnam Veterans Melting into Society," *Los Angeles Times*, November 3, 1975. See also Capt. R. L. Richards's precocious article "Mental and Nervous Diseases in the Russo-Japanese War," *Military Surgeon* 26 (1910): 177–93. For a brief introduction to this subject see my "Shell Shock," *American Heritage* 41, no. 4 (1991): 75–87.

9. Tom Wicker, "The Vietnam Disease," *New York Times*, May 27, 1975, 29.

10. Robert Jay Lifton, *Home from the War: Vietnam Veterans, neither Victims nor Executioners* (New York: Simon and Schuster, 1973).

11. Lifton Testimony, 496, 507.

12. United Kingdom, Parliament, *Report of the War Office Committee of Enquiry into "Shell Shock"* (London: HMSO, 1922), A-2. The most extensive examination of the concept of shell shock, conducted by the Southard Committee, concluded that "shell shock" was a grievous misnomer but "is the popular or vulgar term in general use" and that therefore the term had to be employed in public discourse.

13. Spiller, "Shell Shock," 75–87.

14. Richard J. Barnet, "The Security of Empire," in *After Vietnam: The Future of American Foreign Policy*, ed. Robert W. Gregg and Charles W. Kegley Jr. (Garden City NY: Doubleday & Company, Inc., 1971), 32.

15. George C. Herring, "American Strategy in Vietnam: The Postwar Debate," *Military Affairs* 46, no. 2 (1982): 57.

16. The Gallup Organization, *The Gallup Poll Public Opinion 1937–1997* (Wilmington DE: Scholarly Resources CD-ROM, 2000), 468, 2316–17.

17. Indeed, only 26 percent of those polled in May 1970 would approve using U.S. troops to defend Berlin. This *Time*–Lewis Harris Poll is quoted in Graham Allison, Ernest May, and Adam Yarmolinsky, "Limits to Intervention," in Gregg and Kegley, *After Vietnam*, 49–68.

18. The force structure of all the services declined accordingly. From 1970 to 1974 the Air Force was reduced by 59 squadrons; the Army was reduced from 23 to 16 divisions; the Navy lost 481 ships. These figures, authorizations for FY 1977, are conveniently summarized in John Lewis Gaddis, *Strategies of Containment: A Critical Appraisal of Postwar American National Security Policy* (New York: Oxford University Press, 1982), 322–23.

19. So remembered Henry Kissinger in *The White House Years* (Boston: Houghton Mifflin, 1979), 32.

20. The phrase is Gaddis's in *Strategies of Containment*, 205.

21. Douglas Pike and Benjamin Ward, "Losing and Winning Abroad: Korea and Vietnam as Successes," *Washington Quarterly*, Summer 1987, 77–85.

22. Richard Nixon, *The Real War* (New York: Warner Books, 1980), 122–23.

23. Barry M. Blechman et al., *Force without War: U.S. Armed Forces as a Political Instrument* (Washington DC: Brookings Institution, 1978), 38 and passim.

24. One might even compare this emergency with the seizure of the intelligence-gathering vessel USS *Pueblo* by the North Koreans in January 1968. That incident coincided with the Tet Offensive in South Vietnam. The United States was decisively engaged in fighting there, of course, but it might be difficult to argue that the United States was reluctant to exercise its power elsewhere in the world. The ultimate safety of the crew was a good and sufficient reason to talk a way out of the incident, as indeed occurred.

25. Caspar W. Weinberger, *Fighting for Peace: Seven Critical Years in the Pentagon* (New York: Warner Books, 1990), 159.

26. George Shultz, *Turmoil and Triumph: My Years as Secretary of State* (New York: Charles Scribner's Sons, 1993), 648.

27. The text of this speech forms the appendix of Weinberger's *Fighting for Peace*, 433.

28. Ibid., 402.

29. Shultz, *Turmoil and Triumph*, 649–50.

30. Record, *Perils of Reasoning*, 13, 18.

31. Colin Powell with Joseph Persico, *My American Journey* (New York: Random House), 293. When Weinberger gave his speech, Powell remembered being concerned that these fixed tests might "lead potential enemies to look for loopholes."

32. Ibid., 420–21.

33. For a different view see Record's excellent analysis in *Perils of Reasoning*, 25.

34. Powell, *My American Journey*, 256. See Charles A. Stevenson, "The Evolving Clinton Doctrine on the Use of Force," *Armed Forces & Society* 22, no. 4 (1996): 515–17.

35. Richard Haas, *Interventions: The Use of American Military Force in the Post–Cold War World* (Washington DC: A Carnegie Endowment Book, 1994), 21.

36. See "Major Jette," "The Dread of Incurring Losses on the Battle-Field and the Essential Elements of the Offensive," trans. Col. R. H. Wilson, *Journal of the Military Services Institution of the United States* 51 (1912): 330–40, esp. 340.

37. Joseph C. Arnold, "French Tactical Doctrine, 1870–1914," *Military Affairs* 42, no. 2 (1978): 61–7, esp. 63–64.

38. See Bush's remark in John Mueller, *Public Opinion in the Gulf War* (Chicago: University of Chicago Press, 1994), 45.

39. Steven Kull, I. M. Destler, and Clay Ramsay, *The Foreign Policy Cap: How Policymakers Misread the Public* (College Park MD: Center for International and Security Studies at the University of Maryland, 1997), iii–iv and passim.

40. See the persistence of this "gap" admirably demonstrated in Ronald Brownstein, "Vietnam Is No Longer Part of Iraq Equation," *Los Angeles Times*, September 22, 2002, 1; Charles Moskos, "Our Will to Fight Depends on Who Is Willing to Die," *Wall Street Journal Online*, March 20, 2002; and Henry Kissinger, "The Long Shadow of Vietnam," http://www.newsweek.com, May 1, 2000.

TEN. In the Shadow of the Dragon

Doctrine and the U.S. Army after Vietnam

I n any modern army's hierarchy of professional concerns, military doctrine stands at a second or third order of importance. At the U.S. Army's staff college today students are badgered into memorizing a militarized version of the great chain of being, in which a nation's grand strategy is supposed to set the terms of reference for military strategy, which in turn dictates the character of its military doctrines.[1] Some actually believe this. Orthodoxy tells us further that these doctrines are meant to guide and often to prescribe the manner in which our armed forces will fight.[2] So defined, it is held that doctrine answers the straightforward and practical demands of soldiering and makes it more than possible for a modern American soldier to pass through an entire career never asking any more of doctrine.

But for both students and practitioners of war, doctrine can be made to answer more demands than this. An Army regulation dating from 1965 characterizes doctrine as "the best available thought that can be defended by reason."[3] The image is highly gratifying to contemplate, as are most things fantastic. As a practical matter, however, military doctrine possesses certain properties and behaves much like any other complex, evolving set of ideas. It does not evolve with quite the stately progress that would please theoreticians or romantics, who would impose upon doctrine a structure or meaning as if it were a self-contained body of thought, quarantined from the world in which it is meant to work. This would not be doctrine but dogma.

Military doctrines, fighting doctrines, always have been expressions of their time and place, an artifact in the mental life of a fighting organization. Any armed force operates in accordance with a conception of war that has been formed as a consequence of its history, the state of military knowledge available at the time, the material and technical assets at hand, the objectives to which the force expects to be committed, and, certainly not least, the caliber of those who must attempt to give it life in battle.

Although modern soldiers expect their doctrines to be explicit, professionally authoritative, and officially sanctioned, historically the doctrines under which soldiers fought were rarely so encompassing, prescriptive, or explicit as they are today. Premodern doctrines are best regarded as loose collections of military folkways, "tricks of the trade" handed down by the vets to recruits on the march, in the saddle, or across the bivouac fires. For much the greater part of American military history until this century, fighting doctrines were mostly implied. Soldiers depended for guidance upon what today we would call drill manuals, if they were guided at all.

Retrospectively, one may deduce an army's implied doctrine from how it organizes, disposes, trains, and equips itself. Indeed, this sort of analysis is necessary—to take but one example—in order to understand how the U.S. Army operated against Native American tribes after the Civil War, for there was no doctrine of any kind, and even the drill manuals then in existence were founded upon orthodox European forms of war. Expediency reigned supreme, and if lessons from field operations were passed along, they were conveyed in the most informal and irregular fashion. Soldiers at the time would not have recognized this collection of fighting techniques as doctrine, implied or not.[4] Not until after the First World War was the nature and purpose of fighting doctrine fixed in America as a genuine subclass of military knowledge. It was during the next fifty years that doctrine in its present identity emerged. So from its beginnings American military doctrine has described a rough and twisting path from military folkways toward its contemporary forms. Even so, the most profound changes in the nature and functions of American military doctrine are of very recent vintage. The proximate cause of these changes was America's war in Vietnam.[5]

How an army recovers from a lost war, if indeed it does, is an abiding question in military history, and it is one of some importance to contemporary armies as well. Hard experience has shown that armies must strike a balance between past and future if they are to be prepared for their next war. That experience has also shown that armies, inherently conservative institutions that they are, commonly overvalue their past at the expense of progress. Ancestor worship did much to defeat the French when they fought the Prussians in 1870. The new-model Imperial Japanese Army of 1904–5 achieved an unexpected harmony between tradition and modernity during its encounter with the Imperial Russian Army. As for the Russians in that war, the only discernible effect seems to have been to accentuate the rottenness. Scattered throughout history we can see the wreckage of armies that learned nothing from their experiences, or learned badly, or learned too late.[6]

Of course, some armies do learn from their experiences and are defeated anyway. Here is where the German Army wins good reviews despite having lost every war since 1870. Perhaps Martin van Creveld had the Wehrmacht in mind when he wrote in *Fighting Power*: "Though military excellence is inconceivable without victory, victory is by no means the sole criterion of military excellence. A small army may be overwhelmed by a larger one. Confronted with impossible political and economic odds, a qualitatively superior force may go down in defeat through no fault of its own."[7] But history has a different, brutal, and unforgiving standard: the standard does not award points for stylish conduct, does not insist that an army learn all there is to learn but only enough for victory. And even the most victorious armies must beware, for no sooner is a victory won than the problem renews and reshapes itself, as the French Army would discover in May 1940.[8] Always there is another war, another test, waiting somewhere in the history of the future, waiting to pass judgment on an army's readiness to fight.

For the U.S. Army of the present day, that test revealed itself after years of waiting in the form of the Persian Gulf War. If the

Gulf War was not quite the test that the Army expected to face, a climactic European defense against a Soviet offensive, still it would have to suffice. And suffice it certainly did for President George Bush, among others, who shortly after the war told an audience that victory offered the nation an opportunity to "kick the Vietnam syndrome."[9] Of course, the allies had accomplished their mission handily, but the opportunity of which President Bush spoke was understood by many as the most important dividend of the Gulf War. Many Americans saw the United States' performance in the Gulf War as a deliverance from two decades of struggle against the bitter memories of defeat in Vietnam. In the month following the defeat of the Iraqi Army public opinion polls gave President Bush the highest approval ratings ever received by a serving president, and the armed forces won the highest confidence rating any American institution had received since such polls were taken.[10]

The history of the U.S. Army after Vietnam has yet to be written, but its traces have been drawn in a number of works, some of which are written in the breathless, now-it-can-be-told tones favored by journalists and other literary performers. This body of writing conveys something less than the balanced view one hopes history will eventually produce.[11] In the heady aftermath of the Gulf War American Army officers were not reluctant to pass judgment on what they had accomplished. Indeed, one could argue that for American Army officers of a certain age, the redemptive quality of that war far outweighed their victory over the Army of Iraq. Inside the Army, any suggestion that the Army's performance was less than sterling was viewed as rank disloyalty, or at least unnecessarily troublesome. Instead, the Army produced a quick history of the war whose chief attribute was a drumbeat of triumphalism.[12]

None of this is so surprising. What is more surprising, perhaps, is the idiom in which this chorus of self-satisfaction was expressed. Like their president and commander in chief, American soldiers routinely evoked the Vietnam War in invidious comparison with what they had accomplished in the Gulf. One senior officer observed that "the genesis of the victory in the Gulf was Vietnam" and the commitment of those career officers in the generation after Vietnam who said, "Never again. I will never let that happen to my army again."[13] Set these remarks against those of another officer, spoken nearly twenty-five years before, and one may appreciate the depth of feeling that underscores these attitudes. Said that earlier officer: "I'll be damned if I permit the United States Army, its institutions, its doctrines, and its traditions to be destroyed just to win this lousy war."[14]

The Army very nearly was destroyed. Since the end of the Vietnam War, the most quarrelsome and emotional debate has animated appraisals of the war's origins, conduct, and outcome. So it is all the more remarkable that there is unanimity on one count: that the U.S. Army was an institutional wreck by 1973, when the last of American ground forces were withdrawn from Southeast Asia, and, further, that over the next two decades this army quite deliberately reformed itself into the fighting organization that performed so well in the Persian Gulf.

Nor is that all. This consensus extends to the means by which this transformation is supposed to have been accomplished: these reforms were to be effected through the medium of doctrine itself. If the need for reform was virtually self-evident, it was also true that the usual means of reform were by 1973 largely absent. No civilian reformer in the tradition of a Haldane or Cardwell or Root appeared to rescue the Army from its malaise. The political-military leadership had lost any moral or professional credibility it may have enjoyed. The war had not supplied this army with institutional heroes around whom the faithful could rally. Under the circumstances, neither vision nor visionary seemed possible.

What were the circumstances? Strategic retrenchment was the order of the day. Under the terms of the new "Nixon Doctrine," disengagement from Southeast Asia was but a prelude to general disengagement from all regional conflicts. This disengagement presumed that allies of the United States would provide more support in aid of their own defense. In general, the goal of the Nixon administration was to demilitarize foreign policy by replacing armed confrontation with diplomacy.

For the Army, the new strategic posture of the United States meant a return to the old familiar grounds of what had been its principal interest since the Second World War: the defense of Western Europe. During Vietnam the Army's principal European formation, the Seventh Army, had eroded to little more than way stations, sources of men and equipment for deployment to Southeast Asia. The Vietnam War has been characterized in many ways, but an armored war it most definitively was not. And because the Army had always envisioned defending Europe with heavy armored formations, those were the first to languish during the Vietnam years. The Army's reorientation on the European battlefield heralded, therefore, a happy return to the cradle of orthodoxy after years of exile in the wilds of insurgent warfare.

This orthodoxy was composed of several beliefs that revealed a distinct institutional preference for a certain kind of warfare: defensive Continental warfare dominated by the tank. This defensive conception was highly stylized, enshrined after many years of practice in what was effectively the bible for European war, the War Plan 4102. Strategically and operationally, this plan exercised a much greater influence upon pre-Vietnam European formations than doctrine ever did. Tactically, only one thing mattered: tank gunnery. "Tank gunnery was king," a senior officer recalled from those days. "If you could hit it, you could probably kill it," after which, it was widely assumed, all other tactical problems were rendered mute. Thus, the war's end had simplified the Army's strategic and tactical life.

And, anyway, not much was expected from this army, not by its political masters, not, surely, by the American people. A 1973 public opinion survey of the respect enjoyed by American institutions ranked the military just above garbagemen. America's withdrawal from Southeast Asia in the spring of that year, when combined with the abolition of conscription and the advent of the "all-volunteer Army," may have contributed to the decline in its stature. Since 1969 the public had been treated to accounts of rising drug use among troops everywhere, and certainly in Vietnam, and also to a development that presaged a dark future for this army: "fragging," the killing of superiors by their own troops. Between 1969 and 1971 eight hundred fragging incidents were recorded. Forty-five officers and NCOs had been killed. Driven by the end of the draft to lower its recruiting standards, by the middle seventies half of the Army was composed of those who scored the lowest on aptitude exams. Forty percent of the Army's soldiers had not graduated from high school. By 1974 the Army fell eleven thousand recruits short of its enlistment target and had twenty thousand fewer soldiers than it was authorized to have. Two years later the statistics got worse.[15]

The indiscipline first appeared in Southeast Asia and was translated after the war to the European formations, manifesting itself in numerous racial incidents, drugs, and gang violence among soldiers. Some officers walked their night tours in the company areas with rounds chambered in their side arms. Nor were the signs of institutional decline relegated to the enlisted ranks alone. A succession of five "reductions in force" in the officer corps began even before the war had ended. These reductions were remarkably destructive of officer morale. One officer whose commission dated from 1966 recalled years later that half of his Officer's Basic Course, 163 men strong, had died in the Tet Offensive. Of those surviving, two-thirds had lost their commissions during the postwar purges. Speaking before a session of the Infantry Officer's Advanced Course at Fort Benning in early 1972 while he was still Chief of Staff of the Army, General Westmoreland told his audience that he intended to remove "the scum from the officer corps." According to one report, the general was booed from the stage. Evidently, General Westmoreland repeated his performance later that spring at the Command and General Staff College, where the student body was so uproarious that a cadre of general officers was dispatched from the Pentagon to Fort Leavenworth to counsel the rowdies. One officer, remembering that time, told me: "The senior officer corps was thoroughly discredited by the Vietnam War. The majors were in revolt. They didn't give a shit what the senior officers said." Even five years later bitter resentment was still casually and publicly voiced. As one officer said to me then, "Goddamn this army anyway. We ought to abolish it and start one of our own."[16] The shadow of the Vietnam dragon was long, and it was very dark.

At the head of the men who had inherited this army was Gen. Creighton Abrams, who was under no illusions about the quality of the force that he presided over. His immediate concern when he took office in 1972 was how best to translate the consequences of the Nixon Doctrine into realistic guidance for his army.[17] Abrams was facing a precipitate and, following American traditions, nearly inevitable reduction in the Army's authorized strength. From a strength of over a million and a half in 1968, Department of Defense programs were projecting strength authorizations for 1975 at about half that.[18] In keeping with the new strategy, he was to prepare his army to fight not "two and a half wars" but "one and a half," meaning one major and one lesser conflict. But only four of the thirteen active divisions were then rated as ready for combat. Out in the field at least one junior officer doubted that the Army could contend with even a minor conflict. Speaking of his soldiers to a reporter from the *New York Times*, he said, "You ought to see them, babied, pampered, dumb. Hell, they couldn't even lick the Cubans."[19]

The strength and structure of the Army were to be Abrams's overriding concerns during his tenure as Chief of Staff. But his brief would run only so far: he died of cancer before he had been in office two years. Neither Abrams nor any of his followers perceived at first that doctrine could or would be the means of that reform. Well into Abrams's tenure as Chief of Staff, he and his advisors were contemplating the fundamental roles and mission of the Army in the postwar world. The matter of doctrine played no part in these calculations.[20] Instead, Abrams determined, rather counterintuitively, to increase the number of active divisions from thirteen to sixteen, even as the Army was being demobilized. Furthermore, he intended to ensure that all these divisions were ready for combat.[21]

William E. DePuy was an Abrams loyalist, and as Abrams's illness forced him from the stage, DePuy became, arguably, the most important general in the U.S. Army. He certainly was, and remains, the most important figure in the modern history of Army doctrine.[22] For all his loyalty to Abrams's ideals and aims, DePuy was no sycophant. His character was complete unto itself. From 1969 to 1973 he wielded an important influence over the complexities entailed in designing the new all-volunteer Army. During these four years DePuy perfected a leadership style that had been in the making since his service began in the Second World War.

That war had been DePuy's formative professional experience, and it had not been a happy one. As a young officer in a poorly trained infantry division—the Ninetieth—fighting from Normandy onward, DePuy had decided that few men did what had to be done without being told. Only a few in any given group functioned as they were supposed to function. DePuy thought that the only salvation for such a force lay with professionally competent, sensible, and activist officers.[23] He saw few among his peers or superiors who met his standard. The Ninetieth had the reputation of being one of the very worst divisions the Army fielded during the war. During his time with the division DePuy saw two of his division commanders, several of his regimental commanders, and a number of other officers relieved for incompetence or outright unfitness.[24] DePuy vividly remembered one of his regimental commanders who never left his command bunker, preferring instead to color his tactical maps: green for forests, blue for rivers, black for towns. The regimental sergeant major's job was to keep the commander in crayons. By default, the junior officers ran the regiments, and sometimes with baleful effects. DePuy recalled particularly one whole "terrifying week of almost total failure."[25]

None of DePuy's subsequent professional experience appears to have altered his outlook; on the contrary, his later experience seems to have reinforced it. By contrast with the Second World War, DePuy's Vietnam service was mostly "a distraction." He appears to have been disappointed that the war could not be made to yield to his best efforts. During his tenure as commander of the First Infantry Division he became notorious for relieving commanders and staff officers in numbers not seen since the Second World War. He evidently believed that this was the sort of work a division commander ought to do. He certainly harbored no reservations about this performance later on.[26]

When he became the assistant Vice Chief of Staff of the Army, DePuy's education would be refined as he attempted to translate his values into a bureaucratic environment. In the Pentagon he learned the black arts of defense programming and systems management. Impatient with the sluggishness of the Pentagon staffs and believing anyway that organizations of any sort were mainly good for managing routine and nothing else, DePuy did not hesitate to create ad hoc groups to do the necessary conceptual work his missions required. Once those had completed their work, and only then, DePuy handed the concept over to those who made the trains run on time. He would never surrender his control over the questions he addressed: by the time these got to the staff, indeed, he had already made the critical strategic decisions. Anyone familiar with the U.S. Army knows that this is not the normal approach. If responsible officials hand off a complex problem to their staffs, the quality of the product (the outcome always tending toward the safest, most nearly mediocre answer) is diminished, and, happily for most, this approach diffuses one's direct responsibility as well. In this particular DePuy was different. He was not at all reluctant to assume responsibility, and he was happy to assume the responsibility of others too.[27]

This tendency, when combined with the nature of his work at the Pentagon, finished out DePuy's professional formation. As the principal officer charged by Abrams to cut the Army in half, he could not afford to employ traditional methods of staff work, which emphasize single issues, allow for "ownership" of any given issue, and normally are sequential and highly iterative, allowing for what is generously referred to as "the consensus-building process." DePuy was adept at circumventing these traditions. In this he was aided by a new managerial philosophy that had pervaded all the military services since the advent of Robert McNamara's days as secretary of defense. This philosophy entailed viewing issues on an interdisciplinary, economic, and strictly functional basis. It had long been good enough for any professional officer to say that his position was founded upon his professional judgment. Because professional judgment was ultimately subjective rather than analytical, this approach no longer impressed a headquarters run by the dictates of systems analysis.[28] And anyway, professional judgment had not won the most recent war; why should it be allowed to spoil the peace as well?

In the summer of 1973 DePuy won his fourth star and took charge of a new major Army command whose shape he had a hand in designing. The mission of the new Training and Doctrine Command (or TRADOC), as its name suggested, was to oversee all the military schools and training installations in the United States. DePuy was thus faced with several tasks at once: to organize an entirely new command and to take charge of training and educating all troops and officers. He also wanted to rationalize "combat developments"—the way in which new equipment was researched, developed, tested, and produced—with the way in which equipment was integrated with the standing army.[29]

Notwithstanding the name of the new command, which gave some visibility to the matter of doctrine, the subject of doctrine was not high on DePuy's list of priorities in the summer of 1973. "We started out ignoring it; it just was not an issue," he recalled years later.[30] All of which is only to say that DePuy regarded the matter of doctrine in much the same way as the rest of the Army: as of little real significance to the practical concerns of the Army. Management and training were uppermost in DePuy's mind that summer. As soon as DePuy assumed command, the training revolution in the Army would begin, but it would begin in the absence of doctrine. Instead, DePuy meant to elevate his own ideas about training to the level of a general principle. This, which could be translated roughly as "performance-oriented training," he would apply to his own personal vision of what the military future had in store for the Army. "We are not looking for World War III," he told an audience on the eve of his taking command at TRADOC. Instead, he foresaw a short, nasty, limited conflict, perhaps in the Middle East. In his eyes future wars would be strictly "come as you are." There would be no time for the cumbersome mobilization of the Second World War. Decision would be attained promptly, and very probably that decision would be won by small American forces, if it was to be won at all. To DePuy, this meant that any American unit had to be better by several orders of magnitude than any enemy it was likely to face. This assumption meant that American troops had to be trained to a much higher standard than was customary.[31] In retrospect, it is easy enough to see the doctrinal implications in DePuy's plans for the Army, but these were not at all clear at the time, nor would they become so very soon. At the newly formed TRADOC headquarters at Fort Monroe, Virginia, few epiphanies were available. Initiatives in training were already in the works: DePuy seemed to believe then that the Army could be reformed by means of training alone. Indeed, DePuy would never relinquish his insistence upon the primacy of training over all else. No matter how intensive his efforts were later on in the doctrinal arena, he admitted that his heart was with training.

DePuy enjoyed another prejudice as well. Just as performance was the only sensible way to measure training, so too did he think of performance when considering weapons. Not the weapon itself but its effect and, what is more, its effect against enemy weapons—these were more important considerations for DePuy. Such considerations corresponded nicely with what he had learned during his programming analysis days in the Pentagon. If training could act as a vital additive in combat, overcoming the weight of numbers, DePuy believed that superior weapons whose effects were properly orchestrated were even more important to the new equations of modern battle. Superior training and superior weapons meant superior tactics; superior tactics tilted battle in one's own favor. Wars made of tactics, the war on the ground of the battalion and company-grade officer—those composed the totality of war as DePuy then saw it.[32]

For nearly a generation of soldiering the U.S. Army had not been very attentive to military developments abroad. In late 1973 the Army was in a theoretical limbo. Orthodox military practices had not won victory in Vietnam, yet no body of ideas had so far appeared to supplant or revise those practices. As if to confirm the bankruptcy of the Army's influence over its own fate, Congress had just canceled two weapons development programs that the Army had sought—a new model helicopter and a modern main battle tank.[33] Despite a huge bureaucracy devoted to the development of new material, and despite a large training and education infrastructure, equipment and such doctrine as then existed occupied separate universes. Under the circumstances the Army had difficulty making a case for modernizing its force to congressional committees or, indeed, to itself. The Army's recent past was unsatisfying, its present unpromising, its future as yet indecipherable.

The eruption of yet another Arab-Israeli war in October 1973 was for the American Army a providential event. In its general outline the war corresponded to the military future that DePuy had foreseen only a few months before: it began and ended quickly. It was fiercely lethal. The opposing forces had no time to mobilize further than they had at the outset. The outcome depended importantly upon the quality of the training and the leadership of both armies. There was one critical and major difference, however: the forces did not achieve a decision on the battlefield it-self. The fighting developed only to a point before diplomacy in-tervened. DePuy noticed this difference and incorporated it into his thinking about future war.[34]

Soon after the conclusion of the October War the Army un-dertook an intensive study of its operations and equipment. This study, directed by Chief of Staff Abrams and overseen by DePuy, was to work a profound influence upon the future shape of the Army. That the Army's official attention would be attracted by this war was by no means an inevitability. The 1967 Arab-Israeli War had been fought when the American Army's attentions were fully occupied in Southeast Asia, nor did that earlier war possess such compellingly modern characteristics as the latest war. Be-fore the end of the year a team led by a brigadier general, Mor-ris Brady, from within the Training and Doctrine Command un-dertook a thorough operational investigation of the 1973 War. And although the Brady group issued a final, and still classified, report in the summer of 1974, as early as January of that year DePuy knew enough of what had been learned to tell General Abrams and to react upon his knowledge.[35]

What DePuy learned from the Brady report was that his own army was less well prepared to fight a modern war than even he believed. In three weeks of intense combat the combined tank and artillery losses of both sides were greater than the total in-ventory of American equipment then present in Europe.[36] Ar-mored warfare had reached a state of complexity and lethality that had not been seen since the Second World War and that, in some respects, was unprecedented. Armored forces engaged at ranges as much as 4,000 meters. Employing Soviet-style com-bined arms tactics, Egyptian forces integrated infantry armed with precision-guided antitank missiles with their armored for-mations. Precise, long-range, and well-coordinated fires from protected terrain features exacted a high price from Israeli ar-mored columns, traveling unaccompanied by infantry and at-tempting to fight with scant regard to terrain. Early Egyptian advances had been aided immeasurably as well by a new integrated air defense system composed of radar-guided anti-aircraft guns netted with a surface-to-air missile system farther to the rear. Combined, these systems denied the Israeli Air Force the air superiority they had depended upon in the 1967 war by forming a protective bubble under which ground troops could advance. "On the Suez front," DePuy told Abrams, "the IAF [Israeli Air Force] was effective in CAS [close air support] only when the Egyptians sallied out from under the SAM [surface-to-air missile] envelope." Although the Israelis recovered from the initial shocks of the Egyptian surprise, DePuy doubted whether they "could have sustained an offensive long enough to destroy the Arab forces as they were destroyed in the 1967 war." Notwithstanding the impressive performance of modern equipment on this new battlefield, DePuy believed that the war's implications for training were most important. Had these engagements been run on computer simulations, DePuy told Abrams, "the Israelis would have lost every battle." To DePuy that meant that unquantifiable factors such as "training and leadership weighed more heavily than weapons systems capabilities on the actual battlefield."[37] But it did not mean weapons characteristics and effects were negligible; to DePuy these matters were inextricably associated with the need to train to a new and high standard of combat performance.

Years later DePuy remembered the October War as "a marvelous excuse or springboard . . . for reviewing and updating our own doctrine."[38] The war also supplied the American Army with a new professional reference point uncontaminated by association with Vietnam. This reference point revealed modern war in its most sophisticated manifestation and in such near-clinical conditions that its lessons were seemingly unambiguous. The war painted a picture of Soviet combined arms doctrine and how much the Soviets had modernized their equipment during the Vietnam years.[39] All told, the October War had the effect of organizing knowledge in the absence of operational theory. What had been until now a collection of undifferentiated suppositions and disparate intentions were given substance and an organized framework from which specific reforms could be undertaken. In the process a new professional metaphor had been created that the Army could employ to communicate both within and beyond itself. Drawing upon the lessons of the October War, DePuy mobilized his command and, in his words, "embarked on a program to reorient and restructure the whole body of Army doctrine from top to bottom."[40]

Although TRADOC was still a new command in mid-1974, each of its many moving parts had been assigned its mission. Doctrine belonged to the various advanced schools, which were presided over by the chiefs of the branches. The Infantry School at Fort Benning owned doctrine for the infantry, the Armor School at Fort Knox attended likewise to its specialty, and so on. Only at the Command and General Staff College were the several specialized doctrines supposed to be amalgamated, for combined arms doctrine was thought to fall chiefly within the province of divisional operations. The staff college had the task of indoctrinating students in the art of arranging for dissimilar weapons and organizations to fight as one. The field manual that is meant to prescribe such doctrine is FM 100-5, *Operations*, which sits atop a hierarchy of subordinate manuals, each of which is required to take its cue from the conception of operations found in 100-5. Change 100-5 and one changes, ultimately, the way in which the Army fights. That, at any rate, is the theory, for this doctrinal system is always in motion; 100-5 and the other manuals are always in one stage of revision or another. Still, 100-5 rules the day in doctrine; in the event of a conflict, subordinate doctrine always yields. For these reasons, DePuy needed to focus his attention chiefly on 100-5 in order to conduct his campaign. If he could change this manual and arrange for the rest of the Army to agree, he would be well on the way to his objective.

DePuy conducted this campaign at several levels. His first task was to form a select cadre of loyalists who shared his views. These officers would bear the labor involved in not only the writing but also the selling of the new ways to the Army. That was much the more difficult problem, for the Army was composed, then as now, of numerous constituencies and interests over which powerful brokers ruled. Chief among these was the U.S. Seventh Army in Europe, then made of the V and VII Corps and assorted other units, comprising an important element of NATO defenses. The Seventh Army's agreement to any new doctrine, or even its agreement to be guided by any doctrine at all, was critical to DePuy's success. The Seventh Army's assigned area of operations in central West Germany was the cockpit in which DePuy's new doctrine was then most likely to come to life. If the Seventh Army could not be infused with DePuy's doctrine, it had no other available host. It would be ignored, and it would die. The new doctrine had to apply to NATO Europe or nowhere.[41]

DePuy began in the summer of 1974 by ignoring the organizational boundaries of his own command. From among his school commandants he chose Maj. Gen. Donn A. Starry of the Armor School as his principal confederate. Starry already had a distinguished record of service and was by then a practiced staff officer who had worked with DePuy in the Pentagon. He had been a commander under Creighton Abrams as a young officer, and he had led the Eleventh Armored Cavalry Regiment during the American invasion of the Parrot's Beak in Cambodia during the Vietnam War. While at the Armor School, he would lead a team of writers in the production of an official history of armored operations in Southeast Asia. Like DePuy, he thought little of bureaucratic niceties; even his earliest officer evaluation reports noted his impatience with administration. He shared, and perhaps even outdid, DePuy's enthusiasm for the potentialities of modern armored operations that had been demonstrated in the 1973 War. For anyone who cared to read the signs, Starry was clearly DePuy's professional heir apparent.

Of course, the implicit designation of Starry as the executive agent for the new doctrine reverberated through the corps of general officers under DePuy's command. Immediately, the other schools and their commandants were marginalized, and that included the Command and General Staff College and its commandant, Maj. Gen. John Cushman. Cushman was widely regarded as a military intellectual, and he had an educational and professional background to support the claim. But he had also commanded battalions and brigades in combat, and just before coming to Leavenworth he had commanded the 101st Airborne Division. He was a serious soldier with impressive credentials, his own kind of impatience with bureaucratic inertia, and an outlook toward ideas that was the polar opposite of DePuy's. Cushman would be perhaps the most serious obstacle of all to DePuy's ambitions.

Brig. Gen. Paul Gorman was a third force in this equation. Starry was at Fort Knox, and Cushman was at Fort Leavenworth, but Gorman was at Fort Monroe with General DePuy. DePuy and Gorman had soldiered together in Vietnam and later in the Pentagon. Gorman too had a keen mind and professional sense and was absolutely devoted to the notion of reform. Gorman's forte was training, and it was under his hand that a new system of "performance-oriented" training was quickly instituted, a scheme of training that answered all of DePuy's complaints about his own training in the Second World War. Gorman was the creator of the Army Training and Evaluation Program, a comprehensive task analysis of every critical task a fighting organization must perform in order to capitalize upon its combat power.[42] Gorman had performed well on a mission that was dearest to DePuy's heart, and his influence upon DePuy was considerable.

All of these ambitious young general officers had, of course, been quite attentive to DePuy's interpretations of the 1973 War. All during the spring of 1974, well before the publication of any formal reports, DePuy had been delivering an extensive briefing entitled "Implications of the Middle East War on U.S. Army Tactics, Doctrine and Systems." This briefing, whose primary source was General Brady's report, left no doubt where DePuy stood on the specific tactical and material challenges posed by the war. Already, the Army's training establishment was being bombarded with new "training circulars," written under Gorman's guidance, that incorporated DePuy's tactical outlook. These circulars were meant to convert NCO and officer instructors throughout TRADOC to the new ways of modern war.[43]

If anything, Donn Starry had embraced DePuy's interpretation of the war even more enthusiastically than its author. In April he had advised DePuy to begin proselytizing the new way of war across the Army, opening a free-for-all discussion with field commanders high and low. DePuy understood what Starry was getting at: the convincing was going to be more difficult than the writing. The writing of the doctrine need never take place unless a modicum of consensus could be reached beforehand. But DePuy was not interested in the free interchange of ideas. He was interested in the success of his ideas. "The only way you can judge what is good and what is bad, what works and what does not work, is to judge it in the light of whether it advances you toward your objective or not. If it does not, it is a waste of time. We are not in this business to be good guys," he had told an audience shortly before.[44] Instead of a dialogue, he told Starry and others, he wanted his campaign composed of three sequences. First, he wanted General Gorman's new training bulletins insinuated in all of TRADOC's institutions. Second, DePuy would visit the Army's field headquarters personally to save the savable and admonish the wicked. Then, and only then, would the "dialogue" that Starry wanted be permitted.[45]

What followed in 1974 and 1975 has been characterized as an extended debate, and indeed some did behave as though a debate were under way, but General DePuy intended no such thing. A genuine debate might have asked what was wrong with current doctrine that it must suffer such a wholesale replacement. Nor did DePuy consider the possibility that some experience from Vietnam might still be applicable, such as the hard-won air mobility tactics that were developed largely during active operations. DePuy was not interested in any history but his own history, and then only those parts that he believed had taught him something. To have promoted the free and open exchange of ideas about doctrine would have been antithetical to him and at cross-purposes with his intentions. Even as he managed to infuse the new doctrine with his own tactical preconceptions, he meant the doctrine to serve the larger purposes of explaining the Army to itself, rationalizing the connections between the development of new weapons systems and how those systems would actually be used, and fighting for a rejuvenated Army. But as for what was to go into this manual, under DePuy's hand tactics became war itself.

In the summer of 1974 Starry's enthusiastic promotion of armored warfare as the warfare of the future goaded Gorman into direct opposition. That July Gorman wrote a cautionary memorandum to General DePuy complaining of the promotion of "doctrine by slogan" at Starry's Armor School, where training circulars were punctuated by "nostrums" extolling the virtues of armored warfare over all else. Gorman recommended that DePuy "issue some strong guidance to the effect that Infantry and Armor will fight together."[46] DePuy did not follow Gorman's advice. Starry's aggressiveness seemed to suit him just fine. Years later DePuy remarked that it was imperative to get the infantry out of the "2 and ½ mile an hour mentality."[47]

Not long after Gorman's denunciation of the Armor School, DePuy wrote to his school commandants. Along with his letter he sent an essay on modern tactics, a "draft concept plan," he called it. In fact, the essay was a refined version of the briefing on the implications of the Middle East war he had been giving for several months. Virtually all of DePuy's most fervently held tactical ideas were to be found in this essay: the inherent superiority of the defense in the modern war; the prospect of being outnumbered and outgunned; the new parity in opposing weapons; the superiority of the tank on the modern battlefield; and his conviction that if mass and technological superiority could no longer be assumed, the American Army's only remaining advantage must be found in the quality of its leadership and its training—an advantage that he clearly felt was lacking at the moment.

DePuy did not intend to publish this essay. Instead, he said, it should be like the pot of soup at a French peasant's house, forever cooking over the fireplace: everyone contributes from time to time, and everyone partakes, and the soup keeps getting better. "I view the attached paper somewhat in the same way," he wrote. The "pot of soup letter" has often been cited as evidence of General DePuy's admirable liberality of mind, one anxious to traffic in ideas. But one should remember that this was William E. DePuy's house, his fireplace, and his pot of soup. He meant to allow only certain ingredients in the pot. The "pot of soup" was a fine metaphor after all: DePuy wanted elaboration and improvement, certainly, but not revision. And, importantly, he wanted everyone to have a helping.[48]

To that end, DePuy planned a grand convocation for the fall of 1974. All the school commandants were to meet with troop commanders from Forces Command units in the United States as well as assorted commanders from Europe and Korea for the ostensible purpose of reviewing tactics in light of lessons learned from the 1973 War. The meeting was held at Fort Knox and was called the Octoberfest. The meeting was in fact a carefully rehearsed extravaganza, complete with live-fire demonstrations, all designed to advance the cause of the new doctrine even before it had been written. Too, the widespread infusion of DePuy doctrine by means of Gorman's training circulars would not have been lost upon those who attended. Whether those from the operating forces liked it or not, the NCOs and junior officers joining the field commands in the near future would have been thoroughly indoctrinated already. In the end, through exhaustion or indifference, most seemed to wilt in the face of the TRADOC onslaught. Gen. Walter Kerwin, who commanded Forces Command, admonished the audience on the last day of the meeting to try out the new ideas. This was good enough for DePuy. Now all he had to do was see that the doctrine was written.

IN THE SCHOOL OF WAR

The success of Octoberfest signaled the beginning of an intensive round of meetings between DePuy and his lieutenants. Starry was ever-present; so were Cushman and Gorman, as were the other school commandants. DePuy allowed his subordinates just two months to prepare outlines for FM 100-5 and the most important subsidiary manuals. He left no doubt as to who would be held responsible: "If necessary," he told them, "you must write them yourselves."[49] No one had cause to doubt that DePuy himself would be intimately involved in the process from beginning to end.

DePuy's personal interest and his insistence upon personal involvement from the general officers under his command gave birth to a new stage in the history of doctrine in the U.S. Army. Since the beginning of the century, doctrine had been produced at the Army's various schools by committees of harried military instructors. That early doctrine had borne the imprimatur of the Army General Staff, but it was otherwise faceless. No attention had ever been paid to linking doctrine with either the training establishment or weapons development, with the result that a commander in the field could take or leave current doctrine with near impunity. Since the institution invested so little in its creation, why indeed should anyone have taken this doctrine as in any way authoritative in either an institutional or a professional sense? But in 1974 and afterward William E. DePuy became so intimately associated with the new doctrine that it would inevitably bear his name. Nor was it any secret that a function formerly served by nameless committees was now being attended to by a cadre of general officers. Doctrine had become generals' business, of a very select group of generals in particular.

Notwithstanding the dominant role played by Starry and the Armor School in doctrinal developments so far, responsibility for the manual that was so important to DePuy's ambitions still resided with General Cushman at the staff college. When DePuy and his court gathered once more, at Camp A. P. Hill in December 1974, Cushman's assignment was to deliver an outline draft of FM 100-5. Cushman once defined doctrine as "a search for the truth." None of his other remarks was so telling of his differences with DePuy's philosophy. DePuy believed he had already found the truth, and, indeed, he had committed that truth to paper several times already. Cushman began his draft with a quotation from Gen. George C. Marshall's classic work, *Infantry in Battle*, written in 1934: "Tactics is a thinking man's art. It has certain principles which may be learned but it has no traffic with rules." Such an outlook was anathema to William DePuy. To him, rules were acceptable so long as the rules were right, and he believed fervently that his rules were right. DePuy then gathered his generals about him and produced an outline of the manual he wanted. When the group met again in April of the following year, DePuy assigned a general officer to oversee the writing of each chapter of the new manual. For several days these subcommittees wrote drafts and briefed the others on their work. Then DePuy told Gorman to take all the draft chapters back to TRADOC headquarters at Fort Monroe. Though present, General Cushman did not participate in the writing, nor would he. He and his staff college had been relieved of the responsibility for the new "capstone" manual of the Army.[50]

It was clear enough to DePuy that Cushman's range of vision was insufficient to concoct the sort of doctrine that would serve the Army's purposes, which at the time went far beyond the traditional uses to which doctrine had been put. DePuy thought Cushman's "scholastic" outlook, along with his lofty and formalistic prose, failed to convey "the sense of urgency" necessary to "retrain, reorient and refocus an Army."[51] But perhaps more important, DePuy had other constituencies to deal with that were beyond Cushman's reach, and one constituency in particular was every bit as critical as consensus within the U.S. Army itself. That constituency was made up of the Europeans, mainly, the West German Army.

Since West Germany's rearmament in the 1950s, the Headquarters, United States Army Europe (USAREUR), had been the U.S.

Army's authoritative voice. Short of national-level contacts, this headquarters, also the home of the Seventh Army, had been the principal link between the new West German Army and its American military allies. Shortly after DePuy took command at TRADOC, General Abrams directed DePuy to establish close relations with the German high command. Abrams had given DePuy a golden opportunity to advance his cause by opening an avenue in which the Seventh Army's institutional power over European operations could be circumvented. In effect, DePuy would become the Army's executive agent in a new scheme of army-to-army relationships with the Germans. He moved quickly to institutionalize these relationships by organizing annual staff talks between the Germans and TRADOC officials and taking control of a system of liaison officers assigned to the German Army. As a formality, American staff officers from the European command were included, but as the staff talks evolved, it was clear that TRADOC was supplanting the European command as the voice of the U.S. Army.

DePuy found much in common with the Germans and much to admire as well. His admiration had begun when he was on the receiving end of German tactics in the Second World War, and the new German Army's reorganization of its Panzergrenadier, or mechanized infantry, units had impressed him as just the sort of innovation he was attempting to infuse in the American Army. Germany's geopolitical situation similarly worked to the advantage of DePuy's ambitions. The Federal Republic of Germany saw its chief military task as a defensive one, and any hint of a cross-border offensive was politically and militarily beyond the pale. For their army, that meant a flexible tactical scheme as close to the inter-German border as could be managed. DePuy believed that here was a context in which his new tactics could, and indeed must, be made to work. In this there was nothing unrealistic about DePuy's outlook. Referring later to the set of tactical ideas that came to be known as "the active defense," DePuy observed that "at best, it is a formula for a stalemate or for deterrence." On the inter-German border, and with the correlation of forces opposing one another at the time, victory simply meant not losing.[52]

DePuy played his German card expertly. At every opportunity he evoked his association with the Germans, emphasizing their agreement with the general principles contained in the various drafts of the new manual that TRADOC's staff was now producing.[53] His admiration for the German style of mechanized infantry operations was given as an example of the way American armor and infantry ought to fight in the future. USAREUR might well take exception to General DePuy's programs, but it could hardly disagree with the Germans too. One of the most important constituencies in the Army had been outflanked. Within two years of its establishment as a new command, TRADOC was a power to be reckoned with in the U.S. Army.

Almost from the beginning of DePuy's campaign to rewrite doctrine General Starry had voiced concerns about resistance to change within the Army.[54] The Infantry School had been dissatisfied with Starry's bid for proponency over mechanized infantry doctrine.[55] Time and again DePuy had supported Starry, but he had been careful to include the infantry community in the A. P. Hill conferences. Forces Command, whose forces then comprised the bulk of infantry and airborne units in the Army, expressed displeasure because the new doctrine blithely ignored developments in heliborne warfare that had been perfected in Vietnam.[56] USAREUR objected that little attention had been paid to combat in urban areas and especially to the nuclear dimensions of modern war. Likewise, chemical warfare found little space in the early drafts of 100-5. DePuy's approach to these objections was accommodating. Drafts of the doctrine were distributed throughout 1975 to all the objecting parties along with an invitation that they contribute to the new manual chapters that addressed their concerns. More conferences were held to smooth out objections. None of these objections challenged DePuy's fundamental tactical philosophies. So long as these remained intact, he had no

IN THE SCHOOL OF WAR

objection to others joining the party. Almost insensibly, the Army's hierarchy was becoming attuned to the new importance of doctrine. By these means, as the field manual grew, the various constituencies were mollified. The most political year for General DePuy was 1975.

In February 1976 DePuy wrote a triumphant report on his progress for Gen. Fred C. Weyand, who had succeeded General Abrams as Chief of Staff of the Army. Abrams's tacit support of DePuy's work had been one of his most important advantages. The Chief of Staff's death in late 1974 did not mean, however, that without a patron DePuy's program would be abandoned. It did mean that a power vacuum had been created, and DePuy filled it more than any other general officer. Of all the corps of general officers, only DePuy seemed to have a vision as well as the energy and resources to pursue it. The new Chief of Staff was more nearly DePuy's peer than superior, and what is more, according to DePuy, "he just wasn't intensely interested in the kinds of things we are talking about as I was and as Abe was and as Gorman was and Starry was and so on. He just wasn't."[57] What DePuy left unsaid was that the "kind of things" he and his associates were dealing with were critical to the future of the Army at large, its place in the defense establishment, and its institutional and operational future—matters that were inherently the concerns of any Chief of Staff. General Weyand's uninterest left the field open to DePuy, and only three months earlier he had convened the hard core of his followers once more at Camp A. P. Hill to write the final draft of 100-5. DePuy, Starry, and Gorman personally rewrote the manual, dividing chapters between them. Cushman attended, but only as an observer. No other general officers were present. Less than a month later DePuy briefed all his fellow four-star generals at an Army-level commanders conference and sent them all home with a copy of the draft, asking for comments. This was merely a formality. There was no chance anyone would offer substantive revisions. Barring last-minute serious revisions from the Germans, whom he had also given a draft, DePuy expected to publish the manual he now had in hand.[58] A month later the centerpiece of the new doctrine had also been named: the Active Defense.[59]

DePuy reported all this to General Weyand. He recounted the origins and evolution of thinking that went into the manual as well as the political process by which he had accomplished it all. He cited the concurrence of Israeli, German, and U.S. Air Force authorities, and he admitted the differences remaining between them and his manual. "We are very close on almost all points," he wrote. Nor did he attempt to obscure the eruption of differences within his own army. No doubt General Weyand knew about these already. DePuy recounted how Forces Command had successfully included air mobility tactics in the manual as an example of how he had taken pains to integrate the best available thought into the process. For all its triumphal tone, DePuy's report ended on a philosophical note. He wrote, "It will be several more years before 51 per cent of the commanders in the Army . . . operate instinctively in accordance with the principle of FM 100-5. At that time, it will be genuine doctrine."[60] Speaking before the officers in his headquarters a few days later, he was rather less reserved: "The impact [of FM 100-5] . . . will be a thousand fold. It will be more significant than anyone imagines. [It] will be *the* Army way and it will show up for decades."[61]

DePuy was to be disappointed in these expectations. He intended the manual to be tactically authoritative and comprehensive in its treatment of modern warfare. It was neither. As if to emphasize the tentative nature of the new doctrine, DePuy had directed it to be published in a loose-leaf binder, but given the aggressive, take-no-prisoners manner in which DePuy and his associates imposed their ideas upon the rest of the Army, the appearance of the manual could hardly be taken sincerely. But had DePuy and TRADOC failed to convince the rest of the Army that it must alter its thinking about the future of war, the new FM 100-5 would have been killed by indifference. Whatever else one might say about the Active Defense, it was certainly not ignored.

FM 100-5 was officially published on July 1, 1976. Before the month was out the debate had begun, and in a most unexpected quarter. William Lind, a legislative aide for Senator Robert Taft Jr., had received an early draft of the manual as well as a briefing in which General DePuy himself had participated. Lind was less than convinced on several points and wrote an essay, detailing his doubts. *Military Review*, the house organ of the Command and General Staff College, at first offered to publish the piece. General DePuy was informed, and three days later the offer was withdrawn. DePuy explained later that "it would not serve any useful purpose to have the article published . . . in advance of the FM's distribution to the Army in the field." This episode was reported in the October issue of *Armed Forces Journal International*, which led off with an editorial entitled "Doctrine Developed in a Vacuum?" "There are suggestions," the editorial read, "that the manual is not an Army manual; that TRADOC put it together, got a lower-level DA [Department of the Army] staff chop, then presented the Chief of Staff with a *fait accompli*." This was followed by a book review of the field manual, an unprecedented event in itself, as well as a scathing account of the Lind affair. That accounted that "DePuy hit the ceiling when he heard of this unexpected criticism, and that he ordered the Army to take no notice of the article whatsoever." Since then, Lind had been distributing copies of his paper far and wide throughout the Defense establishment.[62]

Lind's objections to the Active Defense provided the basis for most of the substantive criticism that would follow from other quarters. Lind asked whether "winning the first battle" meant that there would be no second battle; he attacked the doctrine as placing too great a faith on the effect of weapon systems and interpreting those effects always to the advantage of the defender. More pointedly, he thought the new doctrine merely offered nostrums to an army so weak that it could only rely upon slogans to encourage a "can-do" attitude among the doomed. Lind laced his article with historical allusions and examples, marshaled to support his objections, all of which no doubt struck DePuy as completely worthless. Indeed, the TRADOC reply to Lind's criticisms did not even attempt to contest his historical analyses. Not only had doctrine become generals' business, it had become civilians' business as well, and Lind was certainly not the last civilian analyst who would be heard from.

Lind's article, which was eventually published in *Military Review* the following year, effectively signaled the beginning of an unprecedented doctrinal debate involving not only civilian defense experts, some of them self-appointed, but also Army officers. During the next four years nearly eighty essays were published in *Military Review* alone, most of them focusing upon one perceived deficiency or another in the new manual. If DePuy's own standard for doctrine—that it was how 51 percent of the Army fought—then the new field manual was in trouble from the beginning. And it never recovered.

Critics who followed Lind had several objections in common. The new manual was perceived as being entirely too defensive in its orientation. DePuy would have replied, and did, that he was only being realistic and that in any case there was a chapter on the offense in the manual. But critics argued that even the offense pictured in the manual was tilted toward the defense. Alexander Haig, then Supreme Allied Commander Europe, was concerned that the manual was too narrowly focused upon European defense and did not contemplate the possibility that Americans might have to fight elsewhere in an entirely different style. During the bruising encounters between General Cushman and General DePuy at Camp A. P. Hill, Cushman had taken the line that doctrine should not be rigidly prescriptive. But Cushman could not successfully contest DePuy's insistence that doctrine should be precisely that. People had to be told what to do. This approach worked well enough in venues where DePuy was in control, but once the manual was published, he was no longer able to suppress criticism.

Donn Starry had left the Armor Center at Fort Knox in 1976, having been promoted to lieutenant general and been given command of V Corps in Germany. This new perspective impressed some reservations about the doctrine upon Starry. He eventually came to believe that the doctrine did not sufficiently address theater-level problems, and he learned a great deal more about the Soviet threat than had found its way into the manual. Starry would remain with V Corps for only a year before he was promoted to his fourth star. General DePuy retired and handed TRADOC over to Starry. Starry commanded TRADOC for four years. By the time he left the command was well on the way to producing yet another edition of FM 100-5, an edition that was very different from the one he had helped to write at Camp A. P. Hill.

Even today, Starry questions whether the 1982 edition of FM 100-5 repudiated General DePuy's 1976 manual. He argues that it was necessary for the Army to pass through the pain and the controversy that DePuy's manual lighted in order to reach a more balanced doctrine that the Army could accept. Those who participated in the creation of the "AirLand Battle," which is the shorthand term by which Starry's doctrine became known, would argue that their doctrine constituted the real revolution, the real "progress in doctrine," as William Lind would put it.

But by the time Starry's AirLand Battle doctrine was published, the doctrinal revolution was over. That revolution consisted not of the substance of the doctrine but of the unprecedented functions the doctrine had been made to serve and the way in which it had been given life. At a time when there were no incentives but many excuses to do otherwise, DePuy managed to harness doctrine in the service of reform. Never had doctrine been put to such a purpose. No one else wearing an Army uniform had the resources and the energy to make this ambition a reality. The reserves of energy and professional discipline he committed to this task were likewise unprecedented. His intellectual resources were a keen memory of his early service and an analytical mind, neither of which compelled him to the deeper reflections of a more contemplative man. He was a man of action, not of ideas, which were to him things to be consumed or applied if they accorded with his preconceptions. His analytical bent drove his view of tactics as chiefly the sum of weapons systems in action; he was not unmindful of the human dimensions of warfare, as his critics claimed; he merely thought they were subordinate to firepower and capable of producing limited effect on their own. Perhaps this is why, though he knew the political dimensions of steering the new doctrine through the Byzantine collection of interest groups that make up the Army, he did not foresee how these interests might criticize his doctrine once it was finished. For good and ill, DePuy's name was more intimately associated with a military doctrine than any other American soldier had been in over a hundred years.

He shared his enthusiasm and his certitude with only a few others, young and aggressive general officers who were happy to subordinate themselves to the large cause of reform. There were, after all, no other reformers competing with DePuy: they all belonged to him. When by these means doctrine became generals' business for the first time in American military history, the course of doctrine assumed an unprecedented meaning for the institution. It provided a mechanism by which the institution could organize its thinking about future war. Even as DePuy's field manual was being criticized, its critics seemed not to realize that it was DePuy who had created the venue in which they were now thinking.

The doctrinal revolution began as General DePuy's personal creation, and it remained personal while he was in command. His style depended always upon a few loyalists, detached, as it were, on intellectual service to him. But DePuy also commanded a large and complex military bureaucracy that gradually grew to attend to doctrinal issues grand and small. While he was at TRADOC, doctrinal issues were the province of a small, talented, and energetic band of officers who operated under the patronage of a man who had become the most powerful general in the U.S. Army. By the time General Starry took command of TRADOC, an elaborate undergrowth of bureaucracy had been created. Significantly, proponency for the next edition of FM 100-5 was returned to the staff college at Fort Leavenworth. By then the real doctrinal revolution was over, but by then the U.S. Army had become a doctrinally oriented army to an extent hitherto unknown in the American military experience.

Not so long ago General Starry addressed an assembly of military historians at Gettysburg. Few of those in the audience understood who he was, and still fewer understood the significance of the movement in which he had been such an important participant. He spoke of General DePuy, now dead, and of the dark days after Vietnam when the Army was convinced it could not win. He outlined how the American Army had discovered the uses of doctrine and how those uses had helped to make the Army of today. And he recounted how, as he watched with the rest of us the war in the Persian Gulf unfold, he thought to himself, "It all worked."[63]

Notes

The views expressed herein are solely those of the author and do not constitute the official position of the Government of the United States, the Department of Defense, or the Department of the Army. I am especially indebted to Dr. Richard M. Swain (colonel, U.S. Army, retired) and Lt. Gen. Don L. Holder (U.S. Army) for their considerable assistance in the preparation of this paper. A revised version of this paper first appeared in the acta of the Australian Army History Conference for 1995, "From Past to Future," and is now published with the kind permission of the University of New South Wales.

1. I employ the term *doctrine* here to encompass both higher conceptions of war and operational philosophy as well as what the present-day U.S. Army refers to as "tactics, techniques, and procedures." Some of the latter can be quite prescriptive. For the purposes of this paper, my focus is upon the higher conceptions of war and operations as they are addressed in what the Army calls its "capstone manual," Field Manual 100-5, *Operations*, especially in its post-Vietnam editions. Since the mid-1970s especially the Army has taken great pains to ensure that derivative manuals (e.g., those addressing infantry or armor operations) are written in strict consonance with the outlook of FM 100-5.

2. See Field Manual 100-5, *Operations* (Washington DC: Headquarters,

Department of the Army, 1992), iv–vi, 1-1, 1-2, which describe its doctrine as both "definitive" and "adaptable."

3. U.S. Army Regulation 320-5, *Dictionary of Army Terms* (Washington DC: Headquarters, Department of the Army, April 1965), 146.

4. Two especially fruitful examinations of "doctrine" in this period may be found in Robert M. Utley, *Frontier Regulars: The United States Army and the Indian, 1866–1891* (Bloomington: Indiana University Press, 1977), esp. 44–58; and Perry Jamieson, *Crossing the Deadly Ground: U.S. Army Tactics, 1865–1899* (Tuscaloosa: University of Alabama Press, 1994).

5. These observations are more fully developed in the author's "American Military Doctrine," in *The Oxford Companion to American Military History*, ed. John Whiteclay Chambers II (New York: Oxford University Press, 1999), 231–34.

6. A worthwhile set of essays on this subject may be found in Lt. Col. Charles R. Shrader, ed., "The Impact of Unsuccessful Military Campaigns on Military Institutions, 1860–1890," in *Proceedings of the 1982 International Military History Symposium* (Washington DC: U.S. Army Center of Military History, 1984). Especially pertinent to this essay is Col. Harry Summer's "The United States Army's Institutional Response to Vietnam," 296–308.

7. Martin van Creveld, *Fighting Power* (Westport CT: Greenwood Press, 1982), 3.

8. See Robert A. Doughty, *Seeds of Disaster: The Development of French Army Doctrine, 1919–1939* (Hamden CT: Archon Press, 1985).

9. President George Bush, "Remarks at a Meeting of Veterans Service Organizations," March 4, 1991, *Weekly Compilation of Presidential Documents* 27, nos. 1–14 (Washington DC: Government Printing Office, 1991), 248.

10. See "Bush Approval at 89 Percent, Highest in Polling History" and "Victory's Aftermath: American Confidence Soars," *Gallup Poll Monthly*, no. 306 (March 1991): 2, 18–19.

11. The winning entry in the race to publish after the war was Bob Woodward's *The Commanders* (New York: Simon and Schuster, 1991). This was followed in quick turn by James Blackwell, *Thunder in the Desert: The Strategy and Tactics of the Persian Gulf War* (New York: Bantam Books, 1991) and, by the editors of *U.S. News and World Report, Triumph without Victory: The Unreported History of the Persian Gulf War* (New York: Random House–Times Books, 1992). See also the later entries by James Kitfield, *Prodigal Soldiers: How the Generation of Officers Born of Vietnam Revolutionized the American Style of War* (New York: Simon and Schuster, 1995), and James F. Dunnigan and Raymond M. Macedonia, *Getting It Right: American Military Reforms after Vietnam to the Gulf War and Beyond* (New York: William Morrow & Co., 1995). To date, the best works

on the Gulf War that take serious notice of interwar reforms are Col. Richard M. Swain, *Lucky War: Third Army in Desert Storm* (Fort Leavenworth KS: U.S. Army Command and General Staff College Press, 1994), and Rick Atkinson, *Crusade: The Untold Story of the Persian Gulf War* (Boston: Houghton Mifflin, 1993). This theme is employed as the leitmotif in Alvin and Heidi Toffler's *War and Anti-War: Survival at the Dawn of the 21st Century* (Boston: Little, Brown and Company, 1993).

12. Brig. Gen. Robert H. Scales Jr. et al., *Certain Victory* (Washington DC: Office of the Chief of Staff of the Army, 1993). The first chapter is devoted to the history of the Army between the War in Vietnam and the onset of the Gulf War. The remainder of this book is offered as proof of the thesis, set forth in the first chapter, that the Gulf War was the validating event for virtually all the Army's interwar efforts to rebuild itself.

13. Quoted in Al Santoli, *Leading the Way: How Vietnam Veterans Rebuilt the U.S. Military; an Oral History* (New York: Ballantine Books, 1993), 422.

14. Quoted in Guenther Lewy, *America in Vietnam* (New York: Oxford University Press, 1978), 138.

15. These figures are recapitulated from various public sources in Scales, *Certain Victory*, 6–7, 15–16. One should note, however, that public confidence in all major American institutions was in considerable decline during the Watergate years.

16. Ibid., 8; author's notes of a conversation with Lt. Col. Keith Skyles, May 2, 1989; author's notes of a conversation with Col. Richard M. Swain, April 19, 1989. I have spoken with several officers who were either present or had knowledge of General Westmoreland's speech at Fort Benning as well as several who were members of the staff college class of 1972. Any history of the Army after the Vietnam War that does not address the social and cultural stresses experienced by those who stayed on will be incomplete in my view. See also Lt. Col. John H. Moellering, "Future Civil-Military Relations: The Army Turns Inward?" *Military Review* 53, no. 7 (1973): 68–83, which contains the results of a student opinion poll.

17. One general officer, well after the fact, thought that the Nixon Doctrine provided such insufficient strategic guidance that the Army was forced to deduce its proper course of action unilaterally. See Gen. Donn A. Starry, "A Tactical Evolution—FM 100-5," *Military Review* 58, no. 8 (1978): 3.

18. See Capt. Richard J. Hyde, "A New Force Structure," *Military Review* 70, no. 11 (1990): 12.

19. Quoted in Scales, *Certain Victory*, 7.

20. In the spring of 1973 General Abrams formed a small ad hoc study group named after its chief, Col. Edward F. Astarita, to "determine if there was a legitimate role for conventional strategy and for the Army in the post-

Vietnam world." The group produced a secret three-hour briefing that was given throughout the Department of Defense and other executive agencies. The Astarita group was disbanded in the spring of 1974. In 1981 one of the members of the original group, Col. Harry Summers, prepared a written, unclassified version of the group's findings. That paper was presented as an "Occasional Paper" from the Strategic Studies Institute, U.S. Army War College, Carlisle Barracks PA, "The Astarita Report: A Military Strategy for the Multipolar World," typescript, April 30, 1981. No mention was made of the role of doctrine in this paper. See also Gen. (ret.) William E. DePuy, "Presentation to the TRADOC Commanders' Vision '91 Conference, 5 October 1988," in Col. Richard M. Swain, comp., *The Selected Papers of General William E. DePuy* (Fort Leavenworth KS: Combat Studies Institute, U.S. Army Command and General Staff College, 1994), 431.

21. Lewis Sorley, *Thunderbolt: General Creighton Abrams and the Army of His Times* (New York: Simon and Schuster, 1992), 360–67.

22. I am happy to share this view with Dr. Richard M. Swain (colonel, U.S. Army, ret.) in his introduction to his compilation *The Selected Papers of General William E. DePuy*, vii.

23. DePuy's views are reminiscent of those of the post–Civil War doctrine writer and reformer Maj. Gen. Emory Upton, whose *Military Policy of the United States* evokes the same reservations about the qualities of mass armies as DePuy does.

24. This experience, it must be said, was not unique to the Ninetieth Infantry Division. Quite a few of the draftee divisions were even less well officered and consequently less effective. See Robert R. Palmer, Bell I. Wiley, and William R. Keast, *The Procurement and Training of Ground Combat Troops* (Washington DC: Office of the Chief of Military History, 1948), 466–69.

25. Romie Brownlee and William J. Mullen III, *Changing an Army: An Oral History of General William E. DePuy, USA, Retired* (Carlisle Barracks PA: U.S. Army Military History Institute, n.d. [1979?]), 7–16, 35, 45.

26. The characterization is Maj. Paul Herbert's in his *Deciding What Has to Be Done: General William E. DePuy and the 1976 Edition of FM 100-5*, Leavenworth Paper, no. 16 (Fort Leavenworth KS: U.S. Army Command and General Staff College, 1988), 21–23, 125, 131, 140, 152–53.

27. Ibid., 171–75.

28. Ibid.

29. See DePuy's discussion of the problems inherent in the new command in Brownlee and Mullen, *Changing an Army*, 177–79.

30. Swain, *Selected Papers*, 431.

31. "Briefing by LTG DePuy, 7 June 1973, Fort Polk, Louisiana," in ibid., 59–66. The training revolution in the Army largely parallels and in some cases, as above, actually precedes doctrinal reform. The principal author of

training reforms during this period was Brig. Gen. Paul Gorman. For an elucidation of Gorman's ideas see his *The Secret of Future Victory* (Fort Leavenworth KS: U.S. Army Command and General Staff College Press, 1994), III-1–III-42. For DePuy's views on Gorman's ideas see also Brownlee and Mullen, *Changing an Army*, 183 and passim. See also Herbert, *Deciding What Has to Be Done*, 25–29.

32. DePuy's views on war qua tactics suffuse his interview with Brownlee and Mullen; see *Changing an Army*.

33. See Herbert, *Deciding What Has to Be Done*, 27–28. See also a draft of DePuy's memorandum for the Chief of Staff of the Army, January 8, 1975, in Swain, *Selected Papers*, 143.

34. See a transcript of DePuy's handwritten notes entitled "Modern Battle Tactics," August 17, 1974, in Swain, *Selected Papers*, 137–38.

35. See Paul Herbert's discussion of the Brady study and its findings in Herbert, *Deciding What Has to Be Done*, 29–36.

36. Ibid., 30.

37. See DePuy's January 14, 1974, letter to General Abrams in Swain, *Selected Papers*, 69–74.

38. Brownlee and Mullens, *Changing an Army*, 190–91.

39. Swain, *Selected Papers*, 72. American investigators had been surprised, for instance, to see Soviet-model Egyptian tanks, equipped for nuclear and chemical warfare. This finding alone would pose substantial complications when DePuy attempted to fit his new doctrine into the framework of NATO defense.

40. DePuy is quoted in Herbert, *Deciding What Has to Be Done*, 36.

41. I can find only one instance in which DePuy acknowledged, even obliquely, this obstacle to the acceptance of his doctrine. In a letter to Gen. Alexander Haig, then Supreme Allied Commander Europe, he vigorously defended the new doctrine in a kind of shorthand: "It is not a European defense plan." Both officers understood that the European defense plan had for years served as a kind of de facto doctrine in the absence of authoritative doctrinal guidance. Gen. William E. DePuy to Gen. Alexander Haig, October 13, 1976. Copy of letter in the author's possession provided by Dr. Richard Swain.

42. See Herbert's discussion of the Army Training and Evaluation Program and Gorman's role in its creation in *Deciding What Has to Be Done*, 38–39. See also DePuy's recollection of Gorman's accomplishments in the field of training as well as a statement of his own affinity with Gorman's training philosophy in Brownlee and Mullen, *Changing an Army*, 182–87, 202.

43. Herbert, *Deciding What Has to Be Done*, 47. A typescript of DePuy's briefing, "Implications of the Middle East War on U.S. Army Tactics, Doctrine and Systems," n.d. [Spring 1974], may be found in Swain, *Selected Papers*, 75–111.

44. Gen. William E. DePuy, Keynote Address, TRADOC Leadership Conference, May 22, 1974, Fort Benning GA, in Swain, *Selected Papers*, 120.

45. Herbert, *Deciding What Has to Be Done*, 44–45.

46. Gorman to DePuy, Memorandum, July 3, 1974, parts of which may be seen in ibid.

47. DePuy is quoted in ibid., 41. The "2 and ½ mile an hour mentality" was evidently a phrase routinely used at Fort Knox to describe the Infantry School's less than adventurous approach to the problems of modern war. Col. Edwin Scribner, "Doctrine Development by TRADOC, May, 1973–December, 1979," 6. Typescript in the author's possession.

48. Gen. William E. DePuy to Maj. Gen. David Ott et al., July 23, 1974, with enclosure, "TRADOC Draft Concept Paper: Combat Operations," in Swain, *Selected Papers*, 121, 122–35.

49. An account of Octoberfest can be found in Herbert, *Deciding What Has to Be Done*, 47–49; and John L. Romjue, *From Active Defense to Airland Battle: The Development of Army Doctrine, 1973–1982* (Fort Monroe VA: Historical Office, U.S. Army Training and Doctrine Command, June 1984), 4–5.

50. Herbert, *Deciding What Has to Be Done*, 56–59.

51. DePuy's assessment is recorded in ibid., 116 n. 13.

52. Brownlee and Mullen, *Changing an Army*, 192. See also Herbert's detailed discussion of Federal Republic of Germany defense questions and their effect upon American doctrine in *Deciding What Has to Be Done*, 61–67.

53. See, for example, DePuy's letters to Gen. Fred Weyand, Chief of Staff of the Army, April 29, 1975, and again on February 18, 1976, in Swain, *Selected Papers*, 161–62, 181, respectively.

54. Starry's concerns are quoted in Herbert, *Deciding What Has to Be Done*, 42–43, 45.

55. Maj. Gen. Thomas Tarpley, commandant of the Infantry School, opposed Starry's bid for dominance on the grounds that his school would have "proponency for nothing" (ibid.).

56. Ibid., 89–92; Romjue, *From Active Defense*, 4–5.

57. DePuy is quoted in Herbert, *Deciding What Has to Be Done*, 119 n. 1.

58. Ibid., 92–93.

59. An account of the naming of the new doctrine is given in Scribner, "Doctrine Development," 8.

60. DePuy to Gen. Fred C. Weyand, February 18, 1976, in Swain, *Selected Papers*, 179–83.

61. Herbert, *Deciding What Has to Be Done*, 93.

62. F. Clifton Berry, "Doctrine Developed in a Vacuum?"; F. Clifton Berry, "Book Review: FM 100-5, 'Operations'"; John Patrick, "Banned at

Fort Monroe, or the Article the Army Doesn't Want You to Read"; and "TRADOC's Reply," all in *Armed Forces Journal International*, October 1976, 4, 23–26, 27–28, respectively.

63. Gen. Donn A. Starry (U.S. Army, ret.), "Remarks at the Annual Meeting of the Society for Military History, Gettysburg, Pennsylvania, 13 May 1995," 2. Copy in the author's possession. See also Gen. Donn A. Starry, "A Tactical Evolution—FM 100-5," *Military Review* 58, no. 8 (1978): 2–11.

ELEVEN. Urban Warfare

Its History and Its Future

Why should a modern army invest its professional energies in understanding urban warfare? Armies are optimized when they are used in the open. Armies are not built to work best in cities. If one would wreck an army, tradition argues, send it into a city. The functions armies serve, their fundamental organizing principles, their modes of command and control, their operational and tactical doctrines, and even the standards by which they judge their success—all are tuned to the wide-open spaces of the field of battle. In such spaces armies have succeeded more often and more decisively. So goes the argument.

But the origin of these prejudices is rather modern. Frequently, the ancient classic *The Art of War* by Sun Tzu is held up as the ultimate argument against taking war into a city. But Sun Tzu's often-quoted strictures against cities should be interpreted as being in the nature of a protest. Scholars tell us that in the ancient China of his day the arts of fortification and siegecraft were well developed precisely because cities were important in war. Sun Tzu seems most interested in rectifying what he sees as unimaginative tactics in attacking cities. Although he regards attacking cities as the least preferable course of action, his conception of war conduces perfectly with the quickest and least costly way to capture a city—by *chi'i*, that is, by indirect means of feints, espionage, disinformation, subversion, and betrayal. Nor did Sun Tzu think that cities could be ignored. The general who left too many towns and cities behind him as he advanced into the enemy's territory, Sun Tzu wrote, was courting danger.[1]

Once, and for the longest time, cities were integral to the conduct of war. Heavily fortified, snug behind their bastioned walls, cities embodied the strength of the state. Cities could be worth taking: a successful siege—that is, one that was not ruinous to defender and attacker alike—quite often concluded a war decisively. Field engagements, however, did not hold out a promise of decisive victory; one might conduct indecisive operations in disputed zones between one strongpoint and another for years. Decisive field operations were always more difficult than sieges to stage and always posed a sterner test for the armies. Whole wars might pass without seeing a field operation that produced any significant result for those engaged.

Campaigns might simply burn themselves out with no meaningful conclusion at all.[2] Fortresses and the style of war they represented began declining well before the age of gunpowder hurried them along to obsolescence. Fortresses usually were built at command by those who had the resources to give them life. But cities were a collective enterprise, one of the results of constantly redistributing humans and their labors, usually over the course of centuries. From the Middle Ages onward, and especially in Europe, populations were busily rearranging themselves into towns and cities. Between 1100 and 1500 the number of towns in Europe doubled.[3] Most faced their enemies without permanent protection. Even when they were not in the lee of a mighty castle, they managed to survive by putting up fierce and prolonged resistance from behind the crudest defenses. Proper sieges of well-prepared fortresses rarely lasted more than a few months, and certain cities held out just as long. One of the longest sieges recorded in that age was against the city of Acre, which defended itself against Frankish Crusaders for almost three years.[4] While the age of the fortress declined, the modern age of urban warfare was beginning. As Phillipe Contamine has observed, a conqueror might now easily avoid a castle, but "it was absolutely vital to control such centers of economic, administrative, and human resources as were represented by towns."[5]

Cities that were not protected by fortifications posed their own kinds of problems for would-be attackers. An unfortified city, if it was to be defended at all, might be more inclined to defend itself in depth, or along a single avenue of approach, forcing an invader to spend itself from building to building, each of which could be made into a redoubt, until the attacker had dissipated its combat power—or its enthusiasm for the fight. Nor were unfortified cities difficult simply because they could be successfully defended. The very human composition of the city could pose yet another set of difficulties. A city full of terrified civilians or a city swollen with equally terrified refugees could produce a corps' worth of friction without ever firing a shot.

The redistribution of the European population was unprecedented but not unique. The rest of the world matched Europe's new patterns of growth, million for million. In AD 150 the world's population stood at about 300 million. Sixteen centuries of growth were required to double this number.[6] In 1750 the world's population of 600 million began to rise at a rate never before seen. Only fifty-four more years were to pass before the world's population nearly doubled again. By 1804 the world's population had reached 1 billion.[7] The magnitude of this demographic surge is so powerful that neither plagues nor wars nor natural calamities have affected its velocity. During the two centuries since reaching the first billion of population, the world has added 5 billion more.[8] The rate of growth has not subsided, but it has changed shape.

In 1804 London was unique among the world's cities because it had attained a population of 1 million, possibly the first city to do so since ancient Rome. Only one hundred years later, cities all over the world contained more than a million inhabitants. Now one estimate holds that the world contains some 30,000 "urban centers," not megalopolises so much as very large cities. Some of these, such as El Alto, Bolivia, now over 500,000 people, are located close to much larger, better-known cities.[9] By the year 2000 the world contained 387 cities with populations of a million or more—sometimes much more. The most populous urban agglomeration in the world today is Tokyo, with a population of 26.5 million.[10] Not including the city's several contiguous suburbs, the prefecture of Tokyo proper now covers more than 2,000 square kilometers.[11]

IN THE SCHOOL OF WAR

According to a recent UN report, within the next five years global population will be equally divided between urban and rural inhabitants, but virtually all population growth for the next generation is expected to occur in urban areas. Most of these urban areas are in less-developed regions of the world. During the past five years urban growth in these regions was six times greater than growth in the urban areas of developed nations. In the more developed nations 75 percent of the population is already in urban areas, a figure that, by current estimates, will increase to 84 percent within the next generation. However, in the world's largest urban agglomerations, for reasons not explained, populations tend to decline. Yet Dhaka, Bangladesh, and Delhi, India, both defied this trend during the past quarter-century, with populations growing at a rate of 7 percent a year.[12] No evidence suggests that there is any fixed point of maximum urban expansion, a point beyond which a city may no longer serve its purposes.[13] Nor, as noted, is it inevitable that a megacity, once embarked on dramatic expansion, will continue to grow. Mexico City's recent history demonstrates that population surges can indeed abate or even reverse themselves for reasons that have nothing to do with urban dysfunction. In this case a reorientation of national production and consumption was the proximate cause for revising the city's growth estimates downward.[14]

The world's many cities are as varied as the societies that built them. The standard, common, or normal city does not exist. Cities can be broadly distinguished from one another, however. Geography can impose its own kind of tyranny over how a city grows. Cities that are sited on coastal plains, like Tokyo, or that occupy coastal or estuarial islands, such as Lagos, have only so much land available to them. Cities dominated by a particular industry or activity often incorporate it into their design. Capital cities usually fix their national institutions near a ceremonial center where monuments are more numerous than people. This seems to hold true whether the city was originally built for that purpose or later adapted. Washington DC, St. Petersburg, and Brasilia are modern examples of the former. London, Paris, Berlin, and Tokyo did not begin as capitals but eventually assumed the role. It is possible, too, to distinguish between cities by how they respond to certain social or technical developments. Los Angeles and the automobile culture virtually grew up together, with the result that few other cities in the world are so highly integrated with this form of transportation. By contrast, modern Athens was required like so many other ancient cities to transplant modern transport patterns into an urban structure that had not greatly changed in centuries. Comparing cities by one feature or another can be interesting, but it is perhaps not the most effective way to understand the uniqueness of a given city. In this respect a city is more like a book, to be read and understood on its own terms.

Even so, the modern urbanographer and the modern military professional are unlikely to see a city in the same way. Rio de Janeiro's 764 *favelas*—poverty-ridden urban zones distinguished more by the boundaries of the criminal gangs who operate in them than by any division of orthodox government—may seem to the urban planner to be a collection of political, economic, and, above all, social challenges. The military planner may wonder how—if there is no choice—to move large bodies of soldiers through this zone or whether it is even possible for an army to wrest control from the "federation of gangs" that dominates it.[15] While population and urban experts can contend, theoretically, with China's "floating population" of 100 million homeless agricultural workers displaced by rural modernization and collecting in the nation's cities (1 million in Beijing alone), what theories can a commander and military planner draw upon to contend with his mission in densely populated urban areas?[16]

The art of war clearly has not kept pace with the progressively more complex global urban environment. As a consequence, the military profession is ill equipped to meet the unique demands of modern urban warfare. Unable to avoid operating in urban environments, traditional armed forces tend to regress, their tactics devolving to the lowest common denominator, surrendering the initiative to better-prepared adversaries. Forced to resort to expediencies and improvisations, trial and error, and experiments in the face of the enemy, orthodox military forces face the danger of escalation past the point their strategy can sustain and costs they can endure.

But history has never waited for military theory to catch up, so it has been to history that soldiers have turned to prepare themselves for the battlefields of the future. Each of the twelve cases presented in this volume has been the subject of earlier full-length studies.[17] These larger studies focus on the dramatic and unique characteristics of the events they address. The value of studying these cases in a collective set, however, is that they can be held up in each other's light. By doing so one may begin to build a professionally useful body of knowledge about this unique class of military operations.

Just how far urban operations diverge from orthodox military operations can be seen in how differently they are planned and conducted, the constraints under which they labor, how their progress is judged, as well as the results they produce. Sometimes urban operations are so different from orthodoxy that they seem to belong to another war altogether—as if what happened inside the city had little reference to what happened beyond it. No one involved in the battle of Aachen, on either the Allied or the German side, would have seen the city as being important to a larger fabric of operations. The Germans did not intend to hold the city, and the Allies only wanted to get around it. As Christopher Gabel points out in his case study of the battle, the road network would have accommodated the Allies' original strategy quite nicely. Half of the city had already been destroyed by Allied bombing, although exactly why is unclear, because Aachen was not a vital industrial center to begin with. In keeping with the lack of importance both sides assigned to the city, neither side was prepared to fight inside the city. But neither was Adolf Hitler's direct intervention expected, an intervention that had nothing to do with military necessity and everything to do with misplaced sentimentalism. So the German Army did not after all withdraw from the city, the Allies could not leave them there, and thus a city battle was fought for a nostalgic reason as much as any other. Furthermore, while the combat inside the city took on its own character, the rest of the war moved on as before.

Among the cases collected here, the most extreme example of politics and sentiment investing a city with importance is that of Stalingrad. Although Stalingrad is now seen as the archetypical urban battle during World War II, it resembled Aachen in that neither side saw the city as critical to its strategic or operational plans. Neither the German General Staff nor the Soviet Stavka assigned much importance to the place. The German Army would very likely have passed through Stalingrad on the way to greater prizes in the east had not Joseph Stalin made an issue of the place. That done, Hitler complied enthusiastically. Thus, the stage was set for one of the most vicious battles of the twentieth century. While the city might have been of negligible military importance at first, the opposing national leaders ensured that it would grow to strategic proportions.[18]

While neither of the battles for Aachen or Stalingrad could be said to have been intentional and neither was the result of deliberate military planning, the battle for Hue was a critical element in a much larger strategic conception. As Vietnam's old imperial city, Hue was a cultural icon as well as being politically important. Partly because of its significance, all sides had treated Hue as something of an "open" city, immune to the war that had engulfed the rest of the country. For two years North Vietnamese strategists planned the campaign known to history as the Tet Offensive. Operational and tactical preparation for the assault on the city itself began six months before the attack. The North Vietnamese Army (NVA) worked to create complete surprise, and its work paid off. For a time Hue was under control of the NVA.[19] South Vietnamese and American reinforcements to shore up defenses and retake overrun districts were all deployed in the manner of a military emergency—in other words, a think-as-you-go crisis response, always the least acceptable, most expensive course of action.

For all the initial advantages the NVA enjoyed, they were insufficient to guarantee success. The North Vietnamese intended the battle for Hue to conclude promptly and decisively. When their plans were disappointed, they were forced into a series of tactical compromises, including an attempt to reinforce their battle from beyond the city itself. Eventually, the South Vietnamese and the Americans took the initiative away from the NVA. What began as a coup de main ended as a kind of siege in reverse, from the inside out.

Coups de main are not always failures. Nor are coups de main cheap operations, although the importance of subversion, preparation, and speed sometimes may create false expectations of decisive action. Also, unless these sorts of operations are supported properly, they all too often reverse the attackers' fortunes. The NVA's preparations for taking Hue followed the common practice of infiltrating the city well before what the attackers expected would be their decisive blow. The same was true in two other cases here, the Soviet Union's seizure of Kabul and the United States' seizure of Panama City. In both cases the attackers enjoyed virtually overwhelming advantages, and both were so planned.

The Soviets came very close to underestimating the regular forces that would be required to consummate the seizure of Kabul. The Americans, on the other hand, were in the peculiar position of invading themselves, so long and well established was their presence throughout Panama. In both cases the lure of quick, decisive action was too great for the planners to resist. The Americans' concept for invading Panama had a considerably larger scope than the Soviets' concept for Kabul. The Americans planned their invasion to attack many decisive targets as nearly simultaneously as they could to interdict any possible response, but what they wanted in the end was a decision in Panama City. Panama City was the only place, in fact, where a decision could be found. The same was true of Kabul, but there the decision had a much shorter life than the one in Panama. The attack on Kabul merely initiated a decade of unrewarding counterinsurgency warfare from which the Soviets had trouble extricating themselves.

Coups de main have never been quite as easy or quite as decisive as they have seemed. But coups de main may be verging on a new popularity if military thinkers can find ways to win a quick decision with new combinations of specialized forces, precision weapons, and cybernetic attack. Conceived in this manner, the coup de main seems a very modern kind of operation, one that aims at only those elements and functions of enemy power that contribute to his resistance. What is more certain is that the very notion of attacking even moderately large cities such as Grozny in the old-fashioned way—first isolating, then dividing the whole into ever smaller areas, reducing the defenders to their final redoubts—is absurd. Any attacking force that takes on an urban population hoping for a soft, compliant target is risking the dissipation of its combat power well before it meets its primary objective.

The presence of civilians, sometimes in the midst of battle, is one characteristic that makes urban warfare unique among all other forms of war. People trapped in cities by war have persisted in the most inhospitable conditions imaginable. A modern urban population may react stoically to the presence of foreign soldiers, but even noncombatant populations must continue to function, no matter what. For an invading army, even the most welcoming population constitutes a kind of resistant medium in which that army must continue to execute its mission. If the fight for a city is part of a larger campaign (such as in the battle for Aachen), fighting elsewhere might drive a new population of refugees into the city, replacing those who had evacuated earlier and arriving just when city services had been wrecked.

All too often combatant forces have found ways to use civilians to their advantage. In Manila, Hue, Grozny, Beirut, and certainly Sarajevo civilian noncombatants became critical and, at times, decisive elements of the engagement. Most commonly, the influence of noncombatants will work to the advantage of one side or another; they are rarely a "neutral" force. In the battle for Hue, for instance, South Vietnamese and American rules of engagement would not allow the employment of certain weapons,

IN THE SCHOOL OF WAR

but the NVA was bound by no such tactical restrictions. Concern for noncombatant casualties in Beirut was said to have prevented the Israelis from penetrating the city's defenses in 1983. In this instance the Israeli Defense Forces had to contend with the Palestinian refugee camps that worked as a human buffer for the Palestine Liberation Organization defenders behind them in the city proper. By contrast, the siege of Sarajevo was quite explicitly a siege against the noncombatants of the city, inaugurated, as Curt King's essay makes clear, when orthodox military operations failed to deliver the desired result. Sarajevans were, in effect, made hostage to military operations elsewhere, far from the eyes of the international public.

The urban environment, considered in military terms, is a unique environment in terms of both its essential character and its behavior. Faced with the complexities of this environment, military analysts have resorted to explaining cities as a "system of systems," as if cities were only the product of architectural designs and engineers' drawings. Those would not be cities but monuments. The first, most elementary feature of any urban environment is that it is a place where people have collected more or less permanently. It is therefore to the human qualities of the urban environment that the military planner must first look if he hopes to understand how armies can function in such a place.

When a military force acts in an urban environment, its essential humanness guarantees that the environment acts in return; that is, the relationship between a force and a city is *dynamic*. The dynamic interaction between cities and the military forces operating in them redefines and reshapes those forces over time. Because of its dynamic quality, the urban environment works as an important "third force," uniquely influencing the behavior of all sides engaged. This fundamental interaction cannot be ignored by the armies engaged regardless of how long or how intensive their operations.

Nor may we assume that the peculiarities of the urban environment will redound to the benefit of one side or another. As Al Lowe has observed in his essay on the long battle for Rio de Janeiro, early in the Montoneros' career as urban insurgents, they were happy to adopt the style of the *guerrillero*, fighting a war of poverty against orthodox Argentine forces. But as the war dragged on, both sides gravitated toward each other's methods. Unorthodox methods were increasingly adopted by the state, which conducted its own version of guerrilla operations against the Montoneros, including using extralegal death squads. Meanwhile, the methods of the guerrilleros slowly became more orthodox until, paradoxically, the movement's appeal to its power base among the urban poor gradually disappeared. Doubtless, neither side expected the environment itself to exercise this kind of power over its behavior.

The commander who enters a modern city unprepared will soon be forced to acknowledge critical differences in how he must operate if he is to accomplish his mission. The cost of everything will go up. He will need more forces and perhaps different forces; more transport not for his troops but to evacuate noncombatants; more civil affairs specialists to deal with a variety of political and social issues. The presence of refugees and local noncombatants will mean that medical support will be tugged in two directions, toward the rear as well as the front. And in the fighting zones casualties will begin to mount. Indeed, the historical record consistently shows a rapid increase in the consumption rates of all classes of military supply when a force engages in city combat. These differences are so great that the commander might think he had passed from one theater of operations to another. In a way, he has.

Perhaps the first difference the commander would notice is that his mission had to assume a different shape and his force had to adopt different methods. Time-honored combat formations designed for open fighting would reorganize themselves into ever-smaller groups, perhaps even without his intervention. Command and control would not work as it had. The fluidity with which his force had originally maneuvered would be impeded by the medium in which it now attempted to move. Inconsiderable distances would become deliberate advances under full protection.

An attack across a boulevard would take on the character of a river crossing. While the mission tempo would subside, the tactical tempo would intensify. Smaller acts would mean more. Tactical forces would combat smaller targets more fiercely. Buildings would become campaigns, stairs would become avenues of approach, and rooms would become fortresses. In just this way the worst urban battles of the twentieth century assumed their own shapes and purposes. The battles for the tractor factory in Stalingrad, for the Zoo Flak Tower in Berlin, for the fortress at Manila, and for the Citadel at Hue all exploded the best-laid plans of commanders on the spot, forcing them to submit to the tactical demands of the moment.

Modern armies would be mistaken to assume that battles such as these are impossible in the future. The first battle for Grozny that Timothy Thomas describes here, as well as succeeding battles for the city, serves as a warning for those armies that underestimate the challenges of modern urban warfare. Ill prepared, poorly led, poorly supported, and thrown recklessly against a determined defender whose military assets were modest, a ramshackle Russian Army ignored its own history, using firepower as a substitute for thought. Almost a decade after the adversaries began fighting, neither side seems to recognize that fighting is only a means, not an end, certainly not a way of life. So Grozny takes its place alongside those urban battles that have devolved from purpose to habit, where exhaustion rather than the military art offers the only way out. No policy maker or professional soldier should be willing to accept such a verdict.

Modern urban warfare is neither a completely new or completely old military phenomenon; as usual, it is some of both. It is not a phenomenon beyond the reach of professional understanding, and in the past several years a reawakening of professional interest has occurred around the military world. The professional soldier now has within reach a substantial historical and contemporary literature from which the foundation of new military doctrines and practices can be built. This casebook has been written to contribute to that foundation.

Notes

1. By Sun Tzu's reckoning, the general placed his army in "critical terrain." Sun Tzu, *The Art of War*, trans. and ed. Samuel B. Griffith, foreword by B. H. Liddell Hart (London: Oxford University Press, 1963), 38–39, 78–79. See also *Sun-Tzu: The Art of Warfare*, trans. Roger Ames (New York: Ballantine Books, 1993), 111–12, 439.

2. Phillipe Contamine, *The Art of War in the Middle Ages*, trans. Michael Jones (London: Basil Blackwell, 1983), 219.

3. Spiro Kostof, *The City Shaped: Urban Patterns and Meaning through History* (London: Thames and Hudson, 1991; paperback, 1999), 108–10.

4. Contamine, *The Art of War*, 101.

5. Ibid.

6. Kostof, *The City Shaped*, 108–10.

7. The Population Council, "Population," in *The Microsoft Encarta Encyclopedia 99*, vol. 4 (CD-ROM).

8. United Nations (UN), "The World at Six Billion," UN Population Division of the Department of Economic and Social Affairs, New York, 1999, b-2, b-3, http://www.un.org/popin (accessed 1999).

9. Eugene Linden, "The Exploding Cities of the Developing World," *Foreign Affairs*, January–February 1996, 54–55.

10. This figure includes all inhabitants within Tokyo's urban agglomeration as calculated by the UN Population Division. The UN employs the term *agglomeration* to designate only those urban areas that exceed a population of 10 million. The UN employs the term *small cities* for urban areas of 500,000 and less. See UN Population Division, "World Urbanization Prospects: The 2001 Revision; Data Tables and Highlights," UN Population Division of the Department of Economic and Social Affairs, New York, March 21, 2002, 1–3, 172, http://www.un.org/popin (accessed November 2002).

11. Tokyo.gov, "The Official Tokyo Metro Website," http://www.chiji honbu.metro.tokyo.jp (accessed November 2002).

12. UN Population Division, "World Urbanization Prospects," 1–3.

13. This is not to say that once urban growth begins it cannot level off or even reverse itself. Demographic estimates are not predictions of the future. In 1973 estimates of Mexico City's population at century's end ran higher than 30 million, but global and national markets changed radically in the meantime and influenced how economic activity in Mexico was distributed. See Linden, "The Exploding Cities," 54.

14. Ibid.

15. David E. Kaplan, "The Law of the Jungle," *U.S. News and World Report*, October 14, 2002, 35.

16. Linden, "The Exploding Cities," 54.

17. This essay originally appeared in William G. Robertson and Lawrence A. Yates, eds., *Block by Block: The Challenges of Urban Operations*.

18. I have discussed the operational value of Stalingrad more extensively in *Sharp Corners: Urban Operations at Century's End* (Fort Leavenworth KS: U.S. Army Command and General Staff College Press, 2001), 59–60.

19. See Ronnie E. Ford, *TET 1968: Understanding the Surprise* (London: Frank Cass, 1995), esp. 66–86.

Three

Going Public

It is deeply satisfying to be hated by the ignorant. The feeling you get opening a letter or e-mail choked with invective is not to be undervalued. It might even be addictive.

I suspect most historians don't count being reviled as one of their craft's many compensations. It's rare enough anyone takes notice of what we do, but when they go out of their way to attack something we've written or said, we should be grateful. Someone's paying attention. Framing an insult takes some thought—the skill doesn't seem to come naturally—and working up the energy to fire it off does too. There's even the chance of learning something, even if you wonder whether you should check the locks on your door.

As a species, historians are solitary creatures. Some of us make perfectly good company when we leave our desks, but our social skills are no more highly developed than most people's. We prefer to speak from the greater distance of our writing. The largest audience we're likely to face directly is in the lecture hall. Some do brilliantly in that setting, having mastered this minor form of performance art, communing with their audience like actors at the top of their form. Of course, their audiences never see the agonies of self-doubt and recrimination these performers suffer. Even some of the best have confessed to throwing up before they take the public stage.

Then there are those rare historians who seem made for the public life. They've won a spot in the address books of mass media's producers and booking agents. They seem intellectually fearless or even—their detractors say—reckless. Fixtures on opinion pages and talk shows, they take on any subject without misgivings or reservations. They reduce the most complex questions to fifteen-second judgments. They are indefatigable, always on call, accessible and ready, armed for public battle.

When we think about our more public cousins, it is often with disapproval—and envy. We object that public discourse demands too many concessions that sacrifice the nuance and fine detail we've been taught to value most. If this is the public face of history, surely, we argue, it must be history of a lower order. But in between bursts of indignation our curiosity swells up. We wonder how they do it, and then we wonder, How would we do it?

These aren't idle questions. Even if a historian has no taste for public life, the chances of being swept up in the wider world are better than ever. The work scattered across the desk in a quiet study can ignite public interest without warning. When that happens, you learn that this world works by rules and calls on skills different from the ones you ordinarily use.

Different skills, note, not lesser ones.

Richard Snow, managing editor of *American Heritage Magazine*, asked me to serve as a contributing editor in the early 1990s. The magazine had a long career of recruiting historians to write for it who could translate their work into public form without doing violence to their professional standards. The magazine's editors had no agenda, no slant save the conviction that history must in the end be a public art, owned by no one, owned by everyone. That was a cause I had no trouble joining.

The magazine's audience ran to nearly a million readers, a sobering thought for anyone whose ordinary work might reach a few thousand people at most. This fact alone acted as a check against any impulse to toss off an article. If it survived Snow's editors, you could be sure someone in the vast audience waited to skewer any writer who misplaced facts or ventured a dubious interpretation. Writing these pieces was often as much a test of professional skill as writing for a professional journal.

The Internet was not as highly evolved as it is today. Magazines were still a viable channel of public information; back then, aspiring writers fought for a place in traditional print, not blog-

ging on the Net. Snow's magazine received as many as fifty manuscripts a day begging for attention. His invitation to serve as
a contributing editor meant I was free to write anything I liked
with a fair assurance the magazine would publish it.
From time to time Snow would ask for an essay on a particular topic. Sometimes these assignments arrived with tight dead-
lines, forcing everything else to the side of the desk. One day he
called with an idea for a feature he was putting together, a collection of brief appraisals of the most overrated and underrated figures in American history, arranged by certain categories. "Would
you do generals?" he asked. He needed the piece in a week—and
it couldn't go over two hundred words.

The assignment was intriguing and slightly absurd. The length
Snow wanted was ridiculous: how could such a short piece possibly enlighten the magazine's readers? Even if I managed this
kind of near-poetic compression, there was the larger problem
of the subject itself, whose straightforwardness quickly collapsed
the more one thought about it.

For the next several days I badgered my friends and colleagues,
inciting learned judgments and heated arguments along the way.
They all agreed that the generals I chose should enjoy roughly
equal, and high, historical standing. My choices had to be fair:
comparing generals from different wars wouldn't do. Some generals had easier wars than others. That suggested my choices
should come from the same war and that their roles were equally
demanding. Having exhausted my friends' patience, I settled on
Ulysses S. Grant and Robert E. Lee, both grand enough to bear
the burden of the lesson Snow wanted his feature to teach.

What lesson? Simply that in the eternal competition between
historical reputations, injustices were sometimes done. Rather
than acquiescing in history's judgments, we had to give these reputations another look.

So that extra look, reprinted here, was published with a collection of similar pieces in the summer of 1998. My two hundred
words, really a reflection of how reputations sometimes evolved

to the detriment of historical fact, set in motion a minor but bizarre controversy that turned on one remark: rather offhandedly, I'd reminded my readers that whatever else one might say about Lee, he was a traitor to his country.

Both generals had their share of admirers, of course, but Lee's seemed far more passionate about their favorite general, and they lost no time defending his honor. *American Heritage* began receiving letters protesting the injustice done to Lee's name. Not surprisingly, most of these letters came from below the Mason-Dixon Line. Snow happily passed them along to me.

None of the other pieces in the feature caused such reactions. Although a few of the letters challenged the substance of what I'd written (legal briefs on soldiers' oaths of office, the timing of Lee's resignation, states' rights interpretations of the Constitution, and the like), most devoted themselves to assailing the black-hearted heretic who dared slander the Great White Knight of the South.

The growing pile of abuse ran to a certain pattern. Most were typed, but quite a few of the writers showed off their artistic skills too, adding a graphic punch to their opinions just in case language failed them. They usually began making their case with fervent reassertions of Lee's greatness. These were sometimes followed by charges against the magazine for having been fooled into printing the essay. But most of the writers spent their energy describing the kind of person who would perpetrate this crime. To my critics I was clearly:

a Yankee,
a Democrat,
a liberal,
a Communist,
a peacenik,
a hippie,
a draft dodger,
a dope addict,
and a homosexual.

Only some of these were true.

I spent many happy moments contemplating my deficiencies, my defective judgment, my dubious politics, my indiscrete personal traits. Alas, however, the controversy began fading away.

And in ancient times—say, thirty or forty years ago—there the matter would've rested. Now, however, my charge against General Lee attracted the notice of a Web site whose mission was to defend Southern honor against all who offended it. For the convenience of their customers, the Web site's managers published my address, enjoining one and all to write to me directly. My supply of letters was replenished, but, sadly, this wave was shorter than the first. All too soon my enemies no longer cared enough to insult me. The thought occurred to me that I hadn't really held up my end of the transaction. And it was true: I could see this affair stretching out into the distance, a perpetual carnival of triviality. I hadn't cooperated. Instead, I followed the advice given me by an old soldier: Never wrestle with pigs. You both get dirty. And the pig likes it.

Then the White House became involved.

Anyone who's watched daily press briefings at the White House might think they always address great questions of state. We suppose reporters who've earned admission to this rarefied world are at the top of their game. We expect them not to waste time on silliness. And for the most part they honor the seriousness of their position.

That's why President Clinton's press secretary, Mike McCurry, may've been a bit surprised when one of the reporters asked a question that went something like this:

Does the president of the United States agree with one of his employees, a professor at the Army's Command and General Staff College, that Robert E. Lee was a traitor to his country?

McCurry confessed that he didn't know.

Would he bring this matter up with the president?

McCurry said he would see if the president wished to comment.

The transcript of that day's briefing doesn't record what the other reporters thought of this exchange.

Across the river, in the Army's headquarters at the Pentagon, platoons of staff officers commanded by a major general devotedly attend to the Army's public image. Their guiding principle is that any unofficial news is bad news. That goes doubly for any news involving the White House. So adept are they at managing the Army's image that this seldom happens. When it does, the official heart rate rises appreciably.

The first sign that there was a disturbance in the force came from Fort Leavenworth's own public affairs officer, who passed along news of the exchange at the White House and asked for a little background on the question. That given, she rang off, satisfied the Republic was not at peril.

For the next several days, however, I lived in a never-never land between image and reality. Robert E. Lee's historical reputation was obviously not a question that threatened the Army's interests, and in any case one essay was unlikely to overturn it. But for the briefest moment this question became news—about history, about the Army, and about the academic serpent basking in the comforts of the federal government. The reporter's question to McCurry was skillfully phrased: by pointing out that I was an "employee" of the president (as indeed I was, however remotely), he implied I could be disciplined, perhaps fired, for my act of lèse-majesté. Tenure in the civil service such as I had was hardly as sacrosanct as academic tenure. If my elders and betters decided I'd gone too far, they could always cook up a plausible excuse to send me on my way. Over the next few days I imagined staff officers buzzing just outside my door, trying to decide what should be done.

You'd think this would be a good time for me to reconsider my indictment of Lee, perhaps soften it in some way, maybe even apologize for my bad manners. But the reaction to my essay hardened my opinion of what Lee had done. Any sympathy I might've had for Lee dissolved as I thought about the disaster he helped enact. For me, no ameliorating argument could lighten the weight of that burden. What began as a comic reaction to a slight essay became a more important question—and now a personal one. If historians will not defend the truth of the past, regardless of the consequences, who will?

In the end no one ever suggested I revise my views. I'd like to think reason intervened somewhere along the Army's chain of command, but more likely the incident was simply forgotten as it sank back into the white noise of public chatter where it began. I wouldn't have to wrestle with pigs—this time. But I learned that the pigs are always out there, ready and willing for a match.

And the president never called to reprimand his lowly employee.

The canons of historical practice might seem ill suited for public venues, but the appetite for historical knowledge is greater than ever, and the scope of the historian's work now reaches far beyond the light on the desk. Whether we like it or not, inside every historian is a public figure waiting in the wings for a debut. Better to be ready when the call comes to take the stage. That way the stagehands won't have to drag you out there, protesting your innocence. In the age of information, no one is innocent after all.

General

Most Overrated General

Sometimes when I read military history, I get the feeling I'm reading about an Olympic competition in which points are awarded for style as much as for results. In the general-judging business, matters of style and performance are too often entangled. George McClellan was very stylish. He built such a beautiful army that he didn't want to use it. He believed he could choose the kind of war he wanted to fight—an antiseptic war of grand strategies—and ignore the ugly parts. He wandered about his battlefields afterward, and the sight sickened him. The Northern public lionized him, and his soldiers loved him because being beautiful was much more satisfying than being shot down in windrows. The Civil War killed his style.

Robert E. Lee was the most stylish of all our generals and certainly the most overrated. McClellan paid early for his stylishness, but I don't think Lee ever has really been called to account. Lee is truly a tragic figure, a man who by everyone's agreement epitomized high character and soldierly honor but who also was a traitor to his country, a man of formidable military skill whose strategic and operational sense nevertheless was deeply flawed and who led his side from calamity to calamity. But he is the original Teflon general. In many quarters today no hint of blame attaches to him.

Most Underrated General

For these same reasons I think we tend to be a little snobbish about U. S. Grant, this scruffy little man from Illinois who was a failure at just about everything but generaling. His debut was far from promising, and even when he got better, no one could believe he was learning what he had to do. But he did learn. He saw the Civil War for what it was, not what he wanted it to be, not as an exercise in nostalgia or romanticism. Often reviled for his blood-ax methods in the Wilderness, in his classic Vicksburg campaign Grant showed he could also practice war artfully when art was needed. Often said to be devoid of character, he was, on the contrary, the completest character of all our generals, so complete, as T. Harry Williams once wrote, that his countrymen could never quite believe he was real, and we've never given him his due.

For we still want our style, a bit of dash and flash to blind us to what war really is, and while Lee rests in pastoral splendor down in Virginia, up in New York it is always advisable to visit Grant's tomb in daylight.

World War II General

Overrated

Most of the generals of World War II are now forgotten. History has already had its say about which will be remembered. Seen from a distance, generals of high repute make a kind of sense even in their own time. Their reputations are explicable. Qualities of character and mind unbidden by the routines of peace are often called forth by the demands of war. How these men met these demands usually fixes their reputations for good or ill. During the war Lewis Brereton was rated high enough in someone's esteem to draw a succession of important U.S. Army Air Corps commands, rising in rank from brigadier to lieutenant general—no small feat, since he was a kind of Typhoid Mary in uniform. Wherever he landed, disaster was not far behind.

When the Japanese struck the American air base at Clark Field in the Philippines the day after Pearl Harbor, Brereton's B-17s were perfectly lined up on the tarmac, despite MacArthur's orders to guard against surprise attack. The Japanese happily destroyed all but 35 of his 145 aircraft. The year 1943 found Brereton in North Africa, where he put his stamp on planning for an air offensive against the oil fields at Ploieşti in Romania. Brereton had little patience for high-altitude bombing and insisted on a low-level attack. Twenty-five percent of his force did not return. By early 1944 he was in command of the air forces charged with supporting the D-Day invasion, only he didn't think training for the complexities of air-ground cooperation was really necessary, and over this and other issues he quarreled importantly with Field Marshal Montgomery and General Bradley. When Bradley's army tried its breakout from Normandy, Brereton was in command of Operation Cobra, air strikes that killed

Gen. Leslie McNair and a hundred other American soldiers in one of the costliest friendly fire incidents of the war.

Never mind; a new assignment came through just in time. He was given command of the first Allied airborne army in history, with the mission of conducting the most ambitious airborne operation of the war, Market Garden, or, as some came to know it, "a bridge too far." By that stage of the war, however, plenty of incompetent commanders were available to help Brereton drop his troops right on top of several full-strength German divisions.

Someone kept promoting Brereton. Someone kept recommending him for ever more important commands. In someone's eyes Brereton was very highly rated—highly overrated, as it happened.

Underrated

Lucian Truscott is similarly obscure. Truscott's promotions came even faster than Brereton's, and he commanded in battle at every echelon from regiment to field army. During this war the infantry divisions were the hard core of American military power on the ground, and among their commanders were some of the very best soldiers America put into the field. Lucian Truscott was arguably the best American division commander in the war, and for him it was a long war indeed, stretching from Morocco and Tunisia through Sicily to mainland Italy—two amphibious assaults there, at Salerno and at Anzio—and to southern France, where he took VI Corps up the Rhone Valley. He took over the Fifth Army in Italy late in 1944 and finished the war with a campaign against desperate German resistance in the Po Valley. Not one of his campaigns could have been called easy; his troops fought their way over some of the worst terrain and against some of the most determined enemy the European theater had to offer.

Truscott was raised as a cavalry officer. He had wit and dash and a talent to lead, a fine mind, and a ready pen. After the war he wrote one of the best memoirs by any American fighting general, *Command Missions*. But in a miscarriage of history he has disappeared from the view of all but the most serious students of the war. Let Brereton replace him in obscurity.

FOURTEEN. **War in the Dark**

Well before the film's debut we could hear the drumbeat of publicity. Steven Spielberg, America's favorite moviemaker, was going to give us a film about World War II. The title, *Saving Private Ryan*, gave away nothing. Unlike *Schindler's List*, which translated Thomas Keneally's best-selling book on the Holocaust to the screen, *Saving Private Ryan* would build its plot around an obscure incident from the invasion of Normandy. Four brothers from the Niland family had had a very bad war by the summer of 1944: two had been killed on D-Day, and another was thought to have been killed in Burma. The last brother, Fritz, had jumped with the 101st Airborne Division into Normandy, where the odds were that he would make his family's final contribution to the Good War. An enterprising Army chaplain, Father Francis Sampson, found the paratrooper and pulled him out of the fighting. The story was good enough to merit the approval of the most jaded critic, and it was true besides.

But Hollywood could never leave a fact alone. Father Sampson would disappear during the script conferences to be replaced by eight Rangers led by a captain played by Tom Hanks. Having survived their own assault on Omaha Beach, Hanks and his men now have the mission to rescue the last of the brothers. Hanks & Co. have little enthusiasm for this crackbrained idea, but they are experienced combat soldiers and therefore can expect to have acquired an intimate acquaintance with "chickenshit," a wartime term best defined by former second lieutenant of World War II infantry, now Emeritus Professor Paul Fussell, as that which "has absolutely nothing to do with winning the war." Of course, Hanks's squad completes the mission, but not without cost.

Few can doubt that when the history of film in the twentieth century is written, Steven Spielberg will have a place in the front ranks. He has learned to calculate our cultural rhythms so keenly that we invest his work with transcendent significance. We so cheerfully accept his power over our imagination that we forget his other talent as one of America's great entertainment businessmen. His market power is now at least as great as his artistic power. The fabled promoters of movie history, Cecil B. DeMille, Darryl F. Zanuck, and Irving G. Thalberg, are amateurs compared with Spielberg. So what began as a drumbeat became a tightly composed symphony of press releases, photo ops, tie-ins, interviews, and film clips. Web sites and chat rooms began to appear on the Internet. For weeks before the film's release hardly a day passed without reference to *Saving Private Ryan* on television.

The buzz said that *Saving Private Ryan* was going to be a new kind of war film, one that unflinchingly depicted the sharp end of war, the essence of war itself—the infantryman's war. *Saving Private Ryan* was going to be the greatest war film ever made, hands down, no kidding, about any war. When *Saving Private Ryan* hit the screen, it would immediately be recognized as the gold standard for an entire genre of film, and that standard would be founded upon the very action that had always defied being captured on film: combat soldiers, individually and in small groups, more threatened than assisted by the vast mechanical accessories of modern war.

Spielberg and his equally gifted star, Tom Hanks, struck just the right notes too, promoting the film in modest, even reverential tones, selling their movie by understatement. Indeed, the impression conveyed was that this film was not to be seen as entertainment. Dark precautions went out: the first twenty-five minutes, re-creating the assault on Omaha Beach, might be "too intense" for some people. The film had a serious, high-minded purpose. *Saving Private Ryan* would not be an empty military pageant like *The Longest Day*, shuttling platoons of stars across the screen to declaim hollow patriotic rhetoric. Nor would it burden its audiences with cynical reservations about the war or the cause for which it was fought. No need to fear such dialogue as that from *The Naked and the Dead*, uttered in exhausted fatalism by the member of a much less successful infantry patrol, "We broke our ass for nothin'," which elicits the reply, "Higher strategy." No, by telling a simple story, *Saving Private Ryan* would reinvest the Second World War with the straightforward dignity it deserves and by so doing take its audience closer to the essential truth of this war—perhaps any war—than any other film had ever done.

When the film actually appeared, any doubts that this movie was quite as good or as original as advertised were quickly shouted down. Box-office returns, which quickly exceeded fifty million dollars and as of this writing are nearly two hundred million, overwhelmed contrarians like Vincent Canby of the *New York Times* and Louis Menand of the *New York Review of Books*. The thoughtful reviews they offered were widely regarded as acts of lèse-majesté. Other commentators happily perpetrated all manner of rhetorical inanities, using the film to wag reproving fingers at effete baby boomers who were filling up theater seats. We were happy to be insulted, and to insult. On the Web the chat, as captured by John Gregory Dunne in a recent *New Yorker* article, was less than genteel when someone named Brad declined to be impressed. "Let me guess. You are a wannabe hippie. Take your poetry reading, latte-drinking, non-shaving, sandal-wearing BUTT to Arlington National Cemetery and then come back on line, pudboy." This, from Darren, who despises Brad because Brad has the bad grace to suspect that war is not fun. Darren thinks he knows more about war by eating popcorn in the dark. Hell hath no fury like a noncombatant.

So a question worth asking is, How did we come to think we know more about war than we actually do? What body of knowledge did we rely upon before *Saving Private Ryan* came along? The answer is that what most Americans today know of war comes from films—theatrical films, contemporary newsreels, propaganda and training films, documentary films, video films, and now gun-camera films. From the Mexican War onward armies and cameras have gone to war together, producing still photography now easily adapted to film. But if one were to calculate which war dominates film, as Peter Maslowski has done in his fine study *Armed with Cameras: The American Military Photographers of World War II*, the Second World War has no competitors.

All the major armies of the Second World War deployed still and film camera units to document combat action. Millions of still photos, thousands of miles of film were shot on all fronts, at sea, in the air, and on the ground. Some of the American photographic units included veteran filmmakers, among them John Huston, Darryl Zanuck, Edward Steichen, George Stevens, and David O. Selznick. Filming the war demanded not only technical expertise but courage as well, for American cameramen labored under strict instructions not to "reenact" combat footage. Combat film would be shot in combat. The lengths to which photographers went to capture just a few minutes of fighting were extraordinary. On several occasions combat cameramen raced ahead, unprotected, toward enemy lines just to make a shot of an American assault head-on.

But combat proved to be disappointingly un-Hollywood. Shooting footage of air, sea, and land combat posed difficulties unique to each setting, and shots of actual ground fighting were perhaps the most difficult of all to make. Photographers and filmmakers at the time understood their problem very well: ground combat, as practiced, did not easily submit to translation onto film. One of the most fundamental rules of infantry combat was "Never bunch up." A "tight shot" for a camera was also a tight shot for the enemy. Both friendly and enemy fire were disobligingly invisible. If the air was full of lead or shrapnel, combat infantrymen tried to disappear. The most savage firefights seemed to take place on an empty battleground. And if it was nearly impossible to film one's own side in action, getting a shot of enemy action was downright miraculous. In the entire Pacific war, despite near-suicidal efforts by battalions of cameramen, only two sequences of Japanese infantrymen in actual combat were ever captured. The disjuncture between the demands of reality and the expectations of audiences already conditioned by years of cinematic clichés about war and enforced by the prohibition on reenactments of combat was too much for John Huston. Huston's film *The Battle of San Pietro*, acclaimed when it was released to theaters in 1945 and afterward as the most realistic visual documentation of combat in the war, was shot well after the fighting it purported to depict. Sound effects were added in the editing room along with the narration. Screams of pain and anguish were not available for recording, but the Army Air Force Orchestra, the St. Brendan's Church Choir, and the Mormon Tabernacle Choir filled in the blanks. As Maslowski observes, "Watching a video of *San Pietro* with the sound turned off is a supremely dull experience."

If combat cameramen risking their lives around the world contended dangerously with the inherent barriers between film and war, neither was Hollywood free to indulge in artistic license. Especially during the first two years of the war, when an Allied victory was by no means a foregone conclusion, the Office of War Information and the Office of Censorship exercised reviewing authority over both print and film. Not until mid-1943 was a photograph of a dead American soldier shown anywhere in the United States, not in print, not on news film. In the last two years of the struggle, concerned about war weariness on the home front, government officials thought they might reinvigorate domestic morale by permitting more violent representations of the struggle; showing more bodies would remind everyone how serious this war still was, just in case they missed the deliveries of the Western Union telegrams.

Under the circumstances it was hardly surprising that theatrical filmmakers kept clear of reality. Instead, the eighty million people who attended the movies each week were treated to wonderfully forgettable offerings such as *Bowery Blitzkrieg* (1941), starring Leo Gorcey and Huntz Hall, or *Joan of Ozark* (1942), with the redoubtable comedienne Judy Canova. Citizens of College Station, Texas, concerned about Japanese saboteurs in their midst, found alarming confirmation of their fears in *We've Never Been Licked* (1943). They need not have worried; the cadets of Texas A&M were on the job. Newsreels and official films gave the public its closest look at the real war. Those few theatrical films that pretended to depict combat on the ground such as *Sahara, Guadalcanal Diary*, and *Gung Ho!*—all released in 1943—merely increased the distance between the fighting fronts and the home front. The best wartime film, *Casablanca*, was not even about war as such; here the war was simply a great inconvenience, or a great opportunity.

The best American World War II films appeared at war's end and after. By then the public had other sources to draw upon for its understanding of the war: those who had actually fought in it. But combat veterans weren't particularly interested in talking; even if they had been, a public that knew of war only as depicted in the movies knew so little it did not even know what questions to ask them. Too, making a film about war in the victory years was commercially as well as artistically risky; what combat veteran would pay to see a pale version of his experience? How could a filmmaker take on such a job when he knew that thousands of veterans would be looking over his shoulder, critiquing every frame, every shot, every piece of dialogue, every piece of action?

More war films were made anyway, and soon. *The Story of G.I. Joe*, which took its plot from Ernie Pyle's famous wartime eulogy to a beloved infantry captain in Italy, was released in 1945. Pyle's account of one infantry captain's death was highly sentimental, suitably antiseptic for wartime consumption, and it promoted the comforting notion that all soldiers loved and admired their officers. Eisenhower thought it was the best film of the war. But Pyle himself was unable to enjoy its success. He was killed during a mopping-up operation on an obscure Pacific island that year.

Postwar films were about to take on a new, harder edge, antisentimental and antiheroic. High-mindedness was suspect, and life in film became darker, elemental, colored with the fatalistic outlook of a soldier who had seen too much combat. The war found its way into films that had nothing to do with war, but snatches of dialogue still wore combat gear. Life was no longer fair. Honor was a sucker's game. Being good had nothing to do with whether one survived. From the gangster film *White Heat* (1949), listen to this exchange between Paul Guilfoyle and James Cagney:

"You wouldn't kill me in cold blood, would you?"

"No. I'll let you warm up a little."

A Walk in the Sun, based on Harry Brown's novel and directed by Lewis Milestone, who in 1930 had brought *All Quiet on the Western Front* to the screen, came out in 1945 and was the first in a class of hardheaded war films: no patriotic diction here, no improbable heroics, no references to irrelevancies such as grand strategy or the self-important angst of high command, just a morning's march with infantrymen who have had a long war that is getting longer by the minute. For the characters here the war was not about the Four Freedoms; it was about getting through the morning alive, and maybe the afternoon and night too if they were lucky, and then about doing it all again the next day and the day after.

But *A Walk in the Sun* was not going to tell any veteran of infantry combat anything he didn't already know. Only one postwar film spoke directly to the veterans in terms that may have helped them contend with their experiences. *The Best Years of Our Lives* (1946) followed three veterans as they struggled to return to normal life in a world that seemed to understand little and care less about the war they had just survived. The movie won eight Oscars.

As *The Best Years of Our Lives* made plain, memories of the war were already fading, shouldered aside by postwar routines and Cold War anxieties. At some indiscernible point, as if by common, unstated agreement, filmmakers pointed their war films at those who were innocent of war altogether. Like *A Walk in the Sun*, 1949's *Battleground* was unlikely to appeal to combat veterans because it aimed to reproduce their experiences. Producer Dore Schary had trouble finding support in Hollywood for making yet another war film. Even so, audiences in 1949 saw the release of the best-ever movie about war in the air, *Twelve o'Clock High*, and, importantly, John Wayne's now-fabled *Sands of Iwo Jima*.

No two films are less alike. Based on a script by two veterans of the Eighth Air Force's bomber offensive against Germany at the height of the war, *Twelve o'Clock High* follows a bomber-group commander—Maj. Gen. Frank Armstrong in real life—as he fights against the pressures of wartime command, eventually succumbing to its fatigues. Gregory Peck's portrayal of the haunted commander is so appealing that the film is still shown to approving audiences in the military academies.

Sands of Iwo Jima is one of two films that belong in movie history not so much because of how faithfully they reproduce war as because of their influence upon those who saw them. After John Wayne's portrayal of the tough marine, Sergeant Stryker, hit the screen, there were proto-gyrenes all over America, and they took Wayne's cinematic conduct as a standard of behavior with them into their own wars. Veterans of World War II might react suspiciously to Wayne's heroics, but their sons did not. Marine trainees at Camp Pendleton were hired as extras for Tony Curtis's 1961 film biography of Ira Hayes, the Native American who helped raise the flag on Iwo Jima, *The Outsider*. When the director asked them why they had enlisted, half of them said it was because they had been inspired by *Sands of Iwo Jima*.

Six years after Sergeant Stryker died in front of a Japanese pillbox on a Hollywood back lot, a movie was released that would share with *Sands of Iwo Jima* the dubious fame of fixing in the minds of America's youth a picture of combat and how one should behave in combat that has been sustained until the present day. *To Hell and Back* was a war film with a difference: Audie Murphy, America's most highly decorated World War II soldier, played himself, suggesting that here was a chance for the audience to see what combat was really like. What the audience didn't know was that Murphy was still suffering from the after-effects of his real war and would continue to do so for the rest of his life. The experience of trying to reproduce his life in combat was not easy for him, nor did he regard the result as particularly satisfying. *To Hell and Back* was a more highly stylized view of war than any number of war films, and Murphy knew it. He was "a lot braver" in the film than he had been in the war, he said, but his modesty only added to his aura. War could be heroic again, at least until all the future heroes in the audience found out otherwise.

The fifties and early sixties were the heyday of the war movie. War movies with a hard edge were still being produced, but they were not about World War II. In 1951 *The Steel Helmet*, set in the Korean War, came out, followed three years later by *The Bridges at Toko-Ri*. In 1957 perhaps the best World War I movie ever made, *Paths of Glory*, revealed Stanley Kubrick as a director with a decidedly unsentimental view of war. Kubrick's film was banned in France for a time and, notably, from some American military posts. Lewis Milestone filmed S. L. A. Marshall's Korean War saga, *Pork Chop Hill*, in 1959. All these films had much in common with their predecessors. Like the best of the earlier films, they reduced the war to the individual human level. Unlike the worst, they refused to indulge in the easy moralizing that had proved so irresistible so often to Hollywood.

Late in the fifties David Lean's *The Bridge on the River Kwai* inaugurated a subclass of war film that proved to be incomparably more popular. The military extravaganza capitalized upon new film, sound, and screen technology. In Lean's film and the blockbusters that followed—*The Longest Day* (1962), *In Harm's Way* (1965), and *The Battle of the Bulge* (1965)—the screen always had more people on it than were in the audience and more military equipment than one would need to defend a small nation. These were films on the industrial scale, made with the enthusiastic and substantial assistance of the Department of Defense. Grand history, great events, great men provided the rough plots for these panoramas, but beyond that anything that got between the audience and the popcorn was unwelcome. That included reality.

The Vietnam War effectively and promptly killed the war movie, or so film historians say. Why produce a theatrical film about war when the American public saw the war in Southeast Asia on the evening news? Yet even in 1970, as the war was grinding to its melancholy conclusion, one of the most popular war films ever, *Patton*, was released, and so was the dreadful Pearl Harbor extravaganza *Tora! Tora! Tora!* Compared with the war in Vietnam, the Disneyfied version of World War II was more satisfying to contemplate than body counts. Perhaps this was when Studs Terkel conceived his idea of "the Good War."

Once the Vietnam War was safely past, World War II extravaganzas returned to the Pacific with *Midway* in 1976 and *MacArthur* in 1977, the latter proving that films on military egomaniacs don't automatically sell. But *Patton*, portrayed so broadly and with such near-psychopathic glee by George C. Scott, was as satisfying to the war lover as to the most diehard antiwar activist.

Film historians and critics might regard *Patton* and Francis Ford Coppola's *Apocalypse Now* as antithetical. But while filmmakers were still trying to tell a whole story, audiences were reading segments of their films, some no longer than a television commercial, as reference points for themselves. Scott's memorable opening monologue in *Patton*, giant American flag filling the screen, could by itself be made to bear any number of interpretations quite apart from how the director and the actors saw the scene as contributing to the rest of the production. Robert Duvall's burlesque portrayal of the slightly mad Air Cav colonel could be alternately hated or admired without regard for the meaning Francis Ford Coppola invested in it. Today, if I were to ask my students, all professional soldiers, to replay a scene from *Apocalypse Now*, Duvall's scene would be the one, but their interpretations of it would be as varied as they are.

In *The Barefoot Contessa* Humphrey Bogart's character, a director, delivers this line: "Life every now and then behaves as if it had seen too many bad movies." During the Gulf War, as troops in one particular unit began their attack on Iraqi ground defenses, their commander ordered "The Ride of the Valkyries" played over loudspeakers on their tanks and fighting vehicles. I later asked their commander if he had a great number of Wagnerians in his unit. But no, of course he didn't. That was what Robert Duvall had his own loudspeakers play during his heliborne assault on the vc village in *Apocalypse Now* both to unnerve the enemy and to suffuse his own men with Götterdämmerung-like frenzy—a case of life imitating art imitating life. If it wasn't true in the film, real battle would make it so, and the real commander, a decade after, knew exactly the effect he wanted to achieve. This improbable convergence between film and combat was momentary, no doubt. As the more unfortunate among these troops would discover, the distance between film and combat was as great as ever.

At first I had no intention of seeing *Saving Private Ryan*. Having studied with and taught professional soldiers about the experience of combat for twenty years, I had no desire to see an attempt to reduce to film anything I knew about this subject. But I knew, too, that my students would want to know, insist on knowing, what I thought about this movie—not as a film critic but as a military historian. How did this film compare with others of its kind, the ulterior question being, of course, How close does it come to the real thing? In the end avoiding the film seemed like avoiding responsibility. So I went, unenthusiastically, as an obligation, in self-defense.

I saw a good war film, one that was informed by a high purpose, executed with the technical brilliance we have come to expect from its director, played by skilled actors representing the usual collection of American "types": the selfless officer, the tough sergeant, the wise guy, the hick, the intelligent one who will funk it, the medic, and so on. The plotline was, well, dopey, but then the troops drew lots of dopey missions during World War II, and on the scale of dopiness, this one wasn't that high. Any night attack was dopier. The dialogue was noble and pure and thus quite unsoldierly, since the linguistic currency of the World War II American soldier came down mostly to inventive variations on the word *fuck*, made to serve a multiplicity of meanings. But that would have made for a dull script and one completely at variance with the film's high-mindedness. The twenty-five-minute gush of violence on Omaha Beach could hardly have moved a theater audience now inured to the daily police blotter round-ups that pass for the evening news everywhere or nightly television programs featuring "Greatest Disasters on Video." I saw several families, complete with small children, happily munching their way through the whole film. Everyone else seemed pleased to be getting their money's worth.

Aficionados of war films often judge their quality on the basis of accuracy—of historical fact, of military equipment, of technical military procedures. Some will have discovered by now that on the real Omaha Beach the defending Germans did not emplace their machine guns outside the casemates but inside them. Students of the finer points of minor tactics will have noted the highly improbable, near-academic discussion between Hanks and his men on the best way to silence one of said annoying German machine guns. How many discussions on setting up enfilading fire had there been in the maelstrom at Omaha Beach? These characters were supposed to be veterans, and veterans communicate and move in close combat by nonverbal means, signals, a jerk of the head, a wave of the rifle or hand—if even that. They don't talk, because experience will have taught them that no one can hear anything above the din of combat anyway. Screaming is common, however, not to communicate but to expel the overwhelming rush of terrified excitement. Soldiers old and new have testified frequently to being hoarse after a battle, though they don't recall having spoken to anyone.

Afterward, once Hanks and his men embark on their quest for the immensely valuable Private Ryan, it is clear that no one is in any danger as they stroll across the Normandy meadows in perfect view of the cameras, and the enemy too. Showing hours of a seemingly empty Norman countryside of course was beyond even the talents of Steven Spielberg to make interesting. Some acute fans of aerial warfare will also wonder what the marvelously beautiful P-51, an "air superiority fighter," was doing busting tanks when the incomparably ugly P-47s commonly drew ground-support missions and the weapons to do the job. Details of this sort, interesting as they may be to future tacticians and military historians, merely distract us from the uglier facts about what is actually happening in such situations.

As for these ugly facts, including what modern industrial-strength war does to human beings who get in the way, the intense combat action so inventively filmed at the invasion beach, which in reality took several movies' worth of hours to accomplish, would not have made a movie by itself. Cinematic conventions had to be obeyed, and so the combat action does not resume until the end is near, when a highly problematic defense of a village guarding a vital river crossing is hastily mounted. The Germans advance with machinelike confidence, somehow knowing, as we do, that they have the Americans outgunned. Not during the spectacular on Omaha Beach but here, during the fighting for the village, is where we see the single most violent scene. It is also the most intimate. Two soldiers engage in hand-to-hand combat in a grappling frenzy of rifle butts, fists, and knives, reducing the whole war to a small room. We see one soldier consummate his victory over the other slowly, while he whispers soothingly to his enemy as if he were a lover. Outside, the combat builds toward a conclusion we know by now is not going to be a happy one. Of course, the noble Hanks will be killed, but his death is archheroic. His mortal wounds are invisible, but the high-mindedness of his death fills the screen. Horatius is at the bridge again.

Audiences have every reason to be impressed by *Saving Private Ryan*. And Spielberg has every reason to be happy with what he has done. In addition to the box-office returns, he has been acclaimed by veterans' groups and even awarded a medal by the Army to add to his already substantial laurels. Perhaps no other war film has received such approval from old soldiers, who rather more willingly than before have come forward to recount their own experiences. But what, exactly, are the veterans approving? The film may refresh their experiences, but it is highly unlikely that the film will add to their memories. No, the film is for everyone else. Beginning and ending in an American military cemetery in Normandy, it is a eulogy to the victory generation, and it is praise thankfully received.

One of the great myths of war is that fighting in one somehow makes one a better person, someone who has gained admission to a world on the extreme edges of human behavior that everyone else can only imagine. But war still holds its appeal to those who are innocent of the real price required to know it. Some commentators have actually expressed regret they did not fight in World War II (a regret, it should be noted, that is easy to express half a century later). This kind of knowledge cannot be had on the cheap. War in the dark is no substitute. Judged by this standard, there never has been a good war film, and there never will be. But for me the best films about war are those whose makers try to look squarely at war for what it is, not for how they think it should be. Such a standard is not often compatible with artistic or commercial or vicarious ambitions, which is why there are so few good war movies to choose from.

Just as certainly, scenes, bits of dialogue, or expressions of character will be enlisted for the public storehouse of imagined knowledge about modern war. Inevitably, some who have seen *Saving Private Ryan* and others like it will decide that war is an experience worth having. They need not be denied. If they are serious, these cinematic warriors need only go find themselves a war. The world has plenty to choose from. There they will learn that some experiences are better had only on film.

J ust before dawn on August 2, 1990, a war of a sort began in the Middle East. An Iraqi army of 100,000 troops crossed the frontier of Kuwait and swept south toward the capital city. Before the day was out, Iraq had occupied virtually all of Kuwait, and Iraqi formations were seen as far south as the Saudi Arabian border. Neither observers on the spot nor Western intelligence agencies were able to say what the president of Iraq, Saddam Hussein, intended to do next. Hussein offered only the most gossamer justification for the invasion, a revanchist policy based on the dubious claim that Kuwait was actually another province of Iraq, one that had fallen into the hands of a soulless commercial elite and which he was returning to the Iraqi family of provinces. No one was much impressed. On the same day the United Nations Security Council resolved to condemn the invasion and call for the immediate withdrawal of all Iraqi forces. Six months later, on January 17, 1991, the world was able to watch the first air strikes on Baghdad. After six weeks Iraq agreed to an informal ceasefire. By the end of March 1991 Kuwait was free of occupying forces.

In the decade since, these events have had as much difficulty finding a name as Hussein had in finding a justification for them. We have "The Persian Gulf Conflict" or "The Gulf Conflict." For those who wish to emphasize the conflict's significance, nothing less than "The Persian Gulf War" or "The Gulf War" will do. If one grants, for the sake of argument, that what happened was indeed a war, even if not officially declared by virtue of Constitution and Congress, one must admit that ten years later there is some confusion about the shape of the thing. Seen in historical terms only, the Persian Gulf War seems to belong with grand old-fashioned imperial enterprises, a cracking good punitive expedition.

Wars presumably have beginnings, middles, and ends. Only the middle of this one seems clear. Every few days we have news of another air strike against some Iraqi target; in between the strikes allied warplanes enforce a "no-fly zone" over nearly two-thirds of Iraq. UN inspection teams whose mission was to oversee the destruction of certain Iraqi "weapons of mass destruction" are no longer permitted in Iraq. What remains of the UN's sanctions against Iraq may be charitably characterized as being in disarray. Those who like their history neat, who insist on closure, have been disappointed.

We should be able to make sense of the Gulf War by now, should we not? It must have been the object of the most intense media attention in the history of journalism. Allied forces employed sixty military satellites, and upward of three-quarters of a million military calls or messages were exchanged every day. Yet the media consumed twice the bandwidth in reporting the war as did the allied forces in fighting it. The time and treasure consumed by domestic journalism, both in broadcast and in print, are perhaps now beyond calculation.

Despite this intense coverage, the world knew less about the war than it might have thought. Media operations were restricted mainly to "pools" in Riyadh. Military "public affairs" officers assiduously managed a press corps content to be dependent upon the allies for basic support. No small part of the reporting from the Gulf was taken up by the kinds of vapid profiles perfected during intermissions at sporting events, so the world came to know the hulking figure and Pattonesque temper of the American commander in chief, Gen. Norman Schwarzkopf, and learned mostly irrelevant details of his personal history and official life but virtually nothing of anyone else in his chain of command. Whether as a result of something like Douglas MacArthur's media policy during the Pacific War or merely because of journalistic incompetence, no one then or later could name the major commanders on either side of the war. Imagine attempting to understand

World War II without knowing of Göring, or Rommel, or Yamamoto, or Eisenhower, or Patton.

Somewhere just beyond the evening news and the instant "in-depth" analysis lies the vague dividing line between journalism and history. Certainly, the war has been over long enough to generate a literature, but with a few exceptions it tends to be curiously pro forma, reticent, or glib. How successfully does this literature represent the Gulf War before the bar of history? Were one to imbibe the whole of it, would one have a closer understanding of the war ten years after the fact? I wonder.

No doubt there is enough raw material for fact mongering, but some may have noticed that most of the facts originate on one side. To this day we still do not know what Saddam Hussein actually intended to accomplish when he launched his army into Kuwait. Did he want only Kuwait? Or did he harbor the idea of going all the way to Riyadh? We do not know, and history may never tell us.

Whether Hussein's ambitions were limited or grand, his invasion of Kuwait must go down as one of modern history's masterpieces of strategic mistiming. He launched his war at precisely the wrong time. The Cold War was so recently over that the United States and its allies had not had time to begin retrenching. Most of America's readiest, heaviest forces were still stationed in Europe. It was true that they were not the most strategically mobile of our forces, having been fixed in place for going on forty years, but neither were they the only ones available. For all intents, the forces belonging to the Western democracies were newly unemployed. As President Bush himself remarked immediately after the invasion, for the first time in nearly half a century a crisis had erupted that was not somehow a product of superpower competition.

Moreover, the United States was trying on a new military doctrine. As several books about the conflict have shown, the shadow of Vietnam was still influencing how the U.S. foreign policy elite went about managing international crises. At the darkest corner of the so-called Vietnam Syndrome there lay the suspicion that the American people themselves were not up to the challenges posed by military crises and that they would withdraw their support if the war was not going their way. If it is true that this view was ungenerous and distorted, it is also true that this myth formed an important part of the worldview of those who then bore responsibility for the commitment of American military power abroad. Accurate or not, this tendentious reading of recent history helped supplant an operational tradition of gradual, incremental application of American military power. Under the new doctrine, which was especially appealing to the chairman of the Joint Chiefs of Staff, Gen. Colin Powell, and many other officers of the Vietnam generation, only overwhelming military force, applied as nearly simultaneously as possible, was acceptable. In future American wars victory was to be won so quickly that neither the enemy nor Congress nor the American people would have time to react. By the time of the Gulf War the United States had already given the new doctrine a successful test run, during the invasion of Panama.

From the first air strikes in January 1991, the war took forty-two days in all. Iraq had deployed more than 500,000 soldiers dug into defensive positions. The allied coalition had more than 640,000. What the cost in allied casualties would be when these two great forces collided no one could say. Official and quasi-official estimates ran as high as 30,000 casualties. No one suggested calling off the war, but before Schwarzkopf would launch the ground offensive, he insisted that his air forces kill half of the enemy's ground forces. Thirty-eight days later, on February 24, just before dawn, Schwarzkopf ordered the ground offensive to begin. Airpower had done what Schwarzkopf had demanded of it.

What followed in the next one hundred hours has been characterized best by Richard Swain, writing in *Lucky War*, as something akin to a drill bit cutting into a rock face. In only four days allied forces bored into enemy positions and drove what was left toward the Iraqi border. Untold numbers, certainly tens of thousands, of Iraqi soldiers were killed during the allied onslaught.

Large numbers of Iraqi soldiers surrendered, and large numbers, about a third of the total, escaped across the border. Perhaps as much as half of Hussein's elite force, the Republican Guard, escaped with its heavy equipment intact. The allies seemed happy to let it go. In this war, 383 Americans had been killed, 458 wounded. Their allied comrades-in-arms had suffered 510 casualties in all. History records few such tactically decisive wars as this one. But as military thinkers observed long ago, no degree of tactical success can overcome a strategic miscalculation.

The allies' writ ran only to expelling the Iraqi soldiers from Kuwait and returning it to its rightful owners. The United Nations resolution under whose authority the allies operated did not authorize the invasion of Iraq or the overthrow of its government. The Iraqi genie was to be put back in its bottle and kept there. In November 1990 President Bush had promised there would be no "murky ending" to this war, but he was to be disappointed. Hussein survived and revived, and, two presidents later, he still rules in Baghdad. If he did not win control over the oil he wanted, neither did he lose control over his country. In the end, so far as there has been one, the Gulf War won for the allies only status quo ante bellum.

After Vietnam, America's professional soldiers had something to prove, and if they got the chance to prove it in the Iraqi desert rather than on NATO's ramparts, that was just as well. That is why the reader will detect more than a little triumphalism in books like the Army's official account, *Certain Victory*. Here, the years between Vietnam and Iraq amounted to a struggle for professional redemption. For America's professional soldiers and the Bush administration as well, the Gulf War's success banished the ghosts of Vietnam once and for all. Indeed, for many of them it was as if all history since Vietnam had pointed toward that one direction. From those in Washington who set the policies and made the decisions to those who directed their execution in the field, all else sometimes appeared to be irrelevant. As far as the professionals were concerned, they might as well have been fighting to liberate Tibet. For these men, the Gulf War was a war to overturn history itself, and when it was over, they believed they had done just that.

All during the spring and summer of 1991 America welcomed the troops home. In Washington on June 8 a grand review for the president was staged led by General Schwarzkopf himself. The parade seemed to belong to a different age, long past— strangely for a war that had been so technologically advanced. Columns of troops in desert-camouflaged battle dress marched smartly past the reviewing stand, happily rendering their salutes to the commander in chief. The president's public approval rating had soared at one point to 88 percent. But the parades and their memories faded, as parades and memories do, and President Bush was unable to sustain his popularity on foreign victories alone. The admiring soldiers marched away. This was to be his one and only term in office.

Ten years after the war fought its way onto the front pages and TV news, only a few take notice when these dates come around. The decade turned toward new business and left the war to march into history. There it waits patiently with its commanders, its tanks and guns and planes and ships, for the next historian to open time's doors and bring it back to life.

The History Thus Far: A Decade of Gulf War Literature

The books started as soon as the war ended. The *U.S. News & World Report* staff was perhaps first off the starting block with its instabook, *Triumph without Victory*, a compilation of the magazine's reporting on the war. James Blackwell, who became something of a fixture on American television during the war, produced *Thunder in the Desert* at about the same time and to the same effect. Bob Woodward's *The Commanders* was not far behind. It could hardly wait until the conflict was over, and, in fact, it deals mainly with the decision to go to war. *The Commanders* refers not to those who commanded in the field but to the foreign policy elite who directed from afar. Woodward's worshipful depictions of these officials says less about the conduct of modern American statecraft than about the admiring self-image of the conductors.

Rick Atkinson's *Crusade: The Untold Story of the Persian Gulf War* survives as the best of the early books on the subject. Unlike many of his colleagues, Atkinson was conversant with the arcana of modern military operations and with the professional subculture that directs them. He is a critic but not an unsympathetic one, and he is better at the narrative depiction of the war than any writer before or since.

The Gulf War may be notable for many reasons, but the quality of its memoirs will not be one of them. Schwarzkopf's much awaited *It Doesn't Take a Hero* took a year and Peter Petre's help to produce. The book betrays many of the flaws and none of the virtues of most military memoirs. Following their commander's lead, if not his quick start, several military memoirists have attempted their own contributions, with little success. The best of these is a modest volume, published recently by Kent State University Press: *The Eyes of Orion*, a collective memoir by, of all things, a gaggle of lieutenants. If it sometimes descends to the level of *Boy's Own* stories of old, the book is at least a genuinely felt work.

None of the above is likely to teach the informed reader much about what actually transpired during the war or why. Professors Lawrence Freedman and Efraim Karsh finished the first and, in many respects, best of the early analytical studies in their work, *The Gulf Conflict, 1990–1991*. The two seasoned analysts conducted their own field interviews of leading participants in preparation for a television documentary. They used publicly available information and an intimate knowledge of Middle East history and politics to set the Gulf conflict into the longer perspective lacking in other works.

One would expect the passage of time to correct the historical nearsightedness common to books done immediately after war. Instead, the next wave of Gulf War literature was dominated by official writings of varying scope, quality, and objectivity. It tended toward the narrowly technical or bureaucratic, including the General Accounting Office's report on the war. An interesting subclass developed in a contest among the American armed forces to establish how the war was to be interpreted. Mirroring events during the war itself, the competition between the Air Force and the Army was especially bitter, with one or the other running close to claiming to have delivered victory almost unilaterally. The Air Force's remarkable study *The Gulf War Air Power Survey* took World War II's *Strategic Bombing Survey* as its point of reference and produced a work with comparable intellectual and bureaucratic power. Meanwhile, the Army's official entry in the race, *Certain Victory: The U.S. Army in the Gulf War*, was an old-fashioned narrative chronicle written by a committee under the command of a brigadier general.

A far more analytical work, written by the professional officer who served in Riyadh as the Army's theater historian during the war itself, is *Lucky War: The Third Army in Desert Storm*. This was the intellectual counterpart to the Air Force's *Gulf War Air Power Survey*, although its author, Richard Swain, and his project were invisible by comparison. Indeed, Swain's informed criticisms of the Army's operations were regarded by many of his superiors as impudence at best and disloyalty at worst. But if military professionals had been disappointed by the historical and analytical depth of histories of the ground war written so far, after this book appeared they no longer had cause to complain.

Students of the Gulf War will probably have to subsist on these secondary works for some time to come. Only Anthony Cordesman, a longtime student of and prolific author on contemporary strategic and military issues in the Middle East, has since demonstrated the requisite knowledge and persistence necessary to penetrate further into the dark science of planning and executing a modern military operation. The fourth volume of Cordesman's Lessons of Modern War series, *The Gulf War*, may mark the decade's last real contribution to understanding the war that began it.

Four

Experimental History

rnest Hemingway was not one to dispense praise lightly. He was notorious for savaging old friends—Sherwood Anderson, Gertrude Stein, Scott Fitzgerald, John Dos Passos, among many others—who helped him early in his career. Even after he reached the pinnacle of fame he compared his work with that of other writers, imagining himself in the boxing ring, trading literary punches with the best of them, even Shakespeare. He didn't back out of the ring very often. After reading Tolstoy's *War and Peace* he said there was "no need to write a war book." But just in case he was wrong, he was writing *The Sun Also Rises* at the time.

Hemingway knew his war books too. Grant's memoirs, Caulaincourt's *With Napoleon in Russia*, Spaulding's history of the American Army, Ludendorff's memoirs, the 1908 translation of Clausewitz, Ian Hamilton's *A Staff Officer's Scrap-Book*, and several titles from J. F. C. Fuller and B. H. Liddell Hart could be found on his shelves. Alongside these were war novels, among them Stendhal's *Le rouge et le noir*, several works by C. S. Forester, Remarque's *All Quiet on the Western Front*, and Alva Bessie's *Men in Battle*.

Stephen Crane's novel of the Civil War, *The Red Badge of Courage*, was there too. Hemingway called the book "a tour de force."

Maybe Hemingway, despite his combative ego, wouldn't mind being compared with Crane. They were alike in many ways, and in some of these ways Crane stands as a prototype of Hemingway. Two passions drove their lives: writing and war. Both men surrendered themselves completely to their craft, and although both attained a measure of respectability, in the beginning they threw off the constraints of bourgeois life for bohemian adventures around the world. Neither could sit still; they were always on the move, it seemed, and many of their travels took them in pursuit of war. When war was not available, they designed adventures for themselves to pass the time until they heard distant shots.

Hemingway neither needed nor wanted a model, but he knew a good deal about Crane's life. Thomas Beer's 1923 biography, *Stephen Crane: A Study in American Letters*, showed up in Hemingway's library in the 1930s. You can easily imagine Hemingway going through Beer's sometimes inventive book, measuring himself against the young man a later biographer, R. W. Stallman, called "an irresponsible heel."

In their day writers' lives were seldom bound up with what they wrote. Before Crane, only Mark Twain was as famous for who he was as for the books he created. In their generation of writers only Jack London approached the complete fusion of life and art that these two enacted during their careers. London was a short puncher, dying early, and Crane died younger than London, at the age of twenty-eight. But he'd written a classic novel. And he was already a transatlantic celebrity, "irresponsible heel" or not.

Crane's early reviewers didn't know what to make of him or his book. Accustomed to the arid pretentiousness of Victorian high diction, some of them merely ridiculed the plainspokenness of Crane and his characters. Others reacted viscerally to the way Crane used naturalistic descriptions to push his story along. Readers—especially Civil War veterans—applauded those very qualities. One reader's imagination was somewhat overstimulated: he wrote to a newspaper, claiming to have fought alongside the author, a fine, brave fellow.

Readers and critics alike were mystified when word got out that Crane was only twenty-three. They could hardly credit that war could be rendered so truly by force of imagination alone. Surely, critics said, literary precedents could be found that guided this inexperienced youth—a not so subtle suggestion that the kid simply imitated his elders and betters. Émile Zola's sweeping melo-drama of the Franco-Prussian War, *Le débâcle*, was offered up as a possibility. Tolstoy's *War and Peace* was mentioned as another candidate, but Crane didn't get around to reading it until after he finished *The Red Badge*. Aching to escape New York, Crane took off for the West to do a series of articles for a newspaper syndicate, making it as far as Nebraska before going on down to Mexico. On the train from Galveston, Crane wrote to his sister that he was dutifully reading Tolstoy's book while crossing the Lone Star State, but he wasn't impressed and never finished. It just "goes on and on, like Texas," he said.

Crane's life after the book was far more adventurous than his life before it. Chasing from one war to another aggravated the tuberculosis he contracted somewhere, and the disease finally killed him. One day in 1900 at the bat-infested English country house where he'd fetched up, he bent over to pet a dog and his mouth filled up with blood. Not long after, he died at a sanatorium in Germany. Crane had long since adopted the pose of the doomed youth, and he seemed to have regarded his illness as the proper fulfillment of his image.

The Red Badge of Courage has never gone out of print, and it has its own curious history. Early in the book's life it was a grown-up's novel, but as it gradually assumed a place in the canon of modern literature, it became a student's novel, a young man's book about a young man's baptism of fire. By the time I started using *The Red Badge* in my classes, students were dubious about the assignment. "Isn't that a kid's book?" they would say. "I read that in high school."

Yes, but only if you read it like a kid.

After *The Red Badge* came out Crane tried to explain himself, generally a bad idea for any writer then as now. But Crane's answer to his critics was interesting in its own right: he said his book was "a psychological study of fear." The book was not quite the spontaneous act of art some supposed; he said the book "grew" as he wrote it. In the end Crane reached well beyond the novelistic form in which he worked. At a time when the state of knowledge about the psychodynamics of battle was still crude, still more rhetoric than science, still a carnival of half-baked ideas, Crane produced a novel that can still be read as a case study of how the mind works in extremis.

For more than a century literary scholars have disassembled *The Red Badge of Courage* and the mind that produced it piece by piece. Today shelves groan and Web sites bulge with the weight of minute scholarly—and not so scholarly—investigations of Crane's work. Surely by now no part of it has evaded notice. Not a bit of air escapes his academic coffin.

You couldn't find a work more unlike Crane's than Ivan Bloch's *La guerre future*. Published in 1898, three years after *The Red Badge*, this multivolume study of war at century's end was festooned with statistics, charts, and graphs. The study was first published in French but was quickly translated into German and Russian. Bloch was no stylist, and no translator could save his prose; the book was dull in any language. Even so, an intense passion animated his text. Bloch was on an urgent mission: he feared the world—by which he meant the great industrial nations—was on the verge of a great war. Bloch's studies had convinced him that the war he imagined would be fought very soon and that, far from producing victory for one side or another, it would destroy the international economy and lead to national collapse, revolution, and famine. This war would have no victors, only victims. In sum, war was now obsolete and so dangerous to its combatants that any transient successes were more than offset by the larger catastrophe that awaited one and all.

Bloch was careful to frame his argument in the hard prose of economic and military fact, but the centerpiece of his study was founded on an assumption that war had become so violent that modern man could no longer function on the battlefield. War's collapse would begin at the microtactical level: the fragile cohesion of the formations would shatter; soldiers would shrink away to cover; officer casualties would skyrocket disproportionately as they tried to coax their men across the fire-swept fields by leading from the front of their units. Glory and honor and all the manly consolations war offered in the past would be lost in the maelstrom of modern combat.

Bloch thought his hard numbers would persuade even the thickest-headed militarist of war's threat to civilization. But more than a little of Bloch's argument depended on his less than complimentary view of modern man—creatures of congested, soulless industrial life, debilitated by the trials and iniquities of the cities where they collected. Who could expect very much of such men? Bloch expected little at all.

Bloch had no feel at all for history, as some of his critics noticed right away. His knowledge was fixed completely on the here and now. But the history he considered useless could have told him he'd succumbed to an ancient prejudice that said town-bred recruits were inferior raw material for soldiering. You can read this nonsense in Vegetius—fourth century AD—and you can still hear it in places like Fort Benning. Bloch's prejudice was certainly alive and well in his own time; indeed, it was one of the few parts of his argument his detractors agreed with. In Bloch's day the idea went this way:

> Greeklike struggles would be no more. Men were better, or more timid. Secular and religious education had effaced the throat-grappling instinct, or else firm finance held in check the passions.

If, faced with the ordeals of making your way through Ivan Bloch's *La guerre future*, you'd like a faithful rendition of his thesis, this is as good as any. Except Bloch didn't write it. Stephen Crane did—twice, within the space of a few pages, five years before Bloch.

Of course, both men were quite wrong. They had no idea of how far nations and their citizens would go to defend even the most diaphanous cause. Human capacity for suffering seemed to have no limits, and just in case the original point—embodied by

World War I—was missed, we tested it again twenty years later. Not even Bloch at his most pessimistic could've imagined the Second Great War. But by force of their very different imaginations, Crane and Bloch anticipated the collapse of traditional thinking about war. All that Victorian swamp gas about the romance and nobility of war was going to be blown right away.

Since Herodotus historians have danced a long and complex tango with works of the imagination. We're no more or less welcoming to the literary arts than anyone else, but when asked to grant scholarly credence to literature, most historians instinctively turn coy, timidly waiting in the chairs along the dance floor for less intimidating partners. Nowhere is this equivocal relationship between history and literature more visible than among students of the history of war. Military historians agree that fiction and memoirs can get at parts of war that lie beyond their footnotes, and some skillfully deploy pieces of literature to give their work depth and color. In weaker moments some of them may even try their own hands at literature, taking a few cautious steps on the dance floor with this character with pomaded hair and pencil-thin moustache. Fine, a dalliance, but you wouldn't want to marry him, this dubious character called imagination.

All of which is rather self-defeating, because so much of doing military history demands imagination. I don't mean the kind of sloppy fantasizing so common in mass media—"historical" videogames being the most egregious sort of history mongering—but a higher order of imagining, disciplined by a feel for history's crazy randomness and unpredictability, a feel for worlds in which any number of realities is possible. This kind of imagination is the unique product of any historian's upbringing, but the historian's intellectual life is so completely dominated by the task of disentangling these realities that the work seems routine. But what if historians took imagination seriously? What would be the result if we experimented with what the study of history has taught us?

I decided to find out. The essays you'll see here were all experiments, were all meant to test the limits of orthodox military history, simply by using the historical imagination differently. Any experiment runs the risk of being wrong, of course, but in an experiment even failure can advance knowledge. These experiments taught me that the risk was worth it.

All military history begins with a story, so here's one: On the island of Sumatra there lives a hill-dwelling tribe that calls itself the Creech. The tribe has no chief, no matriarch, no war leader. Instead, the tribe looks for its guidance to the one person known to all as the Memory Priest. The Memory Priest serves as the collective memory of the tribe. At certain appointed times, feast days and such, the Memory Priest is called upon to recite the tribe's genealogies, triumphs and transgressions, debts incurred, paid, and defaulted. Several days, perhaps as much as a week, may be necessary for the Memory Priest to recount all he knows of the tribe's history.

Now, the Memory Priest is called to this role at birth. As soon as he is sentient he is taught that he is the embodiment of Creech history. His life is completely taken up with learning all that is known about the tribe's genealogy and with keeping abreast of all that happens in the tribe from the moment of his birth. Aside from learning the bloodlines of his tribe, all the history he learns is new.

The Creech have been characterized as "an outwardly placid people, occasionally displaying fits of violence. Biting themselves in order to show remorse is not unknown, and clawing their faces is commonplace. They are also untruthful and unreliable, prone to thieving, gossiping, gambling, and sudden spasms of the most aggressive behavior."

The Memory Priest is above all this. He has no other duties. He is cared for, cosseted, in fact, because he holds within his mind the tribe's very identity, its view of itself as a society. One might think, then, that the Memory Priest is so honored because he offers the tribe its one reliable anchor in an otherwise precarious way of life by binding its individual and family histories together.

In one way this is true, but not in the way the Memory Priest believes. That is because even though the Memory Priest thinks he knows all the facts about the tribe, there is one fact he does not know, a secret that has been withheld from him his whole life. He does not know that after thirty years have passed, and he is finally an old and toothless man, the Creech will assemble on a special day to hear the Memory Priest recite their history once more. When he is finished, when his memory is finally emptied, he will be killed, roasted, and eaten. Thus are the Creech purified of their past. All debts are forgiven, insults and resentments forgotten, crimes absolved—all history disappears.

The next male child born into the tribe will be named the new Memory Priest, and as he grows he will come to believe that indeed all history begins with him. But while the Memory Priest lives out his comfortable days, behind his back the rest of the tribe revels in its conspiracy and looks forward to the day when he will die and all shame and failure, all record of unpleasantness, will disappear once more and relieve the tribe of the burdens of its history.

You can find this story in Paul Theroux's collection of short pieces entitled *Fresh Air Fiend*.[1] The story may not be true. Sumatra counts no tribe with any such name as the Creech or any of its linguistic variants. Nor can one find, searching through the ethnologies of Sumatra or any other part of Indonesia, any of the more than three hundred ethnic groups claiming this particular custom.

If the story is a fiction, it is not the first time Theroux has played tricks with us. He has written two books of fiction that pretend to be autobiography, and he is not above casting real people—including the Queen of England—in fictional form. And he is not at all apologetic.[2] The fact of it is that this dividing line between fact and faction—between fact and *everything else*, has never been as hard and as fast as we would like to think. And all too often, when we take refuge behind that wall of fact, what we are really doing is avoiding the risk of imagination.

The recent uproar over James Frey's best-selling book, *A Million Little Pieces*, no doubt amused Theroux. He would have been delighted at Oprah Winfrey's discomfort at being publicly flummoxed by that book and by Nan Talese's clumsy defense of her decision to publish it as a memoir.[3]

In the course of that very public controversy, just one critic that I know of pointed out that Frey's book was only the latest entry in a literary tradition that reaches back to the eighteenth century. The book generally regarded as the very first novel in English, Daniel Defoe's *Robinson Crusoe*, was first published as an autobiography and taken as such. Oprah's researchers might have told her, if they knew, that the lately rejuvenated Truman Capote's *In Cold Blood* was not a straight piece of reportage but what he called "novelized history," a form he claimed, rather breathtakingly, to have invented. Of course, he did nothing of the kind. The ghosts of Zola, Hemingway, Solzhenitsyn, and who knows how many others would rise to dispute such a claim.[4]

I'm fond of Theroux's little story, how it navigates its way through fiction toward truth. It is a kind of parable, a cautionary tale for all of us. How the pride of knowledge blinds us to the reality that we don't know quite as much as we think we do, the illusion that we are up-to-date when we are prisoners of tradition. How we don't matter as much as we think. As with the Memory Priest, these fictions pervade the reality in which we military historians work.

Almost instinctively, we historians disapprove of the conflation of fact and fiction we see in the work of Theroux and others. We say that we answer to our own intellectual traditions, so what has any of this to do with us? We say our canons of practice are guided by a different—we might even say higher—purpose: the pursuit of truth about the past. Regardless of which school or method we follow, we are careful never to stray too far beyond Leopold von Ranke's dictum: to recount the past as it actually happened. Even though Ranke could not follow his own rule, it still serves us as a kind of intellectual conscience. The old scholar's finger wags over our shoulder when we are at our desks. Stay close to home, he insists; no adventuring for you.[5]

Fortunately, historians have gone adventuring. The conception and practice of history has traveled to places far from those Ranke prescribed. What would he think of books like Simon Schama's *Dead Certainties (Unwarranted Speculations)*, for instance, or other excursions into counterfactual history, alternative history, novelized history, experimental history? Especially since the Second World War, historians have posed for themselves an ever-expanding range of interpretive and methodological questions, produced a dizzying variety of approaches, divided and subdivided into schools, camps, and tribes—all in an atmosphere of unprecedented intellectual and global foment, a worldwide quickening of pulse. The point is arguable, of course, but I think there never was a time when the possibilities for the advancement of historical understanding were so promising, or so challenging.[6]

In a world now so beset by war, this is particularly true of the practice of military history, where the interrelationship between past and present is so acute and where the connection between thought and action can sometimes be startlingly direct. We must live with the possibility, less remote than one might think, that others may act on what we say and write and that those actions may have mortal consequences. This possibility is not one that much troubles the sleep of many of our colleagues in other fields of history. Even political historians are not likely to feel this responsibility quite so keenly as one who studies war. We cannot evade this responsibility, nor should we wish to.

This responsibility imposes a certain urgency on the work we do. We are more than others obliged to look beyond our immediate interests to the world beyond—to other disciplines for any intellectual, conceptual, or methodological advantage that might advance our work. But we are also obliged to be alert to the shapes and forms of war as it unfolds in the present. Rather than be content with a casual relevance in our work to the conduct of war in our own time, shouldn't we face our connection with the present more directly? Have we met these obligations?

These questions were on my mind recently when I surveyed the seventy or so volumes of the *Journal of the American Military History Foundation*, what is now the *Journal of Military History* (don't ask why; the answer is embarrassing). I'm not sure that what one finds in the journal perfectly reflects the state of military history in the United States at any given time—much less military history as practiced elsewhere around the world. A comprehensive view would have to take into account books, dissertations, many other journals, and popular media, too. But the modern practice of military history in the United States corresponds roughly to the history of the journal itself, and if nothing else the journal has been the one venue in which military history has been consistently welcomed for the past six decades. At least, then, we can think of the journal as a window that has been open during a formative time in the life of our field.

What should we expect to see? Should we see the intellectual currents in other fields of history, or even other disciplines, reflected, however dimly, in the journal's pages? To what extent, if any, does the contemporary world of war make itself felt in the journal? And, should we find answers to these questions, do they really have much to say about the vitality of military history as thought and as practiced now?

Although the American Military History Foundation had been established several years before, the first numbers of the journal did not appear until 1938. The founders framed their interests broadly, as "the stimulation and advancement of historical study of all that relates to war with appropriate emphasis upon American history."[7] A good deal of military history was being written already, but one could not then speak of military history as a field. As Harvey DeWeerd, one of the most important figures in the early history of the foundation, wrote in the summer of 1940, "the objective study of warfare has not been a recognized branch of knowledge in this country."[8]

With a new war on the horizon, the founders went about their work with some dedication, and all too soon war was everybody's preoccupation. Throughout the journal's war years few articles appeared that did not in some way speak to the war in progress. Wartime articles commonly dealt with subjects in the near present or even anticipated issues that lay ahead. As early as 1943 Alfred Vagts was writing about military occupation, and even before the Combined Bomber Offensive began, the journal pointedly ran a review of Giulio Douhet's *Command of the Air*. In that same issue an essay by A. F. Kovacs on the fall of France anticipated interpretations that would only appear in book form years after the war. Toward the end of the war historians were already contributing articles on campaigns barely over. In the summer of 1945 Ben Blakeney's survey of the Japanese high command could have served as a prosecution brief for the Tokyo war crimes trials yet to come.

But the war was not long over before the journal's contributors' interest in the present seemed to wane. A new "antiquarian" section appeared, and alongside reviews of singularly important works such as Bernard Brodie's *The Absolute Weapon* one could now find reviews on the latest books on pistol and revolver shooting, formation badges, and insignia. For several years the journal was full of articles derived from the armed forces' massive official history projects. From time to time articles would address issues of the day such as the ongoing debate over unification of the armed forces, and there was even one article that examined the rationale for dropping the bomb on Hiroshima.[9]

But on the whole, one can see a relaxing of that sense of immediacy that had been so apparent in the journal's wartime days. Even though American foreign and defense policies and structures were radically changing, none of the journal's contributors were moved to express themselves on these developments. If we can imagine a reader whose knowledge of contemporary military affairs depended solely on the journal, that reader would have been wholly ignorant of the integration of the armed forces, the emerging Cold War, the Chinese civil war, postwar occupation and reconstruction, the strategic bombing surveys, or—except for one reprinted speech by Justice Robert Jackson on Nuremberg—a wholly new stage in the history of the laws of war.

Not even a new war was enough to stir the journal's contributors. In the pages of *Military Affairs*, as the journal was then called, the Korean War did not exist. Neither did China or the new arms race. The Soviet Union was invisible until 1957, when Raymond Garthoff contributed an essay entitled "The Soviet Image of the Enemy." That was the only such article until three years later, when the journal ran a piece by James Atkinson on the Soviet theory of war. Colonial wars of liberation in Indochina and Algeria went unremarked altogether during the 1950s save for one essay on Mao's military thought.[10]

Finally, in 1960 the journal devoted an issue to irregular warfare. Not until 1968 did the journal turn once more to contemporary affairs, with the publication of the proceedings of a joint session between the American Historical Association (AHA) and the now renamed American Military Institute entitled "Contemporary History and War," chaired by Peter Paret. Charles MacDonald of the Army's Office of the Chief of Military History read a paper explaining his organization's plans for an official history of the war in Vietnam. C. P. Stacey, Leonard Krieger, and John Shy offered comment. The comments had a sharp, barely civil edge to them and exposed the long-standing fault line between official and academic military history, between those whose work required them to sail so close to the present and those who enjoyed a comfortable distance from their studies. What had been for nearly a generation a wary relationship between the two camps had by 1968 been thoroughly poisoned by the war itself. Krieger in particular questioned whether those in government service, having bound themselves to the government's flawed policies and strategic miscalculations, had surrendered any hope of scholarly independence—a suspicion that is still very much alive today. But it was the intersection of past and present that most disturbed Krieger, that dangerous point where one left fact for the fictions of the present.[11]

The truth of the matter was that these suspicions fell on all military historians at the time, no matter whether they were in government service or not and regardless of what they studied. Nor would these suspicions abate. Just take a look at the most recent newsletter of the Society for Military History, which records a roundtable at the last meeting of the AHA where these suspicions were very much in evidence.[12] Almost from the beginning of the journal, one can find contributors remarking almost as a matter of course on the less than complimentary attitudes of their colleagues toward their work. So the growth of military history during the 1960s must have puzzled our critics. In 1954 thirty-seven universities offered courses in some variety of military history, but by 1960 that number had more than doubled. Between 1949 and 1952 the United States had produced about one hundred doctoral dissertations in the field of military history. Between 1961 and 1970 five hundred were finished or in progress.[13] But just in the middle of this period John K. Mahon gave it as his opinion that "most academic historians" were "revolted by the idea" of studying war. Those of us who came into the profession in these years have no trouble agreeing with Mahon.[14] I was earnestly counseled on several occasions to take up a more humane field of study. I thought at the time, and still do think, that all this was tantamount to confusing physicians with the diseases they treated.

So the disapproval of colleagues seems not to have deterred military historians at all after Vietnam. On the contrary, studies in military history exploded. Their geographical scope, chronological range, scholarly depth, and methodological breadth defied criticism of the field.

At the same time, contributors to the journal seemed as detached as ever from contemporary events. In the years after Vietnam military historians seemed as happy as their fellow citizens to forget about the war, although they would not have been so bold as to claim that their work was free of its influence. In the decade or so after the war only six articles appeared that dealt directly with the war.[15] At a time when American national security strategy and the doctrine and organization of the armed forces were undergoing a sea change, when the Army was a virtual laboratory of social and professional dysfunction, when arms control and disarmament were finally being taken seriously, and when wars in the Middle East and the rise of modern terror were attracting world attention, military historians did not respond in the pages of their leading professional journal. As if by common agreement, military historians stayed as far away as possible from a direct engagement with contemporary military affairs.

One could argue that the work of military historians during the last generation was too vast, simply too energetic, to be accurately represented in the pages of any one journal. I would agree that this is so, but it was not always so. Before the 1960s the journal could claim some authority as the voice of military history, but not after Vietnam. In several issues during the decade that followed the journal carried assessments of the state of military history beginning in 1977, when the institute commemorated its fortieth anniversary. Surveys by Theodore Ropp, Allan Millett, and Gunther Rothenberg fairly bulged with new titles and approaches.[16] No doubt, graduate students on the eve of their comprehensive examinations were plunged into depression after seeing the scope and variety of works they now had to master.

All the varieties of history were entering a time of intellectual experimentation, relaxing their inherent conservatism and narrowness of view. Not only were the old divisions between historical fields dissolving, so too were those between history and other disciplines. Historians were exploring new—or what was said to be new—interpretive and methodological territories.

Military history seemed ready-made, perhaps overdue, for these advances. As long ago as 1940 Harvey DeWeerd had written, rather sarcastically: "It is unfortunate that war is not so academically minded, not so inclined to observe the politely artificial boundaries of our fields of learning."[17] Although military historians were as attracted as ever by drums and trumpets, books were appearing in the 1970s that defied easy classification. On which shelf would one place Paul Fussell's *The Great War and Modern Memory*? What appeared to be a survey of British literature during World War I spawned its own minor industry in books that addressed the idioms by which cultures coped with their experience of war. Do a quick search of amazon.com for books containing the words "and memory," and you'll see what I mean. Surely one of the most important titles of the 1970s was John Keegan's *The Face of Battle*, military history certainly, but, strangely for a field so preoccupied with battle, one that treated the subject in ways that had been only superficially attempted before. The same is true of Eric Leed's *No Man's Land*, which came out a few years later. Where would Ranke place such books?

Including Peter Paret and Michael Howard's translation of Carl von Clausewitz's *On War* with these books might seem perverse, but one could argue that their work was as much a literary triumph as an exercise in military history—and its publication had much to do not only with a rejuvenation of military theory but also with a new and much debated stage in the historiography of the Vietnam War. And could military history lay an exclusive claim even for the new second edition of *The Makers of Modern Strategy* when it contained such pieces as Michael Howard's "Men against Fire: The Doctrine of the Offensive in 1914" and Michael Geyer's "German Strategy in the Age of Machine Warfare, 1914–1945"—pieces that could just as well be regarded as intellectual history?

These advances were real. Of course, one could find precedents, broad analytical works that treated military affairs in their widest context using tools and methods and insights from other disciplines. The difference in the 1970s was that so many works were now drawing on a much wider and more complex foundation of knowledge—so many works, in fact, that they now constituted a movement. And now the movement had a name, for better or worse—the new military history, one that aimed at understanding the phenomenon of war as a whole, not just its parts.[18]

I think it important to emphasize here that these historians were not simply reacting to intellectual fashion. They could as easily have taken Hans Delbrück as their model. Upon finishing his *Geschichte der Kriegskunst* in 1920, he wrote that he would "have no objection if this work . . . were to be classified in the category of works of cultural history."[19] Theodore Ropp's bibliography of the one hundred leading works in military history contains any number of titles predating the "new military history" that would fall under that heading.[20] Nor do I believe Russell Weigley was prompted to write *The American Way of War*, and Gerald Linderman his *The Mirror of War*, and Peter Paret his *Clausewitz and the State* because they were enamored of the new wave of cultural studies then sweeping the profession. I would guess John Shy did not write *A People Numerous and Armed* only because he was interested in new theories of learning.

Inevitably, some worried that the "new military history" had gone too far, whether the field had experienced a "paradigm change"—a question that in itself said much about the field's sensitivity to intellectual currents. If indeed there had been a "gestalt shift," were Michel Foucault and Jacques Derrida and Stanley Fish very far behind? Had military history deserted the battlefield, as some feared? Judging from the range of books published in the last decade or so, clearly not. Military historians seem as interested as ever in battles and leaders, but they are bringing to their work a sensibility that earlier work did not possess. Look at George Rable's study of Fredericksburg or Peter Maslowski and Don Winslow's biography, *Looking for a Hero*, for example. Rable's book is far from the narrative descriptions that once dominated the field, and Maslowski and Winslow's study of one soldier's life is cast in its broadest political, cultural, and psychological context. If there is a new orthodoxy in the practice of military history, works such as these might well represent it.

Of course, traditionalists and modernists will snipe at one another from behind their parapets, but the field has grown too much to be contained by any one school or method. In 1981 the American Military Institute listed 517 members; a decade later, the number had grown 300 percent, and now the Society for

Military History has over 2,200 members.[21] By now, one would hope, all would agree with Peter Paret that "the claim that only certain parts of the subject are important, that history concerned with other parts is marginal and old-fashioned, is destructive of scholarship and inhibits genuine understanding."[22]

So: a great body of knowledge, and a body of talent to use it. Our response to academic fashions has been measured, judicious, conservative—perhaps even too conservative. If we have not gone off into mad deconstructing, neither have we retired into a fortress of tradition. Our faith in fact, our passion for detail, for the mastery of our subject, have not given way to the hypertheorizing that has bedeviled so many of our colleagues. But if military history has reached a certain intellectual maturity, what has been the result? We can agree that military history matters to us, but we may be living a great fiction: that it matters to anyone else. Should it matter?

It should matter.

I want you to consider the caliber of military commentary you see every day, commentary that is remarkable for its ignorance of history; its lack of perspective; its childlike sense of causation, contingency, and the play of chance; its talent for reduction. We can watch self-styled experts deliver judgments based on nothing more than their own immediate personal experience, often translated to the level of a general principle. We are back in Sumatra with Paul Theroux's Memory Priest. The past has been forgiven. History begins anew every twenty-four hours. And we, by our acquiescence, by our reluctance to engage the questions of war in our own time—are we like the Creech, reveling in our secret knowledge?

In a world so much at war, does not our discipline impose an obligation on us to bring our knowledge to bear, to matter more than we have? Our professional upbringing has conditioned us to recoil against involvement with the contemporary world. We have been taught, and rightly so, to be suspicious of drawing lessons from the history we study. All too often we have seen military history treated like a rummage bin of evidence to prove

330   EXPERIMENTAL HISTORY

preconceived notions. But is there no other means by which the historically trained mind can be used? Do our obligations extend only to the verge of the present and no farther?

Historians since Thucydides have said no, that they must extend their gifts into the present. Machiavelli, Clausewitz, Delbrück, Fuller, Liddell Hart—the list is quite long—were not imprisoned by their discipline. They did not take refuge in the fiction of their secret knowledge. They were not reluctant to engage the great questions of war in their own time. To them, engagement did not mean the abandonment of their scholarly principles, the preservation of some supposed detachment from the influence of the present. Clausewitz and Delbrück in particular were careful to draw a distinction between the attainment of knowledge and the use of it, between military history and what they called military criticism. They held that while history and criticism served different ends, scholars could serve both without violating their professional oath. Indeed, they felt it essential that they do so. What they had in mind was not the application of military history so much as the application of the military historian. Military criticism was another means of advancing an understanding of war.[23]

Very few modern military historians have ventured into the world of criticism. What, after all, keeps us in our studies? Some say it is only right that we keep our distance from the present. Contemporary history, as Leonard Krieger argued in 1968, is a contradiction. We should not address a problem until it is over. But how can we tell? As we watch the newest round of exchanges between the United States and Iran, could we say that the atomic age is over or merely embarking on a new chapter? Could we say that the Vietnam War is over when it still casts such a shadow over the conduct of the present war? And can we reasonably say that the war in Iraq is a new war or a continuation of the first Desert War? Another argument has it that other disciplines—international relations, or security studies— are better suited to deal with the present. Once military history could claim primacy as the foundation for any understanding of war, but other disciplines have pressed their claims more successfully. I can find no intrinsic reason why this should be so except for the willingness of their practitioners to involve themselves in the questions of the day.

In the main, military historians have been far too modest about their gifts. The speculative instinct that is at the heart of all criticism is in constant play in the practice of history, and it is especially evident in the practice of military history. When we address the past, we never do so with a blank mind. We have been taught to keep our speculations in check, but our interpretations, our criticisms, would be impossible without allowing some play of what has been called the historian's favorite secret question: "What if?" Think of any often debated historical issue in which the problem is not so much knowing what happened as in explaining what happened. In the task of interpretation we find the very same speculative elements we see in criticism itself, the actual use of the educated imagination. And yet we have been reluctant to use these gifts.

In the spring of 1993 the Institute for Advanced Study in Princeton sponsored a symposium entitled "The History of War as Part of General History" during which Russell Weigley read a paper, "The American Military and the Principle of Civilian Control from McClellan to Powell."[24] Weigley's paper is I think a fair example of the kind of scholarship that conforms to Delbrück's conception of military criticism. Weigley had come to Princeton to register a serious complaint, that at least since the Korean War "conflict and bickering between soldier and civilian had become perennial impediments to the formation of a coherent American foreign and military policy." The catalyst for Weigley's complaint was, as he put it, "a series of vocal military objections to civilian policies in the immediate aftermath of the Cold War." He was particularly critical of General Powell, then serving as chairman of the Joint Chiefs of Staff, for his opposition to any American intervention in the conflict in Bosnia-Herzegovina. Just before the presidential election of 1992 Powell had publicly reiterated his long-standing aversion to limited interventions during an interview with the *New York Times*. This was followed ten days later by an op-ed piece in the *Times* under Powell's own byline entitled "Why Generals Get Nervous." At the same time, President-elect Bill Clinton's campaign promise to liberalize Pentagon policy toward the enlistment of homosexuals had created a toxic environment for the new administration even before the inauguration. Immediately after the inauguration, when President Clinton mooted the question of using his executive powers to set this new policy in motion, opposition from serving and retired general officers was fierce and public. To Weigley, the generals' very public opposition to their commander in chief posed a direct challenge to the American tradition of civil-military relations. He finished his essay with an ominous warning: "The principle of civil control of the military in the United States faces an uncertain future."

As far as I can tell, Weigley's paper was the first instance in recent times in which this issue was raised so directly and frankly in a public forum. More than a decade later we understand very well that the Clinton presidency began its relations with the Pentagon with several strikes against it, and some scholars believe that civil-military relations never achieved a proper equilibrium, that when the Clinton administration dealt with the Pentagon, it was always as a supplicant, never as a master. A considerable body of scholarship since has addressed modern civil-military relations, but none that I have seen quite reveals the depth of personal contempt and disdain of the president I heard expressed almost daily, routinely, and offhandedly by military officers I dealt with during these days, from the rank of captain to four-star general. In his paper Weigley had compared General Powell's reluctance to use force with McClellan's. At the time I thought this comparison was apt on several levels—and I still do.

In addressing a question of such contemporary importance, had Weigley stepped beyond his role as a historian? Some certainly thought so. The proceedings of the Princeton conference were published a few months later in the *Journal of Military History*, and Weigley's paper excited a rebuttal by one of Powell's long-time assistants. Lawrence Wilkerson accused Weigley of allowing "his passion get the better of reason" by indulging in "sweeping generalizations [that defy] the more circumspect principles of professional historians."[25] As Wilkerson's defense of Powell made clear, historians should stay in their playrooms and leave the really important people to the business they know best. For the most part we have obliged Mr. Wilkerson and his friends. They have been safe from any criticism from us.

So, yes, Weigley had taken on the task of military criticism, and to my mind this was long overdue. I would argue that his use of military history in this way, to inform an issue of contemporary importance, followed in the best traditions of Delbrück and others, using their knowledge of military history as the foundation for educated criticism. Weigley's paper certainly did not create this controversy, but the expert way in which he framed it contributed to a depth of understanding that a newspaper article or television segment could not equal. Afterward, Richard Kohn, Peter Feaver, Oli Hosti, and other scholars published their own critical examinations of the issue and inaugurated a decade's worth of valuable research and analysis on a question that is still very much alive today, as Secretary Rumsfeld could attest.[26] But have you noticed? In all the publicity about the public criticisms of military policy by several recently retired generals, few writers seemed aware that anything like this had happened before or that civil-military relations in the United States required a more subtle understanding of the past than ever.

Are there today no questions in which the military historian's knowledge might be usefully engaged? I think we could all make a very long list. The origins and conduct of the present war should have awakened us to the danger of acting as if history never happened and the consequences when scholars turn their backs on contemporary affairs. More than a decade after the end of the Vietnam War Douglas Pike spoke bitterly of "the total failure of the academic community" to come to grips with the war as it was being fought. "Scholars and academics opposed the war," he wrote, "but did so in ignorance. With no basis of knowledge, the counsel was rooted in error, in the field their advice was dismissed, as it should have been, as worthless." And so "when a high-level official—such as Robert McNamara—wanted to know what Ho Chi Minh would think about a matter . . . he would interview himself, asking what *he* would do if *he* were Ho Chi Minh." This was, Pike wrote, "the worst kind of ignorance—what Aldous Huxley calls *vincible* ignorance: that which one does not know and realizes it, but does not regard as necessary to know."[27] We are very well acquainted with this kind of official thinking today. When high-ranking officials run out of arguments, they tend to throw up their hands and say, "History will judge." Well, here, Pike is history, and his judgments on our predecessors should keep us awake at night. Do we have a judgment like this waiting for us somewhere in the future?

So I would like to propose an experiment for you. Set aside some of your time each day to give the same kind of disciplined attention to contemporary military affairs as you do to your other work. You should not be put off by the thought that high officials have access to more and better information than you do or have the advantage of intelligence they cannot reveal. I can assure you from personal experience that those advantages are highly overstated. Look for a question that particularly engages your own interests. Try your hand at writing a piece of criticism under a deadline you've given yourself. Try to rid yourself of the notion that you are somehow betraying your scholarship. Remind yourself that you are not applying history in some superficial or tendentious way, that you are really applying yourself, your own highly educated judgment, and that what you are doing has its own long and honorable and useful tradition. Along the way you will find that what you are learning to do is only different from but not more difficult than the work you ordinarily do. Then look for venues in which you can exercise your newly acquired skills. There are more than ever; find one that suits your tastes and take the plunge.

Then, perhaps, just perhaps, the Creech will not come for you one day. And you will not be roasted and eaten after all.

Notes

1. Paul Theroux, *Fresh Air Fiend: Travel Writings, 1985–2000* (Boston: Houghton Mifflin, 2000), 448–49.

2. See page 2 of Theroux's interview with *Salon*, http://www.salon.com (accessed April 18, 2006).

3. Timothy Noah, "Did Nan Talese Lie to Oprah?" January 27, 2006, http://slate.com (accessed April 19, 2006).

4. Nancy Milford did, in "All the shouting about 'A Million Little Pieces' is part of a long debate that dates to the beginning of writing," *Washington Post Book World*, February 5, 2006, T10. For a countervailing view see Michiko Kakutani's "Bending the Truth in a Million Little Ways," *New York Times*, January 17, 2006, http://www.nytimes.com (accessed January 17, 2006), who seems less interested in literary traditions than in dilating upon what she sees as modern society's increasingly casual regard for truth.

5. Indeed, even in Ranke's own time other scholars were already conceiving of history in radically different ways. See Isaiah Berlin, *Vico and Herder: Two Studies in the History of Ideas* (New York: Viking Press, 1976), xvi–xix, xxiii.

6. Peter Novick, *That Noble Dream: The "Objectivity Question" and the American Historical Profession* (Cambridge: Cambridge University Press, 1988).

7. *Journal of the American Military History Foundation* 3, no. 1 (1939): n.p.

8. Harvey DeWeerd, "Intellectual Preparedness," *Journal of the American Military History Foundation* 4, no. 2 (1940): n.p.

9. See, for instance, Jean Montry, "Unoccupied France and German War Economy," *Military Affairs* (formerly the *Journal of the American Military History Foundation*; hereafter cited as MA) 6, no. 2 (1942): 89–96; Edward S. Mason, "Economic Factors in Military Action," MA 6, no. 3 (1942): 133–42; H. A. DeWeerd, "The Federalization of Our Army," MA 6, no. 3 (1942): 143–52; and Human Roudman, "Evolution of New Fleet Tactics," MA 6, no. 4 (1943): 197–201; Alfred Vagts, "A Memoir of Military Occupation," MA 7, no. 1 (1943): 16–24; S. L. A. Marshall, review of *The Command of the Air*, by Giulio Douhet, MA 7, no. 1 (1943): 44–46; A. F. Kovacs, "Military Origins of the Fall of France," MA 7, no. 1 (1943): 25–40; John North, "Lessons of the North African Campaign," MA 8, no. 3 (1944): 161–68; Ben Bruce Blakeney, "The Japanese High Command," MA 9, no. 2 (1945): 95–113.

10. Raymond Garthoff, "The Soviet Image of the Enemy," MA 21, no. 4 (1957): 161–74; James Atkinson, "The Impact of Soviet Theory on Warfare as a Continuation of Politics," MA 24, no. 1 (1960): 1–6; Francis F. Fuller,

"Mao Tse-tung: Military Thinker," MA 22, no. 3 (1958): 139–45; see also the special issue, "Irregular Warfare," MA 24, no. 3 (1960).

11. Peter Paret, introduction to "Session on Contemporary History and War," MA 32, no. 1 (1968): 1–2; Leonard Krieger, "Official History and the War in Vietnam: Comment," MA 32, no. 1 (1968): 16–19; and John Shy, "Official History and the War in Vietnam: Comment," MA 32, no. 1 (1968): 13–15.

12. Randy Papadopoulos, "Broaching Military History to Wider Audiences: AHA Roundtable Session," Society for Military History Headquarters Gazette 19, no. 2 (2006): 3–5.

13. See Paul Scheips, "Military History and Peace Research," MA 36, no. 3 (1972): 92–93, referencing a survey conducted by Stetson Conn, who was then chief historian of the Army.

14. Mahon is quoted by Theodore Ropp, "Forty Years of the American Military Institute," MA 35, no. 3 (1971): 90.

15. Paul Schratz, "A Commentary on the Pueblo Affair," MA 35, no. 3 (1971): 93–95; Ronald Schaffer, "The 1940 Small Wars Manual and the 'Lessons of History,'" MA 36, no. 2 (1972): 46–51; Ronald Spector, "Getting down to the Nitty-Gritty: Military History, Official History and the American Experience in Vietnam," MA 38, no. 1 (1974): 11–12; George Herring, review of The My Lai Massacre and Its Cover-Up: Beyond the Reach of Law? The Peers Commission Report with a Supplement and Introductory Essay on the Limits of Law, by Joseph Goldstein, Burke Marshall, and Jack Schwartz, MA 41, no. 2 (1977); George C. Herring, "American Strategy in Vietnam: The Postwar Debate," MA 46, no. 2 (1982): 57–63; and Robert J. Graham, "Vietnam: An Infantryman's View of Our Failure," MA 48, no. 3 (1984): 133–39.

16. Theodore Ropp, "Military Historical Scholarship since 1937," MA 41, no. 2 (1977): 68–74; Allan Millett, "The Study of American Military History in the United States," MA 41, no. 2 (1977): 58–61; Gunther Rothenberg, "European Military History in America: The State of the Art," MA 41, no. 2 (1977): 75–78. See also Edward M. Coffman, "The New American Military History," MA 48, no. 4 (1984): 1–5; and John Whiteclay Chambers, "Conference Review Essay: the New Military History: Myth and Reality," MA 55, no. 3 (1991): 395–406.

17. Harvey DeWeerd, "The Total Science of War," Journal of the American Military History Foundation 4, no. 4 (1940): n.p.

18. See Peter Paret's discussion of the "new military history" in his Understanding War: Essays on Clausewitz and the History of Military Power (Princeton NJ: Princeton University Press, 1992), 209–26, esp. 220. An argument could be made that the trend toward new military history as it was

being defined in the 1970s was well under way in the United States and elsewhere long before.

19. Hans Delbrück, *History of the Art of War*, vol. 4, *The Dawn of Modern Warfare*, trans. Walter Renfroe Jr. (Lincoln: University of Nebraska Press, 1985), x.

20. Theodore Ropp, "Military Historical Scholarship since 1937," *Military Affairs, Fortieth Anniversary Issue*, April 1977, 72–74.

21. See Leslie Anders, "Retrospect: Four Decades of American Military Journalism," *MA* 41, no. 2 (1977): 62–67, for a look at the proliferation of other journals and magazines carrying articles on military history. See also D. K. R. Crosswell, "An Analysis of Reader Response for Military Affairs," *MA* 45, no. 3 (1981): 144; John Whiteclay Chambers, "Conference Review Essay: The New Military History: Myth and Reality," *Journal of Military History* (hereafter cited as *JMH*) 55, no. 3 (1991): 398. I am indebted to Robert Berlin, executive director of the Society for Military History, for supplying up-to-date membership figures.

22. Peter Paret, "Military Power," *JMH* 53, no. 3 (1989): 284.

23. See Peter Paret's discussion on Delbrück's distinctions between the military historian and the *Militärschriftsteller*, or *Kritik*, in his "Hans Delbrück on Military Critics and Military Historians," *MA* 30, no. 3 (1966): 148–52.

24. Russell Weigley, "The American Military and the Principle of Civilian Control from McClellan to Powell," *JMH* 57, no. 5 (1993): 27–58. The proceedings of the symposium were published in this issue of the journal.

25. Lawrence Wilkerson, "Communications to the Editor," *JMH* 58, no. 3 (1994): 577–79.

26. See especially Richard Kohn, "Out of Control: The Crisis in Civil Military Relations," *National Interest* 35 (Spring 1994); "The Forgotten Fundamentals of Civilian Control of the Military in Democratic Government," John M. Olin Institute for Strategic Studies, Project on U.S. Post–Cold War Civil-Military Relations, Working Paper no. 13, Harvard University, June 1997; and "The Erosion of Civilian Control of the Military in the United States Today," *Naval War College Review* 55 (Summer 2002). See also Ole R. Holsti, "A Widening Gap between the Military and Civilian Society? Some Evidence, 1976–1996," John M. Olin Institute for Strategic Studies, Project on U.S. Post–Cold War Civil-Military Relations, Working Paper no. 13, Harvard University, October 1997; and also Tom Ricks, "The Widening Gap between Military and Society," *Atlantic Monthly*, July 1997.

27. Douglas Pike, "Conduct of the Vietnam War: Strategic Factors, 1965–1968," in *The Second Indochina War: Proceedings of a Symposium Held at Airlie, Virginia, 7–9 November 1984* (Washington DC: U.S. Army Center of Military History, 1986), 99–119.

A Speculation on the Banality of Evil

April 20, 1945: Fifty feet under the ruined city of Berlin, Adolf Hitler marks his birthday, his fifty-sixth. It will be his last.

Allied air raids have hit Berlin more than eighty times in the last three months. Miraculously, some Berliners still live in the wreckage. Hitler's glittering chancellery, the Reichskanzlerei, has been pounded into a smoldering hulk. No birthday parties there. So a small affair has been arranged below ground, in the claustrophobic warren of bombproof rooms and hallways that serves as the Führerbunker.

Naturally, many well-wishers who would have been happily present for such an important occasion now find it difficult to attend. Most of Hitler's intimates are still within reach, however. Reichsmarschall Hermann Göring can be coaxed from his country estate this one last time. Foreign Minister Joachim von Ribbentropp and Propaganda Minister Joseph Goebbels are only a bunker away. The minister for armament and war production, Albert Speer, has a dangerous commute, but he will go to some trouble to attend this meeting. He feels he must tell his führer personally that he will disobey his orders: the so-called Nero Directives—to deny the enemy any fruits of victory by laying the entire Reich to waste. Reichsführer Heinrich Himmler is plotting a separate peace with the Western Allies at the moment, but he will come into the city too. A few more, some of the lesser lights of the fading Reich, contribute their presence to the grimy air below: Martin Bormann, who in the ever-more confined atmosphere of the bunker is fast becoming Hitler's indispensable man; Artur Axmann, the head of the Hitler Youth who sees in the coming battle for Berlin a great opportunity for his armed children.

Admiral Karl Dönitz and Generals Wilhelm Keitel and Alfred Jodl are in attendance, along with several Berlin area commanders thrown in for good measure. A few days earlier, Eva Braun, Hitler's mistress, arrived without notice to take up residence in the bunker. She seemed an omen. But of what?

As the air raids continued, as the Allied armies fought their way toward the heart of the Reich from virtually every direction, those who remained with Hitler anxiously wondered when he would finally see that it was time to quit the city. He had been heard to say that he would leave Berlin on his birthday, transfer his headquarters to his Alpine redoubt at Obersalzberg, and carry on the war from its mountain fastness. Eva Braun's dramatic arrival cast a new and dreadful light on everyone's speculations. Could it be that Hitler meant to stay to the bitter end? And what would happen then?

Perhaps Hitler knows by now. He is sliding in and out of reality. On occasion he is brutally realistic. The war is lost, so everything is lost. His poisonous worldview tolerates no half measures: success or oblivion, total victory or utter destruction of his nation, its cultural and material wealth, its people, of himself. Then he imagines that the war itself has defeated him, or that the German people have failed him. He wonders whether the German people are worthy of his great ideals. Perhaps he has not been sufficiently demanding. "Afterward," he muses, "you rue the fact that you've been so kind." Then he decides, no. All will go down in ruin, and deservedly so. Even abandoned cities are to be burned.

But in these final days Hitler lives in several worlds. He was a man of whom Lord Tedder would write later that "by ordinary standards would be judged insane." Hitler occasionally dreams that victory may not be lost after all. Burning the cities is not a tacit admission of defeat, but a clever tactical ploy to deny the enemy any possible advantage. Shattered armies can be reconstituted for the final apocalyptic battles on the approaches to Berlin. Seized by imaginings of a rejuvenated Wehrmacht, Hitler visits the front lines for the last time in March 1945, venturing as far east as the Ninth Army's headquarters, then in the castle at Freienwalde. There, the generals and staff officers saw a stooped old man with gray hair and sunken face who occasionally, with an effort, ventured a confident smile. Hitler's old headquarters in East Prussia, at Rastenburg, was the site of the most promising assassination attempt against him, one attempt of forty-two in all, by Richard Overy's count. Since the bomb exploded on July 20, 1944, historians have been tempted to see the explosion as the cause of Hitler's mental and physical decline. But neither the danger of assassination nor the bomb were catalysts of his deterioration. One would expect a certain correspondence between wartime stresses and a leader's mental and physical health, but humans do not react so literally to dramatic events. One of Hitler's physicians thought that until 1940 Hitler looked younger than he was, thriving on the stresses and strains of his megalomania. Between 1940 and 1943, he began to catch up with his age. Even his most admiring followers began to see signs of physical and mental decline. Joseph Goebbels rhapsodized that Hitler's face was that "of an Atlas, bearing the whole world on his shoulders."

By 1943, the quack who served as one of Hitler's attending physicians, Theodore Morell, was administering injections of a brew made up of twenty-eight different drugs. Well before the bomb exploded at Rastenburg, his downward slide had begun. His extremities trembled. His left arm and leg occasionally shook so much as to be useless to him. He began to stoop and shuffle as he walked. Some of those who saw him most often thought he might have Parkinson's disease, but these symptoms as commonly described could just as easily have been hysterical paralysis of a type all too common among soldiers in the Great War. What is quite clear, however, is that Hitler's physicians were of no help to him. Quite the opposite. They contributed importantly to their patient's miseries. By the spring of 1944, Dr. Morell had developed the practice of simply giving Hitler's aides and servants bulk supplies of pills—Dr. Koester's Antigas Pills—containing a mixture of strychnine and belladonna, to be taken whenever the patient demanded. How one might gauge the effect of these minor poisonings upon Hitler is a nice question. Too many other factors must be allowed their influence upon his behavior at the time. One cannot imagine that any of these actually contributed to his command of self or state during the final days of the war.

After the commencement of Operation Barbarossa—the invasion of the Soviet Union—Hitler spent less time in Berlin and more time in his headquarters at Rastenburg. By the end of November 1944, Russian advances forced him to abandon East Prussia once and for all and return to Berlin. Toward the middle of December, he ventured to his Western Headquarters at Ziegenberg near Bad Neuheim to lend his strategic genius to the direction of the Christmas offensive in the Ardennes that collapsed into the Battle of the Bulge. By mid-January, he was back in Berlin, and with the exception of his visit to the Ninth Army's headquarters, there he would remain.

The führer's bunker at Rastenburg had been no palace; it was dark, airless, dank, certainly cheerless. Even Hitler's doctors advised him not to return after the bomb of July 20. But the bunker in Berlin was even more confining than the one in Rastenburg. It was hardly a place designed for recuperation. By February 1945, Hitler's doctors were adding to the list of his symptoms an inability to concentrate and a certain forgetfulness—or was this merely indifference? By then, time had turned itself inside out in the bunker. Daily military conferences began very late in the evening and usually were not finished before six in the morning. Afterward, Hitler, "with shaking legs and quivering hand," stood to dictate instructions to his secretaries and aides. That done, he would collapse on a sofa and engorge himself with his favorite foods, chocolate and cake. During these gastronomic performances, one of his secretaries remembered, "He virtually did not talk at all." Axmann professed to being shocked by his leader's appearance and manner. Hitler seemed to be in his dotage, yet Axmann thought he exuded "willpower and determination" all the same. A much less worshipful description of Hitler at the time comes to us from an "elderly General Staff Officer" who saw a Hitler who "dragged himself about painfully and clumsily, throwing his torso forward and dragging his legs after him from his living room to the conference room of the bunker. . . . [S]aliva dripped from the corners of his mouth."

That day's military conference—Hitler's birthday conference—offered no hope at all that Berlin could escape destruction by the Red Army. General Hans Krebs, who delivered the briefing, told Hitler that the capital would be completely surrounded within a few days at most, or at worst, within a few hours. Only a few Wehrmacht and ss formations survived. Military units depicted on Hitler's situation maps were little more than ghosts of their originals. Hitler imagined them as up to full strength and combat power. He began directing movements and concentrations of these phantom units, creating a gossamer defense against the Red invaders. All these units he placed under the command of ss Obergruppenführer Felix Steiner, and in Hitler's mind, if nowhere else, the so-called Steiner Offensive was born, another phantom flitting through a mind that was fast losing its intellectual cohesion.

Swinging back and forth between lucidity and near-stupor, Hitler announced that he would remain in Berlin after all, that he would not remove himself and his entourage to the Obersalzberg. He told one of his adjutants that the coming battle for Berlin "presented the only chance to prevent total defeat," although precisely how, Hitler could not then say. With General Alfred Jodl, Hitler was more forthright: "I shall fight as long as the faithful fight next to me and then I shall shoot myself."

Word of the führer's intentions was not long in spreading beyond the bunker, throughout the city. On that day, all Reich administrative agencies in Berlin and elsewhere closed for good. Shops, streetcars, subways, police, garbage, mail deliveries all quit even the pretense of operating. The Berlin Zoo closed its gates. On April 20, the office of the commandant of Berlin issued 2,000 permits to leave the city. Himmler found reasons not to visit the Führerbunker again. Reichsmarschall Göring discovered "extremely urgent tasks in South Germany," and decamped hurriedly from his estate with a truck convoy full of loot.

Those who stayed behind with Hitler for the cataclysmic battle will watch a man falling inexorably into a self-dug grave. The military situation outside formed the perfect accompaniment to the atmosphere of Hitlerian *Götterdämmerung* in the Führerbunker. "There is only one thing I still want," Hitler cried out: "The end, the end!" He was, in Hugh Trevor-Roper's memorable phrase, like "some cannibal god, rejoicing in the ruin of his own temples." He would not have to wait long: On the morning of April 21, Soviet artillery began bombarding the outskirts of the city.

Of course it was the Red Army that had aimed itself most deliberately at the Nazi capital. Stalin had feigned indifference to the fate of Berlin, going so far as to tell General Eisenhower that the city had "lost its former strategic importance." In truth, Stalin believed no such thing: Berlin was to be where the Red Army's war would end. Eisenhower had agreed with Stalin that Berlin was "nothing but a geographical location" of little remaining military significance. Characteristically, Stalin assumed Eisenhower was as duplicitous as he himself was, and on the following day Stalin told his defense committee, "the little allies intend to get to Berlin ahead of the Red Army."

A race for Berlin had thus begun, but only the Red Army would be running it. Stalin set his two most experienced generals, Georgy Zhukov and Ivan Konev, against one another to see who could whip his soldiers faster through the crumbling resistance put up by the Wehrmacht and the ss. By early April, Zhukov is slightly closer than Konev. Zhukov has amassed four field armies and two tank armies at the Kustrin bridgehead on the Oder River. For each kilometer of his front lines, Zhukov has placed 250 artillery pieces virtually wheel to wheel. Eleven thousand of these wait to be fired at Berlin. Konev's forces were equally strong and lay alongside Zhukov's, just to the south. Combined, the Soviet armies driving for Berlin numbered more than a million soldiers, happily anticipating revenge. "Berlin for us was an object of such ardent desire," wrote Konev, "that everyone, from soldiers to general, wanted to see [it with his] own eyes, to capture it by force of arms."

The question of which of the Allied armies was going to take Berlin having been more or less settled in the Soviets' favor, there naturally arose the question of what to do with the city and its inhabitants once captured. Inevitably, high-ranking Nazis would be swept up in the last great battle of the European war—perhaps even Hitler himself. On this latter question, Allied policy had yet to take shape. In the meantime, Allied opinions differed wonderfully.

Churchill had considered what eventually was to be done with Axis leaders as early as the summer of 1941, when he was heard to wonder if Hitler and his cronies might be exiled to some remote island. St. Helena, Napoleon's old prison after Waterloo, would not do, however; Churchill "would not so desecrate" the place by putting Nazis on it. The most extreme punishment, he thought, should be meted out to Mussolini: that "bogus mimic of Ancient Rome" should be "strangled like Vercingetorix in old Roman fashion." Naturally, such opinions would grow even less forgiving over the course of the war. Axis leaders were storing up credits for beastliness at a pace that quickly outran any impulse of Allied mercy. After D-Day, Eisenhower startled Lord Halifax one day by arguing that all members of the German General Staff, the Gestapo, and any Nazi above the rank of major should be executed. By the spring of 1945, Churchill and the Foreign Office were of one mind: summary field executions for the highest ranking Axis leaders.

Although Churchill distinguished between the Hitlerites and the rest of Germany, most of his countrymen did not. Nor did the Americans. Roosevelt most certainly did not absolve the German people of responsibility for Nazism. More than once, FDR suggested mass castration of the Germans once the war was safely over, so as to forestall a resurgence of militarism. The president also agreed, at least at first, with his treasury secretary, Henry Morgenthau, who had a plan to de-industrialize Germany and transform it into a permanently impoverished agricultural republic. These were the provisions that seemed to attract the most attention, but Morgenthau also made recommendations for dealing with war criminals that followed Churchill's line. Once a list of Axis "archcriminals" was drawn up and identities confirmed, Morgenthau's plan called for their field execution by military firing squads. One estimate at the time held that many thousands of war criminals all across Europe would be rounded up by war's end.

The American secretary of war, Henry Stimson, was horrified by Morgenthau's plan. At first, President Roosevelt was attracted to the severity of the plan, but Stimson would not hear of it. The Morgenthau Plan was unbecoming of a truly great nation, Stimson argued. The Allies had sacrificed their lives and treasure in defense of the highest moral purposes. Those sacrifices must not be disgraced by the imposition of a Carthaginian peace. Crude vengeance should make way for higher principles of international law and justice. Only a trial by an international tribunal could be acceptable under these circumstances, Stimson insisted. And in this opinion Secretary Stimson could count on the support of none other than Joseph Stalin himself, as Churchill would discover. On a trip to Moscow in October 1944, Churchill had broached this subject with Stalin, and to his surprise found the Soviet leader taking "an unexpectedly ultrarespectable line." Stalin would not budge on the question, Churchill later told Roosevelt. Stalin said "there must be no executions without trial, otherwise the world would say they were afraid to try them." Confronted by an immovable Stalin and a wavering Roosevelt, Churchill gave in to the idea of a trial for the leading Nazis.

Hitler could not have known of Churchill's concession. He almost certainly did know of the Declaration of St. James, an official pronouncement made three years earlier in London by representatives from the nine European governments-in-exile. Constituting themselves as the "Inter-Allied Commission on the Punishment of·War Crimes," the conferees foreswore summary retributions against enemy war criminals, and instead demanded "the punishment, through the channel of organized justice, of those guilty of or responsible for these crimes." The leading Allies would eventually come around to this position as the European War bled to a close. The St. James's declaration of highminded legal purpose could hardly have made any impression on a dictator who had so thoroughly subverted his own nation's legal system. Anyway, Hitler had long thought himself and his party beyond the pale of any law. On the eve of Germany's invasion of Russia in the summer of 1941, Hitler confessed his feeling that they had all passed a moral point of no return. "We have so much to answer for already that we must win," he told Goebbels. Four years later, an international trial was the most humane fate Hitler might have hoped for, but he was in fact contemptuous of any such prospect. He refused, he said, to become "an exhibit in the Moscow Zoo" for the edification of the enemy's "hysterical masses."

By the afternoon and evening of April 22, such prospects as were left to Hitler were disappearing one by one. At the daily military conference in the bunker, it was clear to all present that the Steiner Offensive would never materialize. By then, every Wehrmacht formation in the path of the Red Army was either disintegrating on the spot or falling back in confusion along the roads to Berlin. Virtually all of Berlin itself was now within range of Zhukov's artillery. The city was being drenched in artillery fire, its muffled thumps now discernible in the Führerbunker. Every notion of retrieving the disastrous military situation, of fending off the enemy's advance into the capital, of somehow wresting the initiative from the Russians, of heroic resistance, all these possibilities were rendered impossible by the few reports still being transmitted from the wreckage of the once-proud, seemingly irresistible Wehrmacht.

Hitler listened sullenly as the reports were briefed to him. All of a sudden, casting off any pretense of composure, he unleashed a storm of hysterical ravings. No one was worthy of his regard. All about him were incompetent, corrupt, traitorous weaklings. And so his fit of denunciations went on for who knows how long, draining all those present of self-regard, energy, any reserve of hope. The historian Joachim Fest depicts a scene worthy of a Wagnerian opera: "He shook his fists furiously while he spoke, tears ran down his cheeks; and as always in the disastrous disenchantments of his life, everything collapsed along with the one hysterically magnified expectation. This was the end, he said. He could no longer go on. Death alone remains. He would meet death here in the city." His outburst was so violent, some present thought Hitler had completely lost his senses. On the day after this near-psychotic episode, a corps command of Berlin's defenses, General Karl Weidling, was dismayed to see his führer sitting behind a table strewn with maps, his face puffy "with feverish eyes. When he tried to stand up, I noticed to my horror that his hands and legs were constantly trembling. . . . With a distorted smile he shook hands with me and asked in a hardly audible voice whether we had not met before." Weidling noticed that when Hitler sat down again, "his left leg kept moving, the knee swinging like a pendulum, only faster."

If Hitler was frenzied by the state of affairs as he knew them, what he did not then know would have rendered him completely insensible. Two reports in particular, tumbling down the stairs on top of one another, cast an even darker shadow over the denizens of the bunker, if that was possible. Unknown to Hitler, Himmler had entered into secret negotiations with Sweden's Count Bernadotte for a separate peace with the Western Allies. If anything, Himmler was even less in touch with reality than his leader. Presenting himself to Bernadotte as "the only sane man left in Europe," Himmler was at the same time considering how to colonize the Ukraine with a religious sect that had been brought to his attention by his masseur. Of course, the Allies were in no mood to entertain any alternative to unconditional surrender, and Himmler's negotiations went nowhere, except, late in the evening of April 28, to be announced by Reuters news service. Hitler happened to be in a discussion with Ritter von Greim when a valet appeared with the report. Von Greim reported that his führer turned purple.

This news was followed the next day by reports that Mussolini and his mistress had been taken prisoner by Italian partisans and summarily executed in the small town of Mezzegra. Their bodies had been taken to Milan and hanged by the heels in a garage on the Piazzale Loreto, where a mob wreaked its vengeance on the corpses. Hearing this news, Hitler began preparing for his suicide, a final contribution to the Armageddon he had shrieked out for the German nation that had so disappointed him. He would show them, those "petty bourgeois reactionaries" who thought they had defeated him. Without him, Germany would be leaderless, carrion to be picked over by the wretched Allies.

Most accounts given by those present who survived this final day in the bunker agree that, having spent most of the evening of April 29 writing his "Political Testament," Hitler retired to his rooms with Eva Braun, there to receive occasional visitors from among the dwindling population of the bunker. Sometime in the middle of the afternoon of April 30, Hitler and Braun took their own lives. Braun used poison. Hitler used a pistol. Following his last wishes, several of Hitler's underlings carried the two bodies to the surface, where they were incinerated in the ruins of the chancellery garden, and where the Russians discovered the remains several days later.

So did Hitler take his own life, by his own hand and of his own volition? No doubt he was hysterical, but he was not deranged. Neither madness, nor the approach of the enemy then less than half a mile away in the Tiergarten, nor entreaties from Goebbels or his other courtiers, compelled Hitler to take this course of action. Nor did the deeper impulses of culture drive him toward self-destruction. This was not an act of seppuku. He did not aim to retrieve his honor or ennoble his death in any way. His suicide was an act of spite. He killed himself in the same spirit in which he had issued orders to kill Germany itself. He meant to punish history by absenting himself from it.

Goebbels followed his master not long after. "There must be someone at least who will stay with him unconditionally until death," Goebbels wrote in a codicil to the political testament Hitler had left behind. After a half-hearted attempt to negotiate with the Russians, Goebbels destroyed himself, his wife, and their five children. Heinrich Himmler's dalliance with the role of peacemaker came to a similar end, and he killed himself within days of Hitler and Goebbels. Göring, of course, was still alive, soon to be taken prisoner to stand trial at Nuremberg. The whereabouts of Martin Bormann, after Hitler the most powerful politician in Germany, were unknown. He was believed to have been killed while trying to escape the Führerbunker at the last minute, but no body was found there.

Uncertainties about Hitler's fate were not assuaged entirely. When his death was announced over the radio by Admiral Canaris, Marshal Zhukov thought, "So that's the end of the bastard. Too bad it was impossible to take him alive." Stalin did not believe Hitler was dead. The Soviet historian Dmitri Volkogonov depicts a Stalin intensely interested in the fate of his mortal enemy. "Stalin's triumph would be complete if he could take the Nazi leader alive and have him tried by an international tribunal," Volkogonov writes. Even though Hitler's remains had been discovered by Russian troops, Stalin seems to have been unwilling to trust his own forensic specialists. When Stalin arrived at Potsdam in July for the Allied conference, he startled the American secretary of state James Byrnes by suggesting that Hitler was still alive, hiding somewhere beyond Germany. And Stalin was by no means alone in his suspicion. Rumors of escape continued to fly about, not only about Hitler, but about Bormann too. The Nuremberg prosecutors then preparing charges against the Nazi elite, not at all confident that Hitler was dead, just in case added Hitler's name to the list of defendants.

All of which brings us to an uncomfortable, even unwelcome question. If Hitler had chosen to live, what then? Historians usually find these questions tiresome. Some speculation might be in order, they say, but one ought to be cautious. One may go too far too quickly, slide into fantasy. Besides, simply finding out what did happen is hard enough, sometimes just impossible. Why add to the confusions history already throws in our way? Protests of this sort, against the variant that has come to be called "alternative" or "counterfactual" history, might best be seen as reactions to intellectual shock—reactions that cannot bear the weight of much argument.

For, in one sense, alternative history is history. The confluence of human action creates contingencies and uncertainties that often do not yield an authoritative version of process, event, or person. More often than any historian would prefer to think, one is reduced to educated guessing about which of several versions of the story one ought to accept as credible. In the end one must decide even if there is a chance of deciding badly. History—not only the living of it but the writing of it too—is a chancy business in which a certain tolerance for the calculation of probabilities comes in handy.

In practice, historians exercise restraint bordering on abstinence when they encounter an opportunity to calculate alternatives. Their calculations show up, quarklike, as the merest shadow of a regret that events in a certain case did not turn out differently. Others are a bit bolder, registering disapproval or rendering judgments. Thucydides cast his *History of the Peloponnesian War* as a tragedy because he grieved over the death of Periclean Athens. And he leaves no doubt about what he thought of the second-rate demagogues who succeeded Pericles and led Athens to ruin. A kind of standard is set up, against which successors are made to struggle—this is just one of any number of puzzles the historian may pose for the reader. Indeed, the practice of hypothetical or alternative calculation is so common one might even argue that the doing of history without it is well nigh impossible. As the editor of the present volume has written, "'What if' is the historian's favorite secret question."

The obverse of history in Hitler's particular case, therefore, is not at all hard to imagine credibly. Reacting to precisely the same circumstances, acting upon the very same stew of perception and delusion, Hitler could have just as easily decided not to kill himself after all. Change nothing else but this and one changes everything. One might impose a measure of control over any alternative scenario by asking no more of inventiveness than one might ask of a prediction. How far ahead might one justifiably attempt to see in April 1945? Whatever one answers, one should go no farther than that.

In April 1945, some very real and very important questions about the future awaited answers. Statesmen, policy makers, and soldiers the world over had to guess about what would happen in a most uncertain world. But they did guess. We know, for instance, that there was no agreement between the Allies over how to treat the leaders of the defeated Reich, save that they would not be shot out of hand. What that meant was that for the contingent moment the leading Nazis who were within reach were to be scooped up and interned. Once the Allies agreed on questions of international law and jurisprudence, there remained the business of setting the actual machinery in place, and all of this required some time. Göring spent this interregnum with his wife and daughter in the safety and relatively comfortable custody of the Western Allies. Those taken by the Russians were neither so safe nor comfortable.

So if we may imagine a living Hitler, one who survived the battle of Berlin, we can see now that a good deal of this canvas has already been painted for us. We know that at 12:50 in the afternoon of May 2, General Karl Weidling's chief of staff and several other official representatives flew a white flag at the Potsdam Bridge, that they were escorted promptly to General Chuikov's headquarters, and that an armistice was arranged forthwith. We also know that at about the same time Russian troops took the Reichskanzlerei and, after some confusion, finally discovered the Führerbunker itself. We can easily envision a resigned, even an indifferent Hitler, still alive, having ordered General Weidling to seek a ceasefire. Perhaps Hitler might still have harbored a fantasy of a negotiated peace, but of course he had nothing left with which to strike any sort of bargain. We can also see without fear of contradiction that the Russians would not have been in a mood especially conducive to negotiation, having lost nearly 100,000 casualties in the Berlin campaign alone. No, Hitler would have been hustled off to see one of the Russian commanders, Zhukov or Chuikov. Immediately, a signal confirming his capture would have gone out to Stalin, and then, to the rest of the world. In all likelihood, the prisoner Hitler would have been on his way to Moscow before the day was out.

But, we have now reached the outer limits of a reasonably safe scenario. Before going further, we are forced to consider a less plausible, certainly a less attractive, alternative. How likely was it that Hitler chose escape over suicide—precisely what many suspected at the time? Here, our answers need not be so speculative; we have testimony of just what was required to make good such an escape at this point in time. Escape was possible, but only just. In the chaotic final hours of the war, several small groups took their chances outside, in a wrecked city engulfed by artillery and small arms fire. The chances of success were minuscule. In the aftermath of Hitler's and Goebbels's suicides, an ill-assorted bunch of soldiers, secretaries, and party officials, including Hitler's own secretary Martin Bormann, tried to get out through the New Chancellery exits and into the city with the aim of working their way northwest of the city. All were killed or captured.

But the fortunes of battle favored others. Major Willi Johannmeier, Hitler's army adjutant, was chosen to carry a copy of Hitler's final testament to Field Marshal Schoerner, the newly appointed commander in chief of the Wehrmacht. Two other petty functionaries, Wilhelm Zander and Heinz Lorenz, drew similar missions. This party was rounded out by the addition of a fortunate corporal named Hummerich, presumably assigned to assist Major Johannmeier. Johannmeier, an experienced and resourceful soldier, was detailed to lead the group to the safety of German lines. His skills were about to be tested. The Russians had established three battle lines in a ring around the city center, at the Victory column, at the Zoo station, and at Pichelsdorf. The Pichelsdorf sector was where Johannmeier and his party had to go. At noon on April 29, the four men left the chancellery through the garage exits on Hermann Göring Strasse and struck westward, through the Tiergarten toward Pichelsdorf, at the northernmost reach of the large city lake, the Havel. By four or five in the afternoon, having spent the last several hours evading Russians, the party arrived in this sector. The sector was in German hands for the moment, defended by a battalion of Hitler Youth awaiting reinforcements.

Johannmeier and company rested until dark and then took small boats out onto the lake, making southward for another pocket of defense on the western shore, at Wannsee. There, Johannmeier managed to get a radio signal off to Admiral Dönitz, asking for evacuation by seaplane. After resting in a bunker for most of the day, the small group set off for a small island, the Pfaueninsel, where they would await their rescue by Dönitz's seaplane.

In the meantime, another group of bunker refugees arrived. On the morning of April 29, just as Johannmeier and his party were preparing to leave, Major Baron Freytag von Loringhoven, Rittmeister Gerhardt Boldt, and a lieutenant colonel named Weiss asked received permission to attempt an escape and join General Wenchk's imaginary army of relief. The next day, April 30, they would follow the same but even more dangerous route west as Johannmeier's group. The Russians were as close as a few blocks now, already at the Air Ministry. And they had nearly closed the ring on the Pichelsdorf sector at the Havel. Freytag and his group had set out already when they were joined by Colonel Nicolaus von Below, Hitler's Luftwaffe adjutant. Below seems to have been the last one to leave the bunker before Hitler killed himself.

All of these fugitives collected for a time on the lake, awaiting the salvation of the seaplane. A seaplane did materialize eventually, but owing to the heavy enemy fire, its pilot chose between discretion and valor and flew away before taking on his passengers. Now all were left to their own devices. By ones and twos most of the escapees managed to get away, if only to be taken prisoner later. Johannmeier and his group worked their way down past Potsdam and Brandenburg and crossed the Elbe near Magdeburg. Posing as foreign workers, they passed through enemy lines a few days later. Johannmeier simply continued his journey all the way back to his family home in Westphalia. There in the garden he buried Hitler's last testament in a glass jar. Zander made his escape all the way to Bavaria, as did Axmann, the chief of the Hitler Youth. Nicolaus von Below enrolled in law school at Bonn University. His studies were to be interrupted by the Allied authorities.

All of these men were considerably younger, healthier, and more physically resourceful than Hitler. The vision of Hitler negotiating all these difficulties is an alternative that is defeated by Hitler's psychological and physical states, neither of which, singly or in combination, conduced to the demands of such a choice. By this time, Hitler simply did not have the physical or mental vigor necessary even to attempt an escape, much less actually succeed in one.

But, as the eminent British historian Hugh Trevor-Roper has reason to know, "Myths are not like truths; they are the triumph of credulity over evidence." Immediately upon the conclusion of the war, Trevor-Roper was given access to Allied intelligence and prisoner interrogation reports for the purpose of disentangling the confusions of Hitler's last days, and, by implication, his ultimate fate. Behind Trevor-Roper's assignment were the rumors that swept Europe in the summer of 1945: Hitler had escaped after all, the rumors said. He had gone to ground in Bavaria. Or he was in the Middle East. Or perhaps he had made for the Baltic coast, there to be rescued by submarine and deposited among sympathizers somewhere in South America. These rumors did not merely enthuse the gullible. Stalin startled the American secretary of state at the Potsdam Conference in July by arguing that Hitler was, in fact, alive and in hiding. Allied prosecutors drawing up charges against the leading Nazis took due care to see that Adolf Hitler was indicted, if only in absentia.

But no, given even the unlikely event of survival, it must be to Moscow that he goes. However, this most plausible of alternatives leads us to an important question straightaway. Does he stay there to stand trial, or is he shipped off to Nuremberg for the main proceedings? The Allies had agreed to locate their war crimes trials there because most of the principal defendants had been captured by the Anglo-Americans. The Russians held only a few for the very good reason that the leading Nazis did their best to flee westward, the least immediately dangerous direction, they thought. But if one adds Hitler to Russia's haul of Nazi leaders, the advantage is not quite so certain. The Russians were not particularly difficult on the question of where the trial would be, so long as there was one. Would the Russians have been so obliging if they had held Hitler in the Lubyanka Prison? Would they have insisted upon a grand show trial in Moscow?

There is no way to know for certain. So, one sees, even the most conservative speculation takes one into the shadows of uncertainty quite soon. From this point on, history will insist that we grant more and more "for the sake of the argument," knowing very well that while history is usually explicable, it is often irrational. When dealing with the past, the test of common sense is no test at all.

However, we can be sure enough that a living Hitler would have posed considerable problems for the Allies, assuming he would have been moved to Nuremberg. Most immediately, the question was whether he would have been in a condition to stand trial? Wherever he was imprisoned he would have been treated correctly but certainly not lavishly. Stalin had hoped to put Hitler and fascism on trial, and when the Anglo-Americans finally agreed on the principle of an international tribunal, so did they. A damaged or deranged Hitler would have been less suitable for the event. In prison, no longer in command of his own time, his own diet, or his own medicines, and well beyond the clutches of the malign Dr. Morell, Hitler's physical health might well have improved. Most of the Nuremberg defendants fared well enough. The prison regime even improved the dissolute and rotund Göring. He had been weaned from his addiction to drugs and lost eighty pounds. Had Göring not committed suicide on the day of his execution, he would have gone to the gallows a healthier man.

Imagining Hitler's mental state, once he was captured, is less problematic than one might think. Confinement, in and of itself, could not hold terrors for one who seemed so predisposed to bury himself even when he was at large. As we have seen, first at Rastenburg, and then back in Berlin toward the end, Hitler was downright troglodytic. Of course, Hitler was already familiar with prison life, having served a few months in 1923 for his part in the unsuccessful Munich Beer Hall putsch. This earlier sentence, served no doubt in the presence of admiring wardens, afforded him the opportunity to work on *Mein Kampf*. But even criminals know that every sentence is different. In the event he might have forgotten how to behave in prison, the American Army commandant, Colonel Burton C. Andrus, would have been present to reacquaint him. Andrus imposed very strict rules of confinement upon his charges: only one letter per week, one walk per day, no conversations with fellow prisoners except at lunch, and rations in precisely the same amounts provided to the German refugee population during that severe winter of defeat. What had Hitler done for the past twenty years but write and talk? Denied a freedom of movement, of association, Colonel Andrus would have cast his severe eye over a man who had done little else but talk and write for the past twenty-five years and now was allowed neither. The chances for another *Mein Kampf* would have been very small indeed.

If this strictly regimented environment did not improve Hitler's state of mind, it would not have mattered in the end. Rudolf Hess, whose celebrated flight to Britain in 1941 had shaken Hitler like few other events, arrived in Nuremberg from his wartime confinement as a barely functional amnesiac. He had moments of lucidity punctuated by long spells in which he was detached from reality and barely responsive to social interaction. At first, suspecting him of an elaborate malingering, the Allies subjected Hess to extensive psychiatric examinations and were satisfied that even though he was barely competent he was sufficiently so to stand trial. Hess would spend the rest of his life in Berlin's Spandau Prison. Another defendant, the virulent anti-

Semitic propagandist Julius Streicher, scored so low on his IQ tests that he was examined further by psychiatrists. A third defendant, Robert Ley, leader of the German Labor Front, managed to commit suicide after he heard the charges against him. If we require further evidence that the Allies were disinclined to forgive, postpone, or otherwise soften their prosecution of enemy leaders on any grounds whatsoever, we need only recall that Japan's wartime leader, Hideki Tōjō shot himself in the chest in a botched suicide attempt. He ended up in Tokyo's Sugamo Prison all the same, and at the end of the gallows. Hitler could have expected no less, were he to have stood trial.

Allied officials charged with conducting the International Military Tribunal's business at Nuremberg had any number of worries to disturb their nights. One of them was whether one or more of the defendants would somehow turn the trial to his advantage. More than merely convincing the tribunal that they were not guilty by some means of guile or rhetoric, was it within the power of these once mighty and feared defendants to emerge from the ordeal as heroes or national martyrs? In the event, this fear was groundless. The justices on the tribunal exercised strict control over courtroom behavior. Göring was able to mug and scowl and rustle in his chair to indicate his reaction to testimony, but no more. The white-helmeted military policemen just behind the defendant's box would have removed any unruly defendant from the court's presence had the court's decorum been violated. The behavior of all the defendants, Göring's included, was, like their persons, rather more confined than in ordinary circumstances. Even the most extravagant personality, like the nail that came out too far, would be hammered down. Doubtless, Hitler himself, the most extravagant of these personalities, would have responded along the same lines.

We must return, then, to Hitler himself. Exposed, yet confined in the dock day after day, Hitler, Göring, and the other defendants personified the banality of evil. "There had been quite a metamorphosis," William L. Shirer remembered. "Attired in rather shabby clothes, slumped in their seats fidgeting nervously, they no longer resembled the arrogant leaders of old. They seemed to be a drab assortment of mediocrities. " Hitler's mana would have faded to blandness, as if scrubbed by each of the prosecution's witnesses, until he was made finally to disappear. In the early morning hours of October 16, 1946, the death sentences for ten of the twenty-one convicted defendants at the Nuremberg Trials were carried out. Göring, who was to have gone to the gallows first, had killed himself the night before, perhaps with the aid of a sympathetic guard. Hitler might have managed to do the same to avoid what he had cried out for, *das Ende, das Ende!*

In the end, our alternative scenario would have given Hitler a year and a half more of life. If history would not give him the life he no doubt preferred, it was a great deal more than he had allowed the pathetic millions who died because he lived. One would think humankind would be all too ready to consign Hitler to his well-deserved fate, but as Trevor-Roper has reminded us, "The form of a myth is indeed externally conditioned by facts; there is a minimum of evidence with which it must comply, if it is to live; but once lip-service has been paid to that undeniable minimum, the human mind is free to indulge its infinite capacity for self-deception. . . . When we consider upon what ludicrous evidence the most preposterous beliefs have been easily, and by millions, entertained, we may well hesitate before pronouncing anything incredible. "

The scenarios imagined here, though barely plausible, are more than enough to disturb one's quiet moments with a glimmer of anxiety. At any one moment an infinitude of contingencies await History's choice. When History finally chooses, we say, yes, that must be fitting or right or appropriate to the case. But humankind has seen History make bad choices too. What if Hitler had lived, what if History had been wrong once more?

An Interview with Paul Fussell

The "big push" is how the G-3 journal of the 103rd Infantry Division described its attack against elements of the German Nineteenth Army on November 16, 1944. At H-plus-15 American guns bombarded enemy lines, and the regiments moved forward. In Company F of the 410th Infantry Regiment the future author of *Wartime*, 2nd Lt. Paul Fussell, was about to receive his baptism of fire and his first Purple Heart when shrapnel tore up his elbow. That was near Saint-Dié, on the western slopes of the Vosges Mountains of Alsace.

Nearly five months and a hundred miles later—an eternity for infantry companies and those in them—Fussell "won" another Purple Heart when an excellently placed airburst blew more shrapnel into his back and legs as he and two comrades lay trapped on top of a bunker. The only survivor of this disaster, Fussell spent the rest of the war in the hospital—except that he didn't know it was the rest of the war. His legs buckling under the slightest strain and gasping for breath when he even thought of more combat, Fussell was pronounced fit for duty and reassigned to the Forty-fifth Infantry Division, then preparing for its part in the invasion of Japan. When word came of the bombs at Hiroshima and Nagasaki, Fussell later wrote, he and his fellow soldiers celebrated. Very simply, the bombs meant they would live.

During the bitter winter's combat in Alsace and the Rhineland, Fussell remembers, he was profoundly, irretrievably affected by the insanity of doing again what had been done only a generation before. The same bunkered defenses punctuated the battlescapes where soldiers of the Great War had strained to slaughter one another, and in between the mortal dramas of World

War II combat the soldiers' miseries were hardly different from those of 1914–18.

After demobilization in 1946 and then graduate work at Harvard, Fussell began his academic career as a scholar of eighteenth-century English literature, publishing four books on poetic form, rhetoric, and humanism, including *Samuel Johnson and the Life of Writing*. In 1975 Fussell published *The Great War and Modern Memory*, a work now regarded as the classic evocation of the First World War through its literature and culture. That book won the National Book Award.

Since then Fussell has earned a reputation as one of the most considerable essayists on the American scene, known for deploying the eighteenth century's wit against the culture of the twentieth in a succession of articles and books, including *The Boy Scout Handbook and Other Observations* and *Thank God for the Atomic Bomb and Other Essays*. But by his own testimony he has gone through life since 1945 as a "pissed-off infantryman," as one who looks at the world from the secret places inhabited only by those who have moved, rifle in hand, "against an enemy who designs your death."

In his newest book, *Wartime: Understanding and Behavior in the Second World War* (Oxford University Press, 1989), Fussell attends directly to the war in which he fought, exercising a critical and provocative judgment on its passage into history. It is a passage that he insists has been altogether too happy: from its first shot to its last and ever since, the war has been "sanitized and romanticized almost beyond recognition by the sentimental, the loony patriotic, the ignorant, and the bloodthirsty." Even while the war was being fought, memory was forced to stretch itself around the disaster and grew thinner with every corpse. The ground thus lost by "intellect, discrimination, honesty, individuality, complexity, ambiguity, and irony, not to mention privacy and wit," in Fussell's view, has never been regained. In this interview Fussell discusses how his judgments have been purchased by a lifetime of scholarship as well as by a lifetime's worth of combat.

Now the Donald T. Regan Professor of English Literature at the University of Pennsylvania, Fussell is completing his newest work, *The Norton Book of Modern War* (1990). This interview took place at his home in Philadelphia.

As you make very clear in *Wartime*, the memory of the Second World War has taken a beating at the hands of "euphemizers" and "Disneyfiers," so let's do a pop quiz: What do Walt Disney, Henry Luce, and Edna St. Vincent Millay have in common?

Ignorance, preeminently. Ignorance about the conditions, the real conditions, of human life, as experienced by almost everybody in the world except Americans—who've never been bombed. Who have an abundance of food and goods. And who have never had the experience of most Europeans of almost starving for a six-year period.

Such people as you mentioned seem to me to lack imagination of other people's predicaments and consequently to view the world optimistically, as if the whole world were like Southern California, full of sunshine and good fellowship and fun and superficial pleasures. It's the absence of a tragic sense that I'm suggesting, which is very hard to get over to most Americans because they never really have had the experience, which is highly tragic and ironic. They can't even imagine it. If they would read more *Oedipus Rex* and *King Lear*, under decent instruction, it would help.

This is why my literary interests parallel my political and social and critical interests. It's all one big package. I love teaching eighteenth-century literature because it's ironic and skeptical, and it doesn't hold that people need to be protected against the condition of human foolishness.

Wartime is a book that seems to look forward as well as backward. The first of September 1989 was the fiftieth anniversary of the Polish invasion, which inaugurates for the next six years a great line of fiftieth-anniversary commemorations. Could *Wartime* be taken as a cautionary tale for all those who would launch celebrations?

There's nothing wrong with celebrating the resounding victory, which was moral as well as military, of the Allies in that war. There's nothing wrong with that as long as it is accompanied with an appropriate understanding of the disaster the whole thing visited upon Europe.

Friends who have read pieces of *Wartime* wanted me to ask whether Fussell thinks he may have gone too far in the other direction—that your picture of this war is simply too grim.

No. It would be impossible to go too far in the other direction. War as an institution is so nasty and so vile. I quote Cyril Connolly in the book, saying something that I agree with entirely: that one must never forget that the war *was* a war, and therefore stupid, destructive, opposed to every decent and civilized understanding of what life is like.

So I don't think I went far enough. I didn't go farther because you want to revolt the reader only up to a certain degree; otherwise you wipe out the effect you're trying to create. So part of it is a question of literary tact. I could write a whole book about the disposal of human bodies in Europe, which would be fascinating, but I think nobody would like to read it except medical doctors and funeral directors.

Would you say then that since 1945 the nation really has not come to grips with the actualities of that war?

I do say so. And many of the reasons for that are praiseworthy, actually. It was the beneficence, say, of the GI Bill, from which I profited. It helped pay for my PhD work at Harvard. The beneficence and benignity of that tended to suggest that human nature was benign, whereas the war itself had argued the opposite, that human nature has a very dangerous leaning toward wickedness, original sin, vileness, and delight in destruction and sadism. So it was partly American decency, which is always to be praised and celebrated, that helped wipe out some of the viler memories of that war, and it set us back on a highly American optimistic track again.

How much of that optimism would you be willing to see in our later in-volvement in the Southeast Asian wars?

I think it had a lot to do with it, because it was assumed that any-thing we did must have been done from benign motives, since people imagined that repression of what was called Communism in Southeast Asia was somehow serving the causes embodied in the Declaration of Independence and the Constitution. But I re-member that the original entry into the South Vietnam quagmire was justified in President Kennedy's inaugural speech, where he said that we will bear any burden, et cetera, et cetera, in order to advance the cause of freedom. The problem was that we mis-identified the South Vietnamese government as being connected in any way with the cause of freedom.

But at its start the war could be conceived of as a fairly noble enterprise. It was only as it turned sour that people began to see ways in which it was not. No war starts out vicious. It starts out as an attempt to clean up something that is vile and to redress some injustice. Hitler invaded Czechoslovakia on the excuse of rescuing the Germans there, giving the action a plausible color. Nobody ever says, "Look, I'm going to invade your country be-cause I feel like it" or "because I'm an invader" or "because I want what you've got."

And then the war changes shape?

It inevitably escapes control because that's the nature of modern war. If bombs won't do the job, then you invent atomic bombs, and if they won't do the job, then you invent hydrogen bombs. War takes charge, in other words. And war knows nothing about the ideological reasons that have propelled it. The war is an en-gineering operation.

Your division, as we have noted, went into the line on November 16 near Saint-Dié.

The Germans set fire to Saint-Dié, angering us very, very much. Just after we attacked there was an outpouring of priests and nuns from Saint-Dié soliciting help for the people who'd lost everything in this fire the Germans had set.

After the war I found out something very interesting, which has had a lot to do with my sense that more is going on in the Army than you think is going on. Just before the attack I was assigned to a house between the lines, calling down mortar fire on the Germans, who'd been silhouetted by the fire they'd laid. I got an order from battalion to send out a patrol with an NCO and three or four men to see how deep the river was between our positions and the Germans. So I sent out my best sergeant and three or four of the six or eight men I had with me, and they went out for a couple of hours and reported that the river was nine inches deep and was very easy to cross without bridging equipment.

I sent the news back to battalion. The attack took place the next morning, and it was not terribly successful. They did achieve their mission, but with many casualties. After the war I was in a German town and I found this sergeant and we drank some beer together and he said, "You know, I want to ask you something. You know that night you sent us out, do you really think we went down to that river?"

And I said, "Yes, I did. I really did."

He said, "But of course we didn't. When we went out of the house, we were scared to death. We went down from the house about fifty yards, we lay in the grass for about two hours, we all agreed on the story about the river."

I said, "Okay, thanks for telling me." That happens much more often, I think, than most people are aware.

November and December 1944 were bad enough, the weather getting worse there in the mountains. Then in the third week in January, according to the reports, your outfit was hit by what looked like a panzer division.

We saw no tanks, but we saw a lot of troops. I think they were SS. They were very young and angry and National Socialist. That attack actually took place about five hundred yards to my right in a snowstorm. I wasn't aware of it at all. I had been warned that an attack was very likely, and I was looking out of my slit with my field glasses, and indeed I was seeing troops on the hill far away, German troops in line, moving from left to right, which I reported. The response was, "Well, they're too far away for us to do anything about it; keep us informed."

Those German troops were going through our line on my right, but I was utterly unaware of it. I heard a lot of firing to the rear, but you know, you always hear firing in all directions. And you're not certain where the rear is. It might be your right flank, which might bend back to another adjoining battalion. The line was never given on a map to a platoon leader. The company commander probably doesn't exactly know where it is.

Still, I would have numerous bright ideas. The Germans would carouse in a house within easy range, right in front of us. And I said to my company commander, "Look, may I get a bazooka and get out there some night and give them a big surprise? We'll send a shell right through the wall; we'll kill some of them." And the guy said, "No, you'll just stir them up—it will make things worse. If we sit here quietly, we'll be relieved in three or four days, and we won't have any more casualties, and some new people will come up and deal with the situation." That's the sort of thing you get.

So you don't have much patience with explanations of wartime behavior that depend upon ideology and cause.

If you've been in combat more than ten minutes, you know that it is about survival, and it's about killing in order to survive, and one forgets the presumed ideological motives when one is performing these operations. You're captured by combat, and the only way to get out of the capture is to reduce the threat to your own personal safety, which is to kill the enemy. That's what you're doing in combat.

You did stir up the Germans at some point. When were you wounded?

The first day I was wounded was the first day I was on the line. When I was wandering around innocently and I hadn't yet heard of the 88-millimeter self-propelled gun, a fragment hit me on the elbow. It wasn't bad enough to require much treatment, but it happened. The second time was also a self-propelled gun; it looked like a tank. It hit a tree above me. I was lying on top of a bunker with another officer and my platoon sergeant, both of whom were killed by the same shell. And I was hit in the thigh and in the back.

That was the day of the attack of the Seventh Army, ending ultimately in the crossing of the Rhine, but by that time I was in the hospital, and I stayed there until the war was over.

And since then you've been working up to this book.

Well, I suppose so. The first version of it was *The Great War and Modern Memory*, which is essentially the result of my own war experience and my attempt to make sense of it. Interestingly, I think the idea of that book came to me unconsciously in 1945, when I found myself in Alsace conducting my own platoon war against the Germans in concrete emplacements left over from the First World War. We used those bunkers just as they had been used a generation earlier. I got very interested in the First World War as a sort of prolegomenon to the Second. I wasn't ready to write about my own war, so I thought, I'll put some of my awareness of what combat is like in a quasi-scholarly account of the relation of the First World War to general culture. That's why I did that book.

I remember opening your *Great War and Modern Memory* to the dedication page and seeing: "To the memory of Technical Sergeant Edward Keith Hudson, ASN 36548772, Co. F., 410th Infantry, killed beside me in France, March 15, 1945." I thought that here at last might be a different kind of book about the Great War.

Let me say a word about that dedication. I have always tried to get telling details into my books. In the piece I just finished writing for *The Norton Book of Modern War* I talk about the immense numbers of people involved in the Second World War and the consequent anonymity. When the battle cruiser *Hood* blew up fighting the *Bismarck*, everybody on it, 1,419 men, was killed, except three men. My wife sometimes helps me with research, and I gave her the job of finding out the names and ranks of those three men because I wanted to make the point that these numbers mean nothing when they're detached from individuals. She actually found the names, and I've got them in there.

In the same way—in that dedication to the memory of Sergeant Hudson—I wrote the Army to get his serial number because I knew that would make a very subtle ironic point about this guy's relation to the whole proceeding, and it took them about a year to find it. I'm always anxious for details like that because you convince the reader of your own probity and the verisimilitude of what you're getting at. You're not making this up. You're an accurate and responsible reporter, and the more of that you convey to the reader, the better he'll be prepared to receive the things in your book that are not reporting, that are interpretations.

Historians sometimes get very angry at what I do, and what I have to say is that although I use historical data, I'm essentially writing an essay. One critic thought he was dumping on *The Great War and Modern Memory* when he called it a gothic elegy, but I agreed with him: it is a gothic elegy. If I were really working in history, it probably wouldn't be readable. One has to color it emotionally. One has to make the reader cry and laugh to get anywhere with the sort of work that I want to do.

You've said that though you're a professor of English literature, you've mostly gone through life as a pissed-off infantryman. That refusal to concede anything to sentimentality seems to be disappearing in American letters and certainly in modern American life as the wars recede. What is on the horizon?

Well, I'm not sure that when the Vietnam War veterans get to be my age—I'm sixty-five—we won't have some superb material. Their experience would have been processed through memory, and we'll get some real literature instead of just grievances and complaints. It takes about a lifetime for you to decide in what form you're going to couch your own response to these experiences, and I think this is why it wasn't until my present age that I decided to write about the second war.

Memory, public and official and academic, occupies a great deal of your attention in all your work. I take it you've concluded that memory is so fragile and subject to manipulation and corruption that it is always to be regarded with skepticism and that sometimes these corruptions are so deeply entrenched that they can be uprooted only by satire.

By satire or by documents. Although not a historian, I've learned to distrust almost everything except documents dating from roughly the moment of the event they describe. I treasure the remark by Wright Morris the novelist—a great observation: "Everything processed by memory is fiction." It has to be; otherwise, it doesn't have the form that it requires if you're going to recall it from memory. It has to be a coherent thing, and that means it's got to have plot imposed on it. I've written a lot about how ironic plots make possible wartime memory.

Well before this book was finished, you said that you were still trying to bridge the gap between experience and writing about experience. Has *Wartime* done that?

No, because I wasn't writing about myself, really. When I started writing the book, I put in a lot of personal stuff—sort of shocking stuff that I wanted to remind people of and that I wanted to validate by indicating that I myself had experienced it. At one point we were on an exercise at Fort Benning, very near our graduation as infantry officers, the climactic exercise involving paratroops and live artillery and so on, and we were aware of an anomalous explosion up in the air, up in the sky, about five thousand feet. It proved to have been the moment when a shell hit a Piper Cub that was observing artillery fire. Nothing came down but a shoe, with a foot in it, to our horror and astonishment. And I wanted to testify about that.

I originally had that in the book when I was talking about military blunders. I let a friend, a former student of mine, read that text, and he said, "No, that doesn't belong in there. Either you've got to write an objective account or you've got to write a personal account. But you can't bring them together." So I removed all that stuff.

You wrote in two earlier essays, "My War" and "Thank God for the Atomic Bomb," as well as in Wartime *that direct experience is crucial to understanding the actualities of war, and you've agreed with Walt Whitman that "the real war will never get in the books."*

Eugene Sledge wrote about his experience with the Marines in a book called *With the Old Breed at Peleliu and Okinawa*, and it is one of the finest memoirs to emerge from any war. One reason I like it so much is that Sledge, having really fought, knows that even the people back at battalion headquarters, and sometimes company headquarters, have no idea what's going on three hundred yards to the front and that the troops treat them with something of the same contempt that they reserve for the people at home. They don't know what's going on, and, not knowing, they make you do things that they would never make you do if they knew what those things meant. Like sending out night patrols, for example, which are hopeless, at least with Americans. The Germans might be able to do them, and the Japanese, but not Americans. We're not prepared psychologically for that kind of military work, especially in small units. As I point out in the book, the terrible thing about that war is that it was fought by amateurs, necessarily; it was the first war any of us had ever been in, and nobody knew what he was doing. Even General Eisenhower had never fought in a war before. We were all sort of making it up as we went along.

You mentioned Sledge and his comrades' animosity toward the rear echelons. There's a line in Harold Leinbaugh and John Campbell's book The Men of Company K *that essentially defines the rear as "anybody whose foxhole is behind mine."*

Well, it depends. Anybody who doesn't favor an M-1 rifle is a sissy, I would say. If you favored carbines, it indicated that you weren't a serious combat person and that you were some distance behind the line, because nobody on the line would be content to try to defend his life with a carbine. It's a tiny little thing; it's like a .22. So we regarded even the 60-millimeter mortar section as rear area, because they were so unlikely to get shot at, you know. Counterbattery fire might fall near them, and they would have to move, but they were terribly safe. I had men who would have cut off their arms to be sent back to the sixties, because they were three hundred yards behind.

There is a kind of continuity among soldiers, in whatever war, of imputing tremendous abilities and virtues to their enemy.

Well, I'm still doing it with the Germans, for whom I have intense military respect, which I developed on the line in that winter. They're incredibly good officers. Their junior officers were much better than ours, partly because they were desperate, and they didn't loaf and they didn't screw around the way we did. We knew we were going to win the war, and they weren't certain they were going to lose it until quite a way into 1945, so maybe they fought better.

And they were more disciplined than we were. They took the war more seriously than we did, and they made more out of slimmer resources than we did. We had much more ammunition, we could shoot it off all the time. We never did anything without laying this incredible barrage on the Germans, partly to scare them, partly to assert our own superiority, and we had it in abundance. There was only a week or so when ammunition was short, but if you just phoned in and said, "I'd like a concentration here," it would come. But the Germans had to proceed much more skillfully to make up for deficiencies both in men and in material.

Another thing that has helped disguise the true nature of the war was the strictures imposed on the wartime correspondents. Anything that didn't conduce to the war effort was simply not to be written down.

Right. But much of the censorship was self-censorship, and it was generated by genuine patriotic and moral feeling; it was not really imposed. It was a sense that everybody must get on the team because the issues were so important. And so it's a sort of honorable censorship.

It's not easy to believe that the cause of the war would have been forwarded, or that the war would have ended earlier than it did, if people had been told about body parts flying around on the battlefield and horrible things. They were not told them. So I may imply in the book that the self-censorship was a sort of violation of the spirit of the war, but in a sense it was not. Because the object in the war was to win it as fast as possible, and if lying would do it, if false comfort would do it, if fraudulent representation would do it, these were weapons as honorable as any other.

So it's a very complicated question. I don't know how it would have aided the war if people had known more of the truth about what combat involves than they were told. That would have aided the cause of universal truth and the development of the human intellect, but it wouldn't have won the war any faster. It probably would have slowed it down.

Of course, in later wars there was a great deal of tension between public information officers and the representatives of the media, an adversarial relationship.

The Vietnam War might be still going on if it had been a constitutional war, which would have made it possible to exercise treason statutes against those who were impeding the war effort. But because it was not a declared war, they had to be allowed entire freedom, and consequently they ruined the war effort. The moral is, Don't fight undeclared wars. The Constitution has carefully forbidden them, and every one that we've fought has ended very badly. Even the Korean War ended by killing a vast number of people and accomplishing nothing. It ended where it began and devastated both sides of the country.

So the Founders—excuse my sentimentality, but I care deeply about this—the Founders realized from experience in Europe that a war, bad as it is, must be popular. Everybody must be be-

EXPERIMENTAL HISTORY

hind it, or it won't work. There must be wide popular support for it. So they carefully wrote into the Constitution that war is declared by the Congress. They had no idea that what they also said (largely to honor George Washington), that the president would be the commander in chief of the Army, was going to be used by people like Ronald Reagan as a way of frustrating the popular will.

In this, as in your other works, you attain a mastery of your subject by drawing from unconventional sources.

You get interested in everything that bears upon it—old files of *Life* magazine, the *Saturday Evening Post*, and so on, which I'm fascinated by, and any sort of ephemera that seems to shed light on the subject. When you work with such material, you become extremely sensitive to it; your whole life then is devoted to awareness of these things you may not have noticed before. Consequently, you become conscious of popular music and the way popular music always expresses the popular will; otherwise it won't succeed. You become conscious of the fact that advertising is the real American literature, and that's where you go to find people's secret hopes and dreams embodied, and so I did a lot on advertising, radio commercials, things like that.

I also like to get away from literature. I've learned how to interpret literature, and it's fun for me to learn how to interpret other sorts of documents. I can say wonderful things about sonnets, but there's no fun because I know I can do it. But to say something about a Rinso ad is a challenge.

Did you wonder what Wartime *might be like if you were a German, a Japanese, a Russian, an Italian?*

No, I haven't, but it's interesting. The book probably couldn't be done, because it has to be by somebody who won the war; otherwise, the news that the event was not entirely happy isn't astonishing. The Germans wouldn't be at all astonished to be told that their war was nasty. They were bombed; they know it. Everybody there lost a relative or two or a whole family and all their possessions, so to bring to their attention that the war was vile wouldn't be interesting.

But the very fact that we won the war gives the war a sort of happy atmosphere that needs to be trimmed down a bit. It violates what actually happened in the war.

Before reading the book, I rather expected I would find a chapter on heroism and cowardice.

I don't know why I didn't do anything with that. It just wasn't a subject that interested me. I might have attempted a definition of heroism and cowardice—I dealt with that topic a bit in the section on fear, where people brought themselves finally to recognize that fear was inevitable.

During the war the medics were quick to say, and you say in your book as well, that to anyone who's been on the line, there isn't any such thing as getting used to combat. I take it you think that in such circumstances terms like *bravery* and *cowardice* really aren't useful.

I think *sick* or *well* is better, or *innocent* or *experienced*. I mean, everybody innocent is going to give the impression of courage, as I did the first six weeks on the line. I gave the impression I was incredibly brave because I was stupid and ignorant, and I would lead patrols and I would volunteer for things and place myself in great danger, to the immense annoyance of my platoon, whom I was jeopardizing by these gestures. Gradually, that security begins to wear away until you end just on the brink of what would look like cowardice. You try to give the impression that you're more in control than you know you can be. I think if I had stayed a week longer without being wounded, I probably would have broken down right on the line. I did break down in the hospital after about three or four days.

After you finally realized that you had escaped?

Well, knowing that I had gotten my sergeant killed, feeling guilty that I hadn't given the right orders to save more of my people. The artillery barrage that got us was predictable. We were coming out of the woods, and there was an open space in front of us that we were going to have to cross, and this self-propelled gun was in the woods across the way. It saw our skirmish line beginning to approach, so systematically—some would say Germanically—it began firing from its right to left, and it dropped a shell about every fifty yards in sequence. The one that hit me was about the eighth shell, and you could have seen the pattern by the second or third shell, and I should have. I got my men into the dugouts, so fewer of them were hurt than might have been, but somehow I froze with my sergeant and this machine-gun officer on top of the dugout. We didn't see what was happening. And by the time we perceived it, by the time the penultimate shell hit fifty yards to our left, we realized the next one was going to hit us. But by that time it was too late to do anything. And to have run into the bunker at that point would have been to risk a panic, so we simply stayed there and got hit. There are many reasons why you get hit, and some of them involve questions like that. You know, both ignorance and getting hit are better than what might have happened otherwise. So we just stayed there.

You quote a very affecting passage from Robin Maugham's *Come to Dust* in which just after a tank battle in North Africa he sits down to read Boswell's *Life of Samuel Johnson* while a trapped soldier screams. I showed this passage to a friend of mine who had fought in Vietnam, and it immediately brought to his mind one day when he ate a can of C-rations while studying a beautiful severed hand that lay immediately nearby.

Well, one has to eat. You know, I had a very good platoon sergeant who got wounded and who came back. I saw him again in the Alps when we were occupying there in Austria, and we got drunk one night. I said, "Look, I know you disapproved of me many times, but tell me the time you disapproved of me the most, what I did that annoyed you most."

He said, "It was the time you'd come back from helping Lieutenant Goodman," who'd been shot in the back. I had helped him and put a couple of pads on him, and my hands were covered with blood, and there was no place to wash them, and I was very hungry. And I opened a can of C-ration cheese, great yellow cheese, and with these bloodied hands, which I didn't even notice, I ate the cheese. He said, "At that point I really almost gave up on you. I thought you were incredibly insensitive and bloody-minded and so on," and I said, "Well, I never even noticed." I had to do these two things: one was to help Lieutenant Goodman and get him back to the medics before he died of bleeding, and the other was to eat my cheese. And I did them both.

If someone innocent of combat reads Wartime, *what do you hope he will take from it?*

I hope it will move him to conscientious objection or else impel him cunningly to get into a noncombat branch of the service, if that's possible. It wasn't possible for me, partly because I didn't want to disgrace myself. I was enrolled in Army ROTC in college, and my unit was an infantry unit, and I was enrolled in it for many, many reasons. It was easier than gym. I never liked physical exercise all that much, and I enjoyed certain things about the military. I enjoyed its formality. Formality has always attracted me in literature. I prefer ordered verse to free verse, for example. I prefer eighteenth-century understandings of literary structure to loose understandings.

Knowing what I know now, I would not have been in the infantry. I might have been in the ordnance, which my father was in the First World War. He spent the war riding a horse around an ammunition dump near Bordeaux, a dump of which he had charge. He made a daily inspection around it and had a perfectly satisfactory war. Now, of course, I'd try to get in intelligence or OSS or something involving some kind of intellectual talent. But I was too young in those days to have such pretensions. I was just as bright then as I am now, but nobody knew it.

James Jones has argued that history is too much the story of the top downward. Would you agree?

Well, to a degree, but I talk a lot about the top as well. I talk about Churchill's drinking, and I talk about the difficulty of making top decisions. I end the book, certainly, with a focus at the top. I'd treated the leader class in the book with a degree of disdain up to that point. But I thought I would end by indicating that there is very much another side to it.

You end the book by quoting Eisenhower's revisions to his famous Normandy message, when he drafted a public statement that was to be released in case the invasion failed on the beaches.

He started by trying to sort of sneak out of responsibility by saying, "The troops have been withdrawn," as if some distant, anonymous agency had made the decision. Then he caught himself— I used the word *nobly*—caught himself at it and decided that he had to earn the privilege of leadership by accepting all responsibility, which few people realized. So he said, "If any blame or fault attaches to this attempt, it is mine alone." I thought that was wonderful.

NINETEEN. Rain Stops Play

Hmmm. God! Not another one of these bloody interviews for Southborough's lot. What a waste of time, and with this headache returning it will be agony. Must take some more powders before this chap arrives.

There. Thus fortified—well, a brandy would be better, but as it is still early in the day, mustn't set the others talking.

Right. Where's that dossier? Somewhere in this mess. Ah, there. Might as well have this fellow brought in. Get it over with. How many of these talks have I had? A dozen, two dozen? Every one of them dead certain he's right, and every bloody one of them contradicting the other. It's enough to drive one . . . Miss Banks, has Mr. Rivers arrived?

Ah, splendid, splendid, here you are already! Do please come in. Please be seated. Yes, just there. Splendid.

Well, sir, my name's Fortnum. How do you do, Mr. Rivers. Oh, I do beg your pardon. Dr. Rivers. How foolish of me, of course it is; I see it just here. Ha ha. Well, not a very good start, is it? Early innings, though. Shall I have Miss Banks bring in some tea—I would like some myself. Late night last evening, you know, and our days around here start earlier all the time, what with the reductions. *Après la guerre finie*, perils of peace and all that, you know, economies. Miss Banks, tea, please.

Well, now, sir, I suppose our telegram was not very revealing, so I should just begin by saying how very grateful I am, indeed, how grateful we all are that you have merely taken us at that brief word to interrupt your work and come down to the wo for this meeting. Yes, grateful.

I beg your pardon? Ah, no, nothing really wrong, merely a bit of a headache. Sure it will pass in due course. Let's see, where was I?

Ah yes, well, *de quoi s'agit-il*, eh? Perhaps you will have heard that questions have been raised in Parliament regarding the matter of what has been called, for want of a better name, shell shock. Yes, of course you have. It was in all the papers. Deuced complicated, if you ask me, don't pretend to understand half of it, the medical parts anyway. As for the rest of it, the politics, you know, the Lords have registered concern over whether shell shock is to be regarded as, well, a legitimate, shall we say, authentic war wound, although I must say that I myself can't see how one could come round to such a curious notion. As I say, it's all well beyond me. I wouldn't claim any sort of knowledge about the thing. No.

My role in all this? Yes, an excellent question. Yes, you should not regard me as anything but a minor clerk, you see. My only task is to vet, as it were to examine in advance, those who've been recommended by various authorities as persons who might contribute to the enquiry now in session. Lord Southborough, who I believe initiated the debate in the Lords, has the chair. Viscount Peel accepted Lord Southborough's motion on behalf of government, and the whole was given over to the War Office. That's where I come in, you see, yes. Think of me as a kind of Cerberus, ha ha.

Ah. Miss Banks, you and the tea are just in time. Rather warm in here, don't you think, Doctor? The tea should help. Yes, Miss Banks, just leave it. We'll attend to it ourselves, thank you. Now: thus fortified . . .

Yes, well: I would calculate we've had more than thirty witnesses before the committee thus far, all sorts, and I must say— for myself only, you understand—it has all been deuced interesting. General Lord Horne, of course, Lieutenant General Sir John Goodwin of the medical service, and many others have given most generously of their time and very extensive knowledge of the war. Rather like a history lesson to me, I can tell you. I didn't know the half of it, the part I could fathom. Quite a lot of doctors, too, yes indeed, and, well, I must tell you I have been completely at sea, listening to them go on. Fearfully bright, every man of them. Not the sort of thing a soldier would hear in the mess, I can tell you, no. Still, a chap can learn a great deal just by listening. It gives one a great deal to think about, it does.

Do listen to me go on. Quite absorbing all this is, to me at least, although I imagine you experts take it all on board without any bother at all. Yes. Well. Let me see, I suppose I should add to what I have said already that certain members of the enquiry have voiced a particular concern over the matter of pensions, you see, especially in our present circumstances. The general view seems to be that the cost of these will only rise with the passage of time. That is, veterans who 'til now have not come forward with applications for assistance with their medical problems will inevitably do so.

So we can only look forward to using more public monies, even as the government are trying to recover the costs of the war to the country. There are always the reparations from Germany, of course, but then one can hardly be sure of those, especially as she is in quite dire straits at the moment. None of it looks very good, you see, from any point of view. So I think it was in the way of looking ahead to these problems that Lord Southborough brought the motion in the first place. I've heard it argued in committee already that if shell shock be accepted as a legitimate result of war service, we stand a good chance of being bankrupted by that malady alone, quite apart from the pensions we shall have to pay out for ordinary wounds, amputations, the blind, those who were badly gassed, and such. Well, I mean to say, we already have returns of more than a hundred thousand men claiming medical attention on account of, what's it called, neurasthenia. Deuced if I know what that is.

Well, anyway, I know this must sound quite ungenerous, Doctor, but among the members there is serious doubt that we can afford to recognize this particular disorder by itself as being worthy of a pension.

As against all this, there stands the question of the public's opinion. A goodly number of our fellow citizens, and most especially those on the Labour side of things, have been excited by the whole affair. Indeed, shell shock seems to engender very strong feelings all round. Private clinics and charities popping up everywhere to attend to these chaps. Very odd to me, I can tell you, that a chap who's lost a leg don't signify alongside one who's shell-shocked. Can't account for it myself, most odd indeed.

Too, I would venture to say that the chances of public amity are not at all helped by the rather extravagant arguments advanced by some public figures, the general thrust of which is that the government are taking the side of ingratitude for the sacrifices made during the war, whereas the government were grateful enough when our victory hung in the balance. Throwing up to us that "home fit for heroes" business that came out during the war—promises casually made by members when we were in the thick of it to boost morale and such. I should say, as well, that quite a number of former serving officers have not been helpful to the government side of the question. They seem not at all sympathetic to government's natural desire not to spend a farthing more than necessary. But if we save what we can, it all redounds to the public good in the long run, don't it? You will recognize, of course, how several quite complicated problems meet one another on this ground.

At all events, then, the government must protect against charges of ingratitude, of insensitivity to truly needy veterans, those actually wounded, I mean, as well as against the view that the government are simply niggardly or perhaps incompetent to face up to these challenges, and I should think . . .

What, I beg your pardon?

Well, now that you mention it, I do believe this heat is coming up on me rather. The tea doesn't seem to have helped. I say, I wonder if you would mind awfully if I took a dram or so of brandy? Yes, that should do nicely, if you really don't mind. Would you have one as well? No? Well, so long as you are not put off.

No, actually, as you mention it, I do seem to be having these little spells. Spent some time in the Middle East, you see, before

I went out to France. I may have picked up some bit of unpleasantness along the way; can't quite shake it. Yes, you are quite right, you and my friends agree: I should see a doctor, but, ha ha, isn't that rich? Here I am, sitting right across from one! No, I'm sure this will pass. I shall be quite all right. Don't trouble yourself for a moment. But if you don't mind I believe I shall relieve myself of this tunic, yes, I think I will. Beastly hot in here, don't you think? There. Thus fortified.

That ribband at the top? Oh, well, the MC. A fellow's been around as long as I have is bound to come in the way of something like that, don't you know? Especially if one traveled about France in those days, you know?

Yes. Out in '15 after a year in Palestine and a bit in Cairo. Deuced hot there, I can tell you! Never let up, the heat. Most unpleasant. Mind you, some of the fellows liked it there, couldn't get enough of it. Blazing bloody thermometers as far as I'm concerned, though. Couldn't wait to get to France anyway, felt left out, don't you know? My own regiment went in fairly early on, so my posting out to the fringes of empire, as it were—well, I was left out of the big show, wasn't I? Doesn't do much good, being a soldier, if you aren't permitted to actually do any soldiering. The old ME was just about sweating in headquarters. No life for a solder. Good for the other johnnies, though. Happy to get back, myself. Happy as anything to see the old chums out in France. Good days for me, all in all, though, mind you, we had a few rough patches. Well, you know all about that, I suppose.

Well, what am I saying? I suppose I don't know very much at all about you, and that was to be the purpose of our meeting in the first place. Do forgive me, won't you? All that carrying on about the ME and France and whatnot.

There I go again, you see. Must be age: can't quite keep my mind on a thing very long, ha ha. Well, Sir Frederick Mott put you up for our list of expert witnesses, Dr. Rivers. Quite complimentary, if I may say so. Said you had to be the one to talk to if we called no one else. I wonder if I might inquire, did you actually see service yourself?

No, I'm afraid I don't know Craiglockhart. Sounds a bit out of battery, ha ha. Where was it, Scotland? Yes? My Lord! Farther out than France. And before that? Let me see, somewhere in all this paper, I seem to recall . . . yes, here we are: took degree at St. Bartholomew's, MD in '89, FRCP in '99, by then university lecturer in psychology, elected fellow at St. John's in '02. Most impressive, I must say. But, look here, there's a note about some sort of expedition, good Lord, to the Torres Straits, of all places. Good Lord. And then a book on it all, too. I shouldn't imagine I should understand a word of it: *The History of Melanesian Society*. Perhaps one day you could tell me of your adventures out there. My, my. And so on the basis of your professional standing, as it were, commissioned captain, RMC, in '14, with the following four years, ah yes, here it is right before me, in this Craiglockhart place. Tell me, was it a sort of asylum?

A shell shock hospital? An old hydro? My, my. Didn't know such a thing actually existed. Well, I knew some of the chaps were sent down, as it were, but I never dreamed . . . Most interesting, indeed.

But the front was a deuced big place, don't you know? All sorts of things happening I didn't know about, and happy for it. The regiment held just the tiniest of places; it was our own little world, don't you know? Yes. The world was literally whizzing by, and we saw little of it except the few thousand yards of front and our rear areas. I didn't even get back home after '15. I knew some chaps who took off for old Blighty whenever they could, but I never did. One has to hit a kind of rhythm out there, you see. I think going back home would've spoilt the rhythm out there, you see. I think going back home would've spoilt the rhythm, just when one had got used to it all, don't you know? Yes, two years before I was wounded and sent back. Yes. Close on to three, it was. Started as a lieutenant, came out a major, as you see. Family hardly recognized me. Well, there you are—as it is.

Now, if you would, Dr. Rivers, I don't suppose you could tell me a bit about this, this Craiglockhart place. What was it all about?

What kind of work did you carry on? I must say, an entire hospital, just for shell shock? What sort of men came to you?

Mostly officers? Really. Well, I say. Wouldn't have thought that at all. I don't recall any of our witnesses thus far having made distinctions of rank. Indeed, my impression was those funking it came from the other ranks, don't you know? Well, my, my. I should have thought just the reverse would have been true. I mean, the officer chaps came from good stock, good families, well educated, public school and all. I grant you, of course, the best ones went first—Mons, Ypres, you know. Later on, as the casualties mounted, of course, it was true enough some pretty rum fellows came in behind. Not quite up to the mark, some of them. Funked it pretty badly, they did. But what could we do? No one else available, you see? I can see what you're getting at: after the Regulars were used up and the Kitcheners and Lord Derby's men started coming in, I can imagine your trade improved, as it were, ha ha. Yes.

No? You saw cases like these straightaway as the war began? Among the old sweats? Well, I swear. Never heard of such a thing. Of course, being out in the ME then I wouldn't have known, would I? But look here: those young chaps were top drawer, real gamesmen, you know. Knew some of them before they went over. I mean, it wasn't as though they were the weak sisters. I could understand some in the other ranks, giving way like that, but the early officers . . .

I must say, Dr. Rivers, I wonder if you've got it right? Surely, a man's character stands for something? I mean to say, one could understand a young town fellow, no education to speak of and all, no family—well, none of any distinction, that is—well, they wouldn't really have anything to back on, would they? What I mean is, well, you and I know very well there isn't much self-control in such people. Surrender to any notion that comes into their head unless they're watched over properly, what? Well, I must imagine more than half my time in France was spent trying to keep them out of trouble, just watching over them, seeing they did the right thing, you know?

Oh, well, now that you ask, I didn't pay much attention. I mean, I was hardly the one to mind about that sort of thing anyway, what with the tactical side of the game always in play. I don't know that we had very many shirkers in the RWF. Oh, excuse me, Royal Welsh Fusiliers. It was quite a special mob, you know. May've been a few, of course, always in the other ranks, naturally. Didn't see any among fellow officers that I recall. No. Had a few cases of misbehavior and like that, usual run of things, a few lads not wanting to go out again, going absent after time in the rear areas, that sort. But even those you'd think doubtful at first stood up all right. One fellow, most extraordinary, couldn't bear his manner in the mess—why, do you know he once claimed Homer was actually a woman? Something of a bore. But a good officer, all the same, did his bit, just like everyone else. No, the ones we sent back mostly were all knocked about by shells and the like.

If I had to describe the lads I was with, I'd say they were, well, stoic. Didn't seem to get the wind up, if you know what I mean. Other ranks never blamed of that anyway. Well, if one doesn't have the breeding, er, the background I mean, well, one hasn't the imagination to be afraid. Take things as they come, what?

Well, yes, naturally, there were those who came loose a bit after being shelled and the like, you know, had their voices or hearing or whatnot just blown out of them. One can't imagine the power of those explosions 'til one's been through it. Never felt anything like it. Fairly take your breath away, even if you're not very close. Feel it all through your body, you do. No, a chap don't forget something like that very soon. But with a little rest, one's right as rain, you see. A little brandy or a tot of rum will always help too.

Well, it goes without saying some chaps couldn't repair on their own, and that's where the old MO comes in. Ours were always first-rate chaps. Right flash, some of them, just out from Harley Street. Didn't go around mashing up the technical words, though. Straightforward. Yes, our lads thought the MOs were worth their weight in gold. Chap's got a problem, off to an MO who likely as not was close at hand, right with us in the trenches or not far back. Dash off to the old doc, you know, get some powders, right back, that's what the officers did. Then we made sure the other ranks got to see the doc at regular intervals. In between, if one ran into trouble on patrol or caught one in the trenches, the old docs were right there, yes, right there. Can't say enough about their service.

Helped me a good deal, I can tell you, yes, indeed. Just in the summer of '16, it was, right before the Somme mess began in earnest. The old ME unpleasantness came up on me again, caught a fever or something, couldn't stop shaking, sleep impossible, no appetite, sick to my stomach, that sort of thing. Well, old doc had me up again in no time. Kept me back for a while, let me sleep it out. Brandy without end. Best medicine in the world, brandy and a little sleep. Well, the headaches kept on, but what could anyone do about that, don't you know?

And I would have to say my experience was more or less typical in the battalion. Everyone, man and boy, got the wind up every now and then, you see. Just had to press on, no help for it. Keep yourself under control.

Afraid? No, not after the first bit, is one? What I mean to say is, it's only natural, that first time out and all, that one is bound to get the wind up. But after the first show, why, then, one settles down, gets the rhythm of it. After that, should be all right. That's what I told the lads, I said, "Now lads, it's all right to get the wind up first action, perfectly natural, but then you'll see you can take it, and there'll be nothing to it. Act like you've been doing this all your life, you will," that's what I said to them. Well, I mean, there must be some little germ of fear here and there, don't you know, but then a man controls it, you see? Rather like riding a horse or driving a motor car. One grows accustomed, as it were.

I think our training had a good bit to do with it, too. What I mean to say is, a chap new to the army doesn't know what to do, so we show him, show him what he must do in a certain situation, say, how to cover oneself during a barrage and the like, little things, how to use his rifle, the bayonet, and so on. Well, after all that, he knows what job he has to do, and what job the officers do, and this helps enormously, you see. Steels one for eventualities, as it were.

Mind you, there were some lads who never should've been recruited in the first instance. Not at all up to the mark, and, well, one way or another the front would show them up, so we'd send them away as quickly as we could. A goodly number of those were killed straightaway, however. Just not up to the mark. War has its way, you know, of seeking out those who aren't quite up to the mark. If the shells don't actually get 'em, the concussion will, don't you know?

Of course, that meant the show'd be carried by those who persevered, but isn't that always the way? No small number of the lads picked up the game, time and again, when the weak sisters funked it. Yes, those who stayed out the longest carried the heaviest loads.

Too heavy? I don't quite see what you're driving at. Well, now that you mention it, a chap could see rather more than his share of it. I suppose one could say there comes a point . . . well, I mean, how much can a man take of that sort of thing? One has to admit there is a limit somewhere.

Look here, this war . . . well, one couldn't say there'd ever been another like it, what with the constant shelling and patrolling and sniping and whatnot. And then the bloody MGs, the machine guns, you know, my word, the Boche were awfully good with them! Mow over a whole line while a lark whistled his tune. Bloody dangerous, all in all. Smashed 'em down as best we could, but they always popped up again, you know, just like one of those children's toys. Didn't really have to kill a fellow to do the greatest damage, either. Wounding was just as good, from Fritz's point of view. Always had to tell several lads to drag the wounded back, then Fritz'd take on the stretcher bearers.

Well, I could go on, but you get the idea. That's the sort of thing that'll build up. Some of the lads just hit their limit, that's all. That holds good for the war as well. What I mean to say, no one would have thought it would have gone on so bloody long. Of course, our side won the game, but, you know, I wonder now if anyone really won. One wonders if the war didn't just stop, you know, rather like a game when the weather's heavy. What's that the papers always say? Rain stops play? Weather got too heavy, 's all. No blame there. Have to be sensible about it, you know.

Mind you, some weren't. Brigadier, fellow I knew from before the war, fairly got steamed up about the shell shock thing in '17. Said he wouldn't permit it in his brigade, said anyone claiming it'd be brought up on charges, court-martialed. Just wouldn't have it. Said a man had to control himself, that's all. Saw him at an *estaminet* somewhere round then. Said he'd turned over several to the provost already. Hoped they'd be shot, he said. When I said, "Steady on," he fairly flew at me in a rage. No good talking to him at all. Well, if you ask me, he seemed a bit out of it himself, poor fellow. Caught one in '18, when Fritz made his big push. 5.9 landed right on top of him, they said. Can't imagine what a shell will do to a man 'til one's actually seen it. Most fearsome. Looks like one's been ripped to shreds by some monster, if you can find the shreds, that is.

It was all so fickle, you know. Same thing could happen to anyone, any time. One just couldn't dwell on that sort of thing, just had to get on, you see, do one's duty. Anyway, that's all by way of saying there were some officers, mostly old seniors like this chap, never would give an inch. But for most of us, those on the line, you know, well, one couldn't be so sure . . .

Duty to what? I say, what a funny thing to ask. Well, to stick it, I suppose. That, and one's chums. Yes, that was the thing. One didn't want to let the side down, you see. Had to play up. Ah, no. I see what you mean. No. No. Didn't take long to know where one's real chums were. They were there, right alongside. Not in Blighty, for heaven's sake. Not with the strikers in the munitions palaces, to be sure. That's one of the reasons I didn't go home, you see. I saw too many of the lads come back, spirits all down because no one back there seemed to have any idea of what we were going through out here. Some of them came back hating their families on account of it. Didn't want any part of that. Wanted to keep the war where it belonged, myself. Rather like bad wine, the war—didn't travel well. Best left in the past, you see.

And now you have these shell-shock johnnies, all's they want to do is talk, it seems. Don't know why they don't just . . . well, stop complaining. Goodness knows, there's enough to keep one occupied. Well, I mean there was the flu last year, bloody awful, all those people taken down. Lost my daughter. That sort of thing'll bring you up smart, what? So who are these fellows to complain about their nervousness?

Anyway, the stronger one's character . . . Beg your pardon? Character's obsolete? Well, I swear. Then, if you're right, what's to replace it? What I mean to say, without character, man's not got a leg to stand on. I mean . . . I mean, look here, you don't really fall in with all that German psychological mumbo jumbo? What do they call themselves? Freudians, is it? Like this Meyers fellow, is that his name? Deuced uncooperative, he was. Refused to attend the enquiry at all. Said the establishment wasn't mature enough to hear what he had to say. No. Rum fellow. Heard he resigned his post out in France in '17. Fit of pique, just because no one'd listen to him. And who's this other chappie? Yes, here it is, a Dr. Elder. Bit of a controversy out on Malta. I don't suppose you know either of these fellows? Do you then? Meyers was with you at Cambridge? Well, then, what's his story anyway?

Shell shock is Meyers's invention? My Lord. But I have it on good authority he's dead set against the whole notion. Changed his mind? So the concussions haven't anything to do with it? But look here, Dr. Mott thinks the matter of the brain is deranged by explosion somehow. And didn't Meyers believe the same?

Well, sounds as though he came round to a more sensible notion. Don't quite hold with all that, well, you know, all that rot about hating your mother and such. Wouldn't you know the Boche'd come up with it. Far's I can see, well, they might well've hated their mothers, but no well-bred lad . . . So this Freud fellow's Austrian. Well, much the same, if you ask me.

So I say, what's the game now, as you see it, I mean? You know these chappies, what they think, and you've got your own experience with the shell-shock business. What's your best guess? I mean, is it real?

I say, steady on. You won't get very far with the committee there. Courage is obsolete, or dead already? What do you mean, doesn't work? Well, if it's born into a chap . . . No? Breeding isn't important? Well, yes, I do remember your saying officers dropped out faster at first. All right, I follow, but still, family notwithstanding, a man's in charge of his own behavior, right? Well then, who is?

Sub . . . subconscious? Yes, I've heard some of the witnesses talking about that, though I can't say I quite get the thing straight. You mean, a chap's mind works on a kind of automatic? Yes, I see. I suppose I should make a note or two here. The committee chaps will be, well, intrigued by all this. Mind you, some of them are dead set against . . .

Repression, now what's that? A process and a mental state? Hmmm. Yes. And this comes about because of a conflict. Well, do you mean the fighting? No? A struggle between one's fear and one's sense of duty. Well, I say, this is most original. And what about old Freud's mother? Unnecessary. Well, I'm with you there, Dr. Rivers. Yes, indeed. Don't hold with all that mumbo jumbo, as I said.

Look here: let's say this struggle, as you call it, goes on. Where does it lead? Wait a moment, must write this down: memories, even of recent events, pushed out of the conscious mind into the subconscious mind. Well then, what happens? A kind of rot sets in? Struggle to get out? Nightmares? Paralysis? My goodness, you mean a chappie could lose the use of an arm or leg just because of repression? His eyesight or hearing too? What about the shakes? I mean, could a fellow just not be steady? Suffer headaches and the like?

If I have you right, Dr. Rivers, I must say, your view differs substantially from that of some of our other witnesses. I mean to say, we've had Sir Robert Armstrong Jones in; he says all a chap needs is a bit of electricity and a doctor exercising firm authority to put him right. Says plenty of the lads have responded to his treatments. But it sounds as though, regarding this repression business, he demands that a chap simply put the bad memories out of his mind. I gather you and he are on opposite sides, as it were. Is that about it?

Yes, I can see how you would be. In your scheme a cure comes about when a chap talks it all out, as it were, whereas Jones and others—there's this Yealland chap, for instance—they say just the reverse. Deuced complicated, if you ask me. What's a fellow to decide?

Yes, I agree with that, certainly. See what actually works. Well, did you have a measure of success at your hospital? Could you give me an example?

Sassoon? Why, yes indeed, I did know him. First-class young officer. MC. Quite aggressive. Knocked about quite a lot, he was. Mad Jack, the men called him. Bit on the funny side, liked to go out by himself, hunting the Huns. Ran into a patch of trouble the year before the war was over. Something about denouncing the war and all. Well, I can't say I had any problem with that. Bloody f-ing mess by then, and everyone knew it. He didn't say anything the rest of us hadn't said. Well, he came back anyway. Stayed 'til he was hit again, just before the war was over, as I recall. Yes. Quite a remarkable fellow . . . You mean, he was one of yours? Well. I say. What's he at now? I mean, did he recover?

A poet? Yes, now that you mention it, I did hear something about all that, or, yes, I actually saw a volume in some bookstore or another. There was his name right on the front. I remember thinking, well, what about that. Old Mad Jack. Yes, I do remember. Well, good for him. Good for anyone who got out of the mess more or less whole. Good for us all. Out into the new world, we are, though things don't look quite as bright as they did, mind you.

No. Thank you for asking, my headache is quite gone now. Knew the brandy would do it, after all. Best medicine there is. Good for the heat too.

Well, I think that will be all, Dr. Rivers. I believe on the basis of what I've heard here today that your testimony before the committee would be quite valuable indeed if you would consent to appear. I'm sure the committee will be quite grateful to hear what you have to say, yes, I'm sure of it.

And with that, if you'll just allow me to shake your hand, Dr. Rivers. Yes. Thank you very much for coming down to talk. It's helped me a good deal, too, I must say, what I've understood of it all. Ordinary chaps such as myself can't hope to get it all on one go-round, ha ha, but I think I've got the run of it. Once again, thanks very much. Perhaps we'll see one another again when the committee reconvenes.

Good day, Dr. Rivers.

June 3, 1922

The patient is a thirty-year-old serving officer who joined a distinguished regiment in 1912 after Sandhurst. At the outbreak of the war he was on detached service with the Foreign Office in Cairo and spent much of his time in Palestine. While in the Middle East he married the daughter of a Foreign Office official and had one child, a daughter. He had also spent several months in hospital for recurrent episodes of severe fever of unknown origin but thought to be malaria and was so treated. When his regiment was sent to France, he immediately petitioned for return to battalion duty, and this was granted in due course. He rejoined the regiment on the front in December 1915 and, notwithstanding repeated urgings from his superiors, remained continuously with his battalion until he was severely wounded in March 1918 and returned to England for a period of hospitalization. He was passed by the Medical Board as fit for light duty in August 1919 and was seconded to the War Office. Eventually, he was appointed principal army secretary to the War Office Committee Enquiry on Shell-Shock, in which capacity he was serving during our initial meeting.

On that occasion the patient appeared a fit, mature man of average height and weight. From his manner and mode of speech

I reckoned him to be the product of a good country upbringing, perhaps of the middling class or slightly higher, which he later confirmed as being brought up, as he himself said, during an ordinary untroubled childhood on a small estate in Devon. His family consisted of both parents, two boys of whom he was the eldest, and two younger girls. As he did quite well in school, it was thought he might make a scholar, but he had in mind from his earliest memories to become a professional soldier, a decision of which his parents did not approve but tolerated.

However, when we first met his complexion was somewhat florid, and he sweated profusely and complained in a rather casual way of sleeplessness and headaches. The absence of his right arm seemed to pose no obstacle to his movement or agility. Indeed, he did not once refer to the loss of his arm during the course of a conversation lasting the better part of an hour. He spoke with the rather rapid jollity common to serving officers of his type. Whenever he made reference to his own travails during the war, his manner was rather dismissive, as if these were of no account. He spoke in a normal voice, neither raising nor lowering it unnecessarily, and to all appearance was perfectly at ease with his present situation. His only mention of any difficulty was in the form of an offhand admission that he was treating himself with "powders" and brandy, of which he drank several glasses during our interview. He seemed willing enough, perhaps mildly grateful, to discuss the war with me, even though he may have thought it slightly off-colour to do so, as among fellow officers talking about the war is even now considered bad form.

Two weeks after our first encounter the patient called upon me at surgery. He had been present in chambers during my testimony before the committee and appeared to be listening intently, alternatively frowning and smiling as I spoke. Afterward, he came up to me and thanked me more than profusely for agreeing to appear, saying he was sure the many misconceptions held by the several members would be put right because of what I had said. At the time he offered no hint that he was himself suffering any difficulty or that he would come to see me.

In our subsequent meeting he was as ever polite, calm, and well-spoken. By way of explanation for his unexpected appearance he said that his headaches had steadily intensified, that he had difficulty sleeping all night, and that his appetite was "not what it used to be." Upon further discussion, he admitted occasional sensations on his right side, as though his arm were still present. These sensations took the form of tingling, as when one took a hard knock on one's elbow. At times, he said, these sensations were of such intensity as to prevent his sleeping altogether, whereupon he would rise and take several brandies and eventually doze off just as dawn was breaking. After a short nap he would gratefully dress and go to his offices at the WO, where he would plunge into his work without pause until midafternoon, when he would go to his club and remain until dinnertime.

When asked what he thought was troubling his sleep, he answered that his domestic life had taken a run for the worse after the death of his daughter during the flu epidemic just after the war. His wife had been inconsolable at the time, and as he was himself still in hospital he felt he had badly let her down just when she most needed him. He had convinced himself that he was in some way to blame for the loss of his child, thinking that if he had not been absent he would have been able to protect her from being taken away by the disease. He regretted deeply having missed so much of his child's life. He really had only a year with her before going to the front, and then the awkward months in the hospital, when he was in no condition even to hold her. Since then his wife had become more and more distant, staying with her parents in the country weeks at a time. He had been given to understand that she thought his presence in the house was a poor trade for that of his daughter. He confessed he had no idea how this state of affairs might be repaired.

I agreed at this second meeting to see the patient every few days, as frequently as our respective duties would permit. At the conclusion of this meeting he asked for "something more powerful" to help him through the night, and I agreed on the condition he make an effort to reduce his drinking and on no account to take brandy or any other alcohol at the same time as his medicine. I prescribed one dram of laudanum so highly diluted as to convey only the hint of an effect. To this he readily agreed. He seemed quite satisfied and bade me good-bye in a much more relaxed state than when he first appeared.

As it was evident that this officer had repressed a long war's worth of traumatic memory, my plan was simply to release those memories by revisiting his experiences. His illness was compounded substantially by the loss of his arm, the physically dramatic aspect of which had served to mask his psychological state from view so that his mood and behavior, if remarked upon at all by friends and family, were attributed to it rather than to his mental state. To his wartime complaints were added, at precisely the time when all his reserves were occupied by his physical pains, the very substantial depression brought about by the death of his child. I doubted very much his own version of the domestic events he related and suspected he had attempted to bury this great mental pain alongside all the others he was experiencing. I suspected he was himself the remotest figure in the house, not his wife. All these experiences in combination served to produce the most profound feelings of guilt, which I determined to relieve by means of providing him with a situation in which he could talk about his worries without fear of judgment.

The patient's vague recognition of his difficulties had brought him to me. He had, he said, gone a long way toward adapting himself to the random cruelties of the war, but as the war had gone on so long his toughness, which he considered substantial, had begun to give out. He felt that by the time of his most serious wound—he had been wounded less seriously several times before but had refused evacuation—he was completely worn out, no good to anybody, and had become in fact a poor officer. He had become increasingly concerned he would let his men down and that he could no longer effectively protect them. It was at this very time that he was hit by shellfire during the German attack in '18 that had been so disastrous for our side. He had been out in the open trying to organize evacuation of several dangerously wounded men when a very large caliber shell had landed nearby and nearly buried him completely in an old shell hole whose bottom was composed of glutinous mud. When he came round, he was choking on account of his mouth being filled with this mud. He felt he might drown in it but was eventually pulled from his near grave by a soldier who was himself then killed by another shell. Only when he was clear of the hole and in the protection of the trench did he realize his arm had been mangled beyond repair. Although still addled from shock and in great pain, he put a tourniquet on what remained of his arm and attempted to carry on until he passed out once more. He awoke in a Casualty Clearing Station some time later to learn that nearly everyone in this sector of his trench had been killed and that the whole battalion had been forced to retreat from the attack. He believed his own survival had been nothing less than a miracle, and not an altogether just miracle because so many had been killed.

When, during his subsequent stay in hospital back in England, he was told he was to receive the Distinguished Service Order for his actions, he refused at first, saying that losing an arm was in no way to be celebrated or admired. But the colonel of his regiment called upon him in hospital and prevailed upon him to accept the medal on the grounds that England needed every hero she could get at the moment. Contradictorily, he also implied that the patient should put the war behind him, not only for his own sake but also in memory of those with whom he had served and who had served him so well. The colonel of the regiment also said that it was the patient's duty, as it was every officer's, to set an example by carrying on. The patient finally agreed, not altogether willingly, and not because such arguments as the colonel had made were convincing, but only because he hoped that by doing so he would not be forced to take up again such an unwelcome subject. That was why, during our first meeting, the patient did not refer to his DSO. Indeed, he had never put the ribband on his tunic, preferring instead to wear only his Military Cross, which he'd won, he said, during "happier times" earlier in the war when he was a carefree junior officer.

The circumstances of his wounding, and the events that subsequently transpired, excited considerable anxiety in the patient. By refusing the DSO at first, he was concerned now that his standing in the regiment, which he was most interested to preserve, might in some way have been damaged. He did not wish to be thought of by his fellow officers as in any way a complainer. He feared he had given the impression, too, that he had "given in" to bitterness about the war or his part in it. That was all right for the wartime officers, he said, but it was just not on for a regular. And, with war's end and the demobbing, one's standing was all the more important. A great many officers had been pushed out of service. Every day he read in the papers of former officers appealing to the public for assistance. What with an arm gone missing, he feared, his chances of ever seeing really active service again were bound to be quite small and his future in the army thus jeopardized. He wondered, indeed, whether he would even be permitted to remain in the army. He had a small private income, he said, but not really enough for more than a meager existence for him and his wife in some village. The prospect of such a life filled him with dread. He used the word "barren," a word that took on greater significance when he revealed that his wife had told him she would have no more children even if she could. Because of all this, he said, he felt the world closing in upon him from all sides and sometimes wished he was back in the trenches, when at least "life was simple and straightforward."

Our conversations developed along these lines over the course of several visits. He reported finding it easier to sleep through the night but would not hear of leaving off taking the laudanum, which he reckoned was the reason for his improvement. He said he was taking far less brandy and also that he'd recovered his appetite, though not to the degree of the "old days." His wife's mood, however, had not improved at all. Indeed, she seemed more distant than ever. He began taking long walks in Hyde Park and had recovered some of his old fondness for watching cricket, but he no longer had any use for the riding which had so enthused him as a young man. He said that when he looked at horses now, memories of their slaughter during the war came rushing back to him.

After a month the patient abruptly ceased calling upon me. He sent a note, explaining that his duties at the War Office were very pressing, as the committee was concluding its work and was in the throes of preparing its final report. He said that in a curious way participating in the proceedings had helped him to understand his own situation much more clearly than before. He promised to call upon me again when the press of duties permitted.

A fortnight later notices appeared in the press of the patient's death by his own hand in the room of a commercial hotel near Euston Station. No one having heard the pistol's report, some time had passed before his body was discovered. On the writing table he had left a note, which only read "Rain stops Play."

ACKNOWLEDGMENTS

The essays collected here were written over the course of many years, and so my debts are many and great. They remind me how important old friends and colleagues have been in my education.

The list of those to thank has to begin with the original members of the Combat Studies Institute at the U.S. Army Command and General Staff College: Reg Shrader, Bill Stofft, Bob Frank, Bob Doughty, Jack Binkley, P. D. Jones, Ed Drea, and Bob Berlin. They helped set in motion an important movement in the intellectual life of this army, and one day history will give them their due. My debt to them is beyond reckoning.

Alongside them stand my students at the staff college. As I have already written about them at some length here, I will only say that I hope those who succeeded me draw students like the ones I had the privilege to teach.

Richard Snow, the former editor of *American Heritage Magazine*, played a more important role in the making of this book than he might think. It was Snow in the early nineties who encouraged me to write for broader public audiences and then gave me the platform from which to do it. I was one of his contributing editors at the magazine for more than a dozen years, and I was always a bit startled to see my name alongside true masters of the public art of history. I still suspect Snow made a mistake somehow but refused to confess it.

This is also a good place to proclaim my innocence. This book is not my fault. That it was published at all is entirely due to the badgering I suffered at the hands of my old friend Professor Peter Maslowski of the University of Nebraska. We first met in the

School of War itself, long ago. I do not want to think what the past years would have been like without his friendship.

My wife, Irene, and my son, Galen, have done a wonderful job of just ignoring me all these years when I stared vacantly into space, pretending to think. But I do wonder how many more books they have in them.

SOURCE ACKNOWLEDGMENTS

*Essays in this volume originally appeared in the
following publications.*

"Isen's Run: Human Dimensions of Warfare in the Twentieth
Century," *Military Review* (May 1988): 16–31.

"My Guns," *American Heritage* 42, no. 8 (December 1991):
45–51.

"S. L. A. Marshall and the Ratio of Fire," *RUSI Journal* 133, no.
4 (December 1988): 63–71. Reprinted by permission of the
Royal United Services Institute (www.rusi.org/journal).

"The Price of Valor," *MHQ: The Quarterly Journal of Military
History* 5, no. 3 (Spring 1993): 100–110. Reprinted by per-
mission of the Weider History Group, copyright *MHQ: The
Quarterly Journal of Military History.*

"Cherry Blossoms Falling: Japanese Combat Behavior at War's
End," in *1945: War and Peace in the Pacific: Selected Essays*, ed. Peter Dennis, 1–21 (Canberra, Australia: Australian War Memorial, 1999). Reprinted courtesy of the Australian Defence Organisation, Army History Unit.

"War History and the History Wars: Establishing the Combat
Studies Institute," *Public Historian* 10, no. 4 (Autumn 1988):
65–81. Copyright 1988 by the Regents of the University of
California/National Council on Public History.

"Armies in History, History in Armies," in *A Century of Service:
100 Years of the Australian Army*, ed. Peter Dennis and Jeffrey Grey, 1–11 (Canberra, Australia: Department of Defence, 2001). Reprinted courtesy of the Australian Defence
Organisation, Army History Unit.

"The Vietnam Syndrome: A Brief History," in *The Australian*

Army and the Vietnam War, 1962–1972, proceedings of the 2002 Chief of Army's Military History Conference, ed. Peter Dennis and Jeffrey Grey, 1–15 (Canberra, Australia: Army History Unit, 2002). Reprinted courtesy of the Australian Defence Organisation, Army History Unit.

"In the Shadow of the Dragon: Doctrine and the U.S. Army after Vietnam," *RUSI Journal* (December 1997): 41–54. Reprinted by permission of the Royal United Services Institute (www.rusi.org/journal).

"Urban Warfare: Its History and Its Future," in *Block by Block: The Challenges of Urban Operations*, ed. William G. Robertson and Lawrence A. Yates, 439–50 (Fort Leavenworth KS: U.S. Army Command and General Staff College Press, 2003). Reprinted courtesy of the Combat Studies Institute and the Combined Arms Research Library.

"Overrated and Underrated: General," *American Heritage* 49, no. 3 (May–June) 1998: 19.

"Overrated and Underrated: World War II General," *American Heritage* 53, no. 5 (October 2000): 52.

"War in the Dark," *American Heritage* 50, no. 1 (February–March 1999): 41–48.

"A War against History," *American Heritage* 52, no. 1 (February–March 2001): 82–87.

"Military History and Its Fictions," *Journal of Military History* 70, no. 4 (October 2006): 1081–97. Used by permission of the University of California Press–Journals; permission conveyed through Copyright Clearance Center, Inc.

"The Führer in the Dock: A Speculation on the Banality of Evil," in *What If? 2: Eminent Historians Imagine What Might Have Been*, ed. Robert Cowley, 346–65 (New York: Putnam; London: Pan Macmillan, 2001). Copyright 2001 by American Historical Publications, Inc., and used by permission of G. P. Putnam's Sons, a division of Penguin Group (USA) Inc., and Pan MacMillan, London.

"The Real War: An Interview with Paul Fussell," *American Heritage* 40, no. 7 (November 1989): 126–33.

"Rain Stops Play," in *An Instinct for War: Scenes from the Battlefields of History*, by Roger J. Spiller, 277–99 (Cambridge MA: The Belknap Press of Harvard University Press, 2005). Reprinted by permission of the publisher, copyright 2005 by the President and Fellows of Harvard College.

Studies in War, Society, and the Military

Military Migration and State Formation
The British Military Community in Seventeenth-Century Sweden
Mary Elizabeth Ailes

The State at War in South Asia
Pradeep P. Barua

An American Soldier in World War I
George Browne
Edited by David L. Snead

Imagining the Unimaginable
World War, Modern Art, and the Politics of Public
Culture in Russia, 1914–1917
Aaron J. Cohen

The Rise of the National Guard
The Evolution of the American Militia, 1865–1920
Jerry Cooper

The Thirty Years' War and German Memory in
the Nineteenth Century
Kevin Cramer

Political Indoctrination in the U.S. Army from
World War II to the Vietnam War
Christopher S. DeRosa

In the Service of the Emperor
Essays on the Imperial Japanese Army
Edward J. Drea

The Age of the Ship of the Line
The British and French Navies, 1650–1815
Jonathan R. Dull

You Can't Fight Tanks with Bayonets
Psychological Warfare against the Japanese Army
in the Southwest Pacific
Allison B. Gilmore

A Strange and Formidable Weapon
British Responses to World War I Poison Gas
Marion Girard